Praise for NOT "Just Friends"

"Glass identified alarming new trends, shares intriguing statistical data from her research and disputes common myths. . . . [She] has straightforward, compassionate, nonviolent advice. . . . An impeccably detailed map that lets readers know where the potential hazards lie. An insightful analysis of infidelity."

　　—*The Cleveland Plain Dealer*

"In this long-awaited book, Dr. Glass has provided practical advice that has a scientific basis, as well as profoundly sensitive clinical experience about the highly destructive problem of infidelity. . . . Everyone should read this book! It represents a real breakthrough."

　　—John M. Gottman, Ph.D., author of *The Seven Principles for Making Marriage Work* and *The Relationship Cure*

"I treasure this book, and I treasure Shirley Glass. No one understands affairs better than she does. She offers her traumatized readers compassion, wisdom, and unshakeable common sense. *NOT 'Just Friends'* will save a lot of marriages and a lot of lives."

　　—Frank Pittman, M.D., author of *Private Lies: Infidelity and the Betrayal of Intimacy*

"Most dangerous of all, says long-time infidelity researcher Shirley Glass, Ph.D., . . . author of *NOT 'Just Friends,'* . . . is the growing number of affairs between people who let themselves get too close to a good friend."

　　—*Ladies' Home Journal*

"'The sex differences in infidelity are disappearing,' [says] psychologist Shirley Glass."

　　—*Psychology Today*

"Not only is this the most comprehensive book on affairs that I have ever read, it's the only one that completely reflects the reality of affairs as I have observed it in my twenty-two years of working with this issue. No matter how many other books you have read on this subject, I strongly encourage you to read this one."

　　—Peggy Vaughan, host of DearPeggy.com and author of *The Monogamy Myth*

"It's a relief my mom wrote a great book so I can be totally honest [here]. The sheer ambition of the book is thrilling. *NOT 'Just Friends'* offers one surprising insight after another."

—Ira Glass, host of Public Radio's *This American Life*

"This terrific book presents many new trailblazing concepts, even for therapists already familiar with the issues of infidelity. . . . It is easy to see why Dr. Glass is recognized as an expert. The author, with her thorough knowledge and a light touch, guides the reader through the difficulties in recovering from infidelity. When readers finish this insightful book, they will have taken a journey of healing with someone who has their best interests at heart."

—Rona Subotnik, marriage and family therapist and coauthor of *Surviving Infidelity* and *Infidelity on the Internet*

"I would highly recommend this book for couples who have been through the trauma of betrayal, for those whose relationship has ended in the aftermath of an affair, and for therapists who counsel such men and women. They will all learn a great deal from this wonderful and well-written book."

—Jennifer P. Schneider, M.D., Ph.D., author of *Back from Betrayal*; *Sex, Lies, and Forgiveness*; and *Disclosing Secrets*

"Destined to be the classic for helping couples preserve the love they rode in on. It's a compelling read. You simply can't put it down. If we want to help couples get smart about marriage we also have to help them get smart about infidelity. . . . It's time to wake up, smell the coffee, and be sure everyone reads this book and understands the formula for prevention spelled out so clearly."

—Diane Sollee, founder and director, Coalition for Marriage, Family, & Couples Education, www.smartmarriages.com

"Refusing to pander to audiences expecting Dr. Phil–type quick fixes, Glass . . . scrutinizes affairs and offers well-defined guidelines. Glass's credentials and commitment lend this book credence as a valuable resource."

—*Publishers Weekly*

"*NOT 'Just Friends'* is a thoughtful and attentive book of good advice and welcome hope."

—Booksense.com

NOT

"Just Friends"

REBUILDING TRUST AND RECOVERING YOUR SANITY AFTER INFIDELITY

SHIRLEY P. GLASS, PH.D.

WITH JEAN COPPOCK STAEHELI

FREE PRESS

NEW YORK   LONDON   TORONTO   SYDNEY

*f*P

FREE PRESS
A Division of Simon & Schuster, Inc.
1230 Avenue of the Americas
New York, NY 10020

First Free Press trade paperback edition 2004

FREE PRESS and colophon are trademarks
of Simon & Schuster, Inc.

For information regarding special discounts for bulk purchases,
please contact Simon & Schuster Special Sales:
1-800-456-6798 or business@simonandschuster.com

Book design by Ellen R. Sasahara

Manufactured in the United States of America

40

The Library of Congress has cataloged the hardcover edition as follows:
Glass, Shirley P.
Not "just friends" : protect your relationship from infidelity and heal
the trauma of betrayal / Shirley P. Glass with Jean Coppock Staeheli.
p.   cm.
Includes bibliographical references and index.
1. Adultery.   I. Staeheli, Jean Coppock.   II. Title.
HQ806 .G576 2003
306.73'6—dc21   2002034742

ISBN-13:978-0-7432-2549-6
ISBN-10:   0-7432-2549-X
ISBN-13:978-0-7432-2550-2 (Pbk)
ISBN-10:   0-7432-2550-3 (Pbk)

To my husband, Barry, who has been so much more than a friend. You have fostered my aspirations, creativity, and individuality as we have matured together throughout the years.

CONTENTS

ACKNOWLEDGMENTS

MY GRATITUDE and appreciation are truly heartfelt. So many people have participated in making my vision of this book become a reality. Some knowingly helped me with the actual book, and others helped me throughout the years through shared experiences. This book wouldn't have been possible without the stories I have heard for twenty years by wounded couples struggling to recover from the trauma of infidelity. I have been touched deeply by their pain, inspired by their resilience, and enlightened by them about the multiple meanings of infidelity.

Dr. Tom Wright has been my mentor, dissertation advisor, research colleague, cotherapist, and valued friend. His encouragement when I first came up with the idea of doing research on infidelity at Catholic University in 1975 gave me the courage to embark on what turned out to be a lifelong journey. Our collaboration in research and clinical practice has been the source of the trauma model that is presented in NOT "Just Friends."

Diane Sollee's zealousness about preventing relationship problems before they start through marriage education programs has stimulated the special dimension in this book devoted to "the slippery slope." Diane's enthusiasm for my work has found me a larger audience through her "Smart Marriages" conferences and web site than I could have imagined. Her friendship and nurturing spirit have become mainstays in my life.

My professional writer, Jean Staeheli, has been an author's dream. Her gentle spirit, sensitivity, intellect, and absorption of my voluminous work output has had a profound effect on the book. Our collaboration has been flexible, exhausting, and exuberating. Despite overwhelming personal challenges during the past year, Jean's courage and dedication made it possible for us to continue our collaborative effort. Jean and I had the good fortune to be bolstered by the unflagging support and editorial expertise of her husband, Michael.

I have been blessed with a superlative editor. Leslie Meredith's detailed editorial advice has greatly enhanced the manuscript. Her painstaking scrutiny and astute comments about structure, clarity, and flow have helped me present my message as simply and clearly as possible.

Rona Subotnik, coauthor of *Surviving Infidelity* and *Infidelity on the Internet* read the entire manuscript. Her penetrating insight and humorous comments were provocative and delightful. Dr. Eileen Mager has been cheering me from the sidelines as I have plodded down the arduous trail of first-time author, and she has also offered some sound editing suggestions.

My family has not only been supportive, they have been there to guide me through the publishing maze. My husband, Barry, has given me what I most needed—a guilt-free environment in which I could neglect him for two years while I was sequestered with my computer and long-distance calls to Jean. His perceptive observations during the marketing phase have been very helpful and were accepted by my editor. My daughters, Karen Glass Barry and Randi Glass Murray, have been a wonderful source of professional advice on dealing with agents, editors, and publicists. My son, Ira Glass, has been instructing me and his dedicated audience for years about "narrative arcs." His positive feedback in the early stages gave me the impetus to continue my journey. My dearest friend, Sandy, has been beside me for fifty years through all of my triumphs and travails.

Nina Graybill, my literary attorney, has provided me not only with sound legal advice, but also with encouragement and a shoulder to cry on during many frustrating setbacks. She has become a cherished personal friend.

I have had wonderful support staff. Dorothy Robinson at Free Press has steered me through the editorial process with a positive attitude despite stressful deadlines and capricious computer programs. My own office administrators, Dolores Meadows and Michelle Murray, read early versions of the manuscript and made sound suggestions. Michelle's specialty turned out to be spotting unintentional double entendres. JoAnna Reynolds and Jennifer Thomas, my research assistants, patiently and tediously entered all of the data for more than 300 couples and crunched out lots and lots of numbers. JoAnna did all of the graphs and managed to teach me to use Excel and SPSS.

No matter how promising a book is, it has to be sold. Kris Puopolo's excitement over the proposal gave this book wings. My agent, Suzanne Gluck, believed strongly in the potential of this book and was steadfast in her efforts. Kris Dahl followed up to protect my interests once the manuscript was in process.

Additional thanks: To the individuals who agreed to participate in my dissertation research. To Dr. Bob Athanasiou, who gave me his *Psychology Today* Sex Questionnaire data, and to Dr. Frank Furstenberg and Dr. William Bowers, who sent me the original questionnaires used for Morton Hunt's research on *The Affair* in 1975, when very few people had any data. To the 475 therapists who attended my workshops and willingly completed surveys on attitudes about infidelity. To the workshop attendees and writers of magazine articles and newspaper columns who have expanded my thinking about the complexities of infidelity with their probing questions.

NOT
"Just Friends"

INTRODUCTION

GOOD PEOPLE in good marriages are having affairs. More times than I can count, I have sat in my office and felt torn apart by the grief, rage, and remorse of the people I counsel as they try to cope with the repercussions of their infidelity or their partner's betrayal. In two-thirds of the couples I've treated in my clinical practice over the past twenty years, either the husband, the wife, or both were unfaithful. Broken promises and shattered expectations have become part of our cultural landscape, and more people who need help in dealing with them appear in my office every day.

Surprisingly, the infidelity that I'm seeing these days is of a new sort. It's not between people who are intentionally seeking thrills, as is commonly believed. The new infidelity is between people who unwittingly form deep, passionate connections before realizing that they've crossed the line from platonic friendship into romantic love. Eighty-two percent of the 210 unfaithful partners I've treated have had an affair with someone who was, at first, "just a friend." Well-intentioned people who had not planned to stray are betraying not only their partners but also their own beliefs and moral values, provoking inner crises as well as marital ones.

This is the essence of the new crisis of infidelity: Friendships, work relationships, and Internet liaisons have become the latest threat to marriages. As these opportunities for intimate relationships increase, the boundary between platonic and romantic feelings blurs and becomes easier to cross.

Today's workplace has become the new danger zone of romantic attraction and opportunity. More women are having affairs than ever before. Today's woman is more sexually experienced and more likely to be

1

working in what used to be male-dominated occupations. Many of their affairs begin at work. From 1982 to 1990, 38 percent of unfaithful wives in my clinical practice were involved with someone from work. From 1991 to 2000, the number of women's work affairs increased to 50 percent. Men also are having most of their affairs with people from their workplace. Among the 350 couples I have treated, approximately 62 percent of unfaithful men met their affair partners at work.

The significant news about these new affairs—and what is different from the affairs of previous generations—is that they originate as peer relationships. People who truly are initially just friends or just friendly colleagues slowly move onto the slippery slope of infidelity. In the new infidelity, secret emotional intimacy is the first warning sign of impending betrayal. Yet, most people don't recognize it as such or see what they've gotten themselves into until they've become physically intimate.

Most people mistakenly think it is possible to prevent affairs by being loving and dedicated to one's partner. I call this the Prevention Myth, because there is no evidence to support it. My experience as a marital therapist and infidelity researcher has shown me that simply being a loving partner does not ensure your marriage against affairs. You also have to exercise awareness of the appropriate boundaries at work and in your friendships. This book will help you learn to observe boundaries or set them up where you need to. It will tell you the warning signals and red flags you need to pay attention to in your own friendships and in your partner's.

Most people also mistakenly think that infidelity isn't really infidelity unless there's sexual contact. Whereas women tend to regard any sexual intimacy as infidelity, men are more likely to deny infidelity unless sexual intercourse has occurred. *In the new infidelity, however, affairs do not have to be sexual.* Some, such as Internet affairs, are primarily emotional. The most devastating extramarital involvements engage heart, mind, *and* body. And this is the kind of affair that is becoming more common. Today's affairs are more frequent and more serious than they used to be because more men are getting emotionally involved and more women are getting sexually involved.

Consider this surprising statistic: At least one or both parties in 50 percent of all couples, married and living together, straight and gay, will break their vows of sexual or emotional exclusivity during the lifetime of the relationship.[1] It has been difficult for researchers to arrive at this absolute figure because of the many variations in how research has been conducted, in sample characteristics, and in how extramarital involvements have been defined. After reviewing twenty-five studies, however, I concluded that 25 percent of wives and 44 percent of husbands have had extramarital intercourse.[2] This is startling news indeed.

Vast numbers of Americans are preoccupied by an actual or potential betrayal of an intimate relationship. Their anxiety is not confined to a particular class, occupation, or age. Infidelity can occur in any household, not just in situations where partners are promiscuous or rich and powerful. No marriage is immune.

There are, however, steps you can take to keep your relationship or marriage safe. There are also steps you can take to repair your relationship after emotional or sexual infidelity has rocked it. And there are things you can do to help yourself through the trauma of betrayal. And you'll learn them all in *NOT "Just Friends."*

A Word about Where I'm Coming From

I was prompted to write this book first by my natural desire as a therapist to offer help and comfort to more people. Every time my work on infidelity has been featured in the media, I have received an outpouring from desperate people who say that I've helped them survive their partner's betrayal, rebuild their marriage, and get on with their lives. I have also given relationship advice on the Internet, which has connected me to a large number of people mired in the pain of infidelity and looking for a way out. Although I'm gratified to know that I've helped many people personally through these venues, I am hoping that I can reach many more through this book.

Second, I wanted to bring a new, fact-based, scientifically and therapeutically responsible approach to the guidance that couples receive. Frankly, there are no generally accepted standards for therapists and counselors who treat infidelity. As a result, people often receive bad advice from professional helpers as well as from well-intentioned friends and family members. Many of our cultural beliefs about the behavior of others come from projections of our own attitudes and personal experiences. Unfortunately, these personal biases also affect the work and recommendations of many counselors. In this book, I draw from research and documented evidence to give you solid predictors about who tends to be unfaithful and why, as well as proven recovery strategies for healing your relationship.

Some of the research on which I draw is my own. Twenty-five years ago, my first research project on infidelity grew out of a challenge to my traditional beliefs. At that time, I, like many others, believed that infidelity could occur only in an unhappy, unloving marriage. Then I learned that an acquaintance, an elderly man who had an exceptionally loving marriage, had been having sexual flings for many decades without his wife's ever knowing. Until the day he died, his wife believed that she was deeply and exclusively loved. After this revelation that an affair could indeed happen in a loving marriage, I felt compelled to search the psychological literature on relationships to learn more, but found very little that shed light on this seeming contradiction. The lack of research indicated a void that needed to be filled and I wanted to be the one to do it. So I pursued my investigations into extramarital relationships as a doctoral student at Catholic University of America. As you might imagine, that raised a few eyebrows.

What I discovered from the study I conducted forced me to revise many of my own beliefs about infidelity, which naturally had been limited by my own experience as a conservative young woman who had married at the age of nineteen. Over the years, I've done several other major studies on infidelity that have formed the foundation of my research-based approach to understanding and treating infidelity. My commitment to this field and method is so strong that I am currently writing a book for professionals, *The Trauma of Infidelity: Research and Treatment.*

Here's a brief overview of some of my professional work, so that you'll see the kind of factual information on which I'm basing this book's guidance for you and your relationship. Some of my discoveries are counterintuitive and definitely go against the grain of popular opinion.

- *Psychology Today* Study (1977).[3] This is the study I was inspired to do by the elderly philanderer. It compares the marital satisfaction of people who had affairs early in marriage with those who had them later. At first, I had no idea where I would find subjects for such a study. I ended up calling Bob Athanasiou, one of the authors of a sex questionnaire in *Psychology Today*, who offered to give me the data on the responses of 20,000 people. When I analyzed the data, I found that infidelity in young marriages either meant dissatisfaction or was a predictor of divorce. In addition, I found some very interesting differences between the sexes that piqued my curiosity: *In long-term marriages, unfaithful men were as satisfied as faithful men, but unfaithful women were the most distressed subgroup of all.* I speculated at the time that the reason for these differences was that women's affairs were more emotional and men's more sexual. Today, however, in the new infidelity, both sexes are citing emotional reasons for their affairs.

- The *Airport Sample* (1980).[4] This dissertation research was designed to explore further the sex differences I had found in the *Psychology Today* study regarding reasons for having affairs. I handed out 1,000 questionnaires to people at the Baltimore-Washington International Airport and at a downtown office park in Baltimore. Over 300 mailed them back to me anonymously. I discovered that women's infidelities were about unhappy marriages and falling in love with somebody else, and men's infidelities were more about the desire for sexual excitement than because of an unhappy marriage. An unexpected finding revealed that *the most threatening kind of infidelity combined a deep emotional attachment with sexual intercourse.*

- My *Clinical Sample* (1982–2000). In this recent analysis, the 350 couples I treated alone and in cotherapy with my partner in practice, Dr. Tom Wright, completed the same questionnaires that I used in my dissertation research. These couples exhibit some of the same differences between the sexes in their attitudes toward marriage and infidelity as my previous studies. But it is obvious that *in this new crisis of infidelity, an increased number of unfaithful husbands have deep emotional connections to their affair partner.*

- *Therapist Survey* (1992–2001). In this study, I switched focus and surveyed 465 therapists at thirteen conferences regarding their beliefs about the meaning and treatment of infidelity. The results demonstrate that there is very little consensus among couple therapists about why infidelity happens and how people should be treated in its aftermath.

You'll learn other surprising truths about infidelity, too, from my clinical experience with individuals and couples struggling with infidelity, from my own research into extramarital affairs, and from other research I've conducted in conjunction with Dr. Wright. I also borrow from the collective wisdom of other respected clinicians and researchers. Throughout the book, I use this research to document the concepts and interventions I am discussing, so that you will be comfortable listening to and accepting the guidance I give for protecting your marriage and for getting through your own wrenching experience of infidelity.

I also recount stories of couples that demonstrate how troublesome triangles develop out of friendship. These show the different reasons people break their commitments to each other and what you can do to ease your own pain and suffering. Perhaps you'll recognize a life experience similar to your own in these stories and see a communication technique that could work for your marriage. The stories bring to life the bare-bones statistics on infidelity and demonstrate how this distressing sociological reality intrudes into too many marriages. I've altered all descriptive details in the case examples to protect the couples and maintain their confidentiality, but the actual interpersonal and individual issues are based on factual accounts. For the sake of brevity, some stories are composites of more than one individual or couple. I hope that their stories of breakdowns and breakthroughs will show you that you are not alone and encourage you in your attempt to recover from infidelity.

The Need for a New Outlook

Just because infidelity is increasingly common doesn't mean that most people understand it. So much of the advice on television shows and in popular books about how to affair-proof your marriage is misleading. In fact, much of the conventional wisdom about what causes affairs and how to repair relationships is misguided.

An August 2000 column by the late Ann Landers illustrates this point beautifully—and startlingly. A woman wrote that her husband had casually confessed to a one-time affair and said that it was over. He also said he regretted it, that it had happened only once with a woman she didn't know, and he wanted to come clean and "get it off his conscience." He pleaded with his wife to forgive him. A few days later she came across several bills covering four years that indicated the affair had been ongoing over that period. The wife writes:

I want to know who the home-wrecker is. I told him the only way to prove his love for me is to tell me her name. He refused. I have asked him every day since, saying the only way I can trust him is to know the whole story. Ann, with our marriage at stake, why won't he give me this information? I am worried that he cares more about this woman than he cares about me. What should I do?

Ann's response:

Dear San Diego,
You should stop pressuring him to name the woman and be relieved that she is a thing of the past. Most men would identify her in order to get off the hot seat, but your husband refuses to do that. He may have some integrity after all. If you find it impossible to get past this, please consider seeking professional help.

I would have suggested a quite different response, something like this: "In order for your marriage to heal from the betrayal, your husband has to be willing to answer your questions. Until and unless you find out what you need to know, the affair will remain an open wound in your relationship. So far, the only integrity he is showing is to his affair partner. You have every reason to doubt him."

Popular thinking about infidelity—and the therapy that deals with it—is clouded by myths. The facts, which my research and clinical experience prove, are much more surprising and thought-provoking than unfounded popular and clinical assumptions. Here are a few truths that you will learn from this book:

- *Assumption:* Affairs happen in unhappy or unloving marriages.
- *Fact:* Affairs can happen in good marriages. Affairs are less about love and more about sliding across boundaries.

- *Assumption:* Affairs occur mostly because of sexual attraction.
- *Fact:* The lure of an affair is how the unfaithful partner is mirrored back through the adoring eyes of the new love. Another appeal is that individuals experience new roles and opportunities for growth in new relationships.

- *Assumption:* A cheating partner almost always leaves clues, so a naïve spouse must be burying his or her head in the sand.
- **Fact:** The majority of affairs are never detected. Some individuals can successfully compartmentalize their lives or are such brilliant liars that their partner never finds out.

- *Assumption:* A person having an affair shows less interest in sex at home.
- **Fact:** The excitement of an affair can increase passion at home and make sex even more interesting.

- *Assumption:* The person having an affair isn't "getting enough" at home.
- **Fact:** The truth is that the unfaithful partner may not be *giving* enough. In fact, the spouse who gives too little is at greater risk than the spouse who gives too much because he or she is less invested.

- *Assumption:* A straying partner finds fault with everything you do.
- **Fact:** He or she may in fact become Mr. or Mrs. Wonderful in order to escape detection. Most likely, he or she will be alternately critical and devoted.

NOT "Just Friends" will give you a more complete understanding of what infidelity really is and how it happens. I will provide you with plenty of substantiated information that will help you make decisions about whether and how your marriage can be saved. The following facts, although counterintuitive, are a good place to start:

- You can have an affair without having sex. Sometimes the greatest betrayals happen without touching. Infidelity is any emotional or sexual intimacy that violates trust.
- Because child-centered families create conditions that increase the vulnerability for affairs, the children may ultimately be harmed.
- People are more likely to cheat if their friends and family members have cheated.
- When a woman has an affair, it is more often the result of long-term marital dissatisfaction, and the marriage is harder to repair.

- Most people, including unfaithful partners, think that talking about an affair with the betrayed partner will only create more upset, but that is actually the way to rebuild intimacy. Trying to recover without discussing the betrayal is like waxing a dirty floor.

- The aftermath of an affair can offer partners who are still committed to their marriage an opportunity to strengthen their bond. Exploring vulnerabilities often leads to a more intimate relationship.

- Starting over with a new love does not necessarily lead to a life of eternal bliss. Seventy-five percent of all unfaithful individuals who marry the affair partner end up divorced.

- More than 90 percent of married individuals believe that monogamy is important, but almost half of them admit to having had affairs.

Interesting, isn't it? And not what you'd expect. If you want to maintain your relationship, you need to learn how to prevent affairs and why so many people engage in behavior that goes against their professed values. Even so, knowledge alone is not enough. If you've slipped into an affair, or your partner has, you need a map for your journey to recovery. *NOT "Just Friends"* also gives you the detailed guidance and well-marked routes you need to follow.

Recovering from Betrayal

According to therapists who treat couples, infidelity is the second most difficult relationship problem, surpassed only by domestic violence.[5] It takes years for people to come to terms with betrayal. Like comets, affairs leave a long trail behind them. When an infidelity is revealed, it precipitates a crisis for all three people in the extramarital triangle.

The revelation of infidelity is a *traumatic* event for the betrayed partner. Understanding it as traumatic has important implications for healing. People who have just found out about a partner's affair may react as if they have been viciously attacked. Where they formerly felt safe, they now feel threatened. In an instant, the betrayed spouse's assumptions about the world have been shattered. Commonly, betrayed spouses become obsessed with the details of the affair, have trouble eating and sleeping, and feel powerless to control their emotions, especially anxiety and grief, which can be overwhelming.

I have found that the most complete healing happens gradually, in stages. Because betrayal is so traumatic and recovery takes time, I use an interpersonal trauma recovery plan that parallels the ones recommended for victims of natural disasters, war, accidents, and violence. My clients are living evidence of its effectiveness in their individual healing and in the number of marriages saved with this approach.

Today more couples are willing to try to work through their difficulties in a sustained way. They want to make their marriages "even better than before." They want their suffering to mean something. They want their pain to lead them to insights and new behaviors that will strengthen them as individuals and as a couple. But most people need help learning how to change the bitterness of betrayal into fertile ground for growth. They need constructive ways to confront and understand what has happened to them and how, on a practical level, to repair the ruptures that are breaking their hearts and ruining their relationship.

One of the difficulties of recovering from the trauma of infidelity is that the unfaithful partner must become the healer. It's natural for the un-faithful partner to want to avoid the pained expression on the face of the person he or she has injured, especially when the betrayed partner insists on hearing the excruciating details. But it's important for the unfaithful partner to move toward that pain, offer comfort, and be open to answering any questions. The process of recovery is like steering a ship through a storm. Knowing where you are heading can keep you and your relationship from getting totally lost even when you find yourselves off course.

It *is* possible to emerge from betrayal with your marriage stronger. This book will show you how. You will also learn how to steer clear of such dangerous waters in the future—*if* you both genuinely want to heal and are ready to do the serious work of repair.

Prevention Manual and Survival Guide

Many couples are conflicted about outside relationships that are viewed by one partner as too close and by the other as just friends. NOT "Just Friends" *is for any man or woman in a committed relationship who interacts with interesting, attractive people.* Love alone does not protect you or your partner from temptation. It's not always easy to recognize the thresholds that mark the passage from platonic friend to extramarital affair partner. This book can be a valuable resource for protecting any couple, straight or gay. It will be of interest to anyone who wants to know more about the complex dynamics of how people form and maintain committed relationships. It will help you better understand yourself and your partner.

NOT "Just Friends" does not focus specifically on individuals who intentionally pursue the excitement of extramarital sex. Philandering can be a sign of either entitlement or addiction. The unfaithful partner who engages in sexual affairs with almost no emotional attachment usually operates undetected unless something catastrophic happens that exposes the extramarital liaisons. In any case, I want you to know that recovering from multiple affairs follows the same pathway as that followed by people recovering from a single affair. If the involved partners are genuinely remorseful and committed to remaining faithful in the future, this book can help them too.

NOT "Just Friends" speaks directly to the betrayed partner, the involved partner, and the affair partner at every stage of infidelity. Each individual in this painful situation will find insight and guidance as we chart the course of affairs from their beginning to their end. Here is a summary of how an affair unfolds:

In the beginning, there is a cup of coffee, a working lunch, a check-up call on the cell phone—all of these contacts are innocent enough and add vitality and interest to our days. But when secrecy and lies become methods of furthering the relationship, it has become an emotional affair. When the affair is discovered, the involved partner is torn between two competing allegiances, and the betrayed partner develops the alarming mental and physical symptoms of obsession and flashbacks. Both partners are frightened, fragile, and confused. On their own, they may not know how to cope.

If both decide to stay and work on the relationship, first on the agenda has to be how to reestablish safety and foster goodwill. They may be conflicted about how much to discuss the affair because it's hard to know how much to say and when. It's also hard to know how to remain supportive when a partner is hysterical or depressed and how to live through daily obligations without doing further damage to themselves and each other. NOT "Just Friends" will help guide you through these rocky stages of your recovery.

Rebuilding trust is the cornerstone of the recovery process. Telling the full story and exploring the individual, relational, and social factors that made your marriage vulnerable to an affair is vital for healing and recovery. If you can see through each other's eyes and empathize with each other's pain, then you can be guided in how to co-construct your stories to help you understand the meaning of what has happened. But you need to do this in a healing environment with mutual empathy and understanding. An atmosphere of interrogation and defensiveness will derail your recovery. The technique in *NOT "Just Friends"* will keep you on track in this middle stage too.

After conscious, patient work, you can become strong enough to deal with the hundreds of difficult questions that keep coming up: Will my partner ever forgive me? How can I ever trust my partner again? How do we handle the Other Man or the Other Woman who keeps calling on the phone? Should I share my love letters? What shall we tell the children? How should we handle the moments of pain that continue to intrude months and years after these events are over? *NOT "Just Friends"* addresses all these problems and helps you figure out when it is appropriate to stop being so upset and move on. It also addresses whether to stay and try to work it out and how to know whether your marriage is a lost cause.

It's hard to believe that a marriage can be better after an affair, but it's true—*if* you learn how to handle the nightmarish days after discovery, the traumatic reactions of the betrayed spouse, the revelation of details when the story is told, and the period of construction when the marriage is rebuilt, brick by brick. Even if you choose not to continue your marriage, you still have to recover from the trauma you've been through. The road to recovery can be a stimulus for growth whether you travel it with your partner or you make your way alone. It's a difficult road, but it is passable and well traveled for all its difficulties, and it's important to know that it is there for you and anyone who wants to follow it.

Walls and Windows

Throughout this book, I use the image of "walls and windows" to symbolize the levels of emotional intimacy within the marriage and within the affair. Many of my clients have told me that understanding where the symbolic walls and windows are in their relationship has helped them enormously in explaining the dynamics of their relationship and in articulating their feelings of alienation and jealousy. You can have intimacy in your relationship only when you are honest and open about the significant things in your life. When you withhold information and keep secrets, you create walls that act as barriers to the free flow of thoughts and feelings that invigorate your relationship. But when you open up to each other, the window between you allows you to know each other in unfiltered, intimate ways.

In a love affair, the unfaithful partner has built a wall to shut out the marriage partner and has opened a window to let in the affair partner. To reestablish a marriage that is intimate and trusting after an affair, the walls and windows must be reconstructed to conform to the safety code and keep the structure of the marriage sound so that it can withstand the test of time. You install a picture window between you and your marriage partner and construct a solid or opaque wall to block out contact with the affair partner. This arrangement of walls and windows nurtures your marriage and protects it from outside elements and interference.

To be healthy, every relationship needs this safety code: the appropriate placement of walls and windows. Just as the sharing that parents have with children should not surpass or replace confidences within the marriage, the boundaries in a platonic friendship should be solid. Identifying the position of walls and windows can help you discover whether a dangerous alliance has replaced a relationship that began as "just friends."

In the Afterword, you'll find a quick reference for recovering couples who want to do everything they can to safeguard their relationship against further betrayal. That section of the book is a summary of the successful strategies that make it possible for you to step back from the edge, reestablish boundaries, and commit once more to your primary relationship. It can also help couples who have not experienced infidelity and want to do everything they can to prevent it from happening in the first place.

Best Friends

The ultimate goal in committed relationships is to think of your marital partner as your *best friend*. Nonetheless, rich friendships outside the marriage are also important for a full life, and it is sad when those friendships have to be forsaken after boundaries that protect the marriage have been violated. This is another reason I wanted to write *NOT "Just Friends"*: to give you ways to set appropriate boundaries that will preserve your friendships as well as your committed relationship.

My own life has afforded me the opportunity to nurture and enjoy deep friendships while respecting the sanctity of my marriage. For twenty-five years I have maintained an affectionate and stimulating professional partnership with Dr. Tom Wright, my cotherapist and research partner. Tom and I do not discuss personal matters about our marriages, and we are very much aware of avoiding compromising situations. My marriage to my high school sweetheart, Barry, has lasted over forty years and we regard ourselves as best friends.

Good friendships and a loving marriage: This is what is possible when you value and preserve the differences between them. You can learn how to keep your commitment strong and your friendships safe, so that you will stay in the safety zone and remain "just friends." Otherwise, you can easily cross into the danger zone where infidelity begins, when you are *not* "just friends" anymore. If this has already happened to you or your partner, however, please keep reading.

PART I

The Slippery Slope

In the new crisis of infidelity, platonic friendships and workplace relationships are turning into emotional affairs, usually gradually, often without premeditation. Parties cross boundaries of emotional intimacy, sharing intimate information with a friend that is usually appropriately the exclusive territory of a husband or wife. When emotional boundaries are overstepped, the partner has taken the first step onto the slippery slope leading to emotional and eventually sexual infidelity. Even if the infidelity is "only" emotional, it often leads to a double life of deception and sexuality, threatening once secure marriages.

If you recognize that your friendship *or your partner's friendship* may be in the danger zone of too much emotional intimacy, use this awareness to address concerns about your marriage. The quiz on the next page will help you see where you stand.

Quiz: Has Your Friendship Become an Emotional Affair?*

Directions: Circle Yes or No to the left of each statement.

Yes No   1. Do you confide more to your friend than to your partner about how your day went?

Yes No   2. Do you discuss negative feelings or intimate details about your marriage with your friend but not with your partner?

Yes No   3. Are you open with your partner about the extent of your involvement with your friend?

Yes No   4. Would you feel comfortable if your partner heard your conversation with your friend?

Yes No   5. Would you feel comfortable if your partner saw a videotape of your meetings?

Yes No   6. Are you aware of sexual tensions in this friendship?

Yes No   7. Do you and your friend touch differently when you're alone than in front of others?

Yes No   8. Are you in love with your friend?

Scoring Key:

You get one point each for *yes* to questions 1, 2, 6, 7, 8, and one point each for *no* to 3, 4, 5.

If you scored near 0, this is just a friendship.

If you scored 3 or more, you may not be "just friends."

If you scored 7–8, you are definitely involved in an emotional affair.

---

*This quiz by Shirley P. Glass was first printed in *USA Today* (June 20, 1988) in an article by Karen Peterson, "When platonic relationships get too close for comfort," p. 6D.

1

I'M TELLING YOU,
WE'RE JUST FRIENDS

*You know you're in trouble when
the word "just" appears before the word "friends."*

—IRA GLASS[1]

TWO SIMPLE WORDS: "just friends." We all think we know what that phrase means. We picture two people whose relationship operates within the sanctioned bounds of genuine but limited caring. Friends are comfortable and safe.

The problem is that for more and more people these words are taking on a dangerous connotation. When you express concern about a relationship that seems too close, you are probably not convinced if your partner attempts to reassure you by saying, *"I'm telling you, we're just friends."* It sounds more like a denial than an affirmation.

Your wariness is well-founded. Many individuals who think of themselves as just friends are becoming lovers. Men and women today have the opportunity to meet as equals, develop collegial relationships and mutual interests, and escalate those relationships into love affairs. Therapists and researchers are observing a significant increase in infidelity by married women.[2] Every era has its defining stories, and one of ours may be a new crisis of infidelity.

In the past, the more common type of extramarital involvement was the married man who had casual sex with single women who were not his equal in status or income. There have always been a fairly substantial group of men and a smaller number of women looking for "a little bit on the side." They kept these liaisons separate from their committed relationships, and their escapades usually had no effect on a marriage unless they were discovered.

The same progress and freedom that allow men and women to be business partners, serve together in organizations, and form friendships based on their appreciation of each other as human beings bring with them extra obligations. To both preserve our special friendships *and* keep our vows, we must be more aware than ever before of appropriate boundaries between friends. As I tell my clients, the grass looks greener on the other side of the fence only because we don't have to mow it. Fences allow us to focus on cultivating the good things growing in our own garden and allow others the privacy to do the same. Solid boundaries discourage trespassing.

When you're about to cross the line that separates the richness of friendship from the dangers of something much more intense and destructive, the most obvious red flag is that feeling of attraction that warns you to pull back.

Being Attracted Means You're Still Breathing

Attraction is one of the most dependable constants of our lives. We meet good-looking, dynamic, smart people at work, at class reunions, in restaurants, and on the Internet. As electrically charged beings, we continually respond to the positive charges of others. It doesn't matter whether we are happily married. In the moment of attraction, we are fully alive to the possibilities of potential intimacy.

What is it that allows some individuals to resist the temptation of attraction while others give in to it? The answer lies in the complex interweaving of opportunity, vulnerability, commitment, and values. As psychiatrist Frank Pittman says, "Being in love doesn't protect people from lust." [3] Certainly, the circumstances have to be favorable. You have to meet someone who attracts you when you have the opportunity and the inclination to pursue it. It's worth noting, however, that many people who don't have time for marriage still manage to find time for an affair.

Women who have affairs often consciously detach from their marriages before getting involved. In contrast, men more often withdraw from their marriages as a consequence of extramarital involvement. For both men and women, not thinking about alternatives is a sign of dedication to their marriage partner. Dedicated couples are as protective of their relationship as couples who've just fallen in love. They are cocooned in their own world, blind to the temptations around them, and oblivious of everyone else. Other people are perceived as a threat to their commitment and their relationship.[4] Their friendships have reinforced walls that preserve their commitments.

Being Jealous Could Mean That You're Tuned In

Even in dedicated couples, however, one partner may be oblivious to the subtle manipulations of someone who is attracted to him or her. It's not unusual for a concerned partner to be the first to notice that someone else is trying to slip through the marital wall. You may have felt, on some level, that someone is making a play for your partner, while your partner may deny that such a dynamic exists. Often, concerned spouses will express their uneasiness by saying that their partner "talks about this friend all the time" or, conversely, that it's pretty mysterious that he or she no longer mentions the friend's name. The involved partner may strenuously squash any suggestion of impropriety in an offended tone and even denigrate the concerned spouse as foolish or crazy for bringing up the possibility.

I have often worked with couples where one partner expressed discomfort about a friendship that felt a little too friendly in the absence of any tangible evidence that there was a problem. Warren and Wendy were one such couple, who were in therapy to address other relationship problems. Their progress had frozen, though, and it felt to me as if one of them had a hidden agenda that they wouldn't address. Warren began to remark on certain changes in Wendy's behavior that made him think she was becoming involved with someone else: "All of a sudden, she's wearing new makeup and sexy underwear. She's lost weight, and she's gone back to running after work, like she did when we were first married." He complained that she talked constantly on her cell phone with the door closed when she was home. She claimed she was talking to colleagues and clients about a big confidential project.

Whenever he brought up his uneasiness, his wife made him feel small-minded and overly jealous. "I go back and forth reassuring myself that she won't cheat on me," he said. In the face of her disdain, he dropped his concern, saying that she had never done such a thing before and had always been a good wife: "She's an honest, moral person who would never lie to me." Months later, they were back in my office trying to deal with the affair she had been having.

Wendy had accused Warren of being jealous. There is a big difference between irrational jealousy and rational jealousy. For the irrationally jealous person, things are not what they seem. Normal interactions seem to be strategic moves in the game of seduction; every moment contains the threat of loss. The emotionally jealous person sees only shades of green, not the nuanced hues that color a normal view of life. For example, a husband gets upset when his wife lunches with a male client, or a wife objects to her husband's driving their attractive neighbor to the community association meetings. It doesn't take long for the suspicions of irrationally jealous spouses to be dismissed by everyone. Even when they are correct, no one takes them seriously because of their long-time misperceptions and cries of wolf.

> Men and women are jealous over different things. Research shows that men get more upset about their wives' having sex with other men, and women get more upset about their husbands' being involved in an emotionally satisfying relationship with another woman.[5]

On the other hand, rational jealousy should be taken seriously. Sometimes jealousy is *not* a sign of paranoia but a healthy reaction to valid suspicions. When a not normally jealous spouse suddenly starts getting suspicious, the jealousy is apt to be based on a threat that is real. For instance, Paul and Pam had seen a therapist about her jealousy over letters he was receiving at his office from a former flame, Margaret. Their therapist told them that Pam was suffering from a case of pathological jealousy. But in our couple therapy, I advised Paul to tell Margaret to begin writing him at the house, where he could share their correspondence with Pam. Margaret was enraged that her private communications were being curtailed. The letters that came to the house had a different tone and no longer began with the salutation "My dearest Paul." When it was time for Margaret's birthday, Pam suggested that they send her a birthday card with both signatures on it. Paul was impressed that Pam's hunches about Margaret's intentions had been right on the mark, and her "pathological jealousy" was cured as soon as the walls came down between her and Paul.

Vigilance can be a prudent response that helps the concerned spouse gather more information before deciding how to cope with the situation. It also serves to forewarn a wavering spouse who is teetering on the edge of overstepping proper boundaries and breaking a commitment to the marriage.

Approaching the Slippery Slope

Throughout the book, we will follow one couple in particular, before, during, and after the husband's affair. Their life together represents a common pattern of infidelity and its aftermath.

To Have and to Hold . . .

When Rachel and Ralph got married, they believed that they were equally committed to their promises to remain faithful. Infidelity was not consistent with their values or their loyalty to and love for each other. Besides, they had both witnessed how families could be shattered by extramarital involvements. They wanted to build a family that was safe, secure, and loving.

> In population research by Michael Wiederman, 80 percent of men and women who had engaged in extramarital intercourse said that it was almost always or always wrong.[6]

Ralph and Rachel thought that infidelity occurred in line with the cultural stereotype of men making advances to less powerful but sexually attractive women. They believed it happened to unhappily married men or women who didn't really love their mates. To Ralph and Rachel, people who had affairs were inconsiderate and self-indulgent more than anything else. They assumed that affairs never happened unless something in the marriage went wrong. They considered *their* relationship to be a loving partnership between equals. They naturally assumed that because they were so well matched neither of them would succumb to the attractions of others. Their fundamental commitment and compatibility did not change as they became increasingly preoccupied with daily responsibilities for their two young children.

They could not have guessed that the conditions of their lives would lead Ralph slowly to drift into an affair. He wasn't even aware that he was violating his own principles, except perhaps toward the very end. Like the frog that finds itself in a pan of cool water heating slowly on the stove, Ralph was so comfortable at first that it didn't occur to him to jump out. By the time he perceived that he had a problem, the water was boiling hot and it was too late to escape. Despite his avowed disapproval of extramarital sex, Ralph gradually became involved with Lara, a work colleague whom he considered just a friend.

Step 1: Platonic Friendship/Secure Marriage

As a married couple, Rachel and Ralph were surrounded by a protective wall and looked out onto the outside world through the same window. They had no real secrets from each other. They openly shared their enthusiasms about their friendships with other people because they knew they had nothing to hide. For many years, they succeeded in maintaining appropriate boundaries around their marriage. They followed sensible guidelines for preserving their unity. These are the precautions they took:

- *They didn't discuss relationship problems with anyone who could be a potential alternative to their spouse.* They knew that when you complain about your partner or listen to someone else's sad story, you establish intimacy and signal that you just might be *too* interested and available. Sharing your relationship dissatisfactions with a third party opens a window and begins to create a bond that often crosses the first threshold into an affair.

- *On those occasions when they did need to talk to someone about their marriage, they made sure that the person was a friend of the marriage.* They were right in assuming that an inclination to work out problems and to see the upside can be adversely affected by someone else's negative bias.

- *When one of them had a friend who wanted to talk about personal problems, they were careful about boundaries.* There were times when one or the other wanted to rescue a friend in trouble, but they didn't try to do it alone. When either of them got too involved, they knew they had to take off the Superman cape and include their partner in their helping gestures. Confidential investments in another person's calamities are a well-trodden path toward becoming too emotionally involved.

When Ralph first started working with Lara, they didn't talk about their marriages, except in general, positive terms. This "friendly" wall prevented them from sharing intimate details about all aspects of their lives. As friends, they had small windows into each other's lives, but they didn't get overly personal.

For quite a while, Ralph and Lara were delighted to be such compatible coworkers. They helped each other out; they laughed; they shared the same basic philosophy of life. They bonded over the television show *The Sopranos.* Every Monday morning they would avidly debrief on the previous night's episode. Talking about the characters and their predicaments gave them a way to get to know each other well. Ralph couldn't help contrasting Lara's enthusiasm with his wife's hatred of the program. Where Lara saw humor and deep feeling, Rachel saw violence and the objectification of women.

Step 2: Intimate Friendship/Insecure Marriage

Things began to heat up when Ralph began to fudge on the marriage-saving precautions he and Rachel had always followed. Over time, he began to share more of himself with Lara than with his wife. Part of the reason was simply that Rachel and Ralph had less time together than they used to. When they met, Rachel was a nurse in a pediatric intensive care unit. After they married and had children, they decided it would be best for their family if Rachel worked on the weekend, when Ralph was home. That way she could stay involved with the profession she loved and be available for the children during the week. Because Ralph had more income-earning potential, it made sense to free him to climb the corporate ladder. This arrangement kept Ralph and Rachel so busy with the children that they didn't have much couple time. They spent even less time together when they found out that their seven-year-old had a learning disability, and Rachel had to spend additional hours with him in the evening on reading and homework. Ralph found himself hungry for the stimulating conversations he could have with Lara.

Ralph and Lara went from being glad to see each other, to wishing they didn't have to deal with other people, to sneaking time alone. And when they *were* alone, they began to reveal more and more of themselves. Ralph would say, "I've never told anyone this before." Lara would sometimes cry when she told Ralph about her unhappy marriage and painful childhood memories. When they talked about their desires and aspirations, it felt as if they had never been so close to the heart of their own lives. They allowed their liking for each other to become a major fascination. The problem wasn't that they were attracted, but that they began to act on their feelings as if they had no other primary commitments.

At this point, the window between them was expanding, while the window between them and their spouses was shrinking. Ralph and Lara were sharing more, whereas Ralph and Rachel were sharing less, unaware that the quality of their conversations was deteriorating. Most of their time was spent hashing out the details of family administration and crafting problem-solving strategies concerning their children. There was only a faint trace of the rich exchange of ideas and feelings that had brought them together in the first place.

By now Ralph was spending a lot of time thinking about Lara. And Rachel, who had been hearing about Lara's superlative qualities, also found herself thinking about her. If we could eavesdrop on their private thoughts, this is what we might hear:

> RALPH: *I'm so glad I can wake up and go to work and Lara will be there. When we have lunch together today, I'm going to tell her about the PBS special I saw last night and how I'm feeling inspired to get on the treadmill and work out more. I can really share things with her and be myself. She understands me. Sometimes, with Rachel, things are more difficult. We talk at cross-purposes more than we used to. I feel like we never have any fun together anymore.*

RACHEL: *Ralph sure lights up when he talks about Lara. It's bet-ter than that time when he was so miserable at work. Now, he seems to have more energy and more enthusiasm for work and life in general. Honestly, I may have a pinprick of worry about Lara, but when I stop and think about it, I have nothing to base it on. Things are good be-tween us. Things are fine—I think. We've just been kind of busy and haven't been able to spend much time together. But we still love each other and that's what really counts.*

It's obvious that Rachel is of two minds here. Several months earlier, she had met Lara at a company get-together. She had been uneasy when Lara seemed a little too familiar toward Ralph, referring to a joke only she and Ralph knew and putting her hand on his arm. When Rachel men-tioned her discomfort to Ralph, he brushed her off and told her she was imagining things. His defensiveness made Rachel feel shut out.

Walls and Windows

In many cases, the transition from friendship to affair is barely percepti-ble—to both participants and observers. The boundaries shift slowly. Having a clear, easy way to see where the boundaries are at any given moment can bring both friendship and marriage into sharp focus. One way to determine whether a particular friendship is threatening is to ask *Where are the walls and where are the windows?* This is a useful metaphor for clarifying boundary issues in extramarital triangles.[7]

In a committed relationship, a couple constructs a wall that shields them from any outside forces that have the power to split them. They look at the world outside their relationship through a shared window of openness and honesty. The couple is a unit, and they have a united front to deal with children, in-laws, and friends. An affair erodes their carefully constructed security system. It erects an interior *wall of secrecy* between the marriage partners, at the same time that it opens a *window of intimacy* between the affair partners. The couple is no longer a unit. The affair partner is on the inside, and the marital partner is on the outside.

Asking yourself about the placement of walls and windows can help you determine when an outside relationship has moved beyond friendship into an extramarital relationship. When a friend knows more about your marriage than a spouse knows about your friendship, you have already reversed the healthy position of walls and windows.

Opportunity Is Everywhere

Let's take a look at how people commonly work and socialize. We'll see how easy it is for close, affectionate relationships between men and women to evolve into extramarital affairs. In the past, men and women occupied different spheres: Men worked outside the home and women ran the household and raised children. The rules that governed social and economic behavior inhibited personal freedom. Married men and women were not often exposed to the opportunity for relationships with the opposite sex based on mutual interest and a preference for each other's company.

Today, there are coed dorms, coed workout facilities, open membership in country clubs and civic organizations, sex-blind admission to graduate school, equal access to the armed forces and the professions—all of these changes and others allow individuals to mix freely where once they were segregated and restricted. Women and men live, study, and work together and, not surprisingly, find pleasure in the freedom to come and go as they please.

There are significant differences between men's and women's responses to opportunity. Men desire extramarital sex and often regret lack of opportunity, whereas most women do not understand why a happily married person would want sex with anyone but their spouse.[8] Men tend to be more alert than women to opportunities for extramarital involvement, and they have more chances because of the availability and interest of single women.

In a British survey, 40 percent of unfaithful men had an affair with an unmarried woman.[9]

Of course, opportunity is partly in the eye of the beholder. A happily married woman seems to have a "filter" that screens out other potential

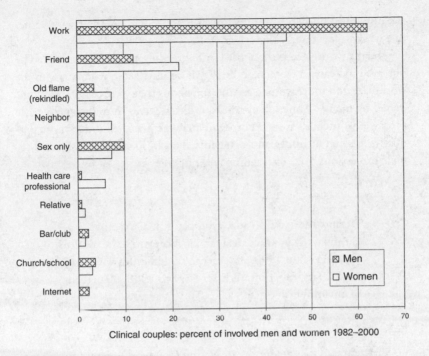

Clinical couples: percent of involved men and women 1982–2000

Unfaithful spouse's acquaintanceship with affair partner

partners.[10] She just doesn't see them; for her, they don't exist. This is a perfect illustration of the general principle that *interest creates opportunity;* conversely, lack of interest creates blindness to opportunity. When a man does make a move, she may even discount it and say, "He didn't mean it. He was just joking."

The overwhelming majority of unfaithful individuals in my clinical practice were not out seeking opportunity. Eighty-two percent of those who had affairs started out being social acquaintances, neighbors, or workplace colleagues with their future affair partners. They never imagined that their friends and coworkers would become co-conspirators in secret love trysts.

Danger Zone: Men and Women at Work!

Work can be hazardous to the health of your relationship. The statistics are alarming; in fact, 46 percent of the unfaithful wives and 62 percent of

the unfaithful husbands in my clinical practice had an affair with someone whom they met through their work.[11]

Today's workplace is the most fertile breeding ground for affairs. The
observed increase in women's infidelity is because more women are in the
workplace and more women are in professions that were previously dom-
inated by men.[12] Annette Lawson found that wives in traditionally male
professions, such as law and corporate management, exhibited more permissive marital attitudes and behaviors than husbands in traditional female professions, such as teaching and nursing.

> During the past decade, workplace affairs among un-
> faithful wives in my clinical sample increased dramatically.
> From 1982 to 1990, 38 percent of unfaithful wives had
> work affairs. By contrast, from 1991 to 2000, 50 percent
> of unfaithful wives had work affairs.

Very few activities are more captivating than working hard together to
achieve common goals. Inspired by teamwork and shared accomplishments, office romances often begin when the pressure of a work deadline
triggers an adrenaline rush that can be misinterpreted as sexual arousal.
The tension and excitement of working closely together for long hours on
demanding projects can charge the sexual chemistry between two people.
Ordering out for Chinese food, loosening your tie, and strategizing victory into the wee hours of the night becomes, intentionally or not, a form
of seduction.

My research and the research of others point to *opportunity* as a primary factor in the occurrence of extramarital involvements.[13] Attractions
are a fact of life when men and women work side by side at the office,
where shared coffee breaks and lunches are commonplace, and where
daily interactions around business projects are the norm. We are so used
to this camaraderie that we hardly notice how habit-forming it can become. But to get another perspective, imagine what you would think if
your best friend called your spouse every night on the way home just to
talk or if your spouse went with your next-door neighbor to share a latte

at the neighborhood Starbucks every morning. You would undoubtedly worry and wonder.

One researcher, Fred Humphrey, calls this phenomenon the "cup of coffee" syndrome.[14] Two people who are married to others begin to meet for coffee breaks. They look forward to the chance to relax and talk. Pretty soon, they are meeting regularly, and the talk becomes increasingly intimate as they share more details of their personal lives. Soon, they can't live without their cups of coffee. Who knew coffee was so potent? Apparently, however, empathic communication can be even more addictive than caffeine.

> In my clinical sample, men who had workplace affairs were married longer when they had their first extramarital sex than men who had affairs in other settings. Fifty-six percent of men involved in workplace affairs had their first extramarital sexual experience after nine years of marriage. Twenty-seven percent of men in non-workplace affairs reported that their first extramarital sexual encounter occurred after nine years of marriage.

Clearly, extramarital involvement is facilitated by careers that offer greater autonomy and freedom from constraint.[15] Some individuals have more opportunity than others for such meetings. People who are home-bound, such as housewives with young children, don't have much personal freedom during the day. Attorneys, on the other hand, have a moderate amount. And traveling salesmen and airline pilots are comparatively free from constraint. (Some airlines now insist that flight attendants change crews with every flight rather than travel with the same group of people several days in a row.) At the high end of opportunity, some professions require out-of-town meetings and conferences where men and women travel together overnight. Finding yourself in a hotel, away from home with plenty to eat and drink and no curfew makes it easy to advance a collegial relationship to a deeper level.

Happily married women often ignore or resist the signs that a man might be interested in more than friendship or a professional relationship. Anna, a young teacher, became confused when Mark, whom she considered her mentor, began to show an interest in her that was more than professional. Mark, a married man in his early forties, was one of the most experienced teachers at this very challenging school and had been her most dependable friend. She had relied on him as a source of sound advice when students became disruptive.

Anna had assumed that because Mark was a sympathetic colleague, she could be honest with him about things that were bothering her. They enjoyed laughing about classroom antics and talking seriously about the books they assigned their students. Anna told me, "He reminded me of my dad, and I assumed he related to me so well because he had daughters of his own. But then he called and asked me to lunch. I went because I was lonely and figured he was safe." His attention was flattering. She didn't think anything bad could happen because she loved her husband, and Mark was a family man who adored his children and was content with his marriage.

During the course of the lunch, he asked Anna if her e-mail was private or if her husband read her messages. That was a big red flag. When he made an offhand remark to the effect that he didn't think Anna's husband was supportive enough, she became anxious. Now she says, "He's started sending me two or three e-mail messages a day. It feels weird and, I have to admit, intriguing." She has begun to compare Mark's maturity and understanding with her husband's lack of sophistication.

Notice that this man has been perfectly honest about his apparently happy family life. Even so, he is drawn to a young colleague who puts him on a pedestal. Although affairs among coworkers are the most common, they do not necessarily mean the partners are in unhappy marriages. James Wiggins and Doris Lederer discovered that involved coworkers generally considered themselves to be happily married and highly compatible with their spouses.[16] At the same time, collegial relationships provided the opportunity to share common interests and mutual admiration on a level that is rare in a long-term marriage.

By and large, people who get involved with coworkers don't set out to turn their friendships into romances. Colleagues and coworkers who drift into affairs are blind to the red flags that mark their passageway. They are so energized by the unreserved acceptance and the support for each other's ideas, skills, and goals that they don't notice how their relationship is changing. The constant proximity and emotional bonding combine to create a powerful aphrodisiac. They are oblivious to the potential chaos and agony that will befall their families if the infidelity is exposed.

> In my clinical sample, 55 percent of husbands and 50 percent of wives who had affairs at the work setting had not had a previous affair.

In Your Own Backyard

Although the majority of emotional affairs happen between coworkers, romance between social friends and neighbors is also common. Among couples I have treated, friends or neighbors were partners in the cases of 16 percent of unfaithful husbands and 29 percent of unfaithful wives. When we understand how thin the line is between friends and lovers, this is not surprising. The ingredients for romantic attachment are already present in a friendship. You like each other, share a history, and are good at talking about your feelings.

Despite the obvious similarities, there are clear differences between friendships and emotional affairs. Emotional affairs are characterized by *secrecy, emotional intimacy,* and *sexual chemistry.* These three elements can combine into a potent brew that intensifies the attraction that already exists. If the relationship is an open book, it is probably a friendship. When attempts are made to hide feelings or interactions, the friendship is becoming something else. When there is more companionship, intellectual sharing, and understanding in the friendship than in the marriage, that's also a warning signal. Sexual chemistry, an undercurrent of arousal and desire, is only enflamed by admissions that a sexual attraction exists but won't be acted on.

It is easier to hide an affair in modern settings where men and women are free to hang out together in public. When you see a man and a woman out in public together, you can't be sure if they are just friends or not. They may be listening attentively to each other, laughing, and speaking in common references. Friends and lovers can be hard to tell apart. Of course, their committed partners can probably tell the difference in an instant by picking up on clues that are invisible to others. But that doesn't obscure the fact that either a friend or a lover can bring you chicken soup when you have a cold, call you late at night with good news, or invite you to lunch.

Men and women tend to view friendship differently. For women, friendship is being vulnerable, open, self-disclosing, and emotionally supportive. For men, friendship is doing things together, side by side. When women treat men friends like their women friends, the emotional intimacy that is natural for a woman can send her male friend a signal she didn't intend. Because husbands tend to save their emotional intimacy for their wives, when they do let themselves become open and vulnerable to another woman it is much more likely to jeopardize the marriage.[17] From the woman's point of view, emotional bonding doesn't become serious until it becomes sexual. Although a man can prove his true friendship for a woman by not pressing for a sexual relationship, the fact is that it is the responsibility of both to put the brakes on.

Often, it's easier to talk with a friend than with a spouse. Friends can be less judgmental, more accepting, and not as likely to overreact because they don't have the same vulnerabilities or expectations from the relationship as long-term partners. In the movie *When Harry Met Sally,* Billy Crystal and Meg Ryan were "just friends" who gave advice freely and welcomed each other's opinions. When Harry told Sally that she wore slacks too often and would look better in skirts, she responded to his observation seriously, almost gratefully. If he had offered this opinion after their relationship had become sexual and when he was more than a friend, he would probably have hurt her feelings. I can imagine her responding defensively and saying, "Oh, I see! Are you trying to tell me you don't like the way I look? I guess you're not attracted to me anymore."

One couple I counseled illustrates how comfortable it can be to open up to a friend who doesn't have to live with our troublesome behaviors or moods. Daryl was afraid he was going to be laid off at work. There had been rumors of layoffs and downsizing, and he'd always had a problem meeting deadlines. He discovered a sympathetic listener in the neighbor next door. He was reluctant to burden his wife, Debbie, who had been preoccupied and depressed because her best friend had just been diagnosed with an advanced stage of ovarian cancer. But besides not wanting to cause his wife further anxiety, he didn't want to hear her words of advice.

Eventually, Debbie discovered how often Daryl was talking to their neighbor and hiding it from her. When she confronted him, he said, "What are you so upset about? We're just friends." And when she confronted the neighbor, her neighbor said, "You have no right to be upset. He needed somebody to talk to, and what he told me was between him and me. It had nothing to do with you."

This friendship had already crossed the threshold of emotional intimacy. Daryl was not telling Debbie how often he was confiding in his neighbor. He was sharing feelings with her that he was not sharing with Debbie, feelings that were increasingly expressed with physical affection: touches on the hand and shoulder. If the neighbor had been interested only in friendship, she would have encouraged Daryl to share his feelings with his wife rather than encouraging secrets between them. Her defensiveness was a red flag too. At first, Daryl couldn't understand Debbie's hurt and outrage because he had not had sex with his friendly neighbor. Eventually, though, he understood that his emotional intimacy with another woman was a violation of his commitment to his wife.

Not all friendships are so dangerous or pose a threat to the marriage. You can have friends who are *friends of the marriage*. They are not in competition with the marriage. They characteristically reinforce the value of marriage in general and their friends' committed relationships in particular. They react to marital complaints with problem-solving approaches that support continuing commitment. Anyone who can be considered an attractive alternative to the marriage partner, however, is a threat *unless* he or she is a friend of the marriage. Single people on the prowl or married people who openly complain about their current relationship are least likely to be friends of the marriage. They represent the highest risk. Potential affair partners often signal their availability or readiness to engage beyond the normal boundaries.

> **A**lmost every unfaithful spouse among my clinical couples was involved with someone who was either unmarried or was already detaching from an unhappy relationship.

Old Flames Burn Hottest

If friendships and collegial relationships can become overheated, former lovers are positively flammable. When they meet again after years apart, they are quick to ignite. They look into each other's eyes and see themselves as they once were: younger, more beautiful, and full of life. Their passion quickly takes root in them again. They know each other, and being together feels like coming home.

People who reconnect and then fall in love again talk about the intensity of their bond and often feel their love is unique. In fact, if their reconnection results in marriage or a committed exclusive relationship, these unions are highly successful. Nancy Kalish has discovered in her study of rekindled romances that 72 percent of these reconnecting partners stay together. If they were first loves who were torn apart by situational factors, their stay-together rate is 78 percent.[18]

When former loves meet, especially those who never consummated their relationships, they have to exert themselves consciously to control their feelings and not pursue the relationship. They cannot meet just once, reminisce casually about old times, and not ignite former feelings. Simply believing that their love for their current partner will stop them is not enough.

Linda learned this lesson, with some loving help from her husband, Richard.[19] They had been married for nine years and had two children. One Saturday afternoon, Linda and Richard took their kids to the local yogurt store. It gradually dawned on Linda that the familiar-looking face of the man in line was her old boyfriend, David. He looked "absolutely gorgeous" with his white hair and nose job.

"It was like everything stopped. I was trying to be nonchalant. But my heart was going ka-boom, ka-boom." After introductions, they chatted and discovered how much they had in common. Linda was a clinical psychologist and David was a psychoanalyst. On the way home, Linda couldn't stop thinking about him.

The next morning, David started leaving messages on Linda's office phone, which she didn't answer. He said he couldn't stop thinking about her. A few days later, he left another message, saying that she probably had her own life, but he couldn't get her out of his mind. Linda found herself becoming preoccupied with him. When he called again and asked her to lunch, she realized how badly she wanted to go.

Linda told Richard that David had invited her to lunch, and she asked him if he minded. She realized that she couldn't look Richard in the eyes because she was so thrilled about seeing David again. At that point, she decided to confess to Richard how fixated she was with David. "Richard was amazing," she said. "When I confessed how obsessed I was, he took me in his arms and held me, and he said, 'Honey, I'm so sorry I can't do that for you anymore.' That's all he said." Linda immediately called David and told him never to call her again. Sharing her feelings with her husband was the best thing Linda could have done.

When we share our hidden feelings about another person with our spouse, the intensity and fascination of that secret are greatly diminished. We let reality into fantasy. When Linda opened a window with her husband, she was able to close an old one with her former boyfriend.

The Intimacy of the Internet

It's easy to understand the power of mutual attraction with interesting new acquaintances or exciting old flames. Our senses move us toward those who are good-looking, funny, smart, or otherwise fascinating. In the privacy of our own thoughts, we are led into a mental betrayal of our partner every day through the seductive realities of a gentle voice, engaging smile, or adoring eyes.

Incredibly, we can now betray our partner through the Internet without receiving any of these physical cues. We can fall in love, or into lust, without ever seeing or touching the object of our desire. Emotional affairs can bloom in any home that has a computer. Researcher Debbie Layton-Tholl found that 27 percent of the respondents in her on-line infidelity study met their affair partners on the Internet.[20]

Internet infidelity is the epitome of extramarital emotional involvement because it meets all three criteria that discriminate between a platonic friendship and an emotional affair. *Emotional intimacy* quickly develops on the Internet because freedom from distractions and lack of social constraints promote a form of free association that allows you to say anything that comes to mind. The wall of *secrecy* that soon surrounds these intimate Internet communications leads to lying, which feeds the obsession with these covert activities. *Sexual chemistry* is fueled by titillating exchanges about sexual fantasies and practical barriers to physical contact. Although some on-line affairs do result in face-to-

face assignations, most do not. Yet actual sexual contact is not a require-
ment for betrayal.

Here's the scene: It's getting late. A woman walks into the computer
room to say goodnight to her spouse, who is ordinarily involved in a
hobby-centered chat room, but notices he seems breathless and mesmer-
ized, so she approaches quietly. He hears her, though, and hits the close
button. A second before the screen goes blank, she sees a flash of a sexually
provocative image, and the words "I can't wait to meet you." She can't believe her eyes. She goes numb and feels as if she's going to pass out. "Are
you looking at pornography?" she stammers. "Of course not," comes the
indignant reply. But suddenly she's not so sure. Now that she thinks about
it, her partner has been wedded to the computer lately, and this isn't the
first time the screen has gone dead when she's walked in unexpectedly.
More than that, her partner has seemed a little, well, strange and distant.
There hasn't been much warmth or much conversation.

This is an upsetting scenario, but it is not unusual. Cyberspace is full
of detours onto very dangerous ground. Anyone can turn on a computer
and meet people who are eager to share personal information and sexual
banter on-line. To the uninitiated or the uninterested, it may seem puzzling that words and images on a computer screen can be so powerful that
they disrupt a person's real life, causing some to lose their committed relationships and even their jobs.

But such on-screen love affairs on the Internet are a new, real threat.
Thousands of people go home every night and can hardly wait to turn on
with their on-line connection. They sit rapt and enthralled by secret relationships that are most fully realized in their imagination. If you've never
had this experience, you might wonder how it could happen. Why would
you ignore the real live person you live with in favor of an unknown and
unseen screen presence you cannot even touch?

From my personal experience as a participant in a message board for
breast cancer survivors, I know how absorbing and intimate on-line relationships can be. We provide each other invaluable medical information,
compassion, support for scary setbacks, and a cheering squad for good
test results. We feel a terrible, lingering loss if someone we have never met
in person dies. Again and again someone on the board says, "Nobody understands me like you all do. I just can't share these kinds of feelings with
my friends and family." An advantage of our on-line relationships is that

we can choose a convenient time to post or respond. Our on-line sisters never say, "Not now. I'm busy."

To get a better understanding about e-lovers, let's look at it from the on-line partner's point of view. In-person relationships are labor-intensive; they take time and, sooner or later, either partner can become disillusioned. You have to hammer out a way to accommodate your two different tastes and living styles, try to mesh two different sets of personal goals, and endure both the boredom and the irritation of actually living in the same space. You take a daily "toothpaste test"; that is, you share the same tube of toothpaste and argue about missing caps and which end to squeeze. You argue about kids and mortgages.

In cyberspace you don't have to do any of that. You can inhabit any persona you choose to create. You can experiment with new roles—sensitive, sexy, or wise. You see each other in the best possible light. Sympathetic correspondence ripens very quickly into intimate connection. Within a few exchanges, you are confiding to each other in the same way you would open yourself to your private diary. You come to feel as if the other person is your soul mate; you find yourself "saying" things you've never said to anyone else before. You can see into each other's hearts and empathize with each other's disappointments and wishes. Some people feel good because they are truly needed; others are relieved that their e-friend is not needy and is willing to cater to *their* needs. Either way, it's whatever your heart desires. You find yourself speaking with a passion and a longing that you haven't experienced since you were fourteen years old, if ever.

And then there's the sex. The two of you have created a secret garden where the sexual chemistry is intensified by titillating exchanges and flights of sexual fancy. The romantic idealization allows you to be anyone you want to be and to project perfect qualities onto your e-lover. Sharing sexual experiences and sexual fantasies in virtual space can be more arousing and more intimate than actually having sexual intercourse with your mate. And, as we shall see, virtual sex leads some of these newly formed couples to meet and consummate their desire in real time.

At any point, of course, this on-line reverie can be rudely interrupted if the real-world partner becomes suspicious and uncovers the private playground. When detective work unearths evidence of a sexually charged, emotionally intimate relationship, the on-line partner usually protests that the effects on the marriage have been negligible. There hasn't been any actual physical contact; therefore, there hasn't been any betrayal—so the argument goes.

But it doesn't feel that way to the betrayed partner. People who discover their partner's on-line emotional and sexual affairs are devastated. Their basic assumptions of honesty and trust have been shattered; the couple's commitment to exclusivity has been broken. As far as the betrayed partner is concerned, there's little difference between adultery on the computer and adultery at a seedy motel on the interstate. The trauma is the same and recovery from it is just as slow. And there is an additional encumbrance: firm household rules must now be established for the use of the computer, which should be used only in a common family area, among other restrictions.

There are many parallels between in-person affairs and Internet affairs. Often, they both start innocently enough. In fact, the first steps are usually deceptively simple. Who would believe that the simple exchange of friendly e-mails could result in divorce and the consequent disruption in the lives of children? Most people never step back to consider the implications of what they are doing. They don't realize that they can use the same precautions that protect committed relationships from in-person affairs to protect them from Internet affairs.

Quiz: Is Your On-line Friendship Too Friendly?

What are the warning signs that you (or your partner) are on the slippery slope to an on-line affair? Take this on-line relationship quiz and see.[21]

Directions: Circle Yes or No to the left of each statement.

Yes No   1. Do you find yourself coming to bed later at night because you are chatting on-line?

Yes No   2. Do you ever exit a screen because you do not want a family member to see what you are reading or writing to a chat room member?

Yes No   3. Have you ever lied to your spouse about your personal Internet activities?

Yes No 4. Would you feel uncomfortable sharing your Internet correspondence with your spouse?

Yes No 5. Have you ever set up a separate e-mail account or credit card to carry on a personal correspondence with an individual on-line?

Yes No 6. Has your Internet correspondence had a negative effect on your work or household tasks?

Yes No 7. Have you ever lied in response to a question from your spouse about your e-mail correspondence?

Yes No 8. Have you ever exchanged photos of yourself with a secret e-mail correspondent?

Yes No 9. Since beginning a secret e-mail correspondence, have you experienced either a loss or an unusual increase in sexual desire with your spouse?

Yes No 10. Have you made arrangements to talk secretly on the phone with your e-mail correspondent?

Yes No 11. Have you made arrangements to meet with your secret e-mail correspondent?

Scoring Key:

Two or more *yes* answers to questions 1, 2, 3, 4 indicate a potential Internet romance is developing. It is time to either share your on-line correspondence with your mate or break off the correspondence and begin to examine how to improve your marriage.

A *yes* answer to any of questions 5, 6, 7 indicates you are crossing the boundary from an Internet friendship to an Internet romance. Acknowledge this relationship for what it is about to become and take action to preserve and enhance your marriage.

A *yes* answer to question 8 or 9 indicates you have begun a fantasy romantic relationship with your on-line correspondent. Even if it never moves to a physical stage, this relationship has great potential to damage or destroy your marriage.

A *yes* answer to question 10 or 11 indicates that you have taken positive action toward initiating an extramarital affair. Consider the impact this will have on your marriage and your children and take steps to sort this out with a professional.

The Prevention Myth

Often after an affair comes to light, outside observers will speculate unfairly and ignorantly that the betrayed wife must have been reluctant or inadequate in the bedroom, or that the husband of an unfaithful wife was spending too much time at work, and *this* explains the affair. Just as uninformed gossips often blame inadequacies or weaknesses in the betrayed partner, women are more prone than men to blame themselves for their partner's infidelity. They think if only they had been more desirable (loving, available, competent, sexy, slender . . .), the affair would never have happened.

This is what I call the Prevention Myth, which states that a loving partner and a good marriage will prevent affairs. This misconception is not supported by any research, even though it is commonly cited as fact on television shows and in popular books about how to affair-proof your marriage. Any advice based on this bad assumption and simplification of a complex issue is misleading. The fact is, sometimes an affair can be understood by exploring deficiencies in the marriage, but often it cannot. If you don't examine all the factors that contribute to an affair, you cannot know. Sometimes the explanation is as simple as attraction, opportunity, and failure to follow precautions. Sometimes it is more complex than that.

Avoiding Fatal Attractions

Most of us would not want to live in a world where we didn't feel some magnetic attraction to other people. But it does make sense to develop a personal strategy for protecting yourself and your relationships from the fallout of acting on such impulses. People who know how to safeguard a long-term relationship may not be able to say exactly how they do it, but you can be sure that they follow, consciously or unconsciously, these basic guidelines:

- *Know that attraction is normal. But just because you feel it doesn't mean you have to act on it. Being attracted to someone else doesn't mean that you've chosen to be with the wrong person.* One of the measures of true commitment is that you don't allow yourself to be pulled away from your priorities by distractions.

  In the movie *Six Days Seven Nights,* the heroine, played by Anne Heche, breaks off her engagement after a week of being stranded with Harrison Ford on a tropical island where they have faced all kinds of dangers. She believes that if her fiancé had been the right person for her, she would never have been attracted to someone else. What a ridiculous assumption! What woman in her right mind wouldn't feel an attraction to a heroic figure like Harrison Ford?

- *Don't let yourself fantasize about what it would be like to be with that other person.* Affairs begin in the mind. The prelude usually involves imagining yourself alone . . . satisfying the curiosity . . . savoring the closeness . . . anticipating the excitement.

- *Don't flirt.* To look is human, but flirting signals that you are available. You've sent out an invitation of receptivity and are ready to see who says yes.

- *Avoid risky situations.* After a skiing accident, former president Clinton never went skiing again. He should have shown similar caution when Monica Lewinsky flirted with him.

In the next chapter, you'll learn how to tell the difference between an emotional affair and a platonic friendship. You will see how emotional affairs intensify when they cross the threshold of sexual intimacy, and how leading a double life requires a balancing act that eventually begins to take its toll.

2

CROSSING INTO A DOUBLE LIFE

We didn't plan it.
After a year of getting closer and closer, it happened.
We fell into each other's arms, and there we were—kissing.

ALMOST EVERY newly married couple expects their relationship to be monogamous. They begin their lives together never imagining that one or both of them would come to consider infidelity acceptable.[1] They probably don't know, however, that pledging themselves to exclusivity will not protect them from thinking, feeling, and doing things they don't want anyone to know about. Even if, during the course of their marriage, they are unfaithful, they may continue to profess monogamy as a value (particularly for their spouse). While they are involved in their affair, they will carry on two different lives: one in public and the other in private. Depending on how careful they are, these two streams will run in parallel channels but will not mix.

Some people begin an affair because of sexual attraction and jump right into sex. But most women and an increasing number of men begin with an emotional connection without any thought of a sexual relationship. They spend time talking and getting to know each other. They delight in their companionship without worrying too much about where it's heading. As they become more intrigued by their friendship, more of their emotional energy is directed away from the marriage.

Step 3: Emotionally Involved Affair/ Emotionally Detached Marriage

Ralph and Lara were beginning to understand that their relationship was more than just a fond friendship. They were aware that they had developed a separate channel of communication and experience, apart from everybody else. They were becoming circumspect in public. Around their colleagues, they were careful not to indulge in any public displays of affection. They treated each other with a certain formality calculated to mask their easy intimacy. But they didn't fool anyone. The electricity between them sparked and crackled, and in the end they gave themselves away.

Far from the observant eyes of their colleagues, on the street or in a restaurant, they relaxed and engaged in a graceful choreography of gestures and body movements. They gazed into each other's eyes. They sat close together and touched each other lightly. They ate off of each other's plates. They finished each other's sentences, their emotions showing plainly through their hands and faces. Anybody looking at them would know they were enthralled with each other.

At home, Rachel told Ralph that she was concerned by some changes she was noticing. Ralph seemed different. He was spending more time at work, and he seemed less interested in the children. She pointed out, with worry in her voice, that he was extremely moody. When she asked him if something was wrong, he said, "Nothing's wrong." He reassured her by telling her how much pressure he was under to meet his sales quotas. He hugged her, and she believed him for the moment. But then he became distant again. She didn't trust her own instincts and mentally put herself down for being suspicious. Thank heaven she was able to focus her thoughts on the remodeling job they had started in the kitchen six months earlier. Staying busy kept her from brooding.

If we could have eavesdropped on Rachel's thoughts, this is what we would have heard:

RACHEL: *Although my gut tells me that something is wrong, I need to believe Ralph. I do wonder why he doesn't talk about Lara anymore, but when I ask him if something is going on with her, he says no. I know he's not the type of man to fool around. And he's always been honest with me. So I think I must be off base. But then I go back to trusting my own intuition, and I know something or someone has come between us. Maybe he's in some kind of trouble and is afraid to tell me. I wonder if it's my fault. I try to be extra caring and accommodating, but it doesn't seem to make a bit of difference. He still seems interested in sex but is less affectionate and hardly ever kisses me when we are making love. I wonder if he's having health problems or money problems he doesn't want to tell me about. Knowing the worst would be better than not knowing at all.*

As relationships become more intimate, people develop a truth bias in which they are more likely to judge their partners as truthful and less likely to detect deception.[2]

When Rachel raised questions about Lara, Ralph told her not to be so hyper, that she was jealous for no reason. He realized that he would have to be more careful about being nice to Rachel. But he was not good about keeping his resolution to make Rachel feel secure because he was so preoccupied with thoughts about Lara.

This is what Ralph was thinking:

RALPH: *I am so happy being with Lara. I feel so special when I'm with her because of the way she listens to me. We are completely tuned in to each other. I feel young and full of energy. I feel a little uncomfortable when I think about Rachel and the kids, so I try not to think about it. Besides, it doesn't really have anything to do with them. I'm not taking anything away from them. How could something innocent like this that makes me feel so good be a bad thing?*

Ralph had a clear conscience. He didn't think he and Lara were doing anything wrong. After all, he was still committed to Rachel. He hoped with all his heart that he could continue to maintain his stimulating relationship with Lara without endangering his marriage. He enjoyed the comfort and familiarity of marriage as well as the novelty and excitement he felt with Lara. Often, however, he thought about how much more fun Lara was. He loved how she looked up to him and put him on a pedestal.

As Ralph discovered, a compelling aspect of emotional affairs is the positive mirroring that occurs. We like how we see ourselves reflected in the other person's eyes. By contrast, in our long-term relationships, our reflection is like a 5x makeup mirror in which our flaws are magnified. In a new romance, our reflection is like the rosy glow of an illuminated vanity mirror.[3]

It is also important to note, however, that the magnetism of forbidden love gives the affair partner an intrinsic advantage when comparing the two relationships. It isn't that spouses are dull and troublesome and affair partners are brilliant and beautiful. Frank Pittman observed that the choice of an affair partner appears to be based on how that person differs from the spouse rather than any perceived superiority to the spouse.[4]

Ralph was convinced that his emotional tie to Lara was a good thing and was not affecting his marriage. His idea of what constitutes an affair was related to his assumption that affairs are about having sex. He felt safe because their relationship was based on a close friendship between two respectful human beings. Because their relationship wasn't sexual, he didn't consider it a "real" affair.

> Men are more likely than women to separate sex and love. In my clinical sample, 26 percent of men and only 3 percent of women said they had had extramarital sex without being emotionally involved.

Despite Ralph's traditional idea that sex defines an affair, his actual behavior signifies the most important new trend for men. The old "sex first" definition of men's affairs is changing. In this new crisis of infidelity, more men are now following what has traditionally been a female pattern, that of emotional bonding first and sex later.

For her part, Lara was having an *easier* time of it at home. She had started being unhappy in her marriage just a few months after the honeymoon, yet had been married for two years. When she started thinking seriously of leaving Lenny, she tried to persuade him to go to counseling with her. He refused to go, so she went by herself for individual therapy. She felt that her marriage had been a mistake, that she had married the wrong person. She was outgoing and sociable, and Lenny was a workaholic. Watching TV was all he wanted to do when he wasn't working. He hardly ever seemed interested in hearing how her day went. Lara told him how unhappy she was and how lonely she felt. In frustration, she nagged and complained.

Then, gradually, because Ralph satisfied her longing for companionship and understanding, she stopped pursuing Lenny. She stopped asking him for attention. Lenny, convinced that her silence meant she was happier, felt secure in the (mistaken) belief that things were better. In reality, she had given up on the marriage and was putting her energy into her closeness with Ralph. Like Lenny, many husbands unfortunately don't realize the meaning of their wife's withdrawal until she withholds sex—or, even worse, packs her bags.

Beginning a Double Life

A useful measure for whether a relationship is a friendship or an affair is the degree of secrecy that surrounds it. Although Ralph was expansive in the beginning about his budding friendship with Lara, he got quieter about it with every passing week. There was a lot he wasn't saying. If their relationship had been strictly platonic, he wouldn't have hesitated to share his encounters openly with Rachel. When it came to their private lunches and special times alone, he became the master of the white lie.

Let's see what the placement of walls and windows can show us that Ralph was either unable or unwilling to admit.

Where are the walls? Ralph stopped sharing the most vital, most interesting, and most gratifying part of his day. He wasn't talking to Rachel about Lara or about the subjects they found so fascinating. This secrecy created a distance between husband and wife. How could it be otherwise? Whenever people carry momentous secrets, they feel different, cut off, and isolated. One woman I know expressed perfectly the kind of communication we should all be striving for in our marriage: "How could I ever have an affair?" she asked. "I would immediately want to tell my husband about it. He is my best friend. I can't keep news like this a secret from my best friend."

Where are the windows? A window of intimacy was opening wide between Ralph and Lara. Although they had not kissed, they had begun confiding their sexual attraction for each other.

Forty percent of the adulterous relationships in a British survey were "affairs of the heart."[5]

In effect, Ralph's emotional attachment to Lara and the secrecy that this engendered was a breach of trust between him and Rachel. The implicit and explicit understanding of their marriage rested on emotional as well as physical exclusivity. They had never agreed that full access to other people would be part of their commitment to each other.

Three Red Flags at the Threshold

Ralph and Lara had stepped over the three thresholds that separate platonic friendships from romantic emotional affairs:

1. *Emotional intimacy* is the most powerful bond of all. Ralph and Lara shared more personal things about their hopes and fears than they were telling their spouses. They turned to each other to discuss troubling aspects of their marriages instead of working on the issues at home. They thought of themselves as soul mates and best friends. Compared with this, their spouses lived in the shadows like half-remembered dreams.

2. *Secrecy* waxes the slippery slope. Their budding romance was bound to thrive in the hothouse environment of the privacy they had built around their friendship. Ralph and Lara created a world well away from the pressure, responsibilities, and routines of ordinary family life. Ralph completely stopped mentioning Lara at home. The secret nature of their relationship automatically increased their intensity and fueled their preoccupation with each other.

3. *Sexual chemistry* is inflamed by forbidden sex. Ralph and Lara began telling each other how much they turned each other on. Both of them fantasized about what their sexual relationship would be like, even though they agreed that they would never act on their mutual desire. But in suppressing it, they found the sexual tension being deliciously increased.

Commitment versus Permission

When a friendship turns into a sexual relationship, people who are married or in an exclusive relationship have already ignored their original commitment and given themselves permission to go ahead. For some people, commitment comes with a mindfulness of the need for exclusivity, about which they have no second thoughts. They seem to have a red stoplight built into their senses. For others, commitment is conditional and seems to come with a yellow warning light that can be heeded or ignored. They split hairs and decide that their commitment permits them to do *this* but does not allow them to do *that*. Their conditional commitment may also be dependent on the state of their marriage. Still others have turned a forbidden transgression into a reasonable option and have given themselves a green light to go full speed ahead.

Red Light: For many people commitment means: "I commit myself to an exclusive physical and emotional relationship with you until one of us dies. No matter what attractive alternative comes into my life, I will not be deterred from my goal of keeping you as my one and only life partner." This is the ideal. It is the default position and assumption in our culture. This is what most people *assume* they are getting and giving when they marry, although very few couples actually discuss it explicitly before they formalize their attachment.

But even if they do talk about it and really mean it with all their hearts *in the beginning,* when the romantic stage of a relationship passes, one or the other may not feel like it anymore. The novelty wears off, the years go by, youth and beauty fade, and quirks that were once endearing become annoying. At this point, a lot of people slip into a more conditional commitment.

Yellow Light: " 'Til death do us part" becomes a commitment to stay, but not necessarily a commitment not to stray. As we have seen, the definition of what constitutes an affair tends to change according to who is doing the defining. I have heard both husbands and wives insist to their spouse that they have honored their commitment either because they never really *loved* the affair partner or they never actually had extramarital *sexual intercourse.*

A distraught wife said to her husband, "How could you do this to me? You always looked down on those men who had affairs and broke up their family." The husband displayed his alternative interpretation of commitment by replying, "I was always committed to you. I never once intended to leave you." She was enraged. "What do you mean, you were committed? How could you be committed when you had sex with another woman?" He answered, "It never meant anything. Why are you making such a big deal out of it?"

Green Light: Ralph was convinced his relationship with Lara was unique, that he wasn't like those other men who have affairs just to prove something. He told himself that their communion with each other provided the perfect setting for profound self-discovery and human insight. He believed he would learn more about himself and about life by pursuing this opportunity to its fullest. He thought about all those admonitions from popular philosophers to take risks, follow your bliss, and live fully in the moment. He made mental lists of people he knew who had died of boredom in stultifying jobs and marriages. Although he was not sure whether or not he loved Lara, he *was* curious about what sex with her would feel like. He missed sexual excitement as part of his married life. He was confident that he could control the risk to his marriage by engineering his relationship with Lara so that no one would ever know.

In my clinical sample, two-thirds of the husbands and wives who had extramarital intercourse regarded *falling in love* as a justification for having an extramarital relationship.

For Lara, the reasons to go ahead were simpler. She was unhappy with her husband and happy with Ralph. She told herself that her marriage had been a mistake and that she was in love with Ralph. He was her soul mate. She wanted to feel alive the way one does at the beginning of a great love affair. When she thought back over her life, she thought she had played it too safe. She was haunted by the sense that if she had been braver, she would have gone after what she wanted and been happier. She didn't want to make that mistake again. Lara knew that there might be obstacles to overcome, but she had no doubt it was worth it. She was able to rationalize her relationship with Ralph because she was in love with him. Like many other unfaithful individuals, she believed that falling in love was the only acceptable justification for having an affair.

Although Ralph and Lara used different personal rationalizations, they were both influenced by how many married people they knew who had had affairs. There is no doubt that we are all affected by what we see others doing. They knew of at least one other work affair in their department, and both of them had friends who were involved, without any apparent penalty. When Ralph and Lara finally did give themselves permission to be physically intimate, the opportunity and the timing were right for them, and their attitudes and experiences had prepared them to justify their decision.

Step 4: The Sexually Intimate Affair/ The Threatened Marriage

An affair that is characterized by full emotional sharing and sexual intercourse is very powerful. It is like a snare that has been woven by intertwining strands of affection, shared experiences, and sexual pleasure. It's not hard to see why such combined-type affairs are the most disruptive to the marriage and the hardest to get over.

What's Happening in the Affair?

It is a bigger leap to that first kiss than it is from kissing to sexual intercourse. After five months of emotional but not physical intimacy, Ralph and Lara's feelings finally spilled over into their first kiss. They were driving together to meet a client for a midafternoon meeting. It was unusual for them to be in the car alone together, as they usually made client calls with other members of their team. On this particular Friday, however, their boss asked them to go together. At the end of the drive Ralph told Lara she was beautiful. She turned toward him, and when he pulled into the parking lot, he reached over and kissed her. It surprised them both, but that first taste was like a drug. They had a hard time regaining their professional demeanor and making the meeting.

Over that weekend, Ralph was a model husband and father. He got up early on Saturday morning, swept the garage, and put out the recycling. In the afternoon, he took his son to soccer practice and suggested that the whole family go out to dinner at their favorite place on Saturday night. Later that night, he made love to Rachel with real attention. On Sunday, he offered to do the grocery shopping and sat with the children during the umpteenth viewing of their favorite movie. There was a bounce to his step. Everything was effortless. Nothing bothered him and nothing tired him.

He tried to think seriously about the implications of his kissing Lara. He had never done anything like this before. He knew it was a violation of his values. His brief attempts to think rationally about what he was doing fizzled into nothing. He kept skipping over the troublesome details and reliving the glorious scene over and over in his mind. He was afraid it might lead to sex, and, at the same time, he was hoping it would.

That first kiss turned Ralph and Lara into teenagers again. There was now no question in their own minds that they were deeply involved. They started taking small risks: touching each other when they were alone in the coffee room, choosing restaurants where they could eat lunch unnoticed in darkened booths, whispering their sexual thoughts to each other as they passed in the hallway. They spent time making out in Ralph's car, inhibiting the desire to go further. They even sent a couple of thinly veiled e-mails through the office intranet. They told each other their fantasies of what it would be like to indulge their desires to the fullest.

> In my clinical sample, 44 percent of husbands and 57 percent of wives reported strong emotional involvement in their affair without sexual intercourse.

Then one day, Lara invited Ralph to lunch at her house on a Friday when her husband was out of town. He knew this was a big step. He was excited, scared, and curious all at the same time. As soon as he stepped inside her house, he held her close and kissed her. She led him to the sofa, where they fondled each other with a sense of freedom and privacy they hadn't known before. They had barely enough time to wolf down the chicken salad Lara had made before they had to get back to work.

The second time Lara invited Ralph to lunch at her house, they picked up lunch at a deli on the way and ate in the car. When they were finally alone in Lara's living room, they stood, touching each other tenderly for a long time. Then Lara told him she'd like him to come upstairs. When Ralph realized she was leading him up to her bedroom, he felt his stomach lurch. He realized that he didn't want to make love on the bed that was hers and Lenny's. Lara understood and suggested they use the twin bed in the guest room instead. As Ralph moved toward the bed, he was aware that everything felt strange. He felt displaced somehow. Mixed in with his excitement was uncertainty about what was going to happen.

Lara pushed him gently down on the bed and stood before him, undressing slowly. He had never seen her without all her clothes on and couldn't help comparing her with Rachel, who was not as firm or as young, but who was still in good shape after having two children.

> Evolutionary psychologists assert that women are looking for power and resources in a mate, and men are searching for youth and beauty.[6]

As Lara started to undress him, he felt overwhelmed by the gravity of what they were doing. He almost stopped her. But his hesitation didn't last long, and soon, all he knew was desire for the beautiful woman who was holding him. They began to make love, and, although it was hard to stop the momentum, Ralph found himself saying that he didn't want to go all the way. Lara was surprised, but she accepted his wishes, and they moved easily on to satisfying each other through oral sex instead. They realized afterward that their feelings of intimacy could hardly have been more complete.

Only when they were finished, lying entwined together, did Lara realize that she was a little disappointed that they hadn't had intercourse. But her regret was fleeting as she relished the excitement and happiness she still felt. Ralph's resistance to making love in her marriage bed made her think that maybe her suggestion that they do it that way was symbolic. Maybe she was ready for Ralph to replace Lenny, whom she increasingly found immature and unsophisticated by comparison.

As Ralph lay in bed with Lara, he was happy, but also uneasy. There was some stirring of nausea, some slight queasiness. He detected inside himself a small voice of anxiety and accusation. What had he done? Would he get away with it? Where would it end? But this voice began to quiet as the hours passed. Two days later, it was completely gone. He could hardly wait to be with her again.

Many men define sexual infidelity as intercourse. For them, other physical intimacies "don't count." This attitude allowed President Clinton to assert angrily, "I did not have sexual relations with that woman." By their own reckoning, Ralph and Lara had been "together" for eleven months and Ralph felt more comfortable *not* having intercourse with Lara. Stopping short of this final pleasure allowed him to maintain a sense of integrity that preserved his sense of himself as a moral person.

> For women, crossing the threshold into infidelity occurs when there is any kind of sexual intimacy, such as romantic kissing. For men, the significant threshold is sexual intercourse.[7]

Things escalated again three months later when Ralph and Lara had their first opportunity to go to an out-of-town conference with two other people from work. After a day attending meetings and renewing professional contacts, they joined their associates for dinner and drinks on Saturday night. At about ten o'clock, everyone else went up to their rooms; Ralph and Lara decided to extend the evening with a nightcap in Lara's room. Although they hadn't discussed it ahead of time, they spent the whole night in each other's arms and had intercourse several times. For the first time, they told each other, "I love you." However, they cautiously stayed away from discussions about the future.

The next morning, before Ralph hurried to get back to his room, they talked about how natural it had all seemed. They began to believe they were destined for each other. They didn't think of their illicit relationship as a commonplace affair, but as a unique love story. They were able to escape their routine lives for a night and express themselves as free and passionate characters in a bold drama.

There were several business trips after that, and those were the best times. They discovered that holding each other all night was just as wonderful as sex.

What's Happening in the Marriage?

Ralph was making love to two women, both of whom he loved, although he loved them in different ways. During the period when Ralph was sexually intimate with Lara but not having intercourse, he was exceptionally turned on at home with Rachel. She was surprised at his sudden interest, taking chances on the living room sofa while their young daughter napped in the next room, kissing her as she stepped out of the shower, coming up behind her as she loaded the dishwasher. He hadn't been this ardent for a long time. Rachel was amused and pleased and took to teasing him in a flirtatious way. He made her feel as if she had inadvertently acquired some magic power to entice him.

But after Ralph and Lara's first out-of-town encounter, Ralph's interest in sex at home began to slow down. Rachel marveled that whatever had ignited his passion a few months earlier had faded. They fell into a kind of rut, the kind of routinized sex that Ralph had once derisively referred to as "missionary sex." He wasn't as spontaneous as he used to be, and when she initiated, he was just as likely to pass up the opportunity as he was to take her up on it.

Rachel noticed some other little changes in Ralph, but nothing that concerned her. She thought of their relationship as ebbing and flowing, as it must in long-term marriages. She was disappointed that he hadn't taken the initiative to plan "romantic" time for the two of them as he used to, although he was willing to spend the weekend at a bed and breakfast when she arranged it. He didn't choreograph a loving birthday for her, although he did buy her an expensive present.

The only big change she was aware of was that he seemed more volatile emotionally. Sometimes he was warm and considerate, and sometimes he was short-tempered and irritable. A couple of times, it almost seemed as though he created arguments to justify being angry at her. He would erupt over something that seemed minor to her and rage out of the house, slamming the door. She would sit bewildered and in tears. She discovered that if she waited a few hours, he would come back, contrite and anxious to make it up to her. She didn't know that he was contacting Lara during his time away from the house. When Rachel tried to talk to him about what was going on, he seemed anxious to avoid anything too intense or intimate. She got the feeling that he was absent in some way. She concluded that whatever was bothering him had nothing to do with her and was nothing he was ready to share with her.

Rachel did wonder, briefly, whether Ralph was involved with someone else. She thought about it and concluded that he couldn't and wouldn't. The only possible candidate was his friend Lara, whom Ralph rarely discussed, and when he did, he sounded matter-of-fact. It's true that there was that *one* time a month ago when Lara had called the house early on a Sunday morning. That was strange. She had said she was sorry but she needed to talk to Ralph about a project that was due on Monday. He hadn't seemed glad to hear from her, and Rachel didn't understand why she had had to call on a Sunday morning. A little pinprick of suspicion had gone through her then, but nothing more came of it, so she had let it go.

The crumbling wall around Ralph and Rachel was made up of the obligations they had to each other as husband and wife and as parents to their children. Ralph still discussed things with Rachel that he didn't share with Lara. For example, they discussed summer vacation plans, whether to send their children to private school, their financial investments, and personal things (such as her premenstrual cramps). It was as though Rachel had become his platonic friend as Lara had become his lover. If asked, he would say that he loved his wife although he was not "in love" with her. When he compared Rachel and Lara, he had to admit that being with Rachel no longer gave him the emotional and physical high he felt with Lara.

When I hear people say that they are no longer *in love* with their spouse, I suspect they are unfairly comparing a long-term relationship with the excitement, singular focus, and idealization of a Stage I relationship. The first stage of romantic love is always exciting. Marriages pass through Stage I, however, into a reality-based love; sharing a past, working toward common goals, and accepting one another's flaws. This middle stage is hard. Affairs seldom maintain the rose-colored aura when they move out of the dark shadows into the light of daily life.

There was no question that Ralph maintained a security wall around his family life. He felt protective of his children and worked hard to provide for their physical and emotional well-being. Once when Lara made a critical comment about Rachel's mothering, Ralph bristled: She had no right to pass judgment on his wife, whom he considered to be a wonderful mother. He cared about Rachel and wanted her to be happy. Sometimes he thought about what it would be like if she, too, had a lover. He couldn't bear the possibility of losing her to another man, but felt his situation was different, of course, because he could handle it all.

The wall he had with Lara was higher and thicker than the family wall. In a sense, he felt less responsible for Lara but more defensive. He knew her every wound, her tender feelings, the nobleness of her character. He wanted to shield her from the brutish disregard of her husband and the jostling of her job. He wanted to lock her away, and himself with her, sheltered from endless obligations and prying eyes.

The window between Ralph and Rachel was cloudy but not closed—sometimes open, and sometimes no more than a sliver. He often found himself pulling down the shade between him and Rachel. It wasn't that he no longer loved her, but being with her made him feel guilty. Although he communicated about mundane events, he was withholding the essence of his life from her. It was painful for him when Rachel continued to share confidences with him as though nothing had changed. He wondered whether she noticed that he wasn't reciprocating.

In contrast, the window was wide open between Ralph and Lara. The only information that didn't pass through was trivia they considered too inconsequential to bother with, or any concern that their idyllic interludes were built on a foundation of deception. They saw each other in the best possible light.

Lara confided in Ralph about Lenny. Ralph knew more about her worries regarding her marriage than Lenny did. Lara felt she had tried to talk to her husband, but he wouldn't listen. In contrast, Ralph didn't discuss Rachel with Lara, because he wanted to keep his worlds separate and he felt a sense of loyalty to Rachel. He knew that Rachel was open to discussing problems in their marriage and that he was the one who didn't want to talk about them.

When Sex Enters an Emotional Affair

Relationships in which sex occurs at the very beginning are less likely to have the deep level of emotional intimacy that occurs when sex is delayed. That's why friendships that build on an emotional level before becoming sexualized are more apt to be experienced as a deep emotional attachment.

> In my clinical sample, 83 percent of women and 58 percent of men who had extramarital sexual intercourse said that they had a strong or extremely deep emotional attachment to the affair partner.

Now that so many more men are having sexual affairs with women with whom they share an emotional bond, the threat to the marriage is greater and divorce is a greater possibility than in the past. Traditionally, men have been more likely than women to become involved in extramarital relationships because of sexual attraction. Men sexualize and women romanticize. When relationships remain primarily sexual, they are seldom a threat to the durability of the marriage unless they are discovered. (And the sex-only affair is less likely to be discovered.)

> In my clinical sample, men who engaged in primarily sexual affairs were as satisfied with their marriages as noninvolved men. However, women in any type of extramarital involvement were less happy in their marriages than noninvolved women.

Women have generally begun extramarital relationships with an emotional involvement that may or may not involve sexual interaction. But unfaithful women who do engage in extramarital sexual intercourse are likely to be in love with the affair partner. That is one of the reasons their

affairs have been associated with lower marital satisfaction and have been
more likely to lead to divorce. Social norms are against sexual involvement for women and emotional involvement for men, so a combined-
type affair is more threatening because it violates societal norms and also
steps into the domains that create the most jealousy.

Complications of the Double Life

For over a year, Ralph and Lara lived their secret life. Then one day, after
they made love, Lara told Ralph she was leaving her husband. She said she
knew that Ralph no longer loved his wife either, and that she didn't see
any reason why they couldn't both get divorced and be together forever.
As she spoke, he felt a jolt of adrenaline and had to calm himself down before he could speak. After a moment of pure panic, he responded carefully, "Let's take it easy. Let's think this through. Let's not do anything
stupid," he said. She said, "I thought you loved me." And they spent the
rest of their time together trying to repair the breach.

This was the first outward sign that the two lovers were no longer totally on the same wavelength. Yet, for some time Ralph had been feeling
guilty about the sex, while Lara continued to enjoy it guilt-free. He also
found himself feeling bad about Rachel, and though he wasn't ready to
end the affair, he noticed that he was more ambivalent about his furtive
trips to the motel and his quick, covert conversations with Lara on the cell
phone.

Now that he knew Lara wanted to divorce her husband, he began to
worry about getting caught. He became super careful. What if he had to
choose between the two women in his life? All things being equal, he
thought he would choose Lara, but all things were not equal. He had kids,
for one thing, and he had made marriage vows to his wife. And then there
was her family, and his family, and their church friends, and the other parents at the school, not to mention his colleagues at work. He began to
have the classic kind of nightmare, where he discovered to his horror that
he was standing in front of his old high school auditorium completely
naked. Every time he thought about getting caught made him feel sick.
He was beginning to fear that, sooner or later, somebody was going to get
hurt.

Ralph was aware that being intimate with two women allowed him to play many different roles, which he enjoyed, but there were times when he got tired of the complications. He didn't like to think of himself as someone who could sustain such an elaborate deception. There were moments when he asked himself what the heck he was doing. How did he go from a devoted family man to a first-class deceiver?

The relationship between Ralph and Lara was more balanced than in some affairs because both of them were married. For married lovers, the marriage is *bread and butter* and the affair is *icing on the cake.* Affairs between married and single people have an imbalance of power because the affair is the one-and-only for the unmarried person, who has to wait in line for time and attention that isn't already allocated to the spouse and kids. Ralph panicked when Lara threatened to leave her husband, because up to that point, his needs were in sync with hers. They were facing the demands of living a double life together. When Lara changed the terms of their understanding, the affair became much less stable and harder to control.

Living the double life is hard work. It entails managing the logistics, including erasing e-mails, hiding cell phones, camouflaging expenses; meeting sites have to be convenient but not places you will likely encounter people you know. The emotional effort of sustaining two relationships, neither of which can be totally authentic, is also difficult. Lying not only erodes personal integrity, it distances you from the person you are lying to. There are two people to share intimacies with, two people to laugh with and cry with, and two people to deceive.

Ralph and Lara had to stay on the alert to cover their tracks. They paid close attention to their calendars, part of which they wrote in code. Ralph had his cell phone bills sent to his office because the phone was a "business expense." Under the pretense of relieving Rachel of the financial duties for the household, Ralph started doing the banking, bill paying, and tax preparation. He kept his last bonus a secret from her and deposited the extra money into a separate account that he could draw on without any explanations.

With every action that strengthened his connection to Lara, there was a corresponding act of deception. He had to remember what he said to whom and what he had promised to whom. He worked hard to keep the two streams of his life separate. Ralph thought it was worth the effort, but there were times when he yearned to live simply and straight. As the months passed, he began to feel more guilty. There were times when Rachel was so giving, so trusting. One time after they made love, she said, "I'm so happy we found each other. I don't think anyone else could make me so happy. I hope I make you as happy as you make me." What he said next was a lie. He knew what she needed to hear and he told her.

Lying

A question that often comes up in my practice is whether people who have affairs are liars. Of course they are. How could it be otherwise? By definition, anyone involved in a secret, forbidden relationship is involved in lies, large and small. If people didn't lie about their infidelities, they'd either have an open marriage or a divorce. Here's the real question: Is this person lying because of the cheating, or is the cheating just another manifestation of ingrained dishonesty? If you are the marital partner of someone who has been having an affair, you have to be able to figure out whether the lying is an idiosyncratic consequence of this particular situation or an embedded trait that is a matter of character and personality.

Lying is not a simple matter. A lie can be motivated by many emotions and intentions, from maliciousness to kindness. It depends on the context. The impact of a malevolent lie may be the suffering of one person or of multitudes. The impact of the humane lie may be the continuation of social relationships. Personal relationships cannot always stand the test of brutal honesty. Telling the truth in every instance could indicate a lack of sensitivity and kindness and undermine the delicate bonds that connect us.

On the other hand, lying in personal relationships to cover up wrongful or deceitful acts destroys trust. Intimate relationships are contingent on honesty and openness. They are built and maintained through our faith that we can believe what we are being told. However painful it is for a betrayed spouse to discover a trail of sexual encounters or emotional attachments, the lying and deception are the most appalling violations.

There is a difference between lies of commission and lies of omission. A lie of commission is the fabrication of information, the making up of a fact or a whole story. Some unfaithful partners go to great lengths to deceive, weaving intricate tales with elaborate details in an effort to endow their lies with a reality that can't be questioned. Others just stretch the truth a little bit to cover their tracks. Ken is an example of someone who put a lot of thought into his deception. To spend a weekend away with his affair partner, he created a flyer announcing a three-day conference; then he had it printed up and sent to his home. When he showed the flyer to his wife, she agreed that attending would be a great advantage to him in his profession. This act of flagrant deception created a huge stumbling block for regaining trust during their recovery process.

Others are not as adept at or as comfortable with deliberate fabrications. They engage in lies of omission. A lie of omission is leaving something out, not mentioning a critical part of the truth, with the intention of deceiving or creating a false impression. I've known people who managed to cover their tracks by extending the duration of their actual weekly appointments with a personal trainer, committee meetings, visits to sick relatives, and adult education classes. They try to conduct their affairs with as few out-and-out lies as possible. But failing to mention time spent alone with a lover or a gift of an intimate nature is as misleading as telling an untruth. Sometimes people think they are on firmer moral ground if they deal primarily in lies of omission; however, as we shall see in the next chapters, the person who is betrayed rarely appreciates the subtleties.

Once you tell one lie, it's easier to tell another and another. Lies begin to cascade until lying becomes a way of being. Inevitably, in an affair one becomes a double liar. To keep both partners satisfied, it is necessary to lie in both relationships. Here is an example of the duplicity that can occur. June was suspicious that her husband, Jerry, was having an affair with Samantha. Even though he denied it, she thought his business trips might be a cover-up to spend time away with Samantha. June decided to make an unexpected appearance at the airport to meet his return flight, so she would know for certain once and for all. When she confronted them as they entered the gate together, an explosive argument followed, and Samantha said to June, "I don't know why you've stayed with him so long when he can't even stand to touch you." June shot back that she and Jerry snuggled in bed every night and fell asleep in each other's arms. Shocked, Samantha cried out, "I feel betrayed!"

Unfaithful persons often say they are protecting their partners from pain, but they are really protecting themselves from exposure so they can continue to live the double life.

Compartmentalizing

Some unfaithful people preserve their parallel lives by putting their thoughts and feelings about the two relationships in sealed compartments. They keep the conflicting story lines of their two different worlds neatly and safely separated from each other. When they're not with the one they love, they love the one they're with. They relish being able to experience different parts of themselves and will go to great lengths to maintain the split self. They can be sober and responsible in one part and risk-taking and pleasure-seeking in another. Stories abound of politicians, celebrities, and sport stars whose numerous affairs run side by side with their commitment to their family. They appear to regard these extramarital relationships as something separate, not relevant, and not threatening to their dedication to spouse and children.

The "monogamous infidel," on the other hand, is a person who *does not and cannot* compartmentalize.[8] This is a man or woman who basically believes in monogamy and cannot be invested in more than one relationship at the same time. For monogamous infidels, the affair takes over and becomes the primary relationship, while the marriage becomes peripheral and detached. They often feel "unfaithful" to the affair partner when they have sex at home.

Mary felt that way about having sex with her husband. Her primary allegiance was to her affair partner, Eddie. It was her extramarital relationship that stirred her passion and her jealousy. She was eager to meet Eddie's live-in girlfriend, Edith, in order to "size her up." She wanted to see for herself what her rival was like. As it turned out, Edith was very sweet and friendly, and she had no clue that anything was amiss. Probably because Mary was married, Edith considered her "safe" and therefore not a threat. She confided to Mary that she wanted to marry Eddie, but he kept saying he wasn't ready. When Mary told Eddie that she felt two-faced about betraying Edith's trust, he couldn't understand why she was upset. He didn't have any remorse about leading a double life and was very good at it.

In this case, Mary is a monogamous infidel and Eddie is someone who splits his relationships into separate compartments. As it happened, things were made more difficult for Mary because her husband became more attentive and more sexually insistent as he sensed her attention wandering. Because Mary could be "faithful" to only one partner at a time, her husband's newly enthusiastic attentions felt "smothering" to her, and she felt the need to pull away even more.

Other Ways of Dealing with Internal Conflict

Besides compartmentalizing, there are other ways to eliminate or reduce the internal anguish caused by a potential disparity between values and behavior. People attempt to deal with the dissonance by lying to themselves about what they are doing. Lying to others is only a partial consequence of infidelity. In affairs, people are as likely to engage in self-deception as in deception of their partners. Self-deception can take the form of denying self-indulgent motives or refusing to acknowledge the potential damage. With practice, people find it easier to hide those unacceptable parts of themselves from themselves. They gloss over aspects that are inconsistent with their internalized values. They tell themselves that what they are doing isn't so bad, that everybody does it and life goes on.

For some people, the way to resolve the internal conflict is to get caught. They may become careless or start leaving clues that would incriminate them. Even an unsuspecting spouse might wonder about a hickey on the neck, charges to a florist on the credit card bill, or a love note stuck in the pages of a book. An unfaithful husband kept his love letters in his briefcase. One day, when he was home with the flu, he asked his wife to look in his briefcase for an insurance form they needed to fill out. Naturally, she found the letters and *he* was found out.

In the next chapter, you will see what happens when clues cannot be denied and suspiciousness turns into devastating reality. When an affair is exposed, all three people must cope with the trauma of revelation. You will learn what helps people live through the difficult hours, days, and weeks that follow.

PART II

The Trauma

There are times in life when everything falls apart. An affair shatters your comfortable, familiar relationships and routines in an instant. This part of the book will help you begin your recovery together with your partner.

When an affair is disclosed or discovered, the betrayed partner is traumatized. How traumatized depends on the nature of the betrayal and the manner of discovery. Trust has been destroyed. In the aftermath of the revelation, if you've been betrayed, you may feel extreme, volatile, traumatic reactions. If you were unfaithful, you're caught in the misery of competing alliances. Even in these first confusing moments, however, you can begin to reestablish a sense of safety by working together as a couple.

Exposure of the double life can leave both partners conflicted about whether to stay or leave. With careful exploration, thought, and the passage of time, you can resolve your ambivalence.

After you commit to working on the marriage, you both still must deal with the post-traumatic symptoms of the betrayed partner. Learning what these symptoms are and how to cope with them will help both of you begin the work of healing.

Rediscovering the places where your connection is still

alive will give both of you hope for the future. As you make deliberate attempts to get back to normal, create goodwill, and communicate with each other compassionately, your relationship will begin to provide you with more pleasure and intimacy. From there, you will be strong enough to sort out and negotiate the complex questions raised by the affair.

3

REACHING THE MOMENT
OF REVELATION

*In that moment, my life was shattered. He says he loves me
but that he isn't 'in love' with me? I don't even know who he is
anymore. . . . It would have been easier if he had died!*

A SINGLE MOMENT can change us forever. After you learn that you've been betrayed, you think in terms of the time *before* and the time *after.* The private calamity of discovering that your partner has become someone you don't recognize and has lied to you as if you were an enemy blows your secure world to pieces. You no longer trust your eyes to see, your brain to comprehend, or your heart to feel what is true.

The journey toward the moment when the affair is revealed is often marked by an awareness that things aren't quite right. After the affair has been exposed, your uneasiness is replaced by many different emotions. The connection between what you *think* you know and your sense of reality has been severed. It doesn't matter whether you were totally in the dark or highly suspicious beforehand. No matter what the circumstances, your assumptions about your partner, your marriage, and yourself have been shattered. They lie in ruins at your feet. This is how Ralph's affair with Lara was revealed to Rachel.

Loss of Innocence

Things hadn't been so good between Ralph and Rachel. He'd been working hard, and she'd been stretched by obligations at home and in her job

67

at the hospital. Rachel was secretly relieved that Ralph hadn't required much from her lately, but she thought she probably hadn't been paying enough attention to him. To get things back on track, she planned a treat for his birthday. After surmising that he had no plans to go out for lunch, she decided to surprise him at the office with a gourmet picnic.

At noon on the big day, Rachel arrived at Ralph's office, picnic basket in hand. She was surprised when the receptionist told her that Ralph wasn't there. She took off down the hall to Ralph's office with the vague thought of leaving him a note. She looked at his Daytimer, which was lying open on his desk, and read "11:30—lunch with L." She felt a wave of panic and confusion. Then she told herself that maybe she was jumping to conclusions. Maybe it wasn't Lara, but someone else in his office. Rachel decided not to leave a note; she picked up the picnic basket and walked quickly back to the car with her heart pounding. She sat in the car and waited until 2 P.M. before driving off with a sick, sinking feeling. As soon as she got home, she threw the champagne, the pâté, and the truffles into the garbage.

When Ralph got home that night, she asked him what he had done for lunch. Caught off guard, he paused briefly, then told her, "I brown-bagged it in the office. I was saving all the birthday fun for you." Then Rachel lashed out at him and told him she knew he had gone out with Lara. She told him she had seen the calendar on his desk.

At first, he denied everything. Then he said that a stockbroker from Legg Mason who was trying to get his business had taken him out to lunch at a fancy restaurant. He hadn't wanted to spoil the special dinner she had made for his birthday by telling her he had a gourmet lunch. He had a rational explanation for every accusation she threw at him. As the hours dragged on, however, things became less rational and more surreal. Rachel kept hammering at him until he was worn down. Finally, just to have some peace, Ralph admitted he'd been having an affair. He cried and asked her for forgiveness, saying he wanted to be with her and that he would break it off with Lara.

As much as Rachel wanted to believe him, she couldn't trust his words. At one moment, the touch and the sight of him nauseated her so much she thought she was going to throw up; the next moment, she held on to him so desperately that her gripping fingers left an imprint on the back of his arms. All that night they were caught in the storm of their emotions, riding the crest of one terrified feeling, barely getting their footing, and then being knocked down by another wave of anger and terror.

A few days later, Rachel called my office for an emergency appointment. When she and Ralph walked in, the tension was palpable. They
both looked exhausted after their all-night marathon and subsequent days
in an emotional pressure cooker. Their emotions shifted back and forth
rapidly. Rachel alternated between being flushed with anxiety, tearful and
sobbing, enraged and shouting, and silently frozen and numb. To her,
everything was unreal. Ralph alternated between being empathic and
comforting, impatient and complaining, avoidant and stonewalling, and
uncomfortable and visibly embarrassed.

During the session, they told me what had happened. At first, Ralph
had denied that his relationship with Lara was anything but a friendship.
Then, under Rachel's probing inquisition, he had admitted a few kisses.
He had become furious when Rachel wouldn't accept his assurances that
that was all there was. She continued her unrelenting accusations until he
finally admitted a sexual affair, but he still claimed his emotional attachment to Lara was minimal.

Even though Rachel had felt something was wrong in their marriage,
she was devastated when she thought that another woman had been the
cause of their problems. She said to him, "It would have been easier if you
had died! You're not the person I thought you were." But in the next
breath, she talked about how much she thought they loved each other and
what a good person Ralph was. She never thought he would be unfaithful
to her because she was convinced they shared the same moral and religious values. Now she didn't know how she could ever trust him again.

The truth is that things will never be the same for Ralph and Rachel.
The innocence and safety that had existed before the affair can never be
reclaimed. Ralph's realization that his double life was over was both a
shock and a relief. He didn't know how he was going to live without being
intimate with Lara, especially since they had to continue to see each other
at work. Rachel didn't know how she could endure the anxiety every
morning when Ralph left for work.

Someone once asked me if it is hard to recover from infidelity without
therapy, and I replied that recovery is hard, even *with* therapy. Ralph and
Rachel, for instance, were in therapy for almost two years until they felt
healed. After a lot of hard work and many setbacks, they were able to rebuild trust by opening a window into the affair and erecting a solid wall
that sent a clear message to Lara that the romance was over. There were
days, though, during that first year of recovery, when Ralph was cold and

distant because he was grieving for the loss of his relationship with Lara. Although it was terribly painful for Rachel to hear Ralph finally admit how emotionally involved he had been, his honesty did ultimately create greater empathy and intimacy in their marriage. Fortunately, both of them were open to exploring the vulnerabilities in their own interaction that had set the stage for his infidelity, and they used the lessons they learned to rebuild their relationship.

Lara also had a difficult year. She took the sound advice of her own counselor to take the next few months to focus on herself and what she wanted out of life. She joined an early-morning yoga class to center herself after the profound loss of her relationship with Ralph. Her life seemed empty. The deficits in her own marriage became even more apparent when Ralph was no longer there to meet her need for emotional closeness. Her affair with Ralph gave her undeniable evidence that she could not remain in a marriage that was an empty shell.

Soon after she left her husband, Lara enrolled in an MBA evening program. As soon as she could, she took a job in another part of the company so she wouldn't be working with Ralph. From that point on, she approached work friendships with married men very gingerly. She wanted relationships only with men who were free to explore the possibility of a long-term commitment.

Before Revelation: Secrets, Lies, and Suspiciousness

Betrayed partners differ considerably in how aware they are of the presence of infidelity in their relationship. Some betrayed partners are completely innocent in the absence of any clues, some overlook subtle clues, some avoid obvious clues, and others are preoccupied with tracking down tell-tale clues. Many affairs are discovered when intuition says that something is wrong and little things that happen just don't add up.

Avoiding Confrontation

Some individuals have definite reasons for choosing not to confront their partner or investigate further. They may be afraid that the marriage would end if the affair were to come out into the open. As one woman said to me, "If I knew for sure, my principles are such that I'd have to break up my family." She decided to do what she could to stop it without finding out for sure how far it had gone. In another case of reluctance, a suspicious husband was afraid that his wife would choose her lover if he confronted her.

Worried partners may choose to deny their suspicions for emotional or practical reasons. They may welcome the decreased pressure for sex or intimacy. One woman admitted that she found her husband much easier to live with when he was in the middle of one of his sexual adventures. Some people choose to ignore infidelity and stay in the relationship for financial reasons or because they don't want to disrupt the family. They apparently believe that a divided loaf is better than no bread at all, even though they might feel they end up with the crumbs.

Unsuspecting Partners

I don't agree with infidelity experts who assert that betrayed partners always know about the infidelity but choose to ignore the signs. Some of these experts even accuse the naïve spouse of actually colluding in the extramarital triangle, an unsubstantiated assumption with which I strongly disagree. My research does not support the view that the spouse always knows.[1]

> In my airport sample, 55 percent of unfaithful wives and 70 percent of unfaithful husbands reported that their spouse did not know about their extramarital involvement.

A lot of secret affairs go unsuspected. Sexual flings that have almost no emotional attachment are the least likely to be suspected or revealed. Unfaithful partners can be so adept at concealing their double life that detection is almost impossible. When involved persons are able to compartmentalize their sexual activities and maintain a loving relationship at home, the infidelity may be totally hidden. Because people in committed relationships tend to have a truth bias that inclines them toward believing what they are told, it seldom occurs to them that they are being betrayed. In fact, unfaithful partners whose infidelities were undiscovered reported little effect on emotional closeness, tension, or distrust in the marital relationship.

> Despite the fact that a high proportion of men and women in my airport survey admitted having had an extramarital involvement themselves, only 10 percent of the men and 19 percent of the women believed that their spouse had ever had an extramarital relationship.

Tracking the Clues

Leaving a trail of multiple or obvious clues can be either intentional or accidental. Carelessness or indiscretion is often the result of a subconscious wish to be discovered. In contrast, the person who doesn't want to get caught is usually very careful about covering his or her tracks and may leave so few clues that only a super-alert investigator could detect the trail. When suspicious partners snoop, spy, and launch inquisitions to uncover infidelity, both partners are likely to be angry and resentful. Suspicious partners resent the repeated, untruthful denials and the necessity for sneaking, and unfaithful partners resent the accusations, incessant grilling, and intrusions into their privacy.

Right in Front of Your Nose: Involved partners who make no real effort to hide their extramarital activities want their spouse to help them end the masquerade. As a matter of personal integrity, if they find it impossible to sustain the lie, they may leave enough evidence around to serve as a confession. When they are asked, they answer questions honestly and do everything they can to work through the pain they have caused. Some may even be signaling for attention from a partner who has not been interested in dealing with pressing issues in the relationship.

Call for Attention: Amanda came to understand the significance of her own affair as a call for more attention from her husband. She was married to an older man who ran his own, all-consuming business. She responded to her husband's neglect by becoming involved with a neighbor. After her lover gave her lingerie for her birthday, she left the box from Victoria's Secret on her night table. When her husband asked whether she was having an affair, she told him right out that she was. She answered all his questions and said that *he* was the man she loved and that she was dying for his time and affection: "I didn't want to throw it in your face. But I wanted you to pay attention to *me.*"

Although Amanda's game was a dangerous one, her affair could become the pivot for some needed changes. Whether her infidelity will act as a positive turning point depends on whether she and her husband make a joint commitment to working on the neglected aspects of their relationship. In addition, although her affair served primarily as an excuse to get her husband's attention, it became yet another problem to be addressed in their marriage.

Exit Plan: Involved spouses who want out of the marriage may let the evidence pile up in a flagrant disregard for their partner's feelings. Stewart's affair was so obvious he might as well have been staging it for his wife's benefit. He told his affair partner it was okay to call him at home; when he went out alone in the evening, he often came home in the middle of the night half-drunk. Then he had the audacity to get angry at his wife's questioning.

After several months of provocative behavior, during which he ridiculed his wife for thinking there was another woman, he simply up and left. He left a message on the answering machine. He told his wife that her crazy jealousy had finally driven him away, that he was gone for good, and who could blame him if he *did* find some comfort in the arms of another woman? As we might expect, his wife was traumatized by his extreme behavior, but his insensitivity to her anguish helped her to see him for the self-centered person he was. After their divorce, she began a wonderful relationship with a widower who was compassionate and caring.

Warning Signs of Infidelity

Sometimes there is no way to know when partners are having an affair because their actions may seem perfectly normal. They might be able to look you in the eye and convince you that nothing is going on. Do not blame yourself if you have been kept in the dark. On the other hand, each potentially suspicious sign could indicate something other than an affair, such as depression or midlife changes. The best clue is probably your own gut instinct, especially if you have never been suspicious or jealous before.

You can't tell whether your partner is having an affair from just one piece of evidence. You need to identify a pattern of unusual behavior. A *change* from the norm or a pattern of opposite behaviors with unpredictable ups and downs is suspicious. Here are some signposts for realistic suspicions:

- *Privacy:* More phone calls taken privately; staying up later and using the computer after everyone is in bed; having the beeper always on hand.

- *Schedules:* More time away from home; longer working hours; more out-of-town travel; more evening or weekend meetings. The explanations for these changes may be overly detailed, or they may be blanket excuses, such as "the new project" or "the planning board" or "my yoga class."

- *Interests:* A sudden and intense interest in a new activity that is deliberately not shared with the partner, such as motorcycles, sports cars, or country-western dancing.

- *Personal Habits:* Preoccupation with personal appearance; abrupt transformation in hair or clothing style, especially a new image more appropriate at a singles bar; efforts to lose weight that involve changes in eating or exercise habits; purchasing new, sexy underwear.

- *Children:* Uneven and inconsistent attention to children, sometimes angry and impatient with them and sometimes lavishing attention on them; not noticing the routine details of children's lives.

- *Money:* Less open about expenditures; checks missing from the family bank account or questionable credit card charges; spending more money on restaurants, hotels, motels, or gifts or on enhancing own attractiveness and desirability.

- *Personal Interaction with Spouse:* Unpredictable behavior that can sometimes be rejecting and critical and sometimes overly clingy; may give the impression that he or she would rather be alone and does not want to talk or be touched; may start arguments and storm out for a few mysterious hours away from home.

• *Sex and Affection:* May have increased sexual desire, and sex may be more passionate; new techniques may be tried or broached, or there may be an avoidance of sexual contact—or both at different times; less spontaneous affection and fewer romantic kisses.

• *Social Life:* Avoids including spouse in familiar social settings with people from work or the neighborhood; or, may want to go out more with others and avoid being alone with spouse.

> **A** survey by Todd Shackelford and David Buss found 170 cues to suspicions of sexual or emotional infidelity.[2] One of the most predictive emotional cues was no longer saying "I love you" to one's partner. Opposite behaviors toward another person, such as increased references or a reluctance to discuss him or her, stood out as other signals of emotional infidelity.

Being a Detective

Persistent accusations that are just as persistently denied may eventually provoke suspicious partners into becoming their own detective. One wife I know checked her husband's tollbooth receipts because she suspected that he was having an affair with a woman who lived on the other side of the bridge. Checking mileage on the odometer or on gasoline receipts is another way to put two and two together. Wives have confirmed suspicions about their husbands' extramarital sexual activities by counting condoms or Viagra pills. Contraceptive devices in women's pocketbooks have set off the alarm for suspicious husbands.

Sometimes the tracks are more subtle. One woman became aware that she didn't know how her husband was spending his Thursday afternoons off. When she asked him, he was evasive. She went rummaging around in his underwear drawer and figured out that every Thursday, he wore his new bikini underpants. That was alarming. She followed the trail and was soon able to answer the question of how he spent his time off.

Sometimes, people want the undeniable evidence of catching their partner in the act. Hotels and motels are notorious locations for affairs and are therefore frequently part of the scenario for discovery. One creative spouse posed as a secretary and called a hotel to ask whether a hotel bill was for a single or double occupancy. In an especially dedicated example of detective work, an anxious husband got on a plane and flew 3,000 miles to confront his wife and her lover in their hotel room. Closer to home, suspicious partners sometimes wait outside the affair partner's house, hoping to catch the suspects going in or out. Parking lot surveillance is common in front of motels, restaurants, or any place that has aroused suspicions.

In December 2000, the first divorce action involving DNA evidence of infidelity went to court. A rejected wife said she found clues that led her to believe that her husband had had a tryst at his farm in Vermont. She had a laboratory examine the sheets for traces of DNA. If her allegations are proven to be true, her husband has violated a no-cheating clause in their prenuptial agreement, which could result in an award of several million dollars for the wife.

Although not as elaborate or expensive as DNA testing, homegrown detectives are supplementing their own instincts with high-tech snooping. Cell phones are a favorite mode of communication by errant spouses, and cell phone bills are a common source of discovery. Most cellular phone companies now list local phone numbers on their bills. Lots of calls to the same mystery number is an obvious signal that something might be going on. Strange calls that are made or received at home can usually be traced by pressing redial or *69. Beepers, too, can provide an electronic record. Beeper codes make it possible to access a list of the previous phone numbers that have called in.

Suspicious partners acquire evidence of betrayal by hiding voice-activated tape recorders behind the front seat of the car, near the telephone in the private study, or under the king-size bed to capture illicit activity while they are out of town. E-mail correspondence, even if it appears private and secure, can be retrieved by computer-savvy sleuths as well as by virtual neophytes who are hot on the trail. Torrid on-line affairs are increasing rapidly, and the cyber trail has become the latest source for uncovering infidelity. Most suspicious spouses, however, will continue to have to rely on their own eyes and ears and on their gut instincts to warn them when their spouse is involved in an extramarital liaison.

Hiring a Detective

By the time a suspicious spouse hires a detective, bitter accusations and heated denials have occurred for months and perhaps for years. The relationship is characterized by distrust and discord. In some cases, the suspicious partner has been accused of being paranoid and pathologically jealous. Detectives often find that there has been an opportunity to consummate an illicit relationship in a private place, such as a motel. They may use video cameras to prove there has been a display of affection. Private investigators who are hired by a suspicious partner are able to corroborate cheating in a preponderance of the cases.

For over two decades, Trent had subjected his wife, Thelma, to questions about her daily activities because of a gut feeling that she was being unfaithful. This was in spite of her apparent devotion to him and their four children. Not only Thelma, but I, as their marital therapist, told him he was being overly possessive and irrationally jealous. Trent finally hired a detective. The detective provided indisputable evidence that Thelma was having an affair with the landscape architect who was designing a lily pond in their backyard. After grueling inquisitions day and night, she eventually confessed that she had been with ten other men since the beginning of their relationship. Trent's rage and humiliation at having been deceived for so long could not be healed by her coerced confession. As their therapist, I was as stunned as Trent by the extent of Thelma's secret life. The marriage eventually ended because they were unable to establish a feeling of trust and security.

Private investigators agree that Valentine's Day is the best time to catch cheating spouses.[3] Unfaithful partners who are having love affairs are apt to plan romantic trysts on that holiday. Men and women use different ploys to sneak out of town with their lover; men may use the excuse that they have to be away on business, and women may say they have to visit a sick relative. One crafty husband first went home to wine and dine his wife. He then had himself beeped so he could rendezvous with his girlfriend.

Confronting Your Suspicions

Confronting is not the same as attacking. Attacking is a hostile offensive that involves accusations, criticism, and abuse. Confronting is meeting face-to-face for the purpose of presenting information for clarification.

Responses to confrontations are varied and may include validation, explanation, alternative perspectives, or defensiveness.

Before You Confront

1. *Know what you hope to gain through the confrontation* and share this goal with your partner. For example, you might want your partner to acknowledge what you already suspect or know to be true. Then you can figure out together whether to work on the marriage or end it. Remaining in the dark about a secret affair is like playing poker with your cards face up while your opponent's whole hand is face down.

2. *Don't set "truth traps."* You want to discover the truth directly, rather than ensnare through devious methods. Don't begin the search for truth with deception or lies. If your child leaves a trail of cookie crumbs, you shouldn't ask, "Did you have a cookie today?" Start out by saying, "I saw the cookie crumbs. Tell me the truth about how many cookies you ate before dinner."

3. *Give yourself time to cool down and become calm.* Your effectiveness depends on how well you have thought through your confrontation. You want to create as little defensiveness in your partner as possible. Excessive emotionality on your part is likely to cause your partner to build a protective shield rather than a bridge to the truth.

4. *Consider writing down your thoughts first* in order to gain clarity. In some cases, a letter is a more effective confrontation than an in-person meeting.

The Confrontation Itself

1. Choose a time and place where you are both unhurried and free from distractions.

2. Do not confront on the telephone.

3. Stick to the facts as you know them:
   - What you know.
   - What you saw.
   - What you've been told.

• The contradictions between what your partner has told you and what you've discovered.

4. Say how these lies or discrepancies make you feel (e.g., betrayed, scared, insulted).

Typical Reactions to the Confrontation

1. Denial: Most people deny at first. They try to find out what the betrayed partner knows.

2. Admission: Whatever they admit is often just the tip of the iceberg.

3. Lying: If the unfaithful partner lies, he or she probably isn't ready to stop the affair but doesn't want to risk losing the marriage.

If your partner acknowledges your accusations, thank him or her for being honest. Say that you would rather know the truth, even though it is painful. Give both of you a chance to cool down before you ask for additional information. If your partner does not admit anything but you are still suspicious, then you can continue to observe, investigate, and confront again.

Jennifer Schneider found that 84 percent of people with patterns of addictive extramarital sex denied any wrongdoing when they were first confronted by a suspicious partner. After some time had elapsed, 96 percent believed that disclosure was the best thing.[4]

When Accusations Are Denied

The accusing partner endures a period of great emotional turmoil when obvious signs of infidelity are denied. A significant issue in the depth of the deception is how long and in what way the unfaithful partner dismisses the legitimate concerns of the worried partner. The individual who is guilty as charged may try to stop further questioning by the intensity of the denial. He or she may attack the partner who would even suggest such a thing. "I'm disappointed that you don't trust me" will stop many inquiring spouses in their tracks. The guilty parties can be very convincing when they say, "I'm telling you the truth. Have I ever lied to you before?" Keep in mind that someone who has nothing to hide is more likely to respond nondefensively and with concern for the distress of his or her partner.

One especially insidious way that untrustworthy, cheating spouses try to disarm a suspicious partner is called "gaslighting." The term comes from the movie *Gaslight*, in which a husband plays a mind game by trying to convince his wife that she is imagining things. In a similar way, a manipulative partner can turn every suspicion or accusation of the innocent spouse into an attack on his or her sanity. Every confrontation attempts to reconfirm that the questioner must be paranoid. The betrayed spouses begin to doubt their own perceptions and lose trust in their own sense of reality.

In an infamous case of adultery, murder, and gaslighting in San Diego, Betty Broderick went to her husband's office and found clear evidence that he was having an affair with his secretary. She went home and cut up all his clothes with scissors. Her attorney/physician husband said she was imagining things and put her under psychiatric care for her delusions. He later divorced Betty and married his secretary (who looked amazingly like a younger version of Betty) on the same date that he and Betty had married. After Betty shot and killed him and his new wife in bed, Dr. Don-David Lusterman testified at her trial that Betty was suffering from post-traumatic stress disorder as a result of her husband's protracted infidelity.[5] The jury, however, found her guilty and she was imprisoned.

Knowing the truth after being suspicious for a long time brings the tremendous relief of realizing "At least I'm not crazy!" You *can* trust your own eyes and ears after all. But close on the heels of relief is fury at having been made to feel overly jealous or weak because of a legitimate suspicion. Soon thereafter a whirlwind of different emotions ensues and you feel anger, disbelief, and affirmation, all at the same time.

The Many Pathways to Discovery

There are as many ways to find out that your partner has been unfaithful as there are unfaithful partners. And although no discovery is easy, the nature of the revelation can make the infidelity itself seem more or less horrible than it might have been otherwise. Couples regain trust more readily after voluntary confessions than after repeated denials that are eventually refuted by indisputable evidence, such as tapes, letters, or photographs.

> **D**isclosure of infidelity leads to divorce more frequently for unfaithful wives than husbands. Still, although telling appears less risky for men, the consequences were three times more negative when men's affairs were discovered by their wives than when men revealed the affairs themselves.[6]

Confessions

Confessions may come after many months of accusations and denials, or like a deadly strike of lightning on a sunny day. Disclosure shock can be so profound that the naïve partner experiences feelings of unreality. He or she feels disconnected, as if the event were happening to someone else. That's how Christopher felt during his wife's confession. He had absolutely no idea that Carly had been having an affair. When she told him in the car coming home from a romantic dinner, without any advance warning, he couldn't believe what he was hearing: "I kept waiting for Allen Funt to appear and tell me I'm on Candid Camera. . . . I couldn't imagine it. . . ."

To end the deception: When Carly decided to tell Christopher about her affair, they had just worked through a difficult patch in their marriage by promising each other greater openness through honest communication. Carly felt that not to tell would violate their renewed commitment. It was hard to upset her husband's newfound sense of comfort in the marriage, but she felt it was the right thing to do. Christopher began to understand that her motivation was to stop deceiving him and to end her affair.

Christopher believed that his wife was sincere when she told him how much she regretted her involvement with the other man. He had faith

that it would never happen again. Carly's honesty was intended to alleviate her guilt and start the next phase of their married life with a clean
slate.

There are many reasons an involved spouse may choose to confess an
infidelity. Obviously, a confession intended to strengthen the relationship
is different from one that is intended to destroy it. Sometimes, though,
the motivation for telling is to trigger a crisis that will lead to separation.

To end the marriage: One night, Tamara confessed to her husband,
Tom, that she was attracted to someone else. She said she expected Tom to
kick her out, but he pleaded with her to stay and work on their marriage.
Surprisingly to him, she refused to answer his questions and would not
offer any explanation for what had happened. All she could say was,
"You're strong. You'll get through this." When he couldn't seem to get
himself together, she suggested that he call his sister. When Tamara
moved out just one week later, Tom felt as if he had been lobotomized.
Because she essentially cut off all contact after that, he had to heal alone.
Picking up the pieces of his broken life was made more difficult without
the opportunity to hear her story and get some closure.

To send a message: Some unfaithful partners confess in order to punish
their partner for unmet needs or to elicit a reaction from an inattentive
spouse. Harold got his wife's attention with innuendoes about his sexual
intimacies with a young woman he had met at the fitness center. He had
complained for a long time about the infrequency of marital sex. When
his wife, Hope, understood that she could actually lose him to another
woman, she realized how much he meant to her. For the first few weeks
after his confession, they had sex every morning and evening. Although
their newfound passion did eventually lessen, his revelation was the catalyst for a new beginning.

To stop the inquisition: Most confessions unfold in a torturous manner.
Beginning with outright denial, the accused partner progresses to foot-
dragging and admissions of minor infractions. Men will initially minimize or deny deep emotional involvement, and women are more inclined
to deny having engaged in any type of sexual intimacy. Just to get off the
hot seat, the unfaithful partner may finally cave in and admit the full extent of sexual and emotional involvement.

Natasha remembered every detail of the morning her husband finally
confessed his affair. "When I told him I knew, he denied it. He insisted
that they were *just friends*. But I kept after him; I didn't let him off the

hook. Finally, he admitted that he had visited her at home one afternoon and they kissed a couple of times. When I told him I didn't believe that that was all, he got furious that I didn't accept his story. Three months later, he admitted they'd gone further."

When evidence has been accumulating, a dishonest denial adds insult to injury. People have a double wound to deal with when they learn long after futile confrontations that their partner repeatedly lied to them with false reassurances and fabricated stories.

The Informant

There is a lot of disagreement about whether friends or family members should inform a betrayed partner when they know that an affair is going on. Ann Landers tended to advise people to MYOB. Other advisors and experts give conflicting advice. My answer is "It depends." Whether or not to reveal an affair depends on the signals a friend or relative is getting from the naïve spouse. Some spouses want to know and others don't. Watch for cues before you decide. A word of caution: In situations where the betrayed partner could become violent or severely depressed after hearing about the infidelity, you might reconsider whether it's beneficial to tell.

A friend: If the informant is a trusted source with legitimate information, telling can be a considerate action. This is what happened to Theresa. She and her husband had been married for fifteen years when her husband's relentless distancing made her ask him if he wanted a divorce. He told her that maybe he did, and they decided together that he should move out. After a few weeks he started calling her to talk about reconciling. Pleased, she agreed that they could start dating each other and see what happened. They spent many happy evenings together and talked seriously about getting back together. Then Theresa got a call from a friend who had attended a birthday party. Guess who had been there as the affectionate companion of one of the invited guests? Theresa's husband!

Theresa was distraught but grateful that her friend saved her from being a fool. The information that her reconciling hubby was acting in public as another woman's boyfriend helped Theresa cut the cord and get on with her life. She knew that she would never be able to trust her soon-to-be-ex-husband enough to attempt a reconciliation.

Anonymous informants: When the informant is an anonymous voice on the other end of the phone or an unidentified letter writer, the tip-off may not be so helpful. It is impossible to judge the intention behind the information or the truthfulness of what is being alleged. Mike found that out when he got a phone call at home from a man who said, "Just thought you ought to know. Your wife's having an affair with her boss." *Click*—the phone went dead. Mike was terribly upset. He had no reason to think his wife was having an affair, but the experience was gut-wrenching. His wife appeared to be as shocked as he was at the phone call and swore it wasn't true. It took many weeks of reassurance and investigation before they could put the matter to rest. Apparently, the call had been made by a colleague of his wife's who was angry because she had rebuffed his sexual advances.

Affair partners as informants: It is not uncommon for the revelation to be made by unmarried affair partners. One woman discovered her husband's affair when his lover forwarded her a sexually explicit greeting card with the husband's seductive message. Another wife found out when her husband's girlfriend showed up at the front door with a packet of e-mail correspondence.

Revelation by the affair partner is more likely to happen when an unfaithful husband has indicated that his wife doesn't understand him and that their marriage is a sham. The affair partner believes him and waits and waits for him to leave his wife so they can be together. After months or perhaps years of waiting for his children's bar mitzvahs, graduations, and weddings, the affair partner takes matters into her own hands; she tells the wife herself, thereby forcing a confrontation, which she believes will resolve in her favor. The crisis of disclosure from the lover most often results in the termination of the affair.

Betrayed partners as informants: I have known betrayed spouses who have called the unsuspecting spouse of the affair partner. They regarded their revelation to another betrayed partner as "obtaining justice." They reasoned, "Why should our marriage be hurt by the affair while their marriage remains unscathed?" One unfaithful husband begged his wife not to call his affair partner's house because he was fearful that her betrayed husband could be violent. She respected his request not to call, and in turn he ended the affair through an e-mail correspondence that she approved.

Medical and legal informants: When the method of discovery is shocking, the betrayals themselves often have serious implications that continue to shape the lives of everyone involved. For example, a doctor becomes the reluctant informer who has to tell a betrayed partner that he or she has a sexually transmitted disease. Will learned that his herpes resulted from an affair that his wife had had with an old boyfriend after Will and she were engaged. I have worked with several couples where the wife discovered the husband's sexual addiction when the police arrested him for soliciting a prostitute.

Even in these extreme situations, couples have recovered from the crisis and created a strong, safe relationship through long-term individual and couple therapy. The recovery process takes place on many different levels and usually lasts several years.

Accidental Discoveries

Melissa called her husband's hotel room at 7:00 A.M. A woman answered and told her that he couldn't come to the phone because he was in the shower. Yvette was walking hand in hand with her lover in a beautiful park when she was spotted by her in-laws, who had taken her children out for a picnic. Needless to say, they did not keep her secret from their son.

For many people, the moment of revelation is frozen in time forever. Every detail is indelibly etched into their memory. For Harriet, it's the image of her husband, Harvey, talking on a pay phone in a beautiful hotel in Rome. They had planned a luxurious trip to Italy for their twenty-fifth wedding anniversary. After they checked into their hotel, Harriet stepped into the shower to refresh herself while her husband went to the concierge desk to make dinner reservations. She dressed quickly and decided to go down to the lobby to look for him. As she rounded a corner, she could hear him saying into the phone, "I love you too, sweetheart. I can hardly wait until I'm home again so we can be together." That was how she discovered Harvey's seven-year affair with his secretary, Kitty. She was so traumatized that they had to fly home the next day. She did recover, but full healing took several years.

Accidental discovery is difficult no matter what the circumstances. But how both partners react in that moment and for the next few hours significantly influences the road to recovery. One betrayed partner was able to make a big leap toward healing her marriage by how she reacted to the news that her husband had been having an affair. She was able to put aside her shock and say to him, "I want our marriage to last. I love you.

But if you determine that she can make you happier than I can, then I will step aside." He was floored. His response to her was, "I never knew you loved me so much." The crisis of his affair was a catalyst that saved their marriage.

The Immediate Aftermath

Disclosure shock is a universal reaction to the betrayal of infidelity. Even suspicious partners are devastated when their worst fears are confirmed. Being betrayed by someone you have trusted feels like a mortal injury. Clearly, it matters *how* you find out that you have been betrayed. Finding out the truth from a remorseful partner is quite different from being forced into hiring a detective to uncover the truth after months of unanswered questions.

At the time of discovery, each partner reacts strongly but differently. Injured partners need to know that the affair will be stopped. They also need to know that all of their questions will be answered. Involved partners can also be in a place of profound suffering: Their lives are in shambles; they're caught in what feels like a no-win situation; they cannot escape the pain they've caused; and they now know that they must relinquish either the affair or the marriage. *Their double life has crashed and burned.*

The involved partner may respond to the revelation with complete honesty, staggered disclosures, or stonewalling. Even if the straying partner eventually comes clean, earlier denials or partial truths hinder healing and recovery. Dragged-out admissions are like driving long distances on a flat tire. Quick attention gets you back on the road fast, but delaying the repair after a blowout can cause irreparable damage to the wheel and axle. Immediate honesty is the best way to rebuild trust.

The betrayed partner may respond to the revelation with tears, numbness, or rage. When tempers are escalating, call a time-out to avoid further scarring. Make an appointment with each other to talk about the issue when you have both calmed down. Don't just walk out without saying something. You can say, "I am ready to explode. I don't want to make things worse than they already are, so I am going to go for a walk. Let's table this discussion for later, when we've both cooled down." Don't follow your partner if he or she is trying to do some damage control. Regard withdrawal as a strategy that can help the relationship at this time rather than as an avoidance maneuver.

What comes next in the hours and days that follow the crisis of discovery depends on how you react to the changes that have torn your world apart. In the next chapter, we discuss how some couples are able to survive disclosure shock together and how others break in two.

4

IN THE WAKE OF DISCOVERY

*The whole thing seemed unreal. I woke up every morning
and couldn't believe that it wasn't just a bad dream.
I don't know how I'll ever feel safe again.*

I F THERE were a Richter scale for emotional earthquakes, the discovery of an affair would register at the outermost end of the dial. Some people manage to recover quickly; the majority, however, feel as if they have been hit by a seismic event in a part of the country where there has never been one before. They are not prepared for the tremor that knocks them off their feet and destroys their home life. In the first minutes and hours after the revelation of infidelity, emotions are out of control.

Traumatic Aftershock: The Emotional Roller Coaster

In the immediate days and weeks that follow, the betrayed partner, the unfaithful partner, and the affair partner are overwhelmed by their enormous losses. The injured partner has lost the positive image of his or her life partner and the assurance of a secure, committed relationship. The involved partner has lost his or her secret love nest and faces the potential loss of marriage and family. The affair partner has lost the romantic cocoon and, usually, the dream of living forever with the lover.

All three are miserable in different ways. Because being deceived is not the same as being a deceiver, however, the betrayed partner is the one who is traumatized and can't imagine how he or she will ever become whole again.

88

Reactions of Betrayed Partners

Even when people think they are prepared for bad news, hearing the worst sends a jolt of adrenaline into the body that sets off a stress reaction. All the body's systems are aroused, and they stay aroused for a very long time. Skin prickles, muscles tense, and reactions are hair-trigger. The body responds as though danger were in every hushed voice and every ringing telephone. You have to be ready to run or fight as if your life depended on it.

> In my clinical sample, 24 percent of the betrayed husbands and wives who knew about their partner's infidelity were severely anxious, and an additional 18 percent were extremely anxious to the point of panic.[1] Thirty percent of the betrayed partners were also clinically depressed.[2]

Irritability and Aggression: Every potential irritation is magnified. The "pea under the mattress" is as big as a rock. The music on the radio makes you want to scream. The baby's fussing feels like an insidious campaign of harassment. Driving becomes a war game, where only the speedy and aggressive survive.

> Male starlings who remained monogamous when they had the opportunity to attract a second or third female were those mated to unusually aggressive females. This aggression was directed toward the potentially home-wrecking females rather than the potentially errant male.[3]

Throwing an object across the room or pounding a fist is not unusual after the revelation is first made. These angry gestures may be a way to express rage without being physically abusive. However, you *must* take any threats of violence seriously. If you are afraid or if you suffer any actual physical assaults, you must have a safety plan or request police intervention. I have treated individuals who have had to remove guns from the house to keep them from killing themselves or someone else. Homicidal fantasies by the betrayed spouse are more often directed toward the lover than the unfaithful spouse.

Numbing: Some people are numb before the revelation because they have turned off their sensors and become oblivious to suspicious signs. Others go numb after the revelation. Marilee went numb when she first heard her husband's confession. She felt turned to stone. She was aware of what was happening, but from a distance. She took in the information without color or feeling, struck dumb by the enormity of the betrayal. She was protected, at least for a time, from a pain that was too difficult to bear.

Obsessing: Betrayed partners commonly review over and over again the period in their life during which the affair was possibly taking place. As soon as they lie down to sleep, they are flooded with images, memories, and unanswered questions. They need to escape, but the whole surreal pageant parades across their vision. During the daytime, they get out calendars and review dates, looking for the missing parts, trying to make sense of what happened in light of their new knowledge. They try to figure out what was going on in their perceived life and how that coordinates with what was going on in the double life.

Sleeping offered Janet little relief. She had a recurring dream of being abandoned and alone that woke her up, sweating with panic. She recounted scenes of her husband, Jim, avoiding family gatherings and working on evenings and weekends. She found it hard to grasp the reality that he had shared his heart and his body with another woman.

Interrogating: The deluge of questions immediately following the revelation seldom satisfies the need to know. Betrayed partners turn into Grand Inquisitors in the weeks and months that follow, until they believe that they have uncovered all of the secrets and lies. It can be terribly difficult for the betrayed partner to show constraint; most want to know everything right now. The midnight interrogation leaves both partners exhausted.

Shifting Emotions: After confronting Jim with evidence of his four-year affair, Janet had, in rapid succession, locked him out of the bedroom and then insisted that he make love to her. Afterward, she felt guilty about having sex with him; she didn't understand that her conflicted feelings were going to alternate between needing reassurance from him that he'd never leave her and wanting to kick him out immediately.

Malcolm told me that when his wife told him she was in love with someone else, he felt as if he was going to pass out. Then he told her he didn't believe it. Then he felt stupid for not figuring it out sooner, and finally he felt so humiliated he wanted to hide. Soon he was out of control with fury. He would cycle through all these emotions (and others besides) over and over again for months.

Reactions of Unfaithful Partners

The immediate reactions of the unfaithful partner in the initial hours after revelation may either transform or solidify as the early weeks and months go by. Defensiveness can turn into openness or persist and become aggression. Ambivalence can turn into clarity or persist and become chronic confusion.

As the implications of the situation become clear, even those who believed they had found their true soul mate are jolted back to reality. It is as though a switch has been flipped, and full attention and energy is channeled back into the marriage. I've observed individuals panic about losing the spouse they had been planning to leave for the perfect relationship. Once the illusion is burst, reality returns. Over time, the fantasy bubble deflates even more if the affair partner acts with impatience and self-interest.

Resentment: Some unfaithful partners understand the need for the betrayed partner's ongoing quest for concrete proof of the affair. Others turn on their partner and attack, as though snooping were an offense worse than infidelity. One man, whose wife read his incriminating e-mail correspondence, turned on her in a rage. He threatened her with divorce if she ever questioned him or checked up on him again.

Impatience: Ambivalent partners may want to do the right thing and make amends, but they don't want to reveal too much about the modus operandi—how they managed to carry off the deception. They are frustrated by the constant hammering for details and searching for clues. They feel smothered by the lack of privacy and personal freedom. When a period of indecision is followed by a commitment, unfaithful partners may feel that they should be welcomed back with open arms. I call this the "*Hi, Hon. I'm back*" maneuver. It's not uncommon to hear, "I said I'm sorry. Why do you have to keep bringing up the past? I'm here now, aren't I? Why can't we go back to the way things were before? I told you it didn't mean anything."

Grief: Although it is quite painful for the betrayed partner to witness the involved partner's sadness regarding the end of the affair, grief can be seen as evidence that the illicit relationship is really over. Most often, the involved spouse is dealing with complex and heartrending issues. It is not uncommon for involved partners to feel shame, loss, and the fear that there is no light at the end of the tunnel. They are forced to ask some frightening questions: Will I lose my spouse and my marriage? Will I lose my affair partner and our romantic odyssey? If we stay together, will my spouse ever let me forget? Can I ever feel as good with my spouse as I did with my lover?

> **At** the beginning of marital therapy, unfaithful wives in my clinical sample were more anxious and depressed than unfaithful husbands: 32 percent of unfaithful wives were severely or extremely anxious compared with 10 percent of unfaithful husbands; 27 percent of unfaithful wives and 14 percent of unfaithful husbands were clinically depressed.

If you're the unfaithful partner, you know that having an affair is both agony and ecstasy. It may have been the most exciting and meaningful thing that has ever happened to you—and the worst. Now that it is exposed, you are probably dumbstruck by how an innocent, life-enriching friendship could ever have turned into such a nightmare. You face a terrible loss with no social support and a lot of social disapproval. Because society at large disapproves of infidelity and frowns on the self-centeredness associated with cheating, the involved partner does not receive much sympathy for his or her unhappiness. More than once, I have heard unfaithful partners lament, "Can't you see that this is hard on me, too?"

Zachary was truly sorry. Looking into Zoë's tearful eyes was harder than he could have imagined. He wanted to console her, but he needed consoling himself. Although he wanted to be caring and available, he grew very impatient with Zoë's over-the-top reactions. Zachary couldn't stand dealing with his wife or his lover, Patti, because of the pressure they were putting on him to choose between them. Despite his good intention to rebuild his marriage, Zachary found that ending the affair was not so easy. Patti made him feel guilty by saying that he had misled her. He wanted to run away and hide somewhere. But being alone made him feel even more conflicted and isolated, and being with either woman was too painful to bear.

A clean break with the affair partner is the surest way for all three parties to start healing their wounds. Affair partners do not always buy into this program of recovery, however, because they have their own agendas.

Reactions of Unmarried Affair Partners

If you're the affair partner, you probably can't believe the affair is over. You may interpret your married lover's concern for you as a sign that he or she still cares about you. This may give you hope that the affair will continue, even in the face of evidence to the contrary.

Some affair partners welcome the crisis of discovery initially, believing that the truth will force their lover to make a choice in their favor. They may have been assured that their lover was planning to leave his or her spouse as soon as the kids were through school or the business was on solid ground. They have dreamed of a life together and had visions of the secure home and family they would make together.

Letting go of a dream is hard. You may have believed that the marriage was unhappy, but you need to realize that someone who could deceive a spouse could also have been deceiving you. You might have been told that the marriage was worse than it really was in order to keep you on the string. Because of society's tainted image of the affair partner, you may feel you are suffering all alone. Instead of sympathy from your friends, you might be hearing a lot of "I told you this was going to end badly."

How affair partners react to the revelation of the affair depends on many factors: what they hoped for, their level of commitment, and how their lover handled the crisis. Reactions typically range from devastated to partly sorry and relieved. When the affair is revealed, it can feel like a painful but necessary step toward resolution.

Most often, however, affair partners suffer great unhappiness. They face tremendous uncertainty and have less control over the outcome than anyone else. In addition, they face the probability that the affair and their intimate partner will be lost to them forever. A single woman involved with a married man may have ignored other romantic opportunities in the hope that the affair would turn into marriage. She may not accept the rejection easily because she is left with false hopes and broken promises.

> Studies have found a very low probability that an affair will result in marriage to the affair partner. Annette Lawson found that only 10 percent of involved partners who left the marriage because of infidelity ended up marrying the affair partner.[4]

Affairs are inherently dangerous, and affair partners who are dropped have the disadvantage of having to heal alone, whereas the betrayed partner and the involved partner can heal together. Individual or group counseling can provide support and insight regarding a tendency to willingly expose oneself to a potentially self-destructive triangle.

Why Some People Are More Traumatized Than Others

The severity of the traumatic reaction is determined by (1) how the discovery was made, (2) extent of shattered assumptions, (3) individual and situational vulnerabilities, (4) the nature of the betrayal, and (5) whether the threat of betrayal continues. These factors interact with one another to determine the intensity, scope, and persistence of post-traumatic reactions.

Shattered Assumptions

All of us operate from a set of basic assumptions about our relationships, our partners, and ourselves. We can describe, at least in a general way, the terms of commitment that characterize our marriages and other significant relationships. Our assumptions provide us with a map of our partner's personality and moral character that predicts how he or she would behave in compromising situations. We are traumatized when these assumptions are shattered because our safe, predictable world is no longer safe or predictable.

Our basic assumptions provide a set of operating instructions for living. They ground us in our identity, allow us to negotiate the complexities of living, and help us to interpret information that is bewildering or complicated. We run our lives following the lines of our assumptions. When these basic assumptions are violated, we are disoriented: "If I can't depend on you, I can't depend on anything in my life." One woman, who had just finished successful treatment for cancer, told her husband, "I wish I had died last year when I was sick—before I learned the terrible truth about you."

Assumptions about the Relationship

A tornado on a summer's day is more devastating than a hurricane. At least you have some warning with a hurricane. When disaster strikes without warning, as it did with the attacks on Oklahoma City, New York, and Washington, D.C., people lose something they can never get back—their innocence. In the same way, our reaction to an infidelity is intensified by how much the betrayal deviates from our basic assumptions about our mutual commitment to monogamy. These are some common assumptions:

- *I assumed we were committed exclusively to each other, no matter what.*
- *I thought we had the same moral values and that we both believed in monogamy.*
- *I never doubted that we loved each other.*
- *I believed I could be safe in this relationship.*

The disparity between what the betrayed partner believed about commitment and exclusivity and the actual behavior of the unfaithful partner determines the extent of traumatization. One young wife thought she and her husband had the perfect marriage: "I knew we were in a slump, but I never thought we weren't totally committed to each other." Believing that she and her husband had a perfect understanding and an unassailable commitment made his betrayal that much more shocking. Another betrayed spouse poignantly expressed this sense of what it is like to know that what you counted on as exclusively yours has been shared with another person: "You took something that was supposed to be mine, which was intimacy, and you gave it to someone else."

Even couples in open marriages have assumptions about their outside relationships. If these assumptions are violated, they feel a terrible sense of betrayal. The rules might be that each person can have multiple sex partners but cannot become emotionally attached or have secret liaisons with another person. If these rules are broken, the devastation is just as great as in a marriage with the assumption of monogamy. One such wife, Colleen, couldn't sleep or eat after learning that her husband was communicating secretly with women on the Internet, although they had engaged in sexual swinging for many years.

Following the discovery of a betrayal, there will never again be the blind trust that existed before. In just a few seconds, the safest haven in the world is turned into the source of the greatest treachery.

Assumptions about Your Partner
- *I thought you were trustworthy.*
- *I thought you would always be honest with me.*
- *I thought you would always do the right thing.*

When you think you know who your partner is and he or she does something absolutely out of character, it is hard to understand what your eyes are telling you. If you believe that you are married to someone with an especially fine moral character, your chagrin is not only about the infidelity but also about the altered perception of your partner. It's like being married to a four-star general and finding out that he's really a Russian spy.

People are attracted to their mates because they admire and respect them. Even after the process of idealization that characterizes a new relationship has stopped, people still want to believe the best of their chosen partner. It is perfectly reasonable to "accentuate the positive and eliminate the negative." You want to feel that the person you are married to is trustworthy. It is devastating to find out that your husband is a liar or that your wife is a cheat. The affront feels very personal. "You're not who I thought you were!" is a common lament of betrayed partners.

Husbands and wives who never had any reason to doubt their mutual commitment to exclusivity are deeply traumatized by the betrayal of infidelity. A betrayed husband expressed disbelief when he discovered his wife with another man: "My wife was a virgin when we married, and she's always been a devoted wife and mother. I would have bet 2 million dollars that that could not have been my wife coming out of a motel with another man." One woman said, "He's religious and hates liars and was never that interested in sex." His affair shattered these assumptions.

In contrast are situations where assumptions of monogamy are shaky to begin with. A couple who had cheated on each other during their engagement were hurt and angry when each of them strayed during the early years of the marriage, but they were not shocked or disillusioned.

Individual Vulnerabilities in the Betrayed Partner

It is not possible to predict with 100 percent accuracy how any individual will react to infidelity according to the nature of the betrayal and the manner in which it was discovered. Betrayed partners also react in a variety of ways based on their personal relationship history, self-worth, and emotional stability. Hopelessness about the future is more prevalent in betrayed partners who blame the infidelity on their own shortcomings and those who fear abandonment. To some extent, this is a matter of in-born temperament: Some people are born serene and nonreactive, whereas others come into this world prickly and hypersensitive.

Who we are is also partly a consequence of the experiences we have had in the past. Our relationship history influences how we will react to interpersonal injuries. To understand why one person stumbles and can't go on and why someone else is able to keep walking in similar circumstances requires an understanding of each person's past. We carry our wounds and our triumphs around with us long after they've actually happened.

Low Self-Esteem
People with low self-esteem will have greater difficulty recovering because they interpret their partner's betrayal as proof of their own inadequacies. Belinda had a chronically ill mother and a supercritical father. Nothing she did was ever good enough for her father. Her mother, on the other hand, was loving but depended on her daughter to take care of her. When Belinda married, she thought she had found her soul mate and would finally get the love and validation she had been searching for. Her whole

world came crashing down when she discovered his love letters to another woman. She couldn't ever feel special with him again. The healing relationship she had expected with her husband turned into another huge scar, although she is working hard to become more independent.

Individuals who had intense sibling rivalries and were the least preferred by their parents are apt to carry into their adult relationships the need to prove that they are worthy of being loved. When their partners gets involved with someone else, it evokes all those old feelings of competition or of being the outsider or the one less favored. Betrayed partners who were scapegoated or neglected as children are vulnerable to viewing a partner's infidelity as a personal rejection.

Men or women who are anxious about their own sexual performance or attractiveness are especially vulnerable to excessive feelings of inadequacy and self-doubt if their partner has extramarital sex. Russ felt as if he had been hit with a club when he discovered that his wife, Rita, had had an affair. She had never seemed that interested in sex with him. When he found out that she had discussed his sexual shortcomings with her affair partner, Russ was embarrassed and humiliated. This guy knew all about him, but Russ didn't know *anything* about the affair partner or his sexual exploits with Rita.

Fractured Trust

Individuals who did not develop basic trust during childhood are especially vulnerable to deception by a loved one. Infidelity brings back all of those childhood wounds for a person who was lied to or whose parents made promises they didn't keep. Those who were physically, sexually, or emotionally abused in previous relationships may be retraumatized when someone they have counted on betrays their trust and dependency. Judith Herman writes, "Trauma forces the survivor to relive all her earlier struggles. . . . Traumatic life events, like other misfortunes, are especially merciless to those who are already troubled." [5]

Parental Infidelity

Witnessing parental infidelity can place people at greater risk of traumatization if they are betrayed by their chosen partner. Gloria thought her life was perfect until she was thirteen. Her father left her mother for another woman, and Gloria's world blew apart. When she talked about her childhood, everything was placed in time as *before* her father's affair (when things were wonderful) and *after* his affair (when her family fell apart). Although her husband knew of her wounds, he had an affair anyway. To Gloria this showed such a lack of regard for her that she could not stay in the marriage.

> Men who witnessed a mother's infidelities are more likely than other men to exhibit pathological jealousy and an inability to let go of a partner's betrayal.[6] In contrast, some women whose fathers were philanderers seem to accept being married to men of the same ilk. They stay while their husbands stray. They look the other way because their expectations were shaped by their family legacy.

An interesting illustration of a father's influence was told to me by a woman from a large ethnic family who was given a piece of advice the day before her wedding. Her father was a man of few words, but he pulled her aside and said, "I want you to know that if you ever learn that your husband has been involved with another woman, that doesn't mean he doesn't love you." When her husband did cheat, she was unhappy but not traumatized.

Pre-existing Stressful Life Events

Disclosure of infidelity is more traumatic when other situational or life events have already created stress or vulnerability. The same life transitions that increase stress, such as unemployment, pregnancy, serious illness, or death of a family member, may push one partner into the escape of an affair—an affair that can push the betrayed partner into a state of collapse. There is no preferred timing for a partner to be unfaithful, but a betrayal in an already burdened relationship feels even more catastrophic.

Pregnancy
Lisa remembered what it was like being pregnant with her second child. She was frazzled keeping up with her toddler and sick to her stomach for

the first four months. She felt trapped and unattractive and in need of special reassurance and support. Instead, her husband got involved with a woman at work and was even less involved and available at home. The affair was painful enough, but the fact that he had betrayed her just when she was most needy and vulnerable made it doubly painful.

Family Illness

Caring for sick and dying relatives obviously puts a strain on a marriage. Constant care and worry draw on the couple's reserves, while their relationship takes a backseat to more urgent obligations. On top of the exhaustion and grief you already have, discovering that your partner is taking advantage of you in such a situation is a serious blow.

Angela had the feeling of being kicked while she was down when her husband had an affair right after her mother died. She considered her mother to be her best friend and was dedicated to caring for her during her terminal illness. After her mother died, Angela was grief stricken. Discovering her husband's fling deepened her depression because she felt totally alone. Her mother would normally have been the person to help her deal with problems in her marriage; now that she was gone, Angela felt she had no one to turn to. Incredulous, she faced her husband, saying, "You had sex with your lover in our bed while I was away taking care of my dying mother?!"

The Nature of the Betrayal

The intensity of the betrayed partner's traumatic reaction is connected with the nature of the betrayal. Each infidelity has its own profile and, therefore, its own character. Infidelity with a stranger is different from infidelity with your best friend. A brief fling at a conference is different from a five-year love affair with the next-door neighbor. Staggered revelations about multiple involvements create a crescendo of shock waves. The length and depth of the deception prior to the disclosure will influence the length of time it takes to recover. Hearing the whole truth earlier in the process enhances recovery.[7] I will give you guidance on how to structure this process in Chapter 8.

One of the things that makes the revelations of sex addicts especially traumatic is that the betrayed partner often hears about multiple sexual encounters staggered over time. One injury is admitted, then another, unexpected one comes later, and then another. Each time the betrayed partners think they have heard it all, they are retraumatized with additional horror stories.

Extent of Extramarital Involvement

How deep was the emotional involvement and what kind of sexual intimacies were experienced? Unfaithful partners tend to minimize the extent of sexual and emotional involvement. Betrayed wives are usually more obsessed with love letters that were written to the affair partner than with revelations of sexual intercourse with casual acquaintances. On the other hand, betrayed husbands are usually more upset by their wife's having sex with another man. Initial denials of emotional attachment by unfaithful husbands and of sexual activities by unfaithful wives indicate that men and women differ in the type of infidelity they consider the most devastating.

Duration of Affair

A clandestine relationship that lasts for years undercuts everything that happened in the marriage during that time. As one husband said, "I can't believe you continued the affair for ten years. It went on so long that all these years our life has been a lie." His memories of those years are now corrupted. Every remembered scene of intimacy and affection is suspect in the light of his new knowledge. All those times his wife told him she loved him now seem like insults and taunts. He cannot believe in the authenticity of any point of connection with his wife that used to bring him joy: "Our whole marriage is a sham."

The death of a wealthy realtor from Connecticut revealed that he had led two entirely separate lives for thirty years.[8] Frank Troy had been happily married to his wife for fifty-eight years while at the same time he lived on weekends with another woman in Rhode Island. The other woman knew he was married but thought he was separated from his wife. He told his wife that he had to be away on weekends to help run the ferry to Block Island. He told the other woman not to call him on weekdays because he had to take care of his sickly sister, who needed total quiet.

Only when Frank died did his wife discover that he had left behind three decades of lying and deceit, along with his sizable estate. On their fiftieth wedding anniversary they had celebrated by renewing their vows in church. Imagine the difficulties she will have coming to terms with the reality that for all those years, she had been married to a man whose double life makes him seem more like an espionage agent than an ordinary husband.

Double Betrayals

The identity of the affair partner is bound to intensify the traumatic reaction of the betrayed spouse. Eve's husband had an affair with the babysitter, whom she had taken under her wing throughout her college years. Cameron's wife had an affair with his business partner, whom he considered one of his best friends. He told me, "This is a double betrayal. I've been screwed over twice!" Leanne sent her husband, Louis, to help out her friend, Maxine, after the tragic and unexpected death of Maxine's husband. Imagine the sense of betrayal Leanne felt when Louis moved out of the house to be with the grieving widow.

These double betrayals involve multiple losses. When the affair partner is a relative, families seldom recover from the shocking treachery. An example is the betrayed wife who discovered that her husband was in love with her sister; another is the husband who found out that his wife had run off with his father. In that case, his wife and his father became outcasts, and the family was split apart forever.

Stolen Treasures

Betrayed partners are hurt when what they longed for in their marriage was given to a rival. Sometimes the spouse has been shortchanged while the lover has been royally treated with gifts of affection, time, and money. One irate wife confronted her husband on just this issue: "We didn't have enough money for baby-sitters, and you spent money for hotel rooms!" Another wife felt cheated and enraged when her quiet, inexpressive husband sent romantic messages to his e-lover. Betrayed partners are deeply chagrined to learn that their workaholic spouse somehow found the time to have an affair.

But there are other kinds of thefts. One husband was willing to make sacrifices for his wife's demanding career, believing that her professional success was good for their marriage and their children. She was often gone in the evenings and traveled several times a year. Her absence was hard for her children and meant that he had to do double duty as both mother and father. When she confessed that she had been having an affair with a man at work, he was outraged that she had enlisted his help in enabling her traitorous behavior: "I thought I was supporting you in your work—all the travel, the late nights. It was all so you could be with someone else."

Flagrant Indiscretions
How obvious was the involved partner? What flimsy lies and subterfuges were employed to cover it up? Betrayed spouses often say they feel stupid about not figuring out things earlier: "It went on right under my nose. How could I have been so blind?" Once they know the score, it all seems so obvious. They have perfect vision in hindsight.

It is also hard when the offending partner is flagrant in his or her disrespectful behavior. What made one husband so angry was his wife's blatant disregard for their family and her lack of discretion: "You took our baby along to the zoo with your lover's children?"

The Gulf between Perception and Reality
How much of a chasm is there between what the naïve partner believed and what really happened? Has a partner been especially attentive, not out of true feeling but as a cover-up? In the early stages of his affair with another woman, one husband took care to be especially loving with his wife. When she found out about his subterfuge, she deeply resented his affectionate ploys: "Just when you were being so nice and so romantic, and I thought you were really committed, I discovered you were hatching elaborate schemes to keep me off the track."

The Threat Continues

An important, ongoing consideration is whether the betrayed partner continues to be threatened. Harriet cried hysterically every morning when her husband, Harvey, left for work. Healing the marriage was particularly difficult because Harvey refused to fire the secretary with whom he had a seven-year affair. He claimed that Kitty's services were indispensable. Although Harvey had ended the affair, Harriet was retraumatized every day that Kitty stayed on the job. Harvey grew impatient and frustrated with Harriet's never-ending harangues because he believed he had answered all of her questions and he was no longer intimate with Kitty. Harriet did not settle down until Kitty moved out of state a year later. Only then could Harriet begin to experience the safety that is necessary for recovery.

Trust has to be earned. Safety has to be reestablished. This is not an overnight process. Just as the involved partner cannot flick a switch to turn off all feelings for the lover, the noninvolved partner cannot shift from betrayal to unquestioning trust in an instant. Each of these common situations carries with it a different flavor of insecurity:

He says they're "just friends" again, and he shouldn't have to cut off all contact.

If the contact continues, the threat continues. It's like a recovering alcoholic who continues to go to happy hour after work every Friday, or an Internet infidel who continues to use the computer at home in the evenings.

She hasn't made up her mind whether she's going to stay or leave.

You feel like a displaced person. Your home as you've known it has been destroyed, and you don't know where you will be or who you will be with from day to day.

He says he's stopped, and I should trust him, but I can't.

You're paranoid if you don't trust him, but you violate your own gut feelings if you do.

He's more sympathetic to her than he is to me.

The other woman rants and raves and screams and yells, and the husband feels sorry for her. But when the spouse gets upset, he thinks, "What a bitch. No wonder I had an affair." If this attitude persists, it's an indication that there may not be enough empathy for the injured partner to allow healing in the marriage.

In each of the preceding situations, uncertainty about commitment to work on the marriage or uncertainty that the affair is over keeps the betrayed partner off balance. If you are certain that the affair is over and there is no contact with the affair partner, recovery is straightforward, although still difficult. The threat has ended, and you can proceed to work through what happened and the meaning of what happened. However, additional incidents of deception are retraumatizing and set the recovery process back to zero.

If the involved partner is ambivalent for too long or continues secret contact with the affair partner, the continuing retraumatization and deception will make healing difficult, whether or not the marriage continues. Depending on how emotionally involved the affair has been, ending it may happen over a long period of time or very quickly. Women are more likely than men to have a prolonged period of letting go; men (and less commonly women), who compartmentalize their primarily sexual affairs, can move on very quickly. Sometimes, in fact, the involved partner dismisses the affair so easily that it's hard for the hurt partner to believe it's really over. Certainty comes through concrete demonstrations of openness and proof that any contact with the affair partner has been cut off.

Establishing Safety: Stop and Share

The first step in recovering from the crisis of disclosure is to establish safety by reversing the position of walls and windows. *The affair must stop, and any intimate interactions with the affair partner must come to an end.* During the affair, secrecy fueled the passion with the lover and diminished the intimacy with the spouse. The involved partner must be willing to open windows inside the marriage and put up walls with the affair partner.

If you are an involved partner, you must *resolve to stop* the affair and *then take steps* to do it. In the beginning you may be more sensitive about hurting your affair partner than about hurting your spouse. The natural thing is to want to check on your affair partner to see if he or she is okay, but your kind intentions are misguided—actually, somewhat cruel, because they give a mixed message to your lover that you are still interested. You have to make a clean break. You are not the appropriate person to provide support for the distress that the breakup caused. It is unfair to offer comfort that will keep the affair partner attached to you instead of moving on. You must also resolve to *share* with your spouse any phone contact or face-to-face encounters with the affair partner.

Honesty now is the only way to undo the legacy of deception and lies. You and your spouse both need assurance that sharing every new interaction will not create new explosions, although some may. The involved partner cannot feel safe in an atmosphere of nasty accusations and emotional storms, anymore than the betrayed partner can feel safe in the absence of honest information. The involved partner believes that telling the truth will only make things worse. The betrayed partner must demonstrate that the distress caused by hearing upsetting information is a short-term reaction, but that the long-term effect is to heal the wounds.

Step 1: Stop All Contact with the Affair Partner

• **What does it mean to stop?** *Stop all personal contact* with the affair partner, if possible; if total avoidance is not possible, stop all personal discussions. Extricating yourself means telling your affair partner that you are committed to rebuilding your marriage and that all intimate communication will stop. Until it is unambiguously clear that the affair is over, your spouse cannot begin to heal and your marriage cannot recover. This means no more phone calls, lunches, or e-mails. If you have a business relationship with your affair partner, as is often the case, there must be an understanding that the relationship will be strictly business. Without closure all three of you will be stuck in a confusing morass of indecision.

• **We were friends before, so why can't we be friends again?** Sometimes after an affair is discovered, the involved partner decides to stay in the marriage but also wants to stay friends with the affair partner. What does that mean? Is the affair over or is it just on hold? Are you trying out the marriage with the option of going back to your affair partner? If the affair is just put on hold, your spouse will remain suspicious. It is an unfortunate reality that someone who has crossed the line into a romantic sexual affair can't go back to the previous state of platonic friendship.

Dora had an intense affair with her doubles partner at the tennis club. There was no question in her mind that she wanted to stay in her marriage, but she also refused to quit playing tennis with her lover and resign from the club. Dennis, her husband, did not accept her reason for continuing. She was adamant that she didn't want to draw notice at the club by abruptly quitting. As far as Dennis was concerned, resigning their club membership and quitting tennis altogether was better than knowing his wife was in continuing contact with the man she had betrayed him with.

Dora's stubborn refusal to stop playing tennis with her lover looks like ambivalence. Although she says she is committed to Dennis, he will not believe it until her behavior demonstrates her commitment. Apologies and promises alone are not enough to rebuild trust; reassurance comes only with observable change. If Dora has been lying for so long, just saying it's over could be another lie. How can Dennis know if she's telling the truth? Only time and devotion to her husband will convince him. A truly remorseful spouse will come home earlier, be more attentive, make his or her partner feel more desirable, and be willing to put up a thick wall with the affair partner. Only then will a betrayed spouse eventually be able to let go of his or her insecurity.

- **What do we do if continuing contact is unavoidable?** It is harder to demonstrate renewed loyalty to a betrayed partner when the two people involved in the affair must have continuing contact. Leonard had a two-year affair with an esteemed colleague in his department at the university. After he got caught, he promised his wife, Linda, that he would end the affair and enter couple therapy to work on their marriage. The problem was that his academic department was small and there was no way he could cut off all contact with his former lover. To make matters even more complicated, they were part of a small research team that was on the threshold of a groundbreaking accomplishment in their field. They *had* to work together. Besides, he still cared deeply for his affair partner and believed that their ability to understand each other was one reason their research was going so well. He was willing to end the affair, but he definitely needed to continue his indispensable working relationship.

In cases where professional collaboration is a necessity, the parameters of the relationship need to be carefully designed and communicated. Here are two suggestions for redrawing those lines:

1. *Limit contact to business only.* If you are serious about reestablishing safety in your marriage and sending clear signals to your affair partner, then you must become a polite but distant stranger to your affair partner. Going out together for coffee, swapping stories about your kids, and trading office gossip are

invitations to intimacy. Telephone strictly for business purposes, and if the other person steers the conversation into personal waters, say, "I'm sorry, but I don't want to discuss that."

2. *Do not talk about your marriage with your affair partner.* If your
ex-lover asks you how your marriage is doing, you can demonstrate that there is a wall around the marriage that cannot be
knocked down by answering, "I'm sorry, but it isn't appropriate
for me to discuss that with you." Refusal to discuss your marriage tells your affair partner where the boundaries are. You
won't be tempted to portray the marriage in a negative light to
protect the feelings of the affair partner, who must understand
that you now have a new commitment to the marriage. You enhance intimacy and rebuild the sense of "we-ness" in the marriage by confining personal information to your spouse.

Step 2: Share All Unavoidable Encounters

- **What does it mean to share?** Sometimes it's impossible to avoid
all contact, so whenever and whatever contact with the affair partner does occur must be told to the betrayed partner, thus opening
a window when there is unavoidable or ongoing contact.

  After disclosure, one husband called his affair partner in front
of his wife to tell her it was over. The next day the affair partner
called him at work and said, "I know your wife made you call me
last night. I could tell. It's not really over, is it?" He told her it was
over. And then he went home and told his wife about the call, even
though she would never have found out about it on her own. His
voluntary honesty gave them a great leap forward into greater
trust.

- **Volunteer *before* being asked.** Up to this point, the injured partner has had to dig up most of the information. The best sharing is
done *before* the betrayed partner has a chance to ask whether there
has been any contact. This suggestion is counterintuitive because
most involved partners wish to avoid initiating any topics that
could stir things up—especially when some calm has been temporarily restored. As one man said, "If I even mention her name,
I'm in for a whole night." But think about what happens if you

don't bring it up and your spouse finds out. *Any contact you admit having with your affair partner is a golden opportunity to gain trust points with your spouse.*

One month after Rudy discovered that his wife, Ruth, was involved with a man who was a client of her firm, he was still feeling shaky about how often they would see each other in the course of their work. One night, when Ruth came home after a long day, Rudy asked her how her day was. "Did anything interesting happen?" "Nothing happened. It was fine," she replied. He then asked her whether she had seen her ex-lover, Steve. "Yeah, he came in, but I didn't have that much to say to him." This was not a good exchange. Rudy felt insecure because he had to pry information out of her, and Ruth felt badgered and scrutinized.

Two weeks later, Rudy again asked his wife, "How was your day?" This time, Ruth said, "I was in line at the bank and guess who was in the car in front of me? Steve! He got out of his car to talk to me. He asked me how things were going with you, and I told him that I really didn't want to talk to him about anything personal." This time, Rudy felt that his wife had given him a gift.

Step 3: Be Accountable

- **Be willing to prove you are trustworthy.** If you are the unfaithful partner and your spouse is constantly snooping around, you might misperceive his or her need to know as an autonomy problem for you instead of a security issue for your spouse. It isn't that your partner has a neurotic need to control your every move. Rather, knowing what is really going on is the only way a traumatized person can begin to reestablish trust. Your approach here can be, "I will help you check up on me." Specifically, you can turn over the beeper, share the cell phone bills, and share your e-mail correspondence. If your affair was an Internet affair, share your Internet history file.

- **Be accountable for your whereabouts.** You may feel smothered, but you owe it to your partner to let him or her know where you are. It may feel as if you are curtailing your freedom, but what you are really doing is taking care of your partner's anxiety. If you are going to be late, call home. It's not fair to create worry. After half an hour, your partner is imagining all kinds of horrible things. Think of what it's like to have a teenager with a new driver's license who doesn't want to wake you up by calling to let you know he or she will be late. You are already sitting on pins and needles, picturing the funeral. In your case, your partner is on pins and needles picturing the rendezvous.

Surviving Day by Day

Recovery from infidelity requires that a couple work together to heal the pain. However, during the early days, both partners may be so depleted from nursing their own wounds that they may not have much left to give each other. I cannot stress enough how important it is that you not deepen each other's wounds during this critical early period. If you cannot muster affection or caring, then be considerate and respectful. At the least, if you *treat each other as nicely as you would treat a stranger,* you are bound to be decent to each other.

In the beginning, with the trauma fresh, you need immediate help in how to survive from day to day. Take care of yourself with exercise, massage, and plenty of rest. If your reactions are extreme (if you cannot eat or sleep, for example), or if either of you has persistent thoughts of suicide or violence, you should talk to your physician about medication and a referral to a therapist.

Develop Support Networks

You need the lifeline of an outside support network to get through the pain. You may feel that you and your partner are in separate boats that are capsizing in the wake of the storm. You will be bailing out together later in the process, but right now you may need other resources for support.

Talk to friends who will help you through these stormy times. Be careful that you do not pick anyone to confide in who will bad-mouth your partner or spread rumors about your situation. Friends of the marriage accept your decision to stay in the process of reconciliation and support it positively. They are empathic, but objective at the same time. They are able to be with you and listen, and they are slow to give advice.

In most cases, it is best not to involve family members (especially children). Family members are usually not able to be as neutral as friends because family members have trouble getting past the hurt you have suffered. Every ugly incident will be an indelible memory. Parents can be very pessimistic about your choice to stay together, and they can hold a grudge against your partner long after you have forgiven each other.

Practice Damage Control

Even now, in these early days, you are setting the stage for the construction of a stronger marriage. Expect peaks and valleys. Intimate, wonderful days are likely to be followed by freaking-out days. Every word that either of you says is likely to be remembered. It can take superhuman patience and empathy to live through this difficult, confusing time, but following some basic guidelines for helpful communication can make all the difference between going down in flames and staying afloat:

1. Knowing that all questions about the infidelity will be answered later is important. Understanding that they need to be answered in a controlled way is essential.

2. Set limits on the midnight talks. Sleep deprivation will intensify negative emotions. Set aside structured time for discussions.

3. Avoid escalating arguments that could result in physical or verbal abuse. Take time-outs if emotions erupt.

4. It is a challenge to construct a disclosure process that unfolds rather than explodes. Traumatic reactions will make it hard for the injured partner to act rationally and with self-control. Fear of consequences will make it hard for the involved partner to be open. Even at this early stage, respectful (albeit angry) questions and thoughtful answers make the road to full understanding easier and more complete.

Lift the Lid a Little Bit

Although it's best to delay discussing the affair until you are on more solid ground, it's unrealistic to expect a sealed lid. Lifting the lid just a little bit can relieve some of the pressure that builds up over unanswered questions. It's important to share a reconstruction of events that allows the betrayed partner to establish the reality of the affair. Betrayed partners have to know the extent of the deception so they can understand what has happened. This means full disclosure of significant facts. Recovery of trust is greatly impaired by the piecemeal, staggered disclosure of basic information. It's critical that there be as few extra, nasty surprises as possible after the original disclosure.

Most likely, questions will focus on both the concrete details and on understanding the meaning of the infidelity. But at this stage it is best to stick to specific facts about *who, what, where,* and *when.* How long has this been going on? When did it start? Where did you meet when you had sex? When you said you went to meet with your boss, were you really with your lover? Who else knows? Do the people at work know? When was the last time you were together? At this point, wild imaginings may be worse than the actual facts. Hearing honest answers about who the extramarital partner is and the extent of the relationship meets a basic need.

As I tell couples who are involved in reconstructing safety in their relationship, not all questions need to be answered at once. Some questions should wait. Even though waiting can be agonizing, questions about motivations and meanings are best kept until later. Answering complex questions requires thoughtfulness and receptivity from both people—qualities that are absent at this moment. Trying to wrestle with them now is futile. These are the kinds of questions that can be tabled for later: Why did you get involved with someone else? Did you think about my feelings when you did this? What's wrong with our marriage? What did I do wrong? What does your betrayal say about what kind of person you are? These questions are best addressed when you've established a sense of safety and commitment to work on the issues.

The intimate details of sex in the affair may satisfy an immediate need to know, but they should be left until later to discuss, if they are shared at all. Sometimes people want to know these details in the beginning but not later. The reason not to share sexual details is that later they can become intrusive and interfere with your ability to be sexual with each other. Sharing sexual details now may create flashbacks or obsessive ruminations for the betrayed partner, even though later on curiosity about these details may disappear as the marriage is on more solid ground.

Nina knew what she needed to know at this early stage to regain some emotional stability. She needed to know whether her husband had lied to her about the need to leave for work at 6:00 A.M. because of extra work. He admitted that he had visited with the other woman at her apartment every morning before going to work and that he had lied about the extra work. Nina was crushed, but she felt some security from his honesty. Hearing the truth made her feel more hopeful about their chances to rebuild their marriage. If he had wanted to continue his affair, he wouldn't have told her.

First Steps of Trauma Recovery

Looking at the immediate crisis as a trauma helps make sense of some of the craziness you are probably experiencing. Traumatic reactions that begin immediately after the revelation can continue for some time. Predictable, necessary stages of trauma recovery will take place over many months and possibly several years. However, be assured that the frequency, duration, and intensity of your traumatic reactions will gradually lessen over time. A detailed description of these traumatic reactions and how to cope with them will be discussed in Chapter 6. For now, let's look at a summary of the first steps in the recovery process.

- *Feel the feelings.* It can be tempting to minimize or deny painful feelings in oneself or the other person. Honest and open engagement about your wishes, hopes, and fears will become the new foundation for a stronger relationship.

- *Reverse walls and windows and establish safety.* The real work of recovery begins when the architecture of the marriage and that of the affair are reversed, so that information flows honestly between the partners and stops flowing to the affair partner. Only when there is a sense of safety in the marriage can the damage be repaired.

- *Cope with traumatic reactions.* Understand that trauma is a normal reaction to the revelation of infidelity. Later chapters provide concrete ways of managing symptoms, such as obsessive ruminating, flashbacks, and hypervigilance. Both partners need to know what reactions to expect and how to cope with them. This is especially important because post-traumatic reactions continue in ever-changing forms throughout the recovery process.

- *Promote goodwill and compassionate communication.* Deposits into the relationship account are fostered by caring actions and words of appreciation. Most couples need guidelines to develop communication that is open, positive, and caring.

Is It Worth the Pain?

During this early stage of emotional upheaval, it can sometimes feel as if it isn't worth the effort it's going to take to rebuild your marriage. Sometimes you wonder whether you'd be better off cutting your losses and ending the marriage now. Unfortunately, there is bound to be pain whichever way you turn. The next chapter discusses whether you should *pick up the pieces or throw in the towel.* I must admit that my own bias is on the side of working on the relationship. Although each individual has to make his or her own decision, I hope that it won't be a hasty one. Please take your time to figure it out while you read on.

5

SHOULD YOU PICK UP THE PIECES
OR THROW IN THE TOWEL?

*"I don't know what to do. I'm damned if I stay
and damned if I go."*

*"Sometimes I feel like we've never been closer,
and other times I feel like I'm sleeping with the enemy."*

I N SOME cases, the revelation of an affair can bring a moment of utter clarity. Some involved partners, as soon as they are on the brink of losing their marriage, know in their bones that they want their marriage to survive. They may have swung easily from spouse to lover when they were living the double life, but once they are faced with the final choice, there is no doubt they want to keep the marriage. It's as though they've been living in a trance and the shock of the revelation snaps them back to reality. Some betrayed partners also react with the same clarity of purpose. They know that no matter what, they want their errant spouse to stay and work with them to make the marriage stronger.

For others, the moment of clarity provides the energy to leave. Years of low-level dissatisfaction or downright unhappiness may be crystallized into the sharp realization that the marriage is over. When one partner externalizes those feelings by having an affair, the betrayal serves as evidence that the marriage is not working. As painful as this revelation may be, either party can use it as a catalyst for deciding to divorce.

Nevertheless, *early decisions to stay or leave are not written in permanent ink.* Even the person whose mind seems to be made up today can have a change of heart tomorrow. The partner who is fed up or emotionally detached one day can initiate romantic overtures the very next day. The partner who is convinced he or she would walk through fire to save the marriage may end up walking into divorce court. Nothing you say or hear this early in the game is set in stone.

> In a nationwide survey, 25 percent of couples who filed for divorce never completed the process.[1]

This chapter is for all of the couples who have *not* experienced discovery as a moment of decisive insight. In a purgatory of indecision, people seesaw back and forth between wanting to stay and wanting to leave. Either partner may doubt that doing the work of trying to resurrect the relationship is worth it. At this point, throwing in the towel can look a whole lot easier than picking up the pieces, *but I urge you to wait for at least three months before you make a final decision.*

It's no wonder that people get tired and feel like giving up. When they are together, they remind each other of the pain. He looks into her eyes and sees his fallen image. She looks into his eyes and sees someone who lied to her. It feels unbearable to both of them. Adding to the sense of unreality are feelings of despair and isolation alternating with moments of passion when they feel an intensity they haven't felt for years.

Whether the affair has triggered certainty or uncertainty, it is productive to remember that at this early point, anything can happen. Ambivalence is common during the first few months after disclosure. Nobody knows in these early days how things will end up.

If you are feeling stuck, give yourself the time you need to make up your mind. Don't give up too soon. The mistake I see most often is people trying to move through the ambivalence too quickly and giving up on the marriage too soon. In these first weeks, everything is still shifting. Aftershocks are still ripping through the marriage, disrupting whatever stability has been hard won. Sometimes it's hard to tell exactly what you feel in the midst of all the confusion and high emotion.

At this point, it may help you to tell yourself that your staying means only that you are committing to a process of grieving and healing. You're taking a close look at yourself and your marriage to face whatever problems there may be. Right now you may not be able to conceive of a time when you and your spouse will again enjoy a relationship based on love and trust, but your job is to work closely with your spouse in forging a new partnership for the future. You will both need time to see how you feel in the aftermath of the trauma, when the aftershocks have subsided.

To figure out a rough timeline for yourselves, you need to look at the timeline of the affair itself. An affair that took a long time to heat up may take a longer time to cool down than one that ignited rapidly. When a friendship slowly progresses after many months or even years into a full-fledged love affair, the unfaithful partners will try to move backward across the timeline and maintain the friendship without the romantic attachment or sexual intimacy. Although this is an unrealistic goal, they are reluctant to put up walls in the affair and can't help sliding the window open just a crack from time to time. Ambivalent partners will have great difficulty following the recommendation to cut off all contact with the affair partner.

Ambivalence Barometer: Walls and Windows

Assessing the relative placement of walls and windows in both relationships provides us with a way of measuring ambivalence. For one thing, walls and windows tell us how far the unfaithful partner has moved back into the marriage. We can get an indication of where current loyalties lie by noticing what communication goes on between the marriage partners versus what remains between the affair partners. Keep in mind that things are constantly fluctuating. The window that's closed today may be thrown open tomorrow and vice versa. But for the moment at least, we can see what the emotional terrain looks like.

Walls

In the first few months after disclosure, there are many walled-off areas within the marriage. Involved partners are often reluctant to expose secrets and reveal continuing contact with their lover because they are not yet sure what they want. They may mistakenly believe that telling the truth about their ambivalence would only upset their spouse. They play their cards close to the vest and do not want any decisions to be taken away from them. If anything, involved partners tend to erect walls in *both* relationships in order to control the situation and keep it from blowing up before they have decided what they want to do.

Sid was walking a tightrope in both relationships. He had not yet decided to end his affair and commit to his marriage. He wouldn't talk to Sally about the affair because he was anxious to preserve its privacy out of loyalty to his affair partner. On the other hand, he refused to talk to his affair partner about how marital therapy was going. It is actually a small sign of progress for the recovery of the marriage when there is less sharing with the affair partner than there used to be, even in cases where the affair has not been totally cut off.

Injured partners may also put up walls to protect themselves from further betrayal. Sally did extensive detective work to see whether Sid was being truthful, but she seldom revealed to him what she had learned. She was keeping the information "on hold" in case they ended up divorcing. She was not ready to be open and vulnerable to the person who had hurt her.

Windows

At the same time that Sally wanted to keep some walls solidly around her own espionage, she kept trying to get Sid to willingly open more windows into the affair. At this point, she knew bits and pieces about the affair. Some of it he had shared voluntarily, but much of it had come out after she repeatedly pressed him for answers.

Sid had opened some new windows with Sally but was still keeping others tightly shut. He told Sally that he occasionally ran into his ex-lover at work, but he made it sound much more casual than it really was. For one thing, he was genuinely concerned about his affair partner, so he kept in touch to see how she was doing since their breakup.

Sid and Sally were both planning contingencies in case the marriage didn't work out. While they were making some efforts to rebuild the marriage, they also wanted to be prepared if their efforts failed. Sid tried to keep his lover "on hold" by checking in with her from time to time "just in case" he was left alone, an indisputable sign of his ambivalence. Sally was also keeping her options open by consulting an attorney on the same day she cooked Sid's favorite dinner for him as a surprise treat.

Two on a Seesaw

The ambivalence of one partner feeds off the ambivalence of the other as they teeter back and forth between staying and leaving. The betrayed partner who is desperate to save the marriage easily becomes discouraged by the outright lack of devotion and remorse. The involved partner who wants to be welcomed back with open arms is put off by the betrayed partner's anxiety and hopelessness about the future. Both of them long to look into adoring eyes that will convince them to stay. They move up and down in reaction to each other's changing intentions to separate or rebuild.

Both partners may demonstrate their ambivalence about working on the marriage by withdrawing, attacking, or failing to initiate caring actions or affectionate gestures. Refusal to appreciate or acknowledge positive actions by the other partner is another indication that commitment to working on the marriage is shaky.

Among couples I have seen for marital therapy, those who had a strong commitment to work on the marriage had a high probability of staying together. Each of them was able to say, "I want very much for my marriage to succeed, and I will do all that I can to see that it does."[2] Separation was more likely for individuals whose commitment to work on the marriage was shaky from the beginning. Their attitude was, "It would be nice if my marriage succeeded, but I'm not going to do any more than I am doing now to keep it going." Of course, a highly committed partner could end up separated despite heroic efforts if the less committed partner is determined to leave.

> In my clinical sample, 47 percent of husbands and wives with low commitment to work on the marriage were separated at the end of therapy, in comparison with 20 percent with high commitment who separated.

Ambivalence in the Involved Partner

Signs: You can recognize ambivalence in your partner by a refusal to be accountable for his or her whereabouts. Lingering loyalty to the lover is shown by unwillingness to reveal details about the affair. Emotional attachment to the lover is unmistakable when there is greater compassion for the distress of the affair partner than for the injured spouse. Unfair criticism or contempt for you as the injured spouse is evidence that your partner is moving away from the marriage.

Reasons: If you are an involved partner, there are many reasons why you are ambivalent about whether to go or stay. You could be afraid of making the wrong decision. It's frightening to think that what you decide now can set the course for the rest of your life. Or you may be paralyzed by the knowledge that one of the people you've attached to will be hurt and abandoned. When you think of the years ahead, you can't bear the thought of living without one person or the other. To lose either individual is excruciating, like having to choose which of your children you love the most.

Making Comparisons

If you have been involved in a romantic love affair, it is normal for you to doubt your love for your spouse. I have heard hundreds of unfaithful partners say to the injured spouse, "I love you, but I'm not *in love* with you." It is common to feel this way right after the affair is discovered and for some time thereafter.

Keep in mind that when you compare your affair partner with your spouse, you are not really comparing two individuals. What you are comparing is how it feels to be in an idealized, romantic relationship with how it feels to be in a reality-based, long-term relationship.

To look at it another way, the choice you are making could be between *the part of you that wants excitement and the part of you that wants comfort and familiarity.* You are choosing between *this* part of you versus *that* part of you. Each relationship calls forth a different aspect of your self. A man may be able to exercise his domestic side with his wife and his adventurous side with his lover. A woman may be conservative and responsible with her husband and sexually daring and carefree with her lover. For people who are torn in two, the prospect of cutting off either relationship feels like cutting off an essential part of themselves.

I have seen people struggling to choose between opposites: between a business executive husband who is meticulous and dependable and a bohemian boyfriend who is disorganized and unpredictable; or between a stay-at-home wife who is warm and easygoing and a career-oriented girlfriend who is ambitious and independent. Strangely enough, the traits you love in your affair partner may be the exact opposite of the traits that originally attracted you to your spouse.

Frequently, what attracts you to your affair partner now can end up being a problem later. For example, the energy and excitement that fire you up in brief binges could be tiring as a steady diet. The jealousy and dependency that make you feel needed could end up getting on your nerves. Although the affair partner might be "a nice place to visit," you might not want to "live there" permanently. Just remember that no relationship can meet all your needs. You can't have it all.

Wanting Both

Randy experienced firsthand how painful it was to discover that he would have to let go of someone he loved. He was a deeply religious man; he was the branch manager in his neighborhood bank; he was well-known in his community for his generosity to others and for his ability to give wise advice to the people who came to him to talk about money and personal matters. His wife, Rianna, was also well liked and from a similar conservative religious background. As a married couple, they were content but admittedly reticent with each other about personal and sexual issues. After twelve years, Randy fell deeply in love with a single woman, whom he considered his soul mate. "I've never been as close to anyone as I am to Sophie. I've never felt as happy as when I'm with her."

After a year, Randy confessed his affair to Rianna because he felt so guilty. He wanted to do the right thing and end the duplicity. But he didn't know which way to turn. In therapy he expressed deep conflict between his moral principles and his love for Sophie. How could he so desperately want something he believed was wrong? How could he destroy his wife, whom he had pledged to love? He didn't know how he was going to live with the decision he had to make, no matter which way he decided.

Like so many other involved partners, Randy couldn't decide which pathway to choose: stay in the marriage, go with the affair partner, try to keep them both, or leave them both. When I hear that involved spouses can't decide, I surmise that they have already decided. What they usually want is to keep *both* relationships. The involved partner's undeclared wish is understandable, but the worst resolution of this dilemma is living with an extramarital triangle.

It might be tempting to think that a way out would be to figure out an alternative arrangement that would allow you and your affair partner to maintain friendly contact. You may believe that you can continue to spend time together—only without the sex. The thought of going cold turkey and never having another shared moment with your lover may seem beyond your powers to imagine.

Certainly, the longer the affair has lasted and the more satisfying it was, the harder it is to let go of. Letting go takes time. The best solution, nonetheless, is to go cold turkey and stop the affair, so that you and your betrayed partner can commit to discovering whether the marriage has a chance of surviving.

Ambivalence in the Betrayed Partner

Betrayed partners show ambivalence about committing to the marriage by holding back when it comes to doing caring things. They may feel entitled to be paid back in full before they are willing to take any initiative to invest in the marriage. Their attitude is to "wait and see" how hard their partner is willing to work to make amends.

In the early weeks after disclosure, the unfaithful partner is too ambivalent and shell-shocked to do much reparative work. Oftentimes, the ambivalence of unfaithful partners is so hurtful and so confusing that injured partners react with their own ambivalence, vacillating between a desperate wish to stay and save the marriage and the wish to leave and save themselves from further harm.

If you are the betrayed partner, you're probably more inclined to work on the marriage if your partner shows a strong commitment to you and goes out of his or her way to be appreciative and attentive. If your partner is still grieving the loss of the other relationship, however, acts of devotion may be slow to appear in the first weeks or even months after discovery.

It's important to stay centered while your partner is bouncing off the walls. Remember, inconsistency probably means that your partner is pulled in opposite directions by these two competing attachments. Take hope if the pendulum seems to be swinging closer and closer to you. Don't push your partner away or try to pull your partner in. Sink your feet firmly in the ground and declare your commitment to work on the marriage alongside your partner, as long as your partner is willing to meet you halfway.

When Nikki found out about Norm's affair, she was shocked and filled with self-doubt. She was unsure whether to end the marriage or try to salvage it. Norm's behavior was so erratic that she didn't know whether she was coming or going. One minute he wanted to make love, and the next minute he told her he had signed a contract to rent an apartment.

I advised Nikki not to be swayed by Norm's instability but to look for behavioral signs of progress, such as increasing honesty and consideration. She made it clear to him that she did not want their marriage to end, but she would not tolerate secret contact with the affair partner. Two weeks after he moved out, Norm begged Nikki to let him move back home. She considered his desire for reconciliation when he agreed to participate in marital therapy. The first few months of marital therapy were focused primarily on helping him resolve his ambivalence and commit to the marriage without reservation.

Damage Control for Both Partners

During this period of instability, you both need to limit damaging interactions that could negatively affect your ability to reconcile. People tend to act out their ambivalence with confusing behaviors. It is preferable to label yourself openly and honestly as ambivalent. If you cannot throw yourself wholeheartedly back into the relationship, admit that you are struggling with your inner conflict.

As a betrayed partner, you should make it clear what you will and will not tolerate. For example, e-mails or phone calls to the affair partner that are open to you and are clearly for the purpose of terminating the relationship might be acceptable. Staying out late with no explanation is probably not acceptable. Don't go berserk when these expectations are violated. Instead, talk about how you feel and give a realistic deadline of a few months' time for making a firm commitment.

Unfaithful partners should make it clear that they take responsibility for the injuries they have caused, but they do not have to accept days on end of verbal abuse. Physical abuse should never be tolerated, no matter what the provocation. If you can't commit to completely severing the relationship with your affair partner, then you must commit to total honesty about the degree of your indecision. Further deception during this time of ambivalence may drive away your partner forever.

A remarkable thing happens when you are honest with each other, even if it is about your ambivalence. You feel closer because taking down walls and opening windows results in greater intimacy.

Getting Off the Fence

Making the decision to go or stay is particularly difficult because both of you are feeling heartsick, stressed, and exhausted. You worry that the damage that's been done cannot be repaired. The involved spouse may be feeling hopeless about coming to a resolution and tired to the bone by the emotional storms that gather and break continually. If you're the betrayed spouse, you wonder whether you will ever be able to stop visualizing your partner with someone else. You don't know if you can ever feel special again. You don't know if you can ever forgive your partner for giving away what you considered sacred to your marriage.

As long as you are ambivalent, there is still hope, because you haven't yet made a definite decision. In this initial stage of indecision, each member of the couple has to decide whether he or she is capable of going through the process of rebuilding intimacy and trust. (Probably the only one at this point who is committed to staying in the triangle is the affair partner.) *Early* decision making revolves around whether to stick with efforts to work through the situation, whereas *later* decision making involves whether to leave the marriage once and for all. *The first decision you need to make is whether you can commit to working on the marriage.*

People have different ways of making life decisions. Some have faith that the unseen forces of the universe will guide them and give them signs. One man felt pressured to choose between his wife and his lover because he was going out of the country on an important business trip and needed to decide which woman he wanted to take. He had just come to a sense of peace about choosing his lover when he picked up the newspaper. In the headline on the front page he saw his wife's maiden name. Even though the story had nothing to do with his wife's family, he felt in his heart that it was a sign that he should be with his wife. And that was the final choice he made.

It is important that you make an active rather than a passive decision to stay and work on the marriage. Brian moved out of the bedroom onto the sofa bed in the den shortly after the revelation of his five-year love affair. When he got the flu and ran a high fever, Bonnie invited him back to sleep in the bedroom because it was more comfortable. When he felt better he didn't move back into the den, but they never discussed what this meant. In fact, they never really processed what had gone wrong in their marriage or what he was going to do about ending the affair. They just drifted back together without any declaration of intent or exploration of vulnerabilities. Two years later, he moved out permanently to live with his affair partner.

Other people are not so comfortable trusting their fate to the vagaries of chance but require a more rational process. Engaging in some head work as well as some heart work is likely to be most helpful for those who are mired in ambivalence. It is helpful to use the *head-heart-gut-groin test* to figure out where you are. The *head* is the rational part that tells whether you like your partner and does an intellectual balance sheet of pros and cons. The *heart* tells you how much fondness and emotional attachment you have. The *gut* is your instinctive sense of what feels right or wrong. The *groin* is an erogenous zone that is influenced by passion and irrational desire. Today, your heart, brain, and gut may be leaning toward staying, while your split heart and groin pull you in another direction. The strongest pull will end up being whichever force you hold most dear.

The worst resolution is a stable triangle. When involved partners stay on an eternal fence, ultimatums given by the spouse or lover move them from one side to the other. They cajole, seduce, and deceive both partners in order to have their cake and eat it too. The spouse and the lover help to maintain the stable triangle by making compromises and accepting whatever crumbs are thrown their way. Children are inevitably harmed by this unhealthy collusion, because it results in underlying tension and open conflict in the home.

Think Things Through Before You Act

If you are tortured by moment-to-moment misgivings about whether to go or stay, declare a moratorium on immediate decision making. For a period of six to twelve weeks, defer making any decisions about leaving. This will provide both of you with a period of safety in which to fully explore your thoughts and feelings. Here are some thought-provoking questions for unfaithful or betrayed partners who are undecided about whether to pick up the pieces or throw in the towel. There are seldom any easy answers. You can explore your thoughts privately, share them with your spouse, or discuss them with a therapist:

1. Visualize the future. Go down the road as far as you can and speculate what it would be like without your spouse. Think about the immediate future, five years from now, and twenty years from now. Picture yourself attending family events separately.

   • How would your life be different?

   • How would your children's lives be different?

   • What difference would it make in your current friendships?

2. Recall the past. Be careful not to rewrite marital history with a jaded view because of the current crisis.

   • What do you remember about the good times you've shared with your partner?

   • What would you miss about your marriage?

   • Have you and your partner struggled hard together to get to this place in your life cycle?

3. See if you can put your disillusionment aside for the moment and figure out your reasons for staying with your spouse.

   • Do you *love* your partner, down deep? (Not liking him or her is different from not loving.)

   • Do you *like* the fundamental type of person your partner is? (Not liking him or her is not the same as the disappointment you may be feeling.)

   • Are you and your partner basically compatible?

4. Assess your own willingness and ability to meet the challenge of working on your relationship.

   • Are you willing to understand what vulnerabilities set the stage for an affair?

   • Are you willing to work toward forgiving and being forgiven for the ways you could have hurt each other?

Questions Betrayed Partners Can Ask Themselves

If you have just heard that your partner has lied to you and been intimate with someone else, you might not be sure whether your marriage is worth the time and effort to sustain it. Because you are probably not in any shape right now to make a permanent decision, take your time thinking through how you feel and what you want to do. How you answer on Day One may be different from how you answer three months later.

> **Of** the partners of sex addicts, 60 percent threatened to leave after the initial disclosure, but only 24 percent who threatened to leave actually left.[3]

1. Ask yourself whether this infidelity is part of a larger picture of cheating and lying.
   - Has this kind of thing happened before?
   - Do you trust your partner to tell you the truth about other things?
   - Is your partner generally dependable and trustworthy?
2. Is your partner understanding about your pain?
3. Is your partner willing to allay your anxiety by being accountable?

Questions Involved Partners Can Ask Themselves

I will never ask you to consider which person you prefer. As I've said before, it's important that you do not make the mistake of deciding on the basis of comparing an exciting, illicit romance with a stable, long-term marriage.

1. Picture yourself with the affair partner in a long-term committed relationship.
   - What would life be like five years from now; twenty years from now?

• Ask yourself whether the affair partner wants to have children. If you already have a family, do you want to be raising another family in the future?

• What would it be like for you and your affair partner to raise stepchildren together?

• How would your children handle your marriage to the person who broke up their intact family?

• What were the things that attracted you to your affair partner? If these traits were to become exaggerated, would you still be attracted? For example, if you like the fact that your affair partner is always frank and direct, imagine what it would be like to be with someone who's brutally honest.

2. What will it be like when the passion of a forbidden love wears off ten years from now? Imagine how forlorn you might have been if something had prevented you from marrying your spouse. You probably would have believed forever that you had lost the one true love of your life.

3. Would you still want to divorce your spouse even if the relationship with the affair partner doesn't work out? This is the central question Lara had to ask herself after Ralph ended their affair. Although Lara was the affair partner in Ralph's extramarital triangle, in her own marriage, she was the unfaithful wife. She ended her marriage to Lenny because of irresolvable problems even though Ralph had made it clear to her that the affair was over.

4. Visualize where you want to be ten or twenty years from now—where you want to be living, how you want to spend your time, and what gives you pleasure. What happened to the dreams you once had about what it would be like to grow old together with your spouse?

Other Considerations

• *Guilt or duty:* Would you be staying out of a sense of guilt or duty? If the only thing that holds you now is a sense of obligation or duty, that's an okay place to start but not an okay place to end. If you feel stuck in the marriage because of financial pressures or religious barriers to divorce, you are signing up for an empty-shell marriage. Your obligation should be to enhance your marital relationship so that good comes out of suffering.

- *For the children:* Would you be staying only for the sake of the children rather than for the relationship itself? Judith Wallerstein's research indicates that many children of divorced parents experience negative effects throughout their adult lives.[4] Nonetheless, marriage as martyrdom is a poor role model for your children's future relationships. Don't dedicate yourself to a life of misery. If you're staying only because of the children, then start connecting with your spouse through family activities but don't let that be the end point. Ultimately, your children will benefit from parents who show them how to be a loving couple.

- *A new perspective:* You might be noticing certain traits in your spouse now that attract you or repel you that you weren't aware of before the affair. You may make your decision according to how he or she behaved in the aftermath of disclosure, rather than basing it solely on the infidelity itself. Couples tend to cope with crises using the same patterns of interaction that have characterized the marriage. Individuals who have been mostly self-serving may appear more entitled than ever before; their narcissism becomes so unmistakable that it's hard to continue to like them enough to stay. On the other hand, compassion and sensitivity that may have been taken for granted before can now be seen as a strong reason not to leave.

- *Repair work:* Leaving a bad marriage without trying to repair it first is like trying to sell your house right after a rainstorm flooded your family room. Once you have finished cleaning and redecorating, you might decide not to put it up for sale. If you leave your marriage when you are feeling devastated, depleted, and demoralized, you'll always wonder whether you made the right choice. Fix it up first and you'll have a better idea of how the finished product suits you.

- *Strength or weakness:* Don't stay because you are too weak to end it and too afraid to be on your own. Stay because you are strong enough to handle the emotional roller coaster. Stay because you

are independent enough to take care of yourself while your partner isn't able to be there for you. Don't leave because you're running away from conflict. Leave because you've done everything
possible for many months and there's absolutely no sign of
progress.

• *Reality check:* For most people, leaving the marriage is not the best
answer. People tend to carry their psychological problems with
them to the next relationship. Old, destructive patterns are per-
petuated unless you deal with them, and second marriages may
have the added strain of blended families and stepchildren. Statis-
tically, there is a 50 percent divorce rate in first marriages and a 60
percent divorce rate in second marriages.[5] If you marry your affair
partner, the probability that it will work out is even worse than the
dismal divorce statistics in second marriages (unless you are marrying an old flame from your youth).[6] Relationships that began
through betrayal and broken trust often end up having their own
problems with trust.

Constructive Separation

For some couples, a temporary separation can be helpful. I am not talking about a separation leading to divorce but a separation to cool things
down. A constructive separation can create a period of stability and calm
for thinking through the complex issues involved. It can strengthen individual boundaries, enhance self-respect, provide psychological as well as
physical distance, and help people discover their degree of voluntary commitment to the marriage.

If a couple agrees on a constructive separation, then the involved partners promise to live alone and have no contact with either spouse or lover
until they can figure out who they are and what they really want. For involved partners who are feeling beleaguered by competing demands and
loyalties and see no way out, a period of abstinence from both relationships can break the dependency bonds and help them to see things more
clearly.

The problem with separating at this point is that trust issues tend to
increase when the couple is apart and strain the marriage even further. If
the involved partner is not ready to stop seeing the affair partner, then it's

better to be honest about that. Involved partners sometimes move out under the pretext of "needing space" but use their new "space" to pursue the affair. *The involved partner who can't promise to be faithful must promise to be honest.* If the separation is really a subterfuge for being with the affair partner, then the couple will have to deal with this added dishonesty if they reconcile. The injured partner will be even more bitter and angry when he or she learns of additional deception.

Whenever violent behavior occurs or the threat of violence is made, a permanent separation should be considered. Be aware that violence often escalates when a victim of physical abuse tries to leave. Your plans to leave should include contingencies for a safe departure, including an escape plan, an extra set of car keys, and a readily available, protected shelter.

Ambivalence Therapy

People who don't know which way to turn can benefit from competent professional guidance. If your discussions turn into escalating fights, the neutrality of a therapist's office can provide a safe context in which to resolve ambivalence. Don't decide to leave until you have explored all avenues, including therapy. If both of you are committed to working on the marriage, it is a good idea to discontinue individual therapy and focus on couple therapy.

The person who refuses to participate in couple therapy but continues in individual therapy may be choosing to work on *me* instead of choosing to work on *us*. Individual therapists can unwittingly replicate the dysfunctional pattern of infidelity because the wall of confidentiality around the therapy excludes the spouse. If you're the injured spouse, you may get the message from the therapist that you'd be better off alone. If you're the unfaithful spouse, you may be creating another extramarital triangle if you use a therapist as your secret confidante.

If the involved partner is working on ambivalence in individual therapy, this should be made explicit to the betrayed partner and the couple's therapist. When the involved partner is not sure he or she wants to stay and work on the marriage, the privacy and neutrality of individual therapy is reasonable. However, the injured partner needs some assurance that the involved partner isn't continuing a double life by saying one thing in couple therapy and something entirely different in individual therapy. If the injured partner believes that the involved spouse has committed to the marriage when in reality he or she is talking to the therapist about whether to go or stay, this is a perpetuation of deception.

Do You Have the Right Spouse but the Wrong Therapist?

Therapists can bring hidden biases about extramarital involvement to marital therapy. Because there is no standard approach for treating infidelity, therapists' attitudes and methods vary widely. Therapists who are unfamiliar with the research literature may be more susceptible to assumptions based on personal experience and unproved theories. Your lack of progress could mean that rebuilding the marriage is a hopeless endeavor, or it could indicate that the therapy itself is ineffective or actually making things worse.

Here are some guidelines to assess whether you have the right therapist for your situation. Is your therapist . . .

- *Lacking in direction?* Ask yourself whether things are improving or seem hopelessly stuck. If things are no better, are you gaining insight about the reasons for lack of progress? Some situations do get worse before they get better. If your therapist just sits back and watches your exchanges without providing any structure or direction, it may be time for a change.

- *Judgmental?* Evaluate whether your therapist's advice is based on personal values rather than on the unique characteristics of each situation. Does the therapist seem either adamantly against divorce under any circumstances or vigorously opposed to staying with an "adulterous" partner?

- *Minimizing?* Does your therapist dismiss the distress of the betrayed partner as a hysterical reaction to a meaningless sexual fling? Is concern about secret friendships and intense emotional attachments perceived by the therapist as irrational jealousy?

- *Unwilling to focus on the affair?* Is your therapist uncomfortable with a betrayed partner's need to know the details of the affair?

You can recognize this problem if your therapist makes such remarks as "Talking about the affair is a way to avoid talking about the real problems"; "Obsessing about the affair is a sign of severe emotional problems"; "Forget about the past."

In Peggy Vaughan's on-line survey, 57 percent of betrayed spouses said that their therapy was mostly frustrating because the counselor focused on general marital problems instead of dealing directly with issues about the affair.[7]

- *Blaming rather than understanding?* Is your therapist attacking the involved partner rather than gaining insight by exploring the vulnerabilities for the infidelity? Or does your therapist blame the injured spouse for causing the infidelity (this is like blaming rape victims for the assault). Therapists who blame the betrayed partner can be recognized by statements such as "Surely you must have known all along about the affair and just turned your head the other way"; "How did you manage to convey that you wanted your partner to have an affair?"

- *Impatient?* Resolving ambivalence and rebuilding after infidelity takes many months. Therapists who are ready to call it quits too soon are not giving you the benefit of time. They can be recognized by statements such as "You should leave if you're only working on it for the sake of the children"; "You should end the marriage if you're not *in love* anymore"; "Leave if your needs aren't being met at home."

In my clinical sample, couples who stayed in therapy for more than ten sessions had a much better chance of staying together than couples who terminated therapy earlier.

If the ideas in this book are helpful to you, you can discuss them with your therapist and find out whether he or she subscribes to the trauma recovery model presented here. You can find a list of helpful books, Web sites, and support groups in the Appendix.

Picking Up the Pieces

It may feel as if this is the last chapter of your marriage, but it could very well be the middle one, especially if you continue working on your relationship. Your challenge during the next year is to put the pieces back together again, but not into the same pattern. A marriage that has endured an affair is like a cracked vase: When the crack is repaired, the superglue makes it stronger than before, but you will always be able to see evidence of the crack.

The heart of ambivalence for the betrayed partner is *Can I ever trust you again?* For both partners, it is *Will we ever have what we had before?* Although I agree that a crucial goal in recovery is to restore trust, I believe the second question is the wrong question. I do not want you simply to have what you had before: I want your relationship to be *different* from what it was. I want you to be stronger, individually and together, without the vulnerabilities that created the conditions for the affair in the first place.

Living with ambivalence for a period of time is terribly unsettling, but it's worth remembering that new circumstances allow for new opportunities. As many couples have discovered, new feelings and new behaviors can emerge out of the chaos that ensues from an affair. A crisis of uncertainty often provides fertile ground for new growth and redevelopment.

In my experience, time is almost always on the side of the marriage if both spouses are patient. Wait at least three months, and try to be hopeful, even when the immediate situation is ambiguous and unresolved. Dealing with the fallout from infidelity should lead to either a better marriage or an unavoidable divorce.

Look for progress from week to week instead of from moment to moment. Setbacks and relapses are common at this stage. Let things play out. You are still dealing with the shock of disclosure and all the traumatic reactions that follow. If you've both decided you want to try starting over, try not to make any final decisions until you've gone through the process described in the rest of this book.

Although Mollie wanted very much to save her marriage, she lost hope when she once again caught Melvin e-mailing Kayla, one of his Internet sweethearts. Melvin said he loved Mollie, but he couldn't seem to stop his on-line romances. Even when their son won a basketball scholarship to college and Melvin realized that Mollie was the only one who could truly share his joy, he still couldn't stop thinking about his e-lover, although his commitment to Mollie was strengthened by this epiphany.

Mollie finally came to the end of her rope when she discovered that he had purchased airline tickets to meet Kayla. Melvin panicked when Mollie told him to pack his bags permanently. He then vowed to stay off the computer except for strictly business activities, and he gave Mollie his password so she could verify that he was being true to his word. Melvin then called Kayla on the telephone with Mollie in the room and told her that the on-line relationship was over for good because he loved his wife. Kayla contacted him a few times after that, and he noticed how self-absorbed she was. He shared these contacts openly with Mollie, who felt hopeful because of his honesty and obvious loyalty to her.

Once you have decided to stay together to try to make your marriage work, you can follow a proven pathway. In the next two chapters specific suggestions for how to begin your recovery process will guide you in coping with post-traumatic reactions together. As you attempt to resume normal activities, I encourage you to share some pleasurable activities that will help you counterbalance the pain.

6

HOW TO COPE WITH OBSESSING
AND FLASHBACKS

I couldn't go to movies or listen to love songs.
Everything became a reminder of how I had been betrayed.

T RAGICALLY, TERRORIST attacks within the continental United
States have given all Americans a more intimate understanding of
what it means to be traumatized. Immediately after the bombings of the
World Trade Center and the Pentagon, people were obsessed with the radio, the TV, and the newspaper. Eventually, most people stopped being
consumed by it, but their lives were irrevocably changed; although they
have resumed normal activities, any new threat can quickly put them
back into a crisis mode.

Post-traumatic reactions can last for days, months, and even years. Although not all traumas are the same, the symptoms of trauma are recog-
nizably consistent. Traumatized partners who are recovering from an
unthinkable betrayal by a loved one have *an obsessive need to hear the story*
in its most intricate details. Their *hypervigilance* about monitoring their
environment and watching their partner with scrutinizing eyes comes
from the realistic fear of further wounding. *Flashbacks* are triggered by
minimal cues that echo the moment of their personal devastation. Coping strategies require a balance between validating these reactions and trying to contain and manage them.

In Chapter 4 we discussed the immediate aftermath of an affair when
it is revealed to the betrayed partner. In this chapter, we discuss how to
cope with the long-term reactions and the crises that continue to erupt for
weeks and even months afterward.

Post-traumatic reactions are particularly severe when they result from the betrayal of important relationships, according to Dr. Judith Herman, a trauma expert.[1] This was vividly brought home to me by Wilma, a psychologist friend of mine who experienced two traumatic events within a short time. Wilma was accosted in her car at a red light in midtown Washington, D.C., by a man who opened her car door, straddled the driver's seat, and pointed a gun at her head. Wilma screamed, and when the light turned green, he jumped out and took her purse. As terrifying as this had been, Wilma said that she recovered from this event more easily than an unanticipated betrayal at work when her colleagues, whom she respected and liked, turned against her.

The betrayal of a close relationship has long-lasting effects that make recovery difficult. Wilma felt she could protect herself in the future by making sure her car door was locked; she was much less sure about being able to protect herself from the backstabbing of ambitious colleagues she had trusted. She was distressed at how little control she seemed to have over her emotions and couldn't believe how long it took to get over it.

Know that it's normal to feel disoriented and confused. Most likely, neither you nor your partner is crazy, and these crazy feelings will not last forever. One of the ironies of healing from infidelity is that the perpetrator must become the healer. This means that betrayed partners are vulnerable because the person they are most likely to turn to in times of trouble is precisely the source of danger. On the other hand, involved partners sometimes find it hard to stay engaged with their spouses when they know that they are the source of such intense pain.

For as long as the first year after revelation, the betrayed partner may have distressing mental, physical, and emotional swings. You may be thinking that you are doing everything right: You're talking more often, and the affair has ended. Why aren't you over these feelings? It's normal to be having these traumatic reactions and they will diminish, but only gradually. First, their frequency will decline; second, how long they last will decline. The intensity of the symptoms is the last thing to go, so it can feel as if you are backsliding despite other signs of progress.

Post-traumatic reactions cluster into three categories: intrusion, constriction, and hyperarousal. These reactions are formally diagnosed as a post-traumatic stress disorder (PTSD) if the threat was physical or life-threatening and if these symptoms last longer than one month.[2] However, betrayed partners whose *psychological* safety is threatened by infidelity commonly display these same clusters of symptoms, and the symptoms can occur over a long period of time. In the following sections, I describe the post-traumatic reactions you may experience and ways you can cope with them.

Intrusion

Intrusion comes from the traumatic images associated with betrayal, such as the moment of disclosure, the suspected intimacies in the affair, or the string of lies preceding the disclosure. You reexperience the psychological distress of the traumatic event when memories, dreams, or flashbacks intrude. TV talk shows, love songs, or even ordinary physical objects that were benign before the revelation now seem electrified with the pain of betrayal. Lovemaking scenes in movies may create vivid images of illicit sex. Words spoken in a patriotic speech, such as "loyalty," can trigger a whole train of intrusive thoughts regarding the treachery in the marriage.

Obsessing

Betrayed partners cannot seem to stop obsessing about the affair until they have all the answers, which can take months. They turn over lies and unanswered questions incessantly in their heads. They develop fixations on visual images, snippets of conversation, and puzzling memories that don't quite add up. They invest a lot of energy in discovering the truth about earlier lies. They question and reexamine all the details of their life together that made perfect sense before, in an effort to reconstruct the real truth.

Reviewing History
The betrayed partner begins to sort out the jigsaw puzzle of past lies into a clear picture of the deception. Forgetting feels dangerous. The entire history of the marriage is reviewed while grappling with shattered assumptions. Elsa had to reconstruct twenty years of her married life after learning about her husband's affair on the same day as her twenty-fifth wedding anniversary.

Elsa discovered that her husband, Elliott, had been involved with other women since the birth of their first child. One incident she recalled was a weekend many years earlier when she and Elliott had gone to the beach with another couple. On Sunday morning Elliott said he was going out to get a newspaper. He was gone all morning. Three hours into his absence, their friends asked Elsa if she was worried that he had been gone so long. She told them he often did this kind of thing. Basically, he was antisocial and needed time alone; he was probably out driving around somewhere listening to music on the car radio. She had come to accept his idiosyncrasies. But when she discovered that he had been unfaithful, she had to undo all her psychological rationalizations and reconstruct past events in a radically new light.

Intrusive Thinking

The need to recapitulate and go over minute details means that the tape of the betrayal runs over and over, on and on, seemingly forever—a continuous loop of details cycling through memory again and again. Belinda found it difficult to work through the damage of her husband's one-year love affair. She was obsessed with a love letter she had intercepted. Although he claimed he wasn't emotionally involved with the other woman, the passionate and loving language told a different story. The poetry, which Belinda hadn't heard from him for many years, haunted her. It was as though Belinda *wanted* to make more pain for herself by contrasting how romantic he was with his affair partner with how unromantic he was with her. Every time she talked with her husband, his reassurances sounded false and hollow. For a very long time, Belinda's reality was that love letter.

Suppressors versus Obsessors

It is generally the rule that at times of emotional stress women tend to obsess and men tend to suppress. It's the contrast between the individual (usually the man) who says, "I'll cross that bridge when I come to it," and the individual (usually the woman) who asks, "What's on the way to the bridge? What's the bridge built of? What's on the other side?" Ruminators analyze and reanalyze and talk about upsetting events, whereas suppressors tell themselves not to think about it. However, *when it comes to affairs, the unfaithful partner suppresses and the betrayed partner obsesses, regardless of gender.*

To escape accountability, the involved partner may promote forgetting by denying or minimizing the magnitude of the betrayal. Before discovery, cheating partners do what they can to discourage or dismiss their naïve partner's worries or suspicions. Now they may try to perpetuate their own guiltlessness by making routine apologies, claiming that the affair was minor or meaningless, redirecting blame toward the betrayed partner, or insisting that it's time to get over it and move on. Anything to avoid having to recount guilty chapter and verse.

Cameron was quite distressed by all the time he spent reliving the crisis of his wife's betrayal with his business partner. He would be doing something quite ordinary, such as mowing the lawn or listening to music, and all of a sudden he would start thinking about an upsetting scene or conversation. Even though he knew that calling it to mind was reopening the wound, he couldn't help following the mental trail back to his wife's lies. Sure enough, once there, he revisited all his intense feelings of outrage and humiliation. For several months, physical contact with her, even when she was tender and wholly present with him, made him vulnerable to distressing thoughts about her sexual actions with her lover. While Cameron was obsessing, his wife became exhausted by his preoccupation with the infidelity.

Secrecy fuels obsessing. Although unfaithful partners would prefer to put the topic of the affair in a locked box, they too can experience intrusive thoughts and flashbacks. They can become obsessed with thoughts of the affair partner or the unmasking of their secret lives. Because secrecy fuels obsession, obsessive thoughts about the lover are intensified by refusing to discuss the affair. Sharing information about the affair allows *both* partners to let go.

Rejection fuels obsessing. Affair partners who have been jilted can also become obsessed. They may engage in hang-up phone calls, constant e-mail messages, and drop-in visits at the home or workplace of their lover. It is hard for them to accept that something that seemed so special could really be over. A cold but clear message from the still married partner is necessary to end this one-sided passionate attachment that keeps all three participants from moving on with their lives. Everyone in the extramarital triangle will be stuck in the past until the affair is clearly over.

How to Deal with Obsessive Thoughts

It is important to understand that *obsessive thinking isn't a pathological response to trauma. It is a normal response.* Until you take steps to grapple with shattered assumptions and construct a story about the affair that makes sense to you, you will be prone to obsessing. In other words, obsessive thoughts may intrude throughout the process of recovery until healing is complete, although they tend to subside as safety and openness are established in the marriage.

When obsessive thoughts are too intense or intrusive, it is important to be able to control them. Following are some techniques that have worked for others.

Write Down Your Thoughts

Writing provides an outlet that helps you "let go," at least for a while. You don't need to clutter up your brain with all these troubling details after you commit them to paper and pen. Writing provides a safe way to express and explore thoughts and feelings without concern about the effect they may have on other people. Give yourself permission to write uncensored thoughts and follow your obsessions to the point of exhaustion. Along the way, you can gain new insights, clarify your own point of view, identify issues you want to follow up on, and uncover new strengths—all in privacy and with freedom.

- *Keep a journal:* When you start to obsess about the infidelity, you can enhance the healing process by expressing your deepest thoughts and feelings in a personal journal. You can write at a regular time or whenever the mood strikes you. You can use the computer, an old-fashioned bound diary, or a plain spiral notebook. You can write as a spectator of these events in the reflective mode of the third person or as a cathartic expression in the first person.

> People who keep journals about their traumatic experiences enhance their immune system through increased T-cell production and report fewer doctor visits and better physical health.[3]

- *Write letters:* You can write to your partner or to the affair partner without monitoring your words. Just let the feelings flow out of you onto the paper. Then put the letter away for a day or two and read it to yourself. Do not send it immediately. You can edit the nasty or damaging parts out of it before you decide whether or not to send it. Your partner can read your letter without being affected by the tone of your voice or the impulse to interrupt you.

Caution: Do not send anything to the affair partner without the support and input of your spouse.

- *Write questions:* Every time you start to obsess over unanswered questions about the affair, write them down. Keep them in a safe place. When you and your partner are communicating with understanding and without blaming, you can let him or her see your list of questions. Your partner can choose which ones to answer right away and which ones need to be deferred until you've established more stability and caring together.

Control Your Thoughts

You can control your obsessional thoughts through several different techniques, such as limiting yourself to specific times of day, distracting yourself with other thoughts, or telling yourself to shut it out of your mind.

- *Schedule worry times:* You can discipline yourself to worry or fret only during certain designated times of the day and for a specific amount of time, from fifteen minutes to one hour. During this time, deliberately revisit any of the disturbing images, memories, or thoughts about the betrayal. Confining yourself in this way will keep your anxiety from contaminating every part of your life. Choose a quiet place to obsess before or after breakfast, lunch, and dinner and possibly before bedtime as well. If a thought intrudes at any other time, tell yourself that you can't think about it now: you have to wait until your next scheduled "worry time." As time goes on, you will be able to cut down on the number of worry sessions and the length of each session.

- *Change the channel:* Imagine a remote control inside your mind that can surf from channel to channel. Whenever you're invaded by unwanted images, switch to another program. If the past is too contaminated, focus on some future event you are looking forward to, or picture your children doing something that makes you laugh or that warms your heart. In the same way that you quickly move past TV programs that are repugnant, you can take control of your inner thoughts and lock out disturbing channels.

• *Practice thought-stopping:* Rona Subotnik and Gloria Harris suggest using the technique of thought-stopping to cope with obsessive thoughts about infidelity. The moment a negative thought or image begins to intrude, try this technique. It is particularly helpful if obsessive imagining of sexual scenes is a problem. Here are several versions:

> Shut your eyes and tell yourself subvocally to "stop" intrusive thoughts or images.
>
> Imagine a red stop sign and think of the word "stop."
>
> Wear a rubber band around your wrist and snap it.
>
> Press your fingernails into the palms of your hand.[4]

Flashbacks

Obsessive thoughts can be controlled, at least to some extent, but flashbacks are involuntary, vivid images that unexpectedly recreate traumatic moments. They can involve sight, sound, smell, or physical sensations. I treated one young woman, Nellie, who had walked onto the porch where her best friend, Ina, had just been murdered by a jealous boyfriend. Years later, Nellie could not figure out why any touch on her shoulder immediately took her back into the feelings of horror she had experienced at the murder scene. She had no conscious recollection of how this was connected to her trauma. Eventually, Nellie recalled under hypnosis how the boy who had killed Ina had then pulled Nellie off the porch and into the neighboring woods by grasping her shoulder.

Flashbacks can be triggered by any cue that has been connected with the infidelity, whether the cue is conscious or not. Flashbacks are distressing because they occur spontaneously, without warning. For the traumatized person, ordinary life is a minefield of explosive triggers. And triggers can be anything: the smell of burning leaves in the fall, getting a busy signal on the cell phone, or sitting down to Thanksgiving dinner (when, two years earlier, he had gone out to pick up ice cream and didn't come back for three hours). Riding past a restaurant where the lovers ate can bring on waves of panic and trembling.

When you have a flashback, it doesn't matter that the truth is known and that things are back on track; you go through it again, almost as if for the first time. One night, Colleen woke up at midnight and realized that her husband hadn't come to bed yet. She got up and found a light shining under the closed door of his computer room. She tried the door, but it was locked. Even though she totally believed that her husband's Internet affair was over and that he was working on his computer project for work, the locked door sent her into a panic. It triggered a flashback to the nights when he used to lock himself in the study at 3:00 A.M. and indulge in sexual affairs on-line. Like others who experience flashbacks, on this night Colleen experienced the physical symptoms that accompanied the original trauma. Even though she knew his shenanigans were over, she endured the same sense of fear, panic, and rage.

Either partner can have flashbacks. Vicky kept flashing back to the moment when her husband knocked on the door of her hotel room and exposed her intercontinental tryst. When she was reminded of that event, she felt as if her heart were jumping out of her ribcage, as though the knock were just happening. As upsetting as they may be, you have to expect that sudden flashbacks will be a normal part of your experience.

How to Cope with Flashbacks
The involuntary nature of flashbacks can be frustrating to both partners. When they occur like a bolt out of the blue during a period of progress and goodwill, it is natural to feel discouraged, as if the uncontrollable emotions will never end. If, however, you notice that you aren't having them as often or that you recover more quickly, you can consider this a sign of progress instead of backsliding. *You will know that healing is nearly complete when flashbacks are twinges rather than painful reexperiences.*

There are approaches for coping with flashbacks alone or with your partner. These will help the unfaithful partner learn how to be a healer and the betrayed partner become active in self-healing.

- *Face flashbacks together:* During therapy, couples receive flashback training based on the compassionate communication skills that are described in the next chapter. The essential lesson is for the betrayed partner to learn how to share flashbacks without blaming and for the unfaithful spouse to empathize and listen. Let's witness the same scene in two takes (just as in the movies). In "Take 1" you'll see what it sounds like when people are just beginning to grapple with flashbacks. "Take 2" shows what it sounds like after successful coaching.

Take 1

Betrayed Partner: I can't even watch TV anymore because of *what you did!*

Involved Partner: I told you not to watch TV. You twist everything into this. Why can't you just put it behind you and get over it? You always ruin everything.

Take 2

Betrayed Partner: I cried all morning because a TV program brought back all kinds of memories. I could sure use a hug.

Involved Partner: I'm really sorry that you're feeling so much pain. I know it's going to take time for you to get over this. Let me hold you until you feel better.

As you can see, flashbacks can provide an opportunity to share the pain and emotionally join in a healing process. The unfaithful partner can take on the role of healer by empathizing verbally and offering physical comfort.

• *Predict flashbacks:* Couples can learn to predict situations that could evoke flashbacks and talk about how they can handle them together. One strategy is to "write over" the memories with reparative experiences. One woman told me that she had experienced a flashback the year before, when she sat down to watch the Miss America pageant on television. In retrospect, she realized that she had been watching the pageant alone on the night she got a call from her husband's affair partner. This year, she wanted to detoxify her poisonous associations and keep from catapulting back into that crisis. She could have chosen to avoid the program, but instead, she asked her husband to sit next to her and watch it with her. When she told him why, he understood and held her hand during the program. Next year, she thinks, there will be no problem.

• *Avoid flashbacks:* Because flashbacks are involuntary reactions that are stimulated by reminders of the trauma, you can learn to avoid situations that are likely to trigger them. Yvette's husband added miles to his daily commute to avoid the city park where she used to go for walks with her affair partner. Even the name of the urban square was upsetting to him, and he saw no reason to revisit his pain every day to and from work. Trauma experts Diana and Louis Everstine caution that after a traumatic event, "The concept of immediately getting back on the horse that threw you is an example of folk wisdom that can cause harm."[5]

• *Ride the wave:* Sometimes flashbacks are unavoidable. Once a flashback begins, you should not try to block it. Trying to stop the process could intensify it. Say to yourself, "This is just a flashback. It will pass." If you stand up to a wave while you're in the ocean, you're liable to get knocked down by its force. Riding the wave will move you safely along toward the shoreline.

Over time, as your recovery progresses, flashbacks do begin to wane. They occur less often as safety is restored. But an unexpected cue, such as seeing the affair partner in public, can still trigger a flashback many years after the traumatic event.

Constriction

Inhibiting thoughts, feelings, and activities that are associated with the traumatic event are signs of constriction. Some traumatized individuals describe feeling numb, show no interest in normal activities, and are detached from other people. Many betrayed individuals vacillate between intrusive thoughts and excessive emotionality on the one hand and constrictive symptoms of avoidance and withdrawal on the other. Although constriction is more prevalent during the early period of suspicion, when the cues that something is wrong are denied, it can definitely occur after the infidelity has been exposed.

Exhaustion caused by preoccupation with the betrayal can lead to a state of not wanting to think about it, hear about it, or talk about it. After all the high drama, emotional constriction sounds like a relief: not to feel anything, not to care. But this is usually a temporary state. I tell people, "First you get numb, and then you bleed."

When Adam learned about Amy's two-year affair with another man, he reacted with almost no perceptible emotion. He was inexplicably calm and uninterested. He didn't want to hear anything about it; he didn't want to confront the evidence that his wife had had other sexual liaisons, including one on the Internet. In addition to avoiding direct knowledge of the infidelity, Adam exhibited another sign of constriction by gradually pulling away from other people in his life. He stopped playing golf with his buddies, withdrew from his children, and made excuses not to socialize with people he used to enjoy. Even those who didn't know him very well noticed that he seemed out of it. He didn't laugh much or express enthusiasm for the things that once gave him pleasure. He was an empty shell, like a war refugee.

Betrayed spouses who appear inexplicably calm after disclosure, who express no feelings, ask no questions, and display almost no emotion are probably numb. This may be a protective coping strategy for events that are too intense or painful to bear, but recovery from infidelity depends on the active involvement of the betrayed partner. During the recovery process, the emotionally constricted betrayed partner gradually thaws out and heats up as the details of the betrayal are integrated into a new reality. This process of emotional integration hurts in the same way that frozen hands ache unbearably as they warm.

Numbing is an adaptive mechanism to survive unbearable pain. Knowing that it usually doesn't last is reassuring. The antidote to numbing is allowing yourself to feel and to verbalize your feelings because feeling the feelings is the first step in trauma recovery. Accepting your partner's feelings is another necessary step for the relationship to flourish. It's not hard to understand why the involved partner may be reluctant to hasten this warming process. However, attempting to freeze the betrayed partner's feelings will shortcut the natural and painful process of healing.

Through individual and couple's counseling, Adam and Amy came to understand why he shut down at first and why it was important for him to start revving up again. At first, he even objected to the word "trauma" and denied that his wife's sexual relationship with another man was really so painful. But as he reclaimed his feelings and acknowledged his hurt, he began to understand why he needed to be more involved in what had happened. He began to ask more questions about who his wife was and why she was unfaithful. Both he and Amy agreed that he needed to stop hiding his head in the sand for their marriage to survive.

The wife of a sex addict became physically ill and refused to listen when her husband started to discuss his actions. His recovery from his addiction was impaired until she was able to accompany him on his journey toward inhibiting his impulses. They became closer than ever, and he was successful in remaining abstinent from promiscuous sex.

Hyperarousal

Long after the revelation of a betrayal, people remain supersensitive and superalert. The nervous system goes into overdrive, ready to react to any additional threat. The betrayed partner who is experiencing hyperarousal is like an automobile engine that is idling on high. Just as it takes one little tap on the gas pedal for rapid acceleration, it takes just one cue to increase the pulse and reactivate the sweat glands. Rational acts of self-preservation become exaggerated into irrational acts of overprotection. Double-checking the facts turns into a full-time preoccupation. Prudent watchfulness becomes paranoia.

Physiological Hyperarousal

Reaction becomes overreaction. Disordered sleeping is common: falling asleep, staying asleep, or getting up in the morning may be difficult. Irritability, outbursts of anger, and difficulty concentrating are other symptoms of hyperarousal. Betrayed partners are easily startled by ringing telephones, dropped glasses, and the sounds of children shrieking happily. Carolyn was still experiencing hyperreactions one month after she found out that her husband, Chas, was having an affair with Roxie, a friend from church. She was so anxious that she felt she was going to jump out of her skin. She had trouble falling asleep and then woke up in the middle of the night. In the morning, she was exhausted and didn't want to get out of bed. She had exaggerated startle reactions when the alarm clock buzzed or a door suddenly slammed shut.

Carolyn couldn't concentrate on anything for very long. Finally, she took a week off from work because she couldn't function adequately, and then she went back on a part-time basis for almost two months. The anti-anxiety medication prescribed by her family doctor deepened her depression, and she began to experience fleeting suicidal thoughts. Continuing therapy and a switch of medication to antidepressants helped stabilize her mood swings after a few weeks.

Your appetite may be sharply affected. Although Carolyn had always been one of those people who habitually put on unwanted pounds during stressful times, she lost her appetite completely. She said, "I've lost weight, but I don't feel thin. I just feel unwell." Anxiety over the potential loss of a secure relationship interferes in a negative way with the capacity to eat. I have seen individuals drop fifteen pounds in one month after they discovered their partner was unfaithful, although they had been unsuccessful with scores of weight-loss programs for many years.

Emotional Hyperarousal

It is important to express emotions without being out of control. Rage and other intense feelings are common, but be careful not to add any more scar tissue. Words used as weapons have infinite power to wound. One man confessed that no amount of time or loving communication had been able to erase the memory of his wife's words when she found out about his affair: "She screamed unspeakable things. She told me that I had been a disappointment to her sexually. She said she hadn't wanted to marry me in the first place." Although this couple decided to stay together and work on their marriage, the husband claims that his wife's words still echo repeatedly in his ears.

Imagine yourself hearing these words from the person you always thought was your dearest supporter and companion: "I never loved you"; "You've never turned me on"; "I've experienced things with my lover I will never experience with you!" And these are some of the less poisonous zingers people throw at each other.

Think about the extra wounds you'll both carry into the future when you hurl such insults at each other. Look for ways to hasten healing instead of continuing to rip off each other's scabs. If you are the involved partner, you can make a conscious effort to concentrate on the best aspects of the marriage and avoid the self-deceptions you've constructed during the affair to justify it. If you are the betrayed partner, you can avoid letting anger or despair distort the best qualities of the past relationship, so that the future isn't so bleak. If either of you feels the need to vent, find a therapist or trusted friend.

Replace hot, raging thoughts with cool, calming ones. Whenever you are overcome by the heat of angry thoughts, you can substitute cooler thoughts for the hot ones:

HOT: How could he do this to me? I didn't deserve it. I was a good wife.

COOL: This isn't about me. Even he admits I didn't do anything wrong. It's about his low self-esteem, and how vulnerable he was because he didn't get the promotion he was expecting.

HOT: She promised she'd never speak to him again, and then she goes and betrays me today by talking to him at the bank.

COOL: She didn't do it intentionally. She didn't know what to say when she ran into him unexpectedly. And the fact that she told me about it means she really is trying.

I don't believe it when people say they can't control their rage. Just suppose that in the middle of one of these tirades, your clergyman rings the doorbell or your child's teacher calls the house. You immediately lower your voice and talk politely. People give themselves permission to be out of control because they feel justified. *You can choose to contain your anger.* Develop methods of containing rage and despair through self-soothing techniques such as hot baths, massage, meditation, and deep breathing.

Hypervigilance

Hypervigilance is one of the most common manifestations of hyper-arousal in traumatized individuals. Hypervigilance is an appropriate reaction to loss of safety. Watching for signs of further danger is an important survival technique. The hypervigilant cancer survivor perceives every twinge as a possible recurrence and insists on repeated lab tests and body scans for assurance or confirmation. With a country on high alert after September 11, 2001, the Atlanta airport was shut down and 10,000 people were evacuated because a man ran up a down escalator to retrieve his lost camera.

In a similar way, betrayed partners who become unrelenting sleuths have turned their internal radar on high alert. They are bloodhounds running down the clues. Every scent of possible betrayal requires immediate investigation.

Olivia felt that she had somehow morphed from a relaxed, trusting person into a paranoid maniac. She hated Oren for having an affair with a customer and turning her into a suspicious person. She had always been comfortable with his staying out late working or playing poker with his friends. Now she was nagging him all the time, badgering him with questions, and double-checking his answers. His work, which had once been a source of mutual interest, was now a source of pain. Olivia couldn't bear to hear the simplest bit of news from his office, but not hearing about his work was worse. Not hearing aroused her suspicion that he was hiding something again.

Despite her wish to avoid the subject, Olivia avidly grilled Oren about every detail of his workday. Despite his complete and rational accountings, Olivia's doubts continued. After all, there were complete, rational accountings before and things weren't what they seemed. What if the explanations that appeared plausible and reasonable now were really all lies? Olivia had been in the room when her husband had called his affair partner on the phone to tell her it was over—and even then, she couldn't be sure. "Every time I call the office and you're not there, I freak out," she told him. "Every time you're fifteen minutes late, I'm convinced you're with *her*."

In this case, Olivia had good reason to believe Oren when he told her the affair was over. He had done everything possible to avoid communicating with the woman with whom he had been involved, including giving her sales account to one of his colleagues. Even so, Olivia had trouble staying convinced because the affair had been so intense and had gone on for two years. There were times when Oren could successfully reassure her about his deep remorse and his total dedication to their marriage, but these moments of security didn't last very long. Only after Oren had maintained a pattern of accountability and safety for eight months did Olivia begin to relax.

Imagine how much more hypervigilant a betrayed spouse is when there is uncertainty about whether the affair has really ended. When Jack confronted his wife, Joyce, about her affair with a man on her bowling team, she was apologetic. Joyce promised to end the affair if Jack would stay in the marriage, but she refused to take steps to distance herself from her affair partner. She wouldn't change teams, or ask her lover to join another team, or quit bowling altogether. Jack wanted to believe her protestations of devotion to their marriage, but Joyce's refusal to get the other man out of her life made him crazy. He wanted to know every detail of every minute she was out of the house and couldn't stomach anything having to do with the activity he associated with his wife's infidelity.

Although *vigilance* in these uncertain situations is appropriate, *unceasing hypervigilance* can destroy the relationship it is intended to preserve. Unfaithful partners who are wrestling with their own ambivalence will be put off by their partner's exaggerated need to know "the facts." They will be worn out by their partner's extreme sensitivity to the suspicion that they are lying again.

How to Handle Hypervigilance

Hypervigilance diminishes as the couple reestablishes some stability and security in their lives during the next months and years. Betrayed partners will remain on high alert until they are convinced that it is safe to trust again. But in the beginning there are shadows and strange noises everywhere. They find themselves on a strange road in the middle of the night with no map and no protection while the unfaithful partner is surviving his or her own version of Hades.

- *Be accountable:* Although extreme hypervigilance is not conducive to recovery, it is reasonable for the unfaithful partner to be accountable for his or her whereabouts. Straightforward answers will alleviate anxiety to such questions as "How do I know you're not going to leave the meeting early and be with her?" "Where did you meet your clients? Which restaurant? What did you order? How long did you stay there?" "When you were using the computer just now, did you write him another e-mail? Every time you use the computer, I panic."

  When Joyce came home from bowling, she became irritable that Jack was waiting up for her. She resented his desperate need for her to report in if she was going to be late. I explained to Joyce that it would be an act of kindness on her part to let Jack know where she was. It was cruel of her to add to his anxiety by refusing to reassure him. Just like the worried parents who can't sleep until their teenagers are safely home in bed, betrayed partners cannot let down their guard until they feel safe from further betrayal.

Separations for business or personal reasons can shake loose any newfound sense of security that may have been established. Because infidelities thrive on secrecy and opportunity, any time the unfaithful partner is out of reach, the injured person feels agitated and scared. Absence makes the wounded heart grow fearful. You can prepare for separations with advance planning that addresses the security needs of the betrayed partner. The unfaithful partner can show consideration for separation anxiety through frequent phone calls and updates about whereabouts and interpersonal contacts.

• *Check it out:* Because hypervigilance results from loss of safety, it can be defused by taking steps to gradually reestablish trust. It is perfectly reasonable for the betrayed partner to become a detective, but it is totally destructive to be an inquisitor. An inquisitor jumps out with twenty questions and tries to find out everything there is. In contrast, a detective checks things out, follows up, and tries to get useful information. If suspicions persist, check them out. Every time something checks out as okay, trust starts to rebuild. But what if you discover more lies? Then the relationship ends up further back than when you started, and you are sadder but wiser. I must admit that my position about being your own detective is not a popular one among most therapists.

> Only 17 percent of the therapists I surveyed agreed with my position statement "The betrayed spouse who becomes hypervigilant and suspicious about the whereabouts of the marital partner after an affair ends should be supported by the therapist in the attempt to track down clues to further acts of infidelity."

Naomi's husband finally confessed to a year-long affair with one of his clients. He swore the affair was over and that he had neither seen nor talked to his affair partner since then. Although Naomi wanted to believe him, something didn't add up. Instead of grilling him or just waiting and wondering, she decided to do some fact checking. The affair had been discovered when she learned that her husband was spending an inordinate amount of time talking to the same mysterious person on his cell phone. To calm her fears she masqueraded as his office administrator and had copies of his office telephone records sent to the house. When they arrived, she saw that he was still making calls to this woman's number. She had been right: the affair was still going on.

- *Invest in a private investigator:* I recommend that couples create a detective escrow fund to be used at the discretion of the betrayed partner to confirm the claims of the unfaithful partner. Before the infidelity was exposed, a wary spouse might have hired a P.I. in secret to confirm or discount his or her suspicions. At this stage of dealing with the affair's aftermath, however, a P.I. is hired for the purpose of getting outside confirmation that the involved spouse can be trusted. As one hurt spouse said, "I want to be able to trust you, but I can't trust your words. I can only trust what I can see and hear."

The unfaithful partner often becomes impatient with having to prove trustworthiness and says, "Either you trust me, or you don't." I tell my couples that trust is not a light switch that is turned on or off. It is more like a dimmer switch that gradually goes from dark to bright.

If you are the unfaithful partner, try to imagine receiving a second bad check from the same person who bounced a check the previous week. You accepted that second check only after being reassured: "Trust me. This check is definitely good." When that same person hands you yet another check, your first task is to call the bank yourself to see if there are sufficient funds. Even if the third check does turn out to be good, you will be calling the bank for a long time before you feel confident about cashing future checks.

- *Let it go:* At some point, the betrayed partner does have to hang up the detective gear. If persistent hypervigilance endures beyond a year despite investigations that corroborate truthfulness, the cause may be unresolved trust issues from previous relationships. On the other hand, I have learned that the instincts of the betrayed spouse are surprisingly accurate in detecting further signs of deception after the initial disclosure. Suspicions of continued involvement might be justified, but if detective work becomes a new lifetime career because your partner keeps deceiving you, you need to either let go and accept that you are married to a philanderer or find a new partner.

New Crises

Let's say that the conditions for recovery are optimum: the affair is ended, the couple has committed to working through the issues, and both partners are actively seeking to create safety and goodwill. They are spending time together with compassion, laughter, and heart-to-heart honesty. *Still,* other shoes are going to drop. Most couples experience relapses and new crises, especially in the early stages of recovery. No matter how well you may be working together as a couple, the behavior of the affair partner, which is not under your control, can also provoke a crisis.

Making the transition from less openness and more lies to more openness and fewer lies will generate new information about previous deceptions. This new information will reverberate painfully until it has been absorbed. When something happens that shatters your fragile new stability into a million pieces, you feel as if you are right back where you started. Realizing that new crises and relapses are part of the territory may allow you to keep these upsetting backslides in perspective.

Uncovering Previous Lies

Crises come in many forms. Bob took comfort in his belief that his wife genuinely cared about the business they were building together, even if she had indulged in a temporary sexual infatuation with another man. When he discovered an e-mail message she had written to her lover that belittled his business acumen, he was crushed.

Sometimes what comes to light is more than revealing messages written under the influence of sexual passion. Sometimes betrayed partners discover elaborate premeditated and hurtful deceptions. The unfaithful partner needs to validate the facts and empathize with the pain of these new revelations. Couples who handle these crises together are more likely to stay together.

Two months after she found out that her husband, Ken, had been taking his assistant with him to out-of-town conventions, Kris was feeling pretty good about the progress they were making in repairing the damage to their marriage. Then one day, for no particular reason, she began thinking about a conference he had supposedly attended six months earlier. She remembered it because he had missed their older son's birthday in order to attend. After doing some careful checking, she put two and two together and discovered that the conference flyer he had shown her had been a fake. He had really spent the weekend at a resort with his lover. It took several weeks for them to resolve the pain created by the revelation of his incredible trickery. However, his remorse went a long way toward helping their recovery.

Surviving Special Occasions

Family life is knit together with rituals and celebrations. Birthdays, wedding anniversaries, graduations, and deaths can provoke crises when they occur before the couple has rebuilt a united front. Having to put on a smiling face in front of others while still feeling unsettled is very unsettling. Putting on the façade of a committed couple when the commitment is unstable is destabilizing.

We connect with those closest to us when we raise a glass or applaud the honoree. And, consciously or not, we tend to compare and contrast how this year compares to last: How do I feel now in contrast to how I anticipated I would be feeling? Any disappointment or discontinuity tends to get magnified at such times, and we end up feeling worse than if it were just an ordinary day.

Major events in the life cycle, such as anniversaries and family celebrations, can be planned for concretely. Talking together about realistic expectations and potential sources of further damage is the key. Six weeks after Karen learned about Karl's affair with his paralegal, their daughter got engaged. They had planned to invite his partners and office staff to the wedding, but his affair partner still worked for the law firm. Karen couldn't bear the thought of her husband's lover, Britney, being present for their daughter's wedding vows. Karl didn't want to incite office gossip by deliberately omitting her from the guest list. After many tears and angry words, the wedding crisis was resolved by limiting the guest list to Karl's law partners.

Handling the Affair Partner's Intrusions

Perhaps the greatest source of crisis is an unplanned encounter with the affair partner. Six months after Ralph and Rachel made the decision to stay together and work on their marriage, they ran into Lara at the mall, and he waved hello to her when she smiled at him. Rachel was furious, especially when Ralph said he didn't want to appear rude by completely ignoring her overture. They didn't talk for two days. They both felt misunderstood, and they perceived each other as insensitive. When the wall of silence came down, they agreed on a plan for future encounters. If they ever ran into Lara again, Rachel would be the one to wave hello while Ralph held Rachel's other hand. Similarly, if a couple knows that the affair partner will be present at a social event they must attend, they can discuss ahead of time how best to demonstrate polite but firm solidarity as a couple.

Often, as the bond between the couple grows stronger, affair partners will ecalate their campaign of sabotage. They may make harassing or self-disclosing phone calls to the betrayed spouse, relentlessly pursue their former lover, or threaten suicide. It is extremely important that the involved partner *not* handle the affair partner unilaterally. It must be clear to the affair partner that there will be no continuation of a secret relationship and that the married lover is committed to the marriage. The betrayed partner must not blame his or her spouse for the affair partner's behavior. In fact, escalating intrusions can be perceived as acts of desperation by the affair partner because the affair is truly over.

After the involved partner has said clearly and forcefully that the affair is over, there is very little the couple can do to control the affair partner's behavior. But they can manage intrusions together by creating a *united front* for dealing with the affair partner. Telephone calls can be screened with caller ID or answering machines. Many couples decide to change to an unlisted phone number. In extreme cases, some couples have had to get a restraining order against harassment by the ex-lover. A smart strategy is to refuse all contact, respond only when you are together, and share all information around any unavoidable encounters.

Relapses

Setbacks are inevitable, so it is important not to confuse a *lapse* or *relapse* with a state of total *collapse*. A *lapse* is a little slip with a quick recovery, and a *relapse* is a regression to a prior state of distress followed by a slow recovery. In contrast, a *collapse* is complete disintegration with little hope of recovery.

Recovery depends on a genuine desire to change, an ability to empathize, and the capacity to exercise self-control. Relapses happen when people under stress get tired, discouraged, fearful, or simply lose focus and revert to previous unconscious patterns. Essentially, they are communications or interactions that go awry. Sooner or later, the betrayed partner will react with bitterness, sarcasm, or blaming to something the involved partner has honestly shared. Inevitably, at some point, the involved partner won't have the patience to endure one more hysterical outburst. Without meaning to, one or the other will have a poor response and set off a chain reaction of emotional explosions.

Triggers for Relapses

In the early months of recovery, relapses frequently occur when things seem to be going especially well. It might seem that there is always a terrible storm or argument after a wonderful night of lovemaking. Emotional and physical intimacy are contingent on letting down walls and taking the risk of being vulnerable. Baring your body and soul may be followed by doubt and self-recrimination. Distancing, fighting, or hateful inquisitions inexplicably appear after intimacy awakens anxiety. These defensive maneuvers serve to create a protective shield.

Relapses can also be triggered by familiar traits that were tolerated before but are no longer acceptable because they evoke fears of further betrayal. Ken had always been a bit flirtatious, and Kris had perceived it as a sign of his warm, friendly personality. However, after his affair, she was easily provoked if he bantered in a joking manner with other women.

Every dinner in a restaurant with an attractive waitress became a battleground where they were armed for conflicting roles of attack and defend. Finally, Ken was willing to examine his behavior through Kris's eyes to prevent the continuous relapses. He learned to be more businesslike with female clerks and other service staff, and Kris learned to show her appreciation over his restraint.

Coping with Relapses

Because it is impossible to avoid relapses, it makes sense to try to understand them when they occur. In the heat of the moment, you can strive for early recognition that you have gotten off track. Then you can short-circuit a chain reaction by suggesting that you both calm down first. After you have some distance, you can discuss the relapse as a source of information about areas in your relationship that need further work. The resulting discussion is an opportunity for the two of you to practice compassionate communication, as described in Chapter 7.

Ask yourselves "What just happened?" and "What can we do differently in the future?" Productive discussions can bring you farther along the road to recovery than if the relapse had never happened. Attitude is everything. If you and your partner are prepared for these retro moments, you will not be derailed by them.

How to Take Care of Yourself

To cope with continuing traumatic reactions, it is important to take care of yourself in the best way you can. Living with continuous stress can lower your immune system and make you more vulnerable to illness. Invigorating mental and physical activities will help to offset the negative impact of traumatic reactions on your health. If your everyday habits are anchored in healthy choices, healing is easier.

Reactivate Fulfilling Activities

Being active is one of the best antidotes for both the jitters and the blues. Schedule satisfying activities back into your life. Some of these activities can be done together, and some of them need to be done apart. One over-wrought wife decided to take piano lessons again as a way to focus her attention and lay out a program of personal accomplishment that would help her regain some sense of self-esteem. One errant husband decided to start swimming laps again, both for the physical benefits and the emotional benefits of time alone to grieve the loss of his lover.

Laughter enhances the immune system by increasing natural killer cells.[6] Watch comedies that tickle your funny bone instead of action movies that make you tense. Energize your weak inner battery by getting involved in a special project that will energize you with its own momentum. If you are too emotionally exhausted for something active, listen to some music that gives you a sense of well-being.

Look Out for Your Physical Health

As far as physical health is concerned, the advice your mother gave you regarding sleep, food, and exercise still stands. Be sure to get enough sleep; sleep deprivation leads to irritability and depressed mood. Some people are tempted to escape through overeating, overdrinking, oversmoking, or overusing drugs. These behaviors compound bad experiences and make them worse. Exercise, eat nutriously, and participate in centering activities such as meditation or yoga. You will maximize the personal resources you need to meet the challenges you are facing.

When you take care of your body, you have the added benefit of taking care of your mind and your emotions, because mind and body are really different aspects of the same organic system. In the process, you improve your mood, boost your confidence, and restore your personal resources.

Look Out for Your Mental Health

Almost everyone going through this difficult experience needs time alone to integrate what has happened and begin to mend. You may need more support than you can provide for yourself. Talking to a therapist can give you a safe place to work through your individual and relationship issues. However, it may not be possible to work on relationship issues until both partners are more stable. Both betrayed partners and involved partners may need antidepressant or anti-anxiety medication to cope with their overwhelming emotions.

Consider seeking help from a licensed mental health professional if:

- Your ability to function in daily life is seriously compromised.
- Your discussions with your partner are explosive with accusations and avoidance.
- The intimacy in your relationship is markedly decreasing as time goes on.
- One or both of you is still ambivalent about whether you want to work on the relationship.
- Either of you is homicidal or suicidal.

So far, we have been working on feeling the feelings and establishing a certain degree of stability. In the midst of coping with debilitating post-traumatic reactions are glimmers of returning to an ordinary life. Taking care of the business of work and family, following daily routines, and creating some pleasure to offset the pain is an important part of trauma recovery.

The next chapter suggests ways to enhance your relationship and foster hope through caring and compassionate communication. These relationship-enhancing suggestions are effective for all couples, even those who haven't suffered from an infidelity.

7

REPAIRING THE COUPLE AND
BUILDING GOODWILL

*I feel more hopeful about our relationship when we are being
nicer to each other. Sometimes things seem back to normal.
And sometimes it's even better than normal.*

I N THE MIDST of all the pain you've been experiencing, a safe harbor
and a glimmer of hope will emerge. From this calm, sheltered place
you and your partner will be able to experience more comfort and pleasure in each other's company than you have for some time. At first, these
small islands of pleasure will be interspersed unevenly over the troubled
waters, but gradually you can use them to build bridges of good faith and
goodwill. To do the hard work ahead of exploring the meaning of the infidelity, you will need to build a foundation of commitment, caring, and
compassionate communication.

If you are reluctant to initiate caring with someone who has disappointed you so much, you can focus instead on giving to the relationship.
Every time you do something good for your partner, you are doing something good for yourself by making the relationship the benefactor of your
giving. Don't wait for your partner to make the first move.

To give up now would be like buying high and selling low. Even if you're
still not sure whether the marriage can be saved, you shouldn't make your
decision based on the lowest point in your relationship. Being the best
partner you know how to be will maximize the potential. Then, if there is
still too great a gap between what you achieve together and what you expect, you can leave with the knowledge that you have truly given it your
best.

You can start making specific repairs to your relationship that will help each of you to feel more connected. It may have been days, months, or even years since you felt good together. Experiencing some kindness and caring in each other's company enhances your chances of rebuilding a satisfying life together. You owe it to yourselves to see how good your marriage can be. You and your partner can work together to create a healing atmosphere that is calm, where information can be shared and where caring begins to bind you together again. Even in this early stage of rebuilding, blame and jealousy can disappear as kindness, consistency, and honesty come to characterize the way you interact.

Repair 1: Getting Back to Normal

First, you can reclaim the couple who used to look forward to time alone together. Some couples may recall how much better things were just a short time ago—before the affair. Others may have to go back many years to a time before the children were born or before their careers took over their lives.

In the midst of chaos, you have to get back to your normal routines and responsibilities. You can begin to bridge the gap between you by collaborating on household decisions. Scheduling family time and couple time is preferable to leaving it up to chance. Planning recreational activities with friends, children, and extended family can solidify your bond. Begin and end each day by sharing information about scheduled activities, daily frustrations, and simple achievements. For example, in the movie *The Story of Us,* the family played the game "high-low" at the dinner table every night. The parents and the children each talked about the high and low points of their day. This is a wonderful way to create a sense of shared experiences.

Take Time Out for Fun and Companionship

One of the first steps in getting back to normal is to increase your enjoyment in each other's company. You are more likely to feel connected when you laugh and have fun together. One husband talked about what it was like to engage his wife in a game of Ping-Pong after the trauma of his affair. "She picked up a paddle and I picked up a paddle, and all of a sudden we were back playing the kind of stupid games we used to play when we were younger. We started laughing and being silly, and I realized how good it could be between us. That was the moment when I knew I could never leave her for another woman."

How long has it been since you planned time together just for fun or for a romantic date? Bring back the activities you used to enjoy doing together. Put fun and companionship back into your life. Set aside time for movie dates, but don't pick anything too heavy. As a matter of fact, screen the content first, so you won't end up reliving your infidelity on the silver screen. Athletic activities, such as tennis, biking, or working out at the gym, provide structured time together when you use up some of your negative energy and come out feeling renewed.

Or just go out for a bite to eat. If you are still in crisis, don't ruin your time out with gut-wrenching conversations. Make your meal together a true *time out*. Stick to mundane discussions, superficial pleasantries, or intellectual sharing about current events or interesting tidbits that you've read or heard. If it feels too awkward to be alone together, create a buffer by asking along another couple who are comfortable and easy to be with.

Make Love, Not War

Renewing your sexual relationship may be a natural, spontaneous act born out of intense feelings. On the other hand, one of you may feel dead sexually. Perhaps you alternate between these two extremes. The bottom line is to respect the feelings of whoever is not yet ready for prime time sex. Do find out what kind of touch or affection your reluctant or uninterested partner would be willing to accept, such as holding hands or goodbye/hello hugs at the front door. Back rubs and foot massages can be a good way to break the ice and achieve some mutual relaxation.

Recall Your Past Together

Remember what it was like when things were better. One way you can begin to foster positive feelings is by reexamining what perceptions and expectations you had for yourselves in the beginning of your relationship, during courtship. Look at your wedding video and talk about what attracted you to each other. I have been touched many times by the visible transformation that couples go through when they begin talking about how they met and what it was like to be falling in love with each other. Even if they had come into my office hurt, angry, alienated, and hopeless, when they start talking about memories, what it was like before things got bad and what it was like when they wanted to be together for the rest of their lives, they create strong images and positive feelings of connection.

Recount for yourselves examples of productive, caring interactions you've had with each other in the past. To make it safe to explore your past together, though, avoid comparing your glorious past with your miserable present: you don't want remembering to become a chronicle of how much you've lost. Ethan and Ellie recalled how they had felt on the same wavelength during their courtship because of their participation in political activism. Now he was working feverishly to get ahead in his law practice while she felt overwhelmed by three preschoolers. His affair was a wake-up call for them to make more time for intellectually exciting, mutual interests.

Use the past as a beacon to highlight the activities you used to enjoy. Paula and Peter used to go hiking and biking all over the Appalachians before their daughter, Penny, was born. When Penny was small, they took her along in a child carrier. But after their move to New England, they gradually drifted apart as Paula's time during the week was devoted to the Parent-Teacher Association at Penny's school and Peter took up golf on weekends. After Paula's affair with a single parent from the school, they realized how their separate activities had created a relationship vacuum. They joined the Sierra Club and started enjoying new friends and outdoor activities together.

Dream about Your Future Together

Look ahead to the future. Think about what your lives together could be like in five years, after you have healed from this trauma. You have so many life events to enjoy together in the future, such as graduations, weddings, grandchildren, and retirement. You have worked hard and struggled through the rough times. Don't give up on your investment before you reap the rewards of your labor.

Work together on the immediate future by asking yourselves the solution-oriented "miracle question": If you woke up tomorrow morning and a miracle had occurred while you were sleeping, what would your relationship look like? What would each of you be doing differently? What would your friends, children, and other family members notice about the way you treat each other?[1]

> According to research by Fran Dickson, couples who were happily married for fifty years had a common vision about how they dreamed their life together would be.[2]

I tell couples that they are not only more likely to stay married but to be happily married if they dream together and plan for their future.

Repair 2: Fostering Positive Exchanges

Every marriage maintains a reservoir of goodwill, a metaphorical line of credit, against which expenditures can be made when needed. Infidelity often bankrupts this joint asset. For a while at least, the relationship balance is in the red. The shock of discovery and its aftermath create large debits, and new credits are few and far between. As soon as you can, though, start making caring deposits that you will be able to draw on during this crisis of deficit spending.

It is not surprising that the betrayed partner feels some jealousy about the time and romance that have been stolen from the marriage or that the involved partner misses the attention and romantic feelings of the affair. Just a few caring gestures will begin to establish the same kind of positive energy in the marriage that were present in the affair. The relationship needs real, tangible solidity that can be built on. The betrayed partner will see that the involved partner has taken steps to walk back into the marriage. And the involved partner will feel hopeful about experiencing the good feelings that were evident in the affair.

The responsibility for building up your joint assets falls on both of you. The betrayed partner shouldn't have to do all of the work so the involved partner will stick around, and the involved partner shouldn't have to make up for the betrayal by doing all of the work. Invest in your relationship now without keeping a tally of who does what. Tell yourself, "It's time for me to concentrate on fixing *us*." This may go against your gut feeling that you don't want to extend yourself first. You may be thinking: "All this caring stuff makes sense, but only if *you* take the first step. I don't want to take a chance getting too close." Or you may be resistant to receiving caring from your partner. Maybe accepting acts of goodwill feels too much like forgiving the betrayal.

Don't make the mistake of *choosing righteousness over happiness,* although the impulse to do so is understandable.[3] If you are serious about making your marriage better, within a few weeks you must begin gradually to soften toward giving and receiving tokens of affection and caring. Caring behaviors are an important way to intensify feelings and strengthen the broken connection. Your mutual commitment and hopefulness will increase through the kind of targeted caring that provides what your partner most wishes to receive. Your emotional link to each other will be directly proportional to how many positive exchanges you share with each other.

> In his extensive research with more than 2,000 couples, psychologist John Gottman found that satisfied couples were those who maintained a ratio of five positive moments for every one negative moment, even if the couple was conflict-habituated or conflict-avoidant.[4]

Ways of Caring

There are so many ways to show you care. Once caring becomes your intention and your approach, you will find many ways to demonstrate in both tangible and intangible ways that your partner's goodwill, health, and comfort are your concern. You will get back to the core of your emotional bond by being caring, doing caring things, and welcoming the caring that your partner initiates.

The security needs of the injured partner may conflict with the autonomy needs of the involved partner. Caring is shown by recognizing and accommodating these opposing wishes. The caring behaviors of the involved partner can focus on making the injured partner feel less anxious and more secure. Caring behaviors by the injured partner can focus on curtailing actions that might feel smothering. Acts of mutual sensitivity include the involved partner calling home if he or she is going to be late and the injured partner supporting autonomous activities such as working out at the gym.

Little Things Mean a Lot

When it comes to caring, small gestures can have big consequences. Turning the steering wheel of a ship just one degree to the right carries the ship miles away from the original destination. Nonverbal behaviors such as smiling eyes and a warm touch on the shoulder are powerful resources to steer your relationship back on course. Positive verbal expressions such as using an endearing nickname can help to rekindle old feelings.

• *Show caring through body language and affectionate gestures.* Sometimes reaching out for each other in simple gestures does more to repair the connection than words can. You can hold hands in the movie theater, speak in a gentle voice, and cuddle up in bed.

• *Show caring by expressing concern and understanding for each other.* Listen willingly to each other's pain. Sometimes, the best thing you can do is allow each other some space. Knowing when to be quiet and let things be as they are for a moment is a healing and, sometimes, a heroic act.

• *Show caring by performing tasks that show consideration.* What a treat it is to have a partner who brings you a cup of coffee and the paper in bed on Sunday morning or who supports your family by handling the arrangements for your sister's visit. Driving the carpool to and from soccer practice gives your partner a much-needed break from the kids and shows respect for your partner's contribution to the family.

Bull's-eye Caring

Bull's-eye caring is when you hit the target right in the center.[5] Too often, our efforts don't hit the right spot with our partner. Task-oriented individuals who love it when their partner cleans out the garage are usually not inclined to initiate the emotionally expressive caring that their partner may desire. Most people give what they wish to receive, rather than what the other person really desires. All this time, you may have been giving not what your partner wants but what *you* want.

I noticed this principle operating in my own life. For example, I like to get affection, so I give lots of hugs. My husband is more task-oriented, so he straightens up the kitchen on weekends and saves me the morning paper each weekday. Finally, I figured out that he would be more impressed by my actions than my expressions of affection. So, to celebrate *his* birthday, I went out and had *my* car washed as one of my gifts to him because he couldn't stand how dirty it was. He expressed his appreciation with a hug instead of buying me a year's subscription to the car wash.

Shirley's Golden Rule of Giving is "Give unto others as others like to give unto you." Caring involves giving in the domain that has meaning for the other person, not just in the domain we prefer or are comfortable with. This is why the traditional Golden Rule, "Do unto others as you would have them do unto you," frequently doesn't work when it comes to caring actions or gift giving.

Stacy complained to me that her husband always gave her a jacket for her birthday and Christmas, when what she really wanted was jewelry. He had given her a leather jacket and a fur jacket; she had given him a chain bracelet and a watch. I suggested that she pull a reverse: ask him to give *her* jewelry and plan to give *him* a jacket. To make it easy for her husband, she gave him a list of ten kinds of jewelry at different price levels that she would be thrilled to receive. She figured a range of options would keep an element of suspense. When he looked at the list, he said in surprise, "But this is all jewelry." It had never occurred to him that this was what she really wanted.

When I saw her after Christmas, Stacy told me, "He just loved his leather jacket." And she was thrilled to show me her new gold watch. Then she added with a smile, "But he also got me a jean jacket."

Express Appreciation

The best way I know to get a positive cycle going is to respond to *any* kind of positive behavior with appreciation. Unfortunately, people tend to react more immediately to negatives than to positives. For example, when you do something mean to me, I tend to react immediately in a negative way. In contrast, when you do something nice for me, I may think "Gee that's nice," but it doesn't have the same immediate effect. Because the negative is more powerful, you need to counteract negative messages by using affirming words and gestures as often as you can.

Give Positive Feedback for Positive Mirroring

It's hard for a long-term marriage to compete with the positive mirroring that went on during the affair. In the affair, unfaithful partners love the way they look when they see themselves reflected in their lovers' eyes. After the revelation of infidelity, they may be consciously avoiding the eyes of the betrayed partner because they are uncomfortable with the tarnished image that is reflected back. The betrayed partner also misses the adoring glances of yesteryear. Both partners long to feel special again. One way to polish the mirror in your marriage is to consciously show appreciation and give compliments.

When you approach your partner and see the appreciation in your partner's eyes, that is positive mirroring. When your partner approaches you and sees caring and affection reflected back, that is also positive mirroring. In a relationship that is working well, both people experience an increase in self-esteem and self-confidence because the other person is sending signals that say "You are a special person." "You are lovable." "You deserve my respect."

In the aftermath of infidelity, both partners have trouble sending positive signals to the other. When they approach each other, they reflect mutual disillusionment. Bert told me the thing he regretted most after his affair was losing the way his wife, Betty, used to look at him with such shining eyes. Betty was equally sad that Bert had tumbled off his pedestal. She had been his most ardent supporter, and, for his part, he had always valued her opinions. They realized it would take time to rebuild their mutual admiration society. When Bert wholeheartedly supported her desire to attend graduate school, Betty knew they had taken a major step forward in restoring her vision of him as her "knight in shining armor."

Give Credit Where Credit Is Due

Learn to give credit when your partner makes an attempt to connect or to repair. I can't tell you how many times I've heard people say "At work and with my friends I can do no wrong. At home I can do no right."

Be alert to the caring things your partner does for you each day and share your appreciation. Recounting moments of caring rewards effort and fires the enthusiasm for continuing to do nice things. Somehow, most people easily recall their own acts of caring but appear to have a memory lapse when asked to recall what kinds of caring they have received. Try to end each day with at least one gesture of appreciation.

Designate one week each month as "family appreciation week." Each day, each family member tells everyone else in the family something he or she appreciates. Schmaltz it up and have fun with it. Thank the children for washing their hands before dinner. Encourage them to thank their siblings for passing the salt. Thank your spouse for small gestures and taken-for-granted tasks, such as taking out the trash or putting the laundry away.

Enhancing Mutual Appreciation and Bull's-eye Caring

When people get a chance to hear how they are appreciated, they are often quite moved and goodwill is enhanced all around. The purpose of the following two exercises is to let your partner know what things you appreciate or would like to see more often as a part of your daily life together.

Privately, fill out *both* forms, "What Pleases Me about You?" and "The Newlywed Game," *before* you follow the instructions about how to share your responses.[6]

Exercise: What Pleases Me about You?

This exercise is a proven way for you and your partner to create an opportunity for positive mirroring.

List ten things that you appreciate about your partner. These could be actions that are pleasing to you when your partner does them, or specifics about the kind of person your partner is that pleases you—either in the past or in the present. Name what pleases you, even if it is a rare occurrence. Be positive and specific.

Example: I really like it when you give me a compliment about how I look.

1. _____

2. _____

3. _____

4. _____

5. _____

6. _____

7. _____

8. _____

9. _____

10. _____

*Now, before proceeding to the Instructions for Sharing (below), go to the next page and fill out the **Guess List** and the **Wish List** for the Newlywed Game. Then come back and continue with the Instructions for Sharing "What Pleases Me About You."*

Instructions for Sharing "What Pleases Me about You"
Sit down facing each other. Alternate turns by going back and forth and sharing one item at a time. Avoid negative comparisons about the way it used to be *before* the affair. As you share each entry, you can say why that particular behavior or personal characteristic is significant, or you can relate a specific example that illustrates your point. Elaborating on each point makes this exercise much more meaningful.

• ***Share the significance:*** One husband told his wife that one of the things that pleased him was that she took a shower every day. She responded incredulously by saying, "You must have really scraped the bottom of the barrel for that one." He explained that in the family he grew up in, people had poor personal hygiene and he was ashamed to bring his friends over. He added, "It means so much to me that you always look and smell so clean." Unless we know the full meaning of the appreciation, we don't know the significance.

- *Share an example:* One betrayed wife told her husband that she appreciated that he was a good father to their children. He accepted her compliment without much feeling. However, he was touched when she described how it warmed her heart to see how patient he was when helping their hyperactive son with his homework. Neither of them had received much attention from their own parents, so his nurturing behaviors with the kids created positive mirroring. Incidentally, she wisely inhibited the impulse to say, "You're a great father, but you've been a terrible husband."

Exercise: The Newlywed Game

In the TV show called *The Newlywed Game,* newlyweds had to guess what their new spouse would say in response to certain questions. It was really a test of how well they knew their partner, and it's fun to play. You will see how well you know your partner's wishes. You'll be comparing your guesses about what your partner wants from you with your partner's actual wish list.

A. Guess List
List five specific things that you believe your partner would appreciate if you did them. Be positive and specific. For example, "You want me to give you a hug when I walk in the door" instead of "You don't want me to ignore you when I come home." Do not refer to the infidelity.

1. _____

2. _____

3. _____

4. _____

5. _____

B. Wish List

List five specific things you would appreciate if your partner did them. Be positive and specific. Don't refer to the infidelity. For example, do *not* request "I want to be able to trust you" or "I want you to stop asking me questions about my lover."

1. _____

2. _____

3. _____

4. _____

5. _____

Instructions

1. You read one item from your Guess List.

2. Your partner tells you whether you have a match with one of the items on his or her Wish List. Continue comparing all your guesses with items on your partner's Wish List.

3. Now it's your partner's turn to compare his or her Guess List with your Wish List, and you tell them whether or not they have a match.

4. After both of you finish reading your Guess Lists, share any of the items on the Wish Lists that were missed or guessed incorrectly.

Scoring

0–1 match = Missed the target.
2–3 matches = Hit the target.
4–5 matches = Bull's-eye.

If you accurately guessed at least three things your partner had on his or her Guess List, then you have a good idea about how to do bull's-eye caring. You probably do not want to spend time and energy trying to please your partner with actions that are on the rim or totally off-target. You got a good idea about the bull's-eye caring that is already going on when you participated in the first exercise and shared what pleases each of you. You can improve your accuracy and achieve even more bull's-eyes with what you have learned in "The Newlywed Game."

If you or your partner weren't too successful on "The Newlywed Game" because you don't know what pleases each other, you may have a communication problem. Perhaps you don't express your wishes clearly and need to strengthen your "I want" muscles. Or perhaps you don't listen to your partner's wishes and need to strengthen your "I hear you" muscles.

Sometimes, a "wrong" guess can uncover an unexpressed desire. Gina guessed that her husband, Gary, wanted her to cook big dinners every night. He said, "Well, actually, I didn't have that written down, but, come to think of it, I would really, really like that." And then she went on: "I think you want me to initiate sex more often." And he said, "Now, *that's* a bull's-eye!"

For his part, Gary learned something new, too. He didn't realize that Gina wanted him to initiate affection that wasn't a prelude to sexual intercourse. They agreed that he would initiate nonsexual affection more often and she would initiate sex in an obvious way by touching him rather than by her usual passive means, such as wearing a new nightgown to bed.

Resistance to Caring

Sooner or later, either partner may feel some resistance to the caring process. Resistance can be to *doing* caring things, to *receiving* caring things, or to *acknowledging* or appreciating caring things. Resistance to caring can indicate ambivalence or anxiety about working on the marriage. It is important to spot the signs of resistance and to understand the reasons one or both partners may be reluctant to reach out with affection and appreciation. Progress will feel at a standstill until resistance to caring is overcome.

Resistance to caring can indicate that the involved partner still has a strong emotional attachment to the lover. The unfaithful partner who acts too loving in the marriage may feel disloyal to the affair partner. In the worst situations, resistance is a sign that the affair isn't over.

Signs of Resistance

One sign of resistance is an unwillingness to please your partner by carrying out specific requests to be more involved at home or to be more loving. Isaac was discouraged because whenever he asked Inez to watch TV with him, she seemed to have some excuse to avoid being alone with him. In another example, Tony kept ignoring Tracie's wish for him to take a bigger role in helping out with the children's homework.

You can spot resistance when you hear someone saying *"Yes, but . . .":* *"Yes,* you cleaned the dishes, *but* you didn't sweep the kitchen floor." When you follow something positive with a *"but,"* the other person will soon learn that nothing is good enough. It's like using a block delete on the computer: it erases whatever positive statement may have preceded it. Think about how it feels when someone says, "Yes, that new outfit is a nice color, *but* the style makes you look a little heavy."

Another sign of resistance is to discount your partner's positive actions or traits. Discounting occurs when the other person makes attempts to be caring, and you minimize or invalidate the efforts: "You're only doing that to look good in front of the therapist," or "I know you really don't want to have sex with me. You never really liked sex. You're only doing it because you don't want me to get angry. You'll probably resent it later." The message here is that no matter what you do, it isn't going to work. Specifically: "No matter what you do, I'm not going to allow it to influence me. I know that you can't really change enough to please me. My mind is made up."

Overcoming Resistance

At this point, if you are staying together only for the sake of the children, you may develop additional, stronger reasons later as your relationship improves. Use whatever resources you have to create a warm, loving family environment. Over time, your original motivation can evolve into staying together because of the pleasures in the marital relationship.

One betrayed wife conveyed what it was like in the beginning of the recovery process, when commitment without caring felt like it wasn't going to be enough: "My husband has recommitted to me after having an affair. That's what I wanted, but I also feel disappointed. A lot of the time, it feels empty. I can see that he wants to be with the kids and for us to be a family, but I don't feel that he has really chosen *me*." Fortunately, she and her husband stuck with it and had the pleasure of falling in love with each other once again.

- *Even if you can't quite manage to be caring yourself and are reluctant to go overboard with appreciation, you can at least notice your partner's efforts.* Comment on actions that indicate considerate behaviors: "I noticed you put all of the dishes in the dishwasher. The kitchen looks nice and clean"; "It was helpful that you called to say you'd be late coming home"; "The flowers you brought home look pretty in the sunroom"; "Dinner tonight was delicious." From these little seeds fully expressed appreciation and mutual caring can grow.

- *Don't wait for your partner to initiate just because you feel that you deserve special treatment.* Resistance can come from either the involved partner *or* the betrayed partner. Sometimes people are scared and don't want to take the risk of rejection, so they wait for their partner to go first. Either one may have a hard time remembering all the good things their partner has done for them in the past. One betrayed husband put it this way: "I can't believe I'm supposed to be nice to my wife after what she did to me. The truth is, a lot of the time I want to hurt her. I want her to feel some of the rejection and hurt that I'm feeling."

- *Walk the walk before you feel the feelings.* Sometimes people are under the mistaken impression that they have to "feel" it before they can do it. It's good to know that behavior can sometimes precede actual feelings. If you can act appreciative even before you feel it, the chances are good that loving feelings will follow. Discover the value of pretending that the changes you desire have already been made. Act *as if* your relationship is as secure and caring as you would like it to be. Small adjustments lead to more permanent and positive patterns of interaction.

- *Be the kind of partner you have always wished for, so that you will know you've done your best.* The attitude "If you do something nice for me, I'll do something nice for you" is an excuse not to change. You are allowing yourself to be controlled and brought down to the level of someone who is not acting very nicely. When you look back, you won't be plagued by all kinds of shouldas/couldas if the relationship doesn't work out. Besides, you just might get the ball rolling in the right direction. If you act the same way you'd behave if you were married to your "dream" partner, your own dreams are more likely to come true.

- *Treat any display of affection as valid "in the moment," not as a sign of eternal commitment.* This will free you and your partner to act spontaneously when you feel some warmth toward each other. Sometimes, openly ambivalent partners deliberately restrain themselves from demonstrating spontaneous feelings of affection to guard against communicating more devotion than they feel. Involved partners may not want to act on their positive impulses of the moment for fear it will be misinterpreted as a firm commitment to stay. At times, involved partners feel the full impact of guilt about what they have done to someone they love and respect. At other times, they fall back on their original story of justification for the affair to help themselves deny their guilt. This internal seesaw can lead to inconsistent caring.

> In research about "the good marriage" by Judith Wallerstein and Sandra Blakeslee, the well-being of the couple was regarded as more important than the separate desires of either partner.[7]

- *Give freely, but don't act as if you're giving in.* There's a big difference between *giving* and *giving in.* If you *give* willingly to please your partner, you will feel like a winner. But if you *give in* out of guilt or because you feel coerced, your resentment will make losers of you both. And if you think that sticking to your guns and refusing to please your partner is a winning position, think again. There is no way that you can win if your partner loses. Think of your caring actions as giving to the *relationship*—a definite win-win situation for both of you. What is good for the relationship will be good for you.

Repair 3: Learning Compassionate Communication

"My spouse doesn't understand me the way you do" is a common refrain in affairs. Unfaithful partners often say that a significant attraction to the affair partner is feeling so accepted. What they are really saying is that their lover was skilled at listening and empathizing.

On a train going from Baltimore to New York, I was captivated by the conversation of the couple sitting behind me. The woman was one of the best empathic listeners I have ever encountered. The interesting part of this story is that they appeared to be strangers. The man was highly opinionated. As he talked about his reactions to different events in his life, she would say, "I understand how you could have felt that way." He gradually opened up more and more. I wondered whether he and his wife had such intimate conversations. If they had had an opportunity to continue their relationship, it could easily have turned into an affair because he felt so well understood and accepted.

Compassionate communication skills are indispensable to the recovery process after an affair. The goal of compassionate communication is to use language as a means of creating a more intimate bond. Whether or not you and your partner were good communicators before the affair, your recovery together requires that you become so now. Couples who have difficulty discussing where to vacation or how to deal with an intrusive mother-in-law are really going to have trouble talking to each other about infidelity. Using four proven tools for compassionate communication will allow you and your partner to forge a more positive bond.

Tool 1: Inhibit, Inhibit, Inhibit

Think about your intent. If your intent is to vent your spleen, then it doesn't matter how you say it. You may feel better afterward because you've gotten rid of all those toxins, but the other person feels poisoned. If your intent is to help the other person understand where you're coming from or make a request for change or to do something differently, how you say it makes a big difference. If you come on strong, even if you're not nasty but merely overly persuasive, the other person will resist being influenced by you.

> *One zinger will erase twenty acts of kindness,* according to researchers Cliff Notarius and Howard Markman.[8]

Inhibit nasty outbursts. So often, after the explosion of discovery, people react by using words as weapons. It is tempting to attack with anger when you are actually afraid and to become insulting when you are hurt or jealous. Staying conscious of your goal to increase safety and goodwill will enable you to exercise some self-control. Popular ideas to the contrary, it is not helpful to "let it all hang out." Too many unmonitored emotional outbursts get in the way of future healing.

Inhibit negative cycling. One of the things that characterize distressed couples is tit-for-tat negativity. This happens when partners feed off each other's words or facial and body expressions until the negativity escalates to a high pitch. You can avoid this negative cycling by refusing to add more fuel to the fire. Don't allow yourself to be triggered by your partner. The best defense is *not* a good offense. When you come to an impasse over some point, table it, take time out, and make an appointment to talk about it later. When you get back together, you can resume the discussion in a more cooperative frame of mind.

You can disagree without being disagreeable. It's natural to disagree, but for your own good you have to hear what your partner is saying. Get to the bottom of the issue that is being discussed. When partners can hear each other and accept each other's point of view (regardless of whether they agree with it), they are making progress. One way to be sure you are getting the point is to acknowledge each other's statements. This usually decreases contentiousness because people tend to soften when they feel they are being heard and understood. A partner who believes you heard the main point is more likely to listen to *your* point of view.

Inhibit rehashing. Don't get into conflicts about conversations that occurred in the past. Couples get hung up on what they did or didn't say last week, and they become furious about their clash of memories. Just let it go, and say, "Okay, let's start fresh. What is your position on this issue *right now?*" After you state your present positions, check it out with your partner that you heard each other accurately this time. If you can't discuss some topics safely, you can come up with a shared list of forbidden topics that you agree not to bring up until safety and goodwill have been reestablished in your relationship.

Inhibit interrupting, contradicting, and confronting discrepancies. Wait for each other to finish before speaking. It takes remarkable restraint to hold back when your partner says something that seems inappropriate or downright dishonest. You might be inclined to stop unwarranted attacks by rushing in to defend yourself, or to stop what you perceive as unmitigated lies, but your partner won't hear your point of view while he or she is still talking. Wait until your partner is completely finished and then state your perspective as calmly as possible.

Inhibit analyzing, mind reading, and editorializing. You will not get any relationship awards for your brilliance at analyzing your partner's motives. In fact, you will probably achieve high honors in the resentment category. Very few people are warmed by the notion that a partner knows their intentions better than they do themselves.

Tool 2: Play Ping-Pong

Too many conversations sound like people at board meetings who remain silent without listening until it is their turn at the mike. Because these ego-driven individuals are interested only in *serving* the ball, they rarely acknowledge others' comments. People who enjoy talking to each other have a rhythm of going back and forth like a good game of Ping-Pong.

Don't hold the ball. Break your message down into short chunks so that the other person can absorb and respond to it. If you hold onto the conversational ball too long, your partner is likely to glaze over and drop out of the game.

Take turns. Dialogues are much more productive than monologues. Only on debating teams does each person make a long speech and then listen quietly for the rebuttal. You are striving for real communication, not a debate where one of you scores points off the other.

Practice alternating between being the speaker and being the listener. As the listener, listen attentively and let your body language signal your receptivity. Don't interrupt. When the speaker is finished, acknowledge what you've heard and then respond with your own perspective.

Research-based communication skills training programs suggest using a square piece of vinyl tile to represent "the floor." Participants in speaker-listener exercises pass "the floor" back and forth as a reminder of whose turn it is to be the speaker.[9]

Tool 3: Use "I" Messages as the Speaker

I have observed that many individuals use "I" and "you" in exact opposition to the techniques that foster compassionate communication. When they are in the role of speaker, instead of saying, "*I* am hurt that . . ." they say, "*You* never think about me." When they are in the role of listener, instead of saying, "So what *you* think about that is . . ." they respond with, "*I* think that . . ."

Focus on expressing your own feelings. First go inside yourself and figure out what you are thinking and feeling. Express yourself directly without emoting, blaming, or interpreting. When you stick to how you feel, your partner cannot argue with you or become defensive. For example, "I get so scared and anxious every time we get a hang-up phone call."

Focus on positive aspects in your requests for change. The basic template is this: When you do A *(this undesirable thing)*, I feel B *(some negative feeling)*. When you do C *(the thing I desire)*, I feel D *(some positive feeling)*. The goal of this kind of communication is for the speaker to express wishes in the manner that will have the greatest likelihood of influencing the other person without creating a defensive response.

Jessica was in the car talking to her husband, John, on the cell phone. He said he would be home from the office at 6:00 and would set the table and make the salad for dinner. She got home at 6:40, but he wasn't home yet. When he opened the front door at 7:00, she said, "When you told me you were going to get home before me and make the salad, I felt happy.

When I came home and saw you hadn't done it, I was disappointed." This was instead of saying: "You never get home when you say you're going to" or "I should have known better than to think you'd keep your word."

> John Gottman found that in loving couples, wives broached touchy subjects with "softened startups," and husbands showed respect by accepting the influence of their wives.[10]

Tool 4: Be a Good Listener

Women often complain that their male partners are poor communicators. Injured partners similarly complain that the involved partners don't communicate with them about their feelings or about the infidelity. What they usually mean is that their partners don't talk enough. The complaining partners think that they themselves are good communicators because they have a lot to say. However, communication is not a two-way street in which you talk and then I talk. If we just talk and talk, nobody is listening. Without listening, there is no real communication.

Communication is a four-way street, in which messages are not only sent, but received: you send → I acknowledge receipt of your message → I send → you acknowledge receipt of my message. The best way to encourage your partner to talk more is for you to listen more and talk less.

Each of you can demonstrate with nonverbal behaviors that you are listening. Maintain eye contact and nod your head if you resonate with what is being said, or engage in back-channeling utterances like "Uh-huh," which means *I hear you.* You will both gain confidence that your partner is willing to participate in the process of healing the rift.

Acknowledge what you hear. The heart of active listening is to acknowledge that you heard not only your partner's words but also his or her inner voice. You can demonstrate active listening on three different verbal levels:[11]

1. *Reflecting* is the foundation of active listening. A reflecting response is a mirror that acknowledges what you just heard, like a

sounding board that echoes the transmission. For example, "So, what you're saying is that it makes you very anxious when we get hang-up calls."

2. *Validating* is the next level of active listening. When you validate your partner, you substantiate the validity of what he or she is saying. For example, "You're right. We have been receiving a lot of hang-up calls lately, and it could be [the affair partner] trying to contact me."

3. *Empathizing* is the deepest level of listening. You exhibit empathy for your partner when you show that you understand the underlying emotions behind the message. For example, "You must feel a wave of panic when we get one of those hang-up calls because it might look to you like my affair isn't really over."

Provide support without problem solving. Put your fix-it remedies in storage until your partner actually asks you directly, "What do you think I should do about this?" Try to relate to your partner's emotions without trying to solve the problem.

Gayle told Gordon at dinner how impossible her boss had been that day. When Gordon said, "I told you that you should quit that job," Gayle thought, "Next time, I'll keep my frustrations to myself." What she really wanted was a sympathetic shoulder to cry on. Gordon learned that Gayle was more comforted when he said, "I know you had a really rough day today. I understand how upsetting it is to have a boss who is such a jerk."

Provide support without empty reassurances. It may be counterintuitive, but validating your partner's worst fears is actually helpful. You may be afraid that by validating the negative, you will intensify your partner's negativity. Many people believe that acknowledging the reality of their loved one's fears will only make things worse. But minimizing feelings will make your partner feel all alone, and the burden will seem even heavier. As strange as it may seem, taking your partner's concerns seriously is not only validating but actually relieves some of the emotional distress.

It is difficult to listen to a partner's pain in any case, but this is particularly true if you are the cause of the injury. A natural response is to offer reassurances, such as "Don't think about it. It's going to work out fine."

However, reassurance does not feel like support. *Reassurance feels like cheerleading in the middle of a funeral.*

Instead of saying "Time heals all wounds," you can comfort each other by acknowledging "Of course you're upset. Anyone would be upset."

Compassionate Communication Do's and Don'ts

DON'T SAY	DO SAY
You had time for an affair, but you don't have time to help me with the kids.	I realize that you are under a lot of pressure at work. That's why it means so much to me when you are able to help out with the kids.
What did you do all day that you didn't have time to call the plumber?	I know that you had a busy day, but I was hoping you'd call the plumber. I'm worried that the septic system might back up.
All you seem interested in is having intercourse. You never seem interested in foreplay.	Do you have any idea how turned on I get when you kiss my face and my neck?
Why can't you seem to make time for us to go away together? You must not want to be alone with me.	I feel disappointed that you're too busy for us to go away together. I'd feel so excited and hopeful if we had a trip to look forward to.
You pushed me into somebody else's arms because you didn't give me enough attention.	I was feeling lonely so I was vulnerable to attention from somebody else.
You shouldn't make such a big deal out of my little fling. You're only pushing me away with your superdramatics.	I feel so uncomfortable when you get so emotional that I feel like running away. I never realized how much this would hurt you because it didn't mean that much to me at the time.
I bet you didn't talk nasty to your boyfriend.	I get really hurt when you are sarcastic to me because I picture you speaking sweetly to your boyfriend.

Creating an Empathic Process

One of the best predictors of how successful a couple is going to be in saving their marriage after infidelity is how much empathy they have for each other. More important than the actual problems that exist in the marriage is whether each person can walk for a while in the other's shoes. Can the involved partner feel what the betrayed spouse is going through and understand the humiliation, the anger, and the need to go over and over what has happened in the past? Can the betrayed partner feel the loss and the guilt that the unfaithful spouse is living through?

Here's a concluding example of how both partners shifted into an empathic process after a false start. An unfaithful wife was scheduled to go to her company picnic, where her former affair partner was going to be present. Spouses were not invited.

Husband: I don't want you going to the office picnic because he'll be there.
Wife: I have to go. Politically, it's not good for me if I don't go.

This first interchange wasn't nearly as productive as the one that took place later that day. At that point, they delved deeper into the risks involved *to them as a couple* of either going or not going. Notice that this time, they approach it as a joint problem that they are trying to solve together.

Wife: What would it be like for you if I went to the office picnic?
Husband: It makes me uncomfortable.
Wife: Is there any way I could make it easier for you?
Husband: What are the consequences if you don't go? Is there anything we could do for damage control?

This couple shifted from playing singles and being on opposite sides of the tennis net to a doubles game where the fallout from the affair was tackled together. Every little step you take toward each other counts. Little investments that you make now can lead to big dividends. Find the place inside your relationship where you are still connected by caring and affection. Expand that spot until it grows larger. Know that there is reason to hope. The communication skills you learn and practice now will always serve you well. Exploring the meaning of the affair can be accomplished only in an atmosphere of caring, commitment, and compassionate communication. Of course, there will be setbacks, ups and downs. They are part of the normal process of recovery.

So far, we have worked on feeling the feelings, establishing safety, and coping with traumatic reactions. Now it is time to construct a story about who each of you is and what has happened in your marriage and in the affair. From the stories in Part III, you will come to understand why the affair happened and what you can do to rebuild a strong and happy marriage that will be less vulnerable in the future.

PART III

The Search for Meaning

A vital part of trauma recovery is telling the story of what happened. The only way for anyone to comprehend what seems an incomprehensible event is through the search for meaning. After any personal loss or unimaginable catastrophe, we need to piece together what happened and talk about our experience. Rescue workers receive debriefing, bereaved family members join support groups, and trauma victims create a narrative of their experience. Expressing the emotions and telling the story is the best pathway to healing. This applies to the trauma of an affair, too. If you don't know the story of the affair, you may recover but you will not heal—the wounds will always be there.

When you're telling the story of the affair, how you talk together is even more important than what you say. The story of the affair is not just about what happened in the affair itself. The story must include the context in which the affair occurred. This part of the book will help you explore infidelity from different perspectives. The story of the marriage will provide a framework to understand whether relationship vulnerabilities set the stage for an affair. The unfaithful partner must be understood through his or her personal history, attitudes, and unmet needs. Looking at outside influences is also an essential part of the story since infidelity flourishes in an environment of social approval. Understanding the dynamics of the unmarried affair partner will be helpful for all three people affected by the extramarital triangle.

In the process of exploring each of these perspectives, the couple discovers what created vulnerability to an affair in the first place. Four Vulnerability Maps (Individual, Relationship, Social, and Single Woman) in each relevant chapter will help you to assess your susceptibility to becoming involved in an extramarital triangle. Vulnerabilities must be understood before a couple can weave their stories into a meaningful narrative that accounts for what led to the affair, what sustained it, and how it was resolved.

8

THE STORY OF THE AFFAIR

Everybody, including our therapist, tells me I'm crazy
to keep on digging for details.
I only know that I can't rest until I know the whole story.

THE BETRAYED partner's drive to hear about the inner life of the affair is more than just a desire to satisfy curiosity or uncover more lies. Knowing the true story behind a trauma is the only way the victim can stop obsessing and begin to heal.[1] Betrayed partners need to discuss what they had been feeling, what they suspected, and what they already know. Then they need to fill in all of the missing pieces.

Because affairs are secret, betrayed partners can't resolve their grief over their loss of innocence until they know *what really happened.* Unfaithful partners who lie about the details cause more harm than good because the only way to restore a betrayed partner's sanity is to be honest about what has, up to now, been concealed.

The burning question for betrayed partners is: "How do I know you won't betray me again?" They can answer this only by knowing what led to the infidelity and what kept it going. In the first stage of discovery, unfaithful partners either lied or were brutally honest, and betrayed partners were both fragile and attacking. But discussing the affair now that goodwill has been established will help put it to rest for both partners. The final story of the affair should be co-constructed by both partners to account for all of the secrets, unanswered questions, and contrasting interpretations and attributions.

Although involved partners might resist sharing the story of the affair, it's important to realize that anything that is good for the relationship will ultimately be good for them personally. Also, involved partners need to tell the story for their *own* recovery: to understand how and why they crossed the line into an affair. Letting the secrets out of the bag helps them detach from the affair partner and dissolve the romantic fantasy.

Why It's Important to Tell

I'm convinced that it is crucial to tell the story of the affair. My conviction is based on my own clinical experience with couples as well as the experience of trauma therapists and other infidelity researchers. But not all therapists agree with me. Many of them believe, right along with their unfaithful clients, that the less said about the affair, the better. To complicate matters, well-intentioned friends and family members usually advise "Be quiet. Talking about it just makes it worse."

> Of the 465 therapists in my survey, 41 percent believe that "a spouse's desire to know details of the partner's extramarital involvement should be discouraged by the therapist."

Yet betrayed partners themselves verify that knowing the details is beneficial. Peggy Vaughan's on-line survey of 1,083 betrayed partners found that couples who thoroughly discussed the affair were more likely to stay married. Open discussion and honest communication led to restored trust and an improved relationship that was even better than before the affair.[2]

> In Vaughn's survey: (1) when the unfaithful spouse answered all questions, 86 percent of couples remained married and 72 percent rebuilt trust; (2) when the unfaithful spouse refused to answer questions, 59 percent remained married and 31 percent rebuilt trust.

Research by Jennifer Schneider and her colleagues found that honesty is crucial for both sex addicts and their spouses.[3] Nearly every betrayed wife of a male sex addict felt that she should be the one to decide how much to be told. Most did not ask for information they were not ready to hear.[4]

Telling the Truth Rebuilds Trust

To cleanse the lying that occurred during the affair and in the early stages of revelation, the involved partner needs to be totally honest. Only information offered freely can clear the air.

Fill in the Missing Pieces

Telling the story of the affair replaces a fictionalized account with the truth. It is totally shattering and disorienting to find out that intrigue and deceptiveness were going on while you were assuming everything was normal. That's why both partners need to get out their calendars, discuss the receipts, and review the cell phone calls. Things won't make sense to the betrayed partner until all the missing pieces are accounted for.

After Rachel discovered Ralph's affair, she needed to make sense of the time before she was aware of his involvement with Lara. She zealously scrutinized the calendar as a key to what had really happened. She had many questions she still wanted Ralph to answer:

- When we had such great sex at the beach, were you still turned on from being with Lara the day before?
- When you surprised me with our club membership, was that to throw me off the track because you wanted to get in shape for her?
- When you couldn't come with me to visit my sick aunt, was that because you thought you could take advantage of my time away to be with her?
- When you bought me that expensive watch for my birthday, was it out of love or guilt?

Sometimes, the betrayed partner's inability to let go of obsessive thoughts points to missing pieces. Cliff remained uneasy about his wife's recounting of her infidelity, even after Cheryl had told him a credible story about a brief fling with an acquaintance that was now over and done with. She answered every question put to her, was empathic about his pain, and dedicated herself to being a better wife. And still . . . Cliff realized he wouldn't let go because there was something about her story that didn't sound right. He couldn't accept her version of events and had to find out the truth.

After a night of tossing and turning, Cliff woke Cheryl up and told her he wasn't satisfied that she was telling him everything. He told her they were not going back to sleep until he got the full story. Finally, Cheryl confessed that she hadn't had sex "a couple of times," as she at first claimed, but had had a two-year affair. Cliff's relief that he finally had the truth was greater than his distress at the seriousness of his wife's involvement.

Clear Up Misperceptions
Unlike Cliff, whose intuition about greater involvement was confirmed, Melissa learned that her husband's infidelity was not nearly as deep as she had feared.

Melissa inadvertently discovered that Morty had a one-night stand while he was away on a business trip. When she called his hotel room at 7:00 A.M., a woman answered and said that Morty was in the shower. Upon Morty's return home, Melissa was very upset and said she couldn't rest until she had "all the details." Fortunately, Morty was eager to repair the damage and was willing to answer her questions honestly.

In the abbreviated transcript that follows, their therapist provided a safe place for Melissa to ask her questions without blame or accusations on her part and without defensiveness or stonewalling on his:

Melissa: So, you met her in the hotel bar . . . What did she do to arouse your interest and turn you on?
Morty: She flattered me. She said appealing things about my looks. She wasn't looking for a long-term thing. She made it clear she was sexually attracted to me and was feeling horny.
Melissa: How did you feel?
Morty: Excited. Intrigued, not aroused.
Melissa: Did she have a great body?
Morty: Not bad.
Melissa: Did she have big breasts?
Morty: Average.

Melissa: Bigger than mine?

Morty: A little bit bigger, but kind of saggy.

Melissa: What happened when you got into your room?

Morty: When I came out of the bathroom after five minutes, she was in bed. I thought, "Holy mackerel, this is really going to happen." . . . She tried to kiss me on the mouth, but I gave her my cheek. I was physically excited, but mentally mad at myself. . . . It went very fast. It was over very quickly.

Melissa: Did you talk to her at all?

Morty: From the bathroom . . . just general bullshit. Once I walked out, nothing.

Melissa: No other talking, during or after?

Morty: After we started, I wanted it over as quickly as possible. After ten minutes it was awful. I couldn't wait to get out of the room. I regretted it very badly. . . . I rolled over. I had to get some sleep. I got up at 5:30, showered and dressed in the bathroom. At 6:30 I left and told her to have a good trip home.

Melissa: Sounds like she got to you through flattery.

Morty: Yes, but I ended up losing my own self-respect. I responded to her wanting me. My guilt is so great. I'll never do it again. I feel like a real piece of dirt. It's a huge betrayal of trust.

As painful as these details were, they satisfied Melissa's need to know what had happened that night. She could feel her husband's basic loyalty to the marriage, and she could hear how much he regretted his behavior. It turned out that the truth wasn't so awful because he wasn't emotionally attached and the sex wasn't as good as she had imagined.

Expose the Modus Operandi

Willingness to expose the *modus operandi* (way of operating) of the affair goes a long way toward reestablishing the credibility of involved partners. They need to reveal what the cover-ups were and how they managed to find the time and place for a liaison. Exposing the secret maneuverings limits the possibility that the affair will continue and gives the betrayed spouse the inside scoop.

Cliff insisted on knowing how Cheryl had carried out her deception. She reluctantly told him how her best friend, Sandy, had provided her house for Cheryl's lunchtime trysts. Sandy had also covered up for Cheryl when Cliff called to find out where Cheryl was. Cliff was greatly relieved by this information. He regarded it as evidence that Cheryl's affair was over because she had revealed the time, place, and accomplice. Cheryl was upset when Cliff insisted that she end her friendship with Sandy, but she understood how betrayed he felt by Sandy's complicity in the affair. The tension between them was greatly diminished when Cheryl severed her connection to Sandy in order to rebuild trust with Cliff.

Telling Releases the Secret Ties That Bind

Forbidden fruit is exotic and exciting. As long as the affair is kept in a glass bubble and worshipped as a sacred happening, the romantic attachment to the affair partner is more apt to persist. Talking about the affair in some detail takes it out of that bubble and exposes it to the cool light of realistic scrutiny. It loses its magical power.

In *The Bridges of Madison County* Francesca spends four days with the handsome stranger, Robert Kincaid, and the rest of her life savoring the memory.[5] She doesn't leave with the wandering photographer, not only because of her sense of responsibility to her husband and children, but because she's aware that the untouched fantasy is better than any real-life relationship could ever be. She tells her secret lover, "I want to keep it forever. If we leave we lose it. I want to hold onto it the rest of my life."

From then on, each year on the same day, she secretly takes out a manila envelope with cherished photographs and clippings. Her husband, Richard, is aware that there is something inside her he can't reach. Just before Richard dies he tells her, "Francesca, I know you had your own dreams, too. I'm sorry I couldn't give them to you." She regards his dying words as the most touching moment of their whole life together. His honesty and clear vision pierces the barrier that her fantasy life had built.

Keeping a secret is an act of *thought suppression*. Some fascinating research by Daniel Wegner and his colleagues on thought suppression illustrates the power and allure of past relationships that remain secret.[6] People who hide old romances remain obsessed with them. Keeping the relationship secret intensifies arousal and makes the partner appear more attractive and exciting than he or she would otherwise have been. Secret relationships are overvalued because thought suppression creates an irrational perspective.

Debbie Layton-Tholl found that unfaithful partners experience greater arousal and preoccupation with their lovers after ending an affair if they never disclose the affair to their spouses. Once an affair is disclosed, the freedom to discuss the relationship diminishes the obsessive thoughts and feelings of excitement connected with the affair partner.[7]

> Among the 1,200 unfaithful spouses in Layton-Tholl's on-line survey, those who had multiple affairs were less likely to report increased arousal, obsessive preoccupation with the lover, or difficulty holding the secret than people having only one affair.[8]

Telling Increases Marital Intimacy

Keeping secrets erects barriers. Whenever you're trying not to spill the beans, you are inhibiting your own natural impulses with internal warnings: Be careful! Don't tell! Don't show! Instead of being free and authentic, you become artful, subtly crafting your verbal responses to influence your partner's impressions and reactions. It's hard to be truly close to someone when you're hiding something of significance from him or her.

Stan had a child with his lover. He and his wife, Stella, offered financial support far beyond the legal requirements because they both felt it was the right thing to do. Even so, Stan and Stella had discussed only the superficial facts of his affair. When Stella worked up the courage to ask questions after many months had elapsed, the answers filled her with great despair. She said, "Of course, I knew you had an affair. After all, you got her pregnant. But I never really pictured you actually having sex with her. It wasn't a reality for me until now." Although she was very upset, what happened next was that Stan and Stella made love for the first time in over a year. Their silence about the affair had created a wall that their open discussion finally tore down.

If the involved spouse protects the identity of the lover or the nature of the relationship, then the betrayed spouse is the outsider in an extramarital triangle. Sharing the details is an act of positive demolition. The involved spouse dismantles the structure that kept the injured spouse outside in the cold and replaces deceit with hope.

After Drew permanently ended his lengthy Internet affair, he was very happy and relieved about his decision. However, his firm refusal to disclose the real name or screen name of his e-lover confirmed to Debbie that he was protecting his affair partner instead of being totally loyal to his wife. Debbie couldn't stop obsessing about it, so she threatened to leave if he didn't tell her the identity of the mystery woman who had virtually torn them apart. Drew reluctantly revealed it under great duress because he didn't want to lose his wife. Debbie then felt free to invest in the marriage without further reservations because the boundaries and loyalties were now clear.

How to Tell

How couples talk together about the infidelity is even more important than *what* they talk about. A constructive process creates hope and healing, whereas a destructive one creates hopelessness and despair. You will need to draw on all of the compassionate communication skills you learned in Chapter 7. Your goal is to shift from an adversarial process to an empathic process for discussing the story of the affair.

Pitfalls to Avoid

Avoid getting locked into escalating power struggles. In a pressurized atmosphere, the more the betrayed partner pushes for information, the more the involved partner pulls away. The more the involved partner retreats into a corner, the more the betrayed partner applies coercive tactics to open up. Both play a significant part in creating a constructive interaction for sharing thoughts, feelings, and memories.

For Betrayed Partners

If you are a betrayed partner who wants to get your spouse to open up and tell you what you want to know, there are specific things you can do to avoid gridlock.

- *Control destructive outbursts:* If you go ballistic every time your partner shares, you are teaching him or her that it's better not to share. If you want openness and honesty, you must show that telling the truth will make things better—not worse, as feared. For example, you can say something like: "I'm glad you told me. Hearing it made me cry, but I want you to know that the truth is helping me to heal." Painful experiences can create intimacy, but explosive reactions build their own walls. Who wants to get close to a volcano?

One unfaithful wife wrote to me: "When I answer my husband's questions truthfully, sometimes he lashes out: 'You whore! You're lower than a sleazy slime!' He tells me I'm not allowed to get angry when he says those things because then he just gets more upset. . . . I'm willing to go through this verbal barrage if it's valuable for my husband. He says everything he has read says these reactions are normal and healthy for betrayed spouses; that he has to get them out in order to heal. When do things go 'too far?' "

I told her that her husband is *not* reacting in a healthy way. He is being emotionally abusive. He will never learn the true story of the entire affair—why it happened—unless their interaction evolves beyond bitter name-calling. Although it is normal for the hurt partner to be angry, this husband will have to develop some empathy and self-control. If he doesn't, his wife will have little incentive to do the hard work of healing the relationship.

- *Silence is golden:* You will learn more if you close your mouth and open your ears. Don't interrupt or contradict. When your partner starts to open up, pretend you are sitting behind a one-way mirror where you can see and hear but cannot be seen or heard. When your partner's story triggers a question or a retort, write down your comments for later. If you step in too quickly and pull your partner off track, you'll never know what else you would have heard.

- *Curtail your interpretations:* Diagnosing your partner's problems is not relationship-enhancing, even if you happen to be a licensed psychotherapist. For example: "The reason you got involved was that you never got enough love from your father." This feels intrusive to the partner who is being analyzed. You want to convey: "I'm trying to understand what you were feeling." Unsolicited interpretations might make *you* feel good, but I'll bet that your partner won't feel better as a result.

For Involved Partners

Involved partners tend to shut down or become defensive when injured partners want to discuss the infidelity. If you are the involved partner, you may not want to talk about the infidelity or even think about it. I realize that it can be humiliating to discuss actions that you now regard as wrong. It may be painful to expose events that could create hurt or rage, and it may be difficult to recall memories of a secret world that was shared with someone other than your spouse. But if you respond in any of the following ways, you are demonstrating limited commitment to rebuilding your marriage.

- *Avoidance:* You may resist getting into the deep waters of the affair to avoid dealing with painful subjects. Perhaps your usual pattern is to avoid anything that creates conflict. If that's the case, you can use this crisis to become more assertive by telling the whole story and facing up to your partner's negative reactions.

- *Denial:* Denying the basic facts concerning the affair will perpetuate mistrust. You are heading for divorce court if you acknowledge only details that are the indisputable bits of evidence dug up by your betrayed partner.

- *Stonewalling:* Retreating and refusing to talk may be your usual way of avoiding discomfort or conflict. If, however, this is not your normal pattern and you are withdrawing now because you feel attacked every time you attempt to share, let your partner know. Tell your partner that the tongue lashings are teaching you to hold your tongue.

- *Discounting:* Refusing to accept the seriousness of the problem is a way to deny responsibility. Using the words "yes, but" may indicate the absence of genuine remorse. Admitting your wrongful acts doesn't make you a bad person; admitting the hurts you have inflicted makes you a better partner.

You can overcome your resistance and hang in there until you have shared the full story of your affair. It's natural to be frustrated, but the reality is that your partner cannot relax until you have overturned every stone. Persistent unwillingness to discuss or deal with problems that stem from the infidelity will inflame wounds, intensify distrust, and increase the probability of divorce.

Although addressing the same questions over and over again is irritating, each time gives you an opportunity to shed more light on the topic. It's not helpful to say "It's been three months; when are you going to get over it?" It is helpful to show empathy by saying something like "If you had done this to *me*, I'd be even more of a basket case than you are."

The Three Stages of Disclosure

The way couples interact when they talk about the affair changes over time. At first, they confront each other in an adversarial truth-seeking inquisition. Then they engage in a more benign process of neutral information seeking. Finally, they cooperate together in a healing exploration characterized by an empathic search for deeper understanding. Obviously, this last stage is the ultimate goal. Some couples evolve along this pattern naturally; others have to work harder at it.

Not everyone proceeds through all three stages of disclosure. Some couples remain mired in a destructive truth-seeking process, and others never get beyond a neutral information-seeking process. Even couples who reach the stage of empathic sharing will occasionally backslide into an earlier stage, especially when they can't agree on what constitutes the truth.

Stage 1: Truth Seeking
During truth seeking, the dialogue sounds like an NYPD interrogation of a criminal who is withholding incriminating evidence. The betrayed partner launches the inquisition by setting truth traps, and the unfaithful partner covers up until cornered with undeniable proof of wrongdoing. This adversarial process is never a recommended way to get at the truth.

When Kris first confronted Ken about his affair, she turned on the heat while he tried to wiggle his way out of answering her questions. As you read the following dialogue, you can see Kris firing these questions at her husband without giving him a chance to catch his breath:

> *Kris:* Did you go to Boston alone in January?
> *Ken:* Of course I did. Why are you so insecure?
> *Kris:* Did you eat dinner out with anyone?

Ken: Look, I was on a business trip. I didn't know anybody there except the people I do business with, and I ate dinner alone.

Kris: Then why did your check from the hotel restaurant indicate that two people were at the table?

Ken: It's probably a clerical mistake. You know how hard it is to get good help these days.

Kris: You ordered gin and tonic and a pink zinfandel. You don't drink pink zinfandel. That's a woman's drink.

Ken: How did you get the sales check? I really resent you snooping around when I haven't done anything wrong.

Kris: You've been acting very suspicious lately, and I needed to find out for myself. I hired a detective in Boston, and the detective said that you got into a cab at the airport with a tall brunette.

Ken: That's ridiculous. It wasn't me.

Kris: Then it must be your twin. I have pictures to prove it.

Ken: Oh yeah. Now I remember. There was this woman going into the city, and I offered to share my cab with her.

And so forth and so on. When both partners are hostile and feel alienated, it's impossible for any honesty or healing to come out of such a destructive process. The goal is to move forward into a collaborative process of sharing information and move away from the act of detecting lies. The story of the affair can't unfold in such an environment of mutual mistrust.

Stage 2: Information Seeking
Before you can know the meaning of the affair, you have to gather some data. What counts most is *how* you do it. The best way is to engage in a neutral process of information seeking, as if you were a reporter covering a story. In this way you and your partner might sound like an interview on the *Larry King Show:* professional and cordial, but not especially close.

Betrayed partners can get out the exhaustive list of questions they've been collecting. As more of the truth is revealed, you need to be prepared for earlier lies to be unearthed. It is likely that your involved partner will say things that differ from what he or she said before. Before embarking on this exploration, you need to assure your partner that you will not use any new information as a weapon. If you do, you put the whole disclosure process at risk.

If you are the betrayed partner, don't use the new details to point out old lies. Instead of dwelling on how much you were deceived during the affair, show appreciation that your partner is being honest at last. Think how hard it must be for your partner to face you and admit all of the deceptive words and actions. You might feel better if you accept that the lies and cover-ups were a frantic attempt to keep you from discovering the truth and leaving the relationship.

If you're the involved partner, try your utmost to discuss matters that you'd prefer to keep in a locked box, either because you cherish the memories or because you feel ashamed. Don't muddle your brain by inventing new lies that you will have to keep track of. There is very little you can say that your partner hasn't imagined or already proven. If your partner's initial reaction is despair, disgust, or anger, see whether the days that follow show less obsessiveness and more healing. If you're worried about how your answers affect your partner, ask him or her *"How is this information going to help you to heal?"* Then, answer truthfully.

Using the *fishbowl technique* I developed, Opal and Oscar were able to create a neutral process for information gathering after many months of resistance. The fishbowl allows betrayed partners to present all their questions in a nonthreatening way, and it allows unfaithful partners to choose the time and sequence for answering specific questions.

Opal's obsession with Oscar's infidelity was fueled by his repeated promises, denials, and continued deception over a four-year period. The only truthful information she got was through her own detective work. When his affair finally ended, he was reluctant to discuss any details in his desire to forget the past and start over. But Opal had seven pages of questions she wanted answered. Some of the questions were traps to test his honesty; some were complex questions of intent and meaning; and some were looking for specific facts and details.

Opal placed each question on a separate piece of paper inside a clear glass bowl. When Oscar was in the mood to answer a question he would go to the fishbowl on his own and pull out questions until he found one that he could answer without too much discomfort. Opal tried to accept his answers without a challenge and told him how helpful the information was to her. One weekend, they went to a hotel where they had all their food brought in by room service. They stayed until they had gone through every single question in the fishbowl. This was a giant step toward bonding and building a trusting relationship after years of dishonesty and betrayal.

After you clarify the factual details and form a joint account of the traumatic events, you're ready to discuss the story of the affair with an empathic process that creates a shared meaning.

Stage 3: Mutual Understanding

In Stage 3 you focus on understanding what the affair means to both of you. The dialogue you engage in sounds like two people who love and care about each other working together to understand the beginning, middle, and ending of the affair. You're reaching consensus about what happened in the past and optimism about your future capacity to cope.

Conversations become introspective, respectful, sensitive, and free-flowing with information. They contrast sharply with earlier interactions that were glib, slippery, or hostile. You will be able to see through each other's eyes and sense each other's feelings. It hurts, but you want to understand. The betrayed partner might say, "I know it will take time to get over the loss of the friendship you had with [the affair partner]." The unfaithful partner might say, "I understand that it will take a long time before you will be able to trust me again because of the lies I told you."

Ironically, it's not uncommon for some couples to experience a honeymoon period as they share their deepest and most intense feelings with each other. They may lie in bed at night holding each other while talking about the affair. Couples who get to this level of intimacy have a rare opportunity to know each other in a deep way that unblemished couples may never have the opportunity to realize.

From Stage to Stage

The following story illustrates how one couple went through all three stages of disclosure after the wife's discovery of her husband's emotional infidelity. Their discussions gradually evolved from an adversarial process into an empathic process with shared meaning.

Revelation: At the company Christmas party, Georgia accidentally overheard George being teased about his daily coffee breaks with a young female employee. Georgia's rage was directed at the secrecy of the liaisons and the realization that she had been deceived for several years about his private little tête-à-têtes. She had assumed that she and George were completely open and shared everything. Although she believed George's protestations that he did not love the other woman and had not been sexually involved with her, Georgia was prepared to end a thirty-two-year marriage that had been close and sexually satisfying because she felt so deeply betrayed.

Truth seeking: At first, Georgia threw angry questions at George in rat-a-tat-tat punishing barrages. George's initial response was to clam up, except to say over and over, "It was completely innocent; she's *just a friend.*" He told Georgia to stop being hysterical over nothing.

Information seeking: As Georgia softened and began to ask for information without interrupting or being sarcastic, George began to answer her questions. Yes, there was some sexual innuendo, but no touching. Yes, there was some shared personal information about his medical problems and difficulties with his supervisor at work, but he never talked about Georgia or their marriage. Yes, he was flattered by her attention, but he never considered having a relationship outside of work. And yes, he knew he was doing something wrong by keeping it a secret all these years.

Mutual understanding: Eventually, after several months, Georgia believed that her husband had told her all there was to tell about this relationship. Knowing the details, she began to put herself in his place. She could feel the pleasure he must have felt in having this break in the day to look forward to. She began to understand this "friendship" in the context of his worries about pressures at work and his deteriorating health. He understood how his lies of omission had shattered her trust. Although Georgia never forgot his betrayal, she let go of her anger because she understood how it had happened.

Believe it or not, over time, as pain diminishes, couples may be able to tease each other with private little jokes about the affair partner and something that happened during the affair. By the following year, they were making jokes about George and his fondness for coffee.

What to Tell

The betrayed spouse's need to know is the determining factor for how much detail and discussion is necessary. Some want to know everything; some seek only basic facts. Each couple must figure out what details to share by following their own unique path. You will learn through trial and error what is healing and what adds more scar tissue. Information that quells the obsessive need to know is healing, but information that seems to fuel obsessiveness is retraumatizing and should be avoided. For most people, pressing to hear about graphic sexual details or to see love letters is a mistake because the vivid images can become intrusive and interfere with intimacy. The desire to know often recedes as the relationship becomes more comforting.

If you are the betrayed spouse, ask yourself whether you can heal without seeing or hearing things that would be upsetting. If you are unsure of the consequences of knowing, ask your partner to discuss one sensitive issue. Notice if the answer makes you feel worse about your spouse or yourself, or if the information helps satisfy your hunger to know it all. Pay attention to whether you feel better a day later or whether the details are haunting you. If they are haunting you *but* you also feel better, then there is a part of you that is healing. Let your partner know so he or she can see the part that's healing as well as the part that's hurting.

For some individuals, an obsessive need to know the details is characteristic of their innate coping strategies. These are the people who get on the Internet and know more about a disease than their doctors do. These are the people who do six months of research before buying a camera. There is no way in the world that such people can let go of their partner's infidelity until they have heard it all.

Reconciling Different Perspectives and Mistaken Beliefs

Betrayed partners have trouble accepting stories that differ from what they believe to be true. Their reality can come from authenticated facts that they have ferreted out on their own or from erroneous perceptions. I've never heard a betrayed partner's version at the outset that wasn't based on projections, anger, and misperceptions. Infidelity researchers Kristi Gordon and Donald Baucom assert that initial inaccurate explanations by injured partners must be balanced by information that reflects what actually did happen.[9] Because it's not unusual for unfaithful partners to confound the truth through deliberate distortions that minimize involvement, it can take months for betrayed partners to develop an accurate version.

Many of our beliefs about the behavior of others come from how we explain our own actions and feelings. As the betrayed partner, your attempts to hear and understand your partner's story is commonly sifted and filtered through your own beliefs and experiences. What you believe about the affair is distorted by projecting your own point of view onto your partner. These projections lead to *the error of assumed similarity.* When we engage in the error of assumed similarity, we assume that something has the same meaning for our partner that it has for us.

Part of the hurt and confusion of an affair is the sudden, wrenching realization that your partner does not think or feel exactly as you do. After all these years, you find that your assumption about how much alike you are is really an illusion. Ian said, "I don't understand how anyone who prays in church every Sunday could commit the sin of adultery." Ian believes that he would never violate the teachings of their church, so he can't understand how his wife, Ilene, could ever have been unfaithful.

Many errors of assumed similarity are derived from sex differences. Men and women generally have different perspectives on sex, love, and infidelity, yet they assume that their partners feel and think the same way they do. Women tend to view their husbands' affairs through the lens of love, whereas men tend to view their wives' affairs through the lens of sex.

Many a betrayed wife has said, "I don't believe you didn't love her. You must have loved her if you had sex with her." Like this wife, most women cannot understand how a "happily married man" would want sexual intercourse with another woman, whereas sexual variety appears to be a reasonable desire to men.[10]

One man who caught his wife meeting secretly with a coworker found it almost impossible to believe that she could have been emotionally involved without having sex. When she told him that they had sat in the car talking for hours, her husband rejected her explanation and insisted that this man must have appealed to her because he was able to give her multiple orgasms. Nonetheless, her affair had been emotional only.

> In my clinical sample, 83 percent of involved women and 61 percent of involved men characterized their extramarital relationship as more emotional than sexual. In the airport sample, 71 percent of involved women and 44 percent of involved men characterized their extramarital relationship as more emotional than sexual.

Early discussions about affairs will be more comfortable if men ask women first about their emotional involvement and women ask men first about their sexual involvement. Women are reluctant to reveal sexual intimacy and men are reluctant to reveal emotional attachment because each of them senses what type of involvement will be more distressing to their partner.

Questions to Answer

Questions about specific details are frequently an entryway into a deeper story. For example, questions about what gifts or cards were exchanged are really probing for how invested the unfaithful partner was in the affair—emotionally and financially. One unfaithful wife and her affair partner made cassette tapes for each other with special love songs. Although it was extremely painful for the betrayed husband to listen to the romantic words of the songs, it helped him realize why it was so hard for his wife to let go of the affair. He was also shaken by what he had neglected. Ultimately, he was inspired to bring more romance back into their marriage.

The following ten questions will guide your exploration of the circumstances of the infidelity and the meaning behind it. Some of them are typical questions posed by betrayed partners, and some of them are questions I use in my clinical practice to bring a slightly different perspective on the underlying motivations. Discussing them will give you the raw material from which to co-construct your story.

1. What did you say to yourself that gave you permission to get involved?

There are all kinds of reasons for not stepping over the line that would normally stop you from entering forbidden territory. Vulnerabilities and values will be revealed by the thoughts and actions that came up as you crossed thresholds into the extramarital relationship. Most likely, discussing these questions will uncover the magnetism of the relationship, the sense of curiosity, or the belief that nothing bad would come of it. One of the most revealing thoughts is whether the unfaithful partner considered the consequences of getting involved or only of getting caught.

For example, how did Ralph decide to go ahead with that secret lunch date he had with Lara? What was he anticipating? It's important to understand how a platonic friendship can shift into an affair. When people confide to opposite-sex friends about problems in their marriage, they are revealing a weak spot and signaling their availability at the same time. Although women share deep feelings with lots of people, particularly other women, men are usually most comfortable sharing their feelings in a love relationship. As a result, when a relationship becomes emotionally intimate, men tend to sexualize it.

Through discussions with his wife, Lisa, Les figured out how he let himself be drawn into an affair with Fiona, a new colleague at work. He recognized that it started off with his compassion for Fiona's situation. He was moved by her tale of a distressed marriage, a disabled child, and a terminally ill father who lived with her.

Les admitted that he was flattered by Fiona's idealizing him when she compared him to her insensitive husband. He pictured himself as her protector rescuing her from her troubled life. One freezing Sunday, when he got a call from Fiona asking him to drive over and give her dead battery a charge, he did share it with Lisa. Later, he and Lisa agreed that when he stopped talking about Fiona at home and started keeping his weekend phone calls secret, the friendship had shifted into an emotional affair. Sexual intimacy developed as Les became convinced that he was "in love" with Fiona, and he began to detach emotionally and sexually from the marriage.

Fiona had grown up in a working-class family without luxuries. She was thrilled when Les took her out to a simple lunch at a restaurant that had table service. In contrast, when Les and Lisa went to five-star restaurants, they took it for granted as part of their lifestyle. Les felt gratified that he could add a little joy to Fiona's troubled life.

Because Les and Lisa talked about how he felt sorry for Fiona, it became clear to both of them that he was vulnerable to rescuing maidens in distress. He vowed that in the future, he would erect distinct boundaries with unhappy, attractive women who touched his kind heart. When involved partners share their feelings on this level, they are letting their betrayed spouse inside their mind and reforging their bond. They not only are discussing what occurred, but together they are gaining insight into the underlying dynamics.

2. After the first time you had sex, did you feel guilty?

Asking about guilt reveals the internalized values of the unfaithful partner. Some people never feel any guilt about getting involved. People who anticipate guilty feelings before they act are more inclined to avoid dangerous crossings. Others feel guilty after they act, although guilt after the transgression doesn't necessarily keep them from repeating their "sin."

Some people feel so disgusted with themselves after their first extramarital sex that they get together again with the affair partner as soon as possible: another dose of the aphrodisiac offers them a temporary escape from their self-loathing. Some get rid of their guilt and continue the affair by rationalizing that nobody is getting hurt because they are "not taking anything away" from their spouse or family. Others transform guilty feelings by taking responsibility and terminating their extramarital behaviors long before they are discovered.

3. How could it go on so long if you knew it was wrong?

Affairs are both messy and glamorous. The forbidden, unstable nature of secret affairs keeps passion flowing years beyond what's common in a stable relationship. Unfaithful spouses often appear to be addicted to their lovers. They fail in their efforts to end the affair time and time again, pulled back by a magnetic force they can't seem to resist. Only with great determination are they able to break the spell.

Comprehending what started an affair is different from comprehending what kept it going. It may have started out of a shared interest or sexual attraction but continued because of a deepening emotional attachment. Or it may have started as an emotional affair and continued because the sex was so great. Or it may have started because the marriage was in a slump but continued because it assumed a life of its own long after the marriage improved.

It is as important to understand how the affair ended as it is to understand what sustained it. The ramifications of an affair that was ended by the unfaithful spouse before disclosure are very different from an affair that was ended either by the affair partner or by the ultimatums of the betrayed partner. If the affair ended abruptly, the attachment will be harder to break than if the affair died a natural death. It's easier to put a relationship behind you if you're the one who made the decision to leave.

4. Did you think about me at all?

If the unfaithful partner had been thinking about the betrayed partner, he or she wouldn't have gotten so involved in the first place. The act of infidelity is not about the person who was betrayed—it is about the person who did the betraying. Betrayed spouses often see themselves as a central character in a spouse's affair and believe that every step was taken with them in mind. "How could you do this to me?" they ask. The reality is that the involved spouse probably didn't consider his or her partner much at all. Simply put, unfaithful partners seldom anticipate the tragic consequences or the pain they inflict.

It will probably be hurtful for betrayed partners to learn that although unfaithful spouses have difficulty suppressing thoughts of their lovers at home, they are unlikely to think about their spouses while they are in their love nests. Intrusive thoughts of lovers flow from the necessity of maintaining secrets, but it takes little energy to suppress thoughts of socially sanctioned marriages.[11]

> **D**ebbie Layton-Tholl found that 87 percent of involved partners think of their lover while with their spouse, but only 47 percent ever think of their spouse while with their lover.

5. What did you share about us?

This question addresses the issues of loyalty to the marriage and the nature of emotional intimacy in the affair. The betrayed partner has an understandable interest in knowing how much of a window the affair partner had into the marriage. The betrayed partner might also want to know how he or she and the marriage were portrayed.

Some unfaithful partners give positive accounts of their marriages and glowing descriptions of their spouses, to the bewilderment and chagrin of their affair partners. Others describe their spouses as cold or distant. It's hard to know whether this is an attempt to deceive by making the marriage look bad or whether it is a misguided unburdening of real marital woes. In any case, if you are the unfaithful partner, it's important for you to talk to your spouse about real problems in the marriage that you've discussed only with your affair partner. The next chapter will help you both review the story of your marriage and address these problems together.

In the event that the marriage was shielded and the betrayed spouse was never discussed, why were these topics *not* discussed with the affair partner? Some unfaithful partners try to keep their double lives completely separate by compartmentalizing. They may delude themselves into thinking that they are honoring their marriage by shielding it from the scrutiny of the person they are cheating with.

6. Did you talk about love or about a future together?

Talking about love is likely to bring to the surface errors of assumed similarity. The betrayed partner might insist that love and marriage were part of the picture and won't believe otherwise. If the involved partner *does* confess to being in love, this admission can make sense of events in a way that rote denials never could. It would explain why the affair went on so long and why it took so long to recover from the loss.

If you are the involved partner, however, you should not fabricate a story of unrequited love just to satisfy your partner's misguided projections. Be honest about whatever romantic declarations or talk of the future did occur. Otherwise, your betrayed partner may fill in the blanks with scenarios that are far more painful than the actual truth. Admit it if you ever shared dreams of "riding off into the sunset" together or said "I love you" in the heat of passion. I have seen it backfire when betrayed partners found incriminating love letters or e-mails after involved partners denied exchanging words of love or dreams of the future.

If you are the betrayed partner, make a strong effort to hear the story without filtering it through your own subjective lens. Infidelity does occur without falling in love. You must be open to versions that vary from your belief system unless you have valid evidence that you are getting a watered-down rendition.

7. What did you see in the affair partner?

The betrayed partner will already have a portrait of the affair partner, but it is almost never the whole picture. Betrayed spouses are prone to place all the blame on the affair partner, preferring to believe that their gullible spouse was manipulated and seduced. They may not be willing to accept that the person to whom they're married took an active role, and therefore displace a lot of the anger and rage onto the affair partner. Involved partners must recount the ways they encouraged the affair and invested energy to keep it going. It is less likely that an infidelity will happen again when the involved partner owns up to having been a full participant.

Al and Amber quarreled about their divergent perceptions of his affair partner, Zelda, who worked for him. Amber regarded Zelda as "a bitch and a manipulative slut who was out to get Al's money." In reaction, Al glorified Zelda's competence and loyalty. But the more Al talked about Zelda, the more he realized that he could never have maintained a long-term relationship with her because of her mood swings. Amber, on the other hand, grew to understand that Zelda's constant praise and high energy appealed to Al. Finally, they arrived at a combined picture of Zelda as a hard-working woman with a charged personality who used flattery to get what she wanted.

Betrayed partners vacillate between glorifying the lover as an incomparable rival and disparaging him or her as a despicable human being. Questions about physical appearance, personality, and intellect are attempts to see whether they measure up to their rival in sex appeal and achievement. These questions aren't helpful, as they seldom reveal the lure of the affair partner. In fact, many betrayed partners are astounded to see affair partners looking rather ordinary. The appeal of the affair is frequently in the positive mirroring or the sounding board it provides, rather than in the lover's charisma.

8. What did you like about yourself in the affair? How were you different?

Instead of focusing on what the affair partner was like, it is more productive to focus on what the *unfaithful partner* was like in the extramarital relationship. New relationships allow people to be different: more assertive, more frivolous, or more giving. A strong attraction of affairs is the opportunity to try on new roles: the insensitive, detached husband becomes energized by his own empathy and devotion; the sexually uninterested wife is exhilarated by newfound passion and erotic fantasies. In long-term relationships, the potential to develop a different persona is constricted by familiarity. For example, a man who is a powerful CEO in a large corporation is regarded and teased in his family of origin as "the baby."

A good question for the involved partner is: "What did you experience about *yourself* in the affair that you would like to experience in the marriage?" Perhaps the marriage can begin to foster these positive aspects of the self. In fact, the betrayed partner may have been wishing to see those qualities all along and may find it hurtful that the involved partner enjoyed them first with somebody else.

9. Were there previous infidelities or opportunities, and how was this time similar or different?

This is an opportunity to examine any patterns of infidelity or near misses that may be relevant to how this affair unfolded. Discuss how you or your partner handled previous temptations, even if no lines were crossed. Explore past experiences of slippery slopes and blurred boundaries. If this is not the first incident, ask how this infidelity is different from or the same as the others. Were there earlier experiences that were "only oral sex" or "sex without love" or "love without sex"?

Partners who were too accepting of an earlier infidelity can mislead their spouses into thinking it's no big deal to be discovered. One unfaithful husband told me that his affair had been worth it. It had taken him only two weeks to pay for something that had felt good for six months.

Not every couple takes the time or has the guidance and support to work through betrayals that have occurred before. Although you might prefer to move ahead without dredging up all that old, miserable stuff, past affairs that are not dealt with will continue to contaminate your relationship.

10. Did you have unprotected sex?

Sad to say, this is one of those questions that you must ask. Ignoring the risk of disease or pregnancy is a thoughtless act. Some unfaithful partners give an adolescent rationale: "We were swept away by love and didn't want it to look like it was preplanned." Although relying on birth control pills or diaphragms may protect from unwanted pregnancies, those methods still expose the participants to sexually transmitted diseases. Few people regard their affair partners as a possible source of infection, so they don't take the necessary precautions to have safe sex.[12]

Based on data from a National AIDS Behavioral Survey, low levels of condom use were found among married subjects age eighteen to forty-nine reporting extramarital sex: 60 to 64 percent did not use condoms with the extramarital partner.[13]

Unprotected sex is a painful reminder of how inconsiderate and reckless the unfaithful partner may have been during the affair. Regardless of protestations, both spouses should be tested for AIDS and other sexually transmitted diseases. Willingness to submit to these humbling medical exams and tests is an act of consideration and accountability by the involved partner that will remove another obstacle to resuming safe marital sex.

Search for Meaning

It takes many conversations before a couple is able to reach a consensus on the complex issues involved in infidelity. And it is unrealistic to expect that they will agree on all dimensions. Here are two examples of couples who found the meaning of the infidelity through a collaborative effort.

Karla had an affair with her husband Kent's best friend. They described a breakthrough they had at home during a search for understanding and how relieved and close they felt as a result:

Kent: This has been so hurtful . . . I was betrayed by my wife and my best friend.
Karla (acknowledging empathically): I felt you didn't love me because you didn't desire me sexually.
Kent: That's because I was anemic. I didn't have any energy. I've always loved you. Since I've been taking medication, sex hasn't been a problem. What does that have to do with love?
Karla: Because of my emotional deprivation growing up, I realize that I have gone to sex as a way of getting love. I remember doing that in college. I had lots of brief sexual relationships when what I was really looking for was affection and approval.
Kent: You're saying that my not desiring sex meant to you that I didn't love you, so you went outside our marriage.
Karla: It was a terrible thing to do. I know now that you must love me if you're staying with me. I realize that the support and acceptance you give me is a true sign of your love.

In this discussion, Kent and Karla share information and are thoughtful, introspective, and open. Both felt that it brought them to a new level of intimacy.

One of the greatest obstacles to the recovery of Grace and Gavin was their dispute about the meaning of his extramarital sex. Grace went ballistic when he said he had always been committed to her and was only having a little fun. According to Grace, a sexual relationship that went on for two years was clearly an affair. Gavin would not agree that he had an "affair" because he had never been in love with Tina.

After several months of conflicting perceptions, Gavin and Grace were finally able to agree on the meaning of his sexual infidelity. Gavin realized that he was afraid of aging and declining sexuality. He had been avoiding sexual intercourse with Grace for the year preceding his infidelity because of erectile dysfunction. Tina's attention was flattering because she was much younger; he felt as if he had found the "fountain of youth." His excitement temporarily overcame his impotence. He had had many casual sex partners before marriage, so he didn't perceive occasional sex with Tina as an "extramarital affair."

When they were able to see his infidelity through each other's eyes, they felt more deeply connected. Gavin finally understood that what was trivial sex to him was a profound betrayal to Grace, and Grace accepted that Gavin's sexual affair was not about love or a failing marriage. They were able to commit themselves to Grace's definition of fidelity for the future.

Through the process of talking, telling, sharing, and listening, you are rebuilding trust. The driving need to know becomes a positive energy source that changes the way you interact. You are learning to be together as two hurting people who care about each other and want to understand each other's pains and fears.

No story of an affair is complete without discussing the complex factors that set the stage for infidelity. The vulnerabilities that create the context for an affair are discussed in the ensuing chapters in the stories of the marriage, the individuals, the outside influences, and the affair partner. Understanding what led to the affair is not a simple recounting of attraction and opportunity but a complex weaving of personal and relationship vulnerabilities.

9

THE STORY OF YOUR MARRIAGE

I thought we had a good marriage.
Now I'm hearing that you've been unhappy for years.

AFTER ELSA told her mother that Elliott had been cheating on her for most of their married life, she felt criticized rather than consoled. Her mother said, "What did you do wrong? People don't cheat unless something is missing at home." Elsa's mother mistakenly believed the Prevention Myth: *A happy marriage is insurance against infidelity.* Despite research evidence to the contrary,[1] even many therapists consider affairs to be an unmistakable sign of a faulty marriage.

> In my therapist survey, 53 percent of the female therapists and 39 percent of the male therapists disagreed with this statement: *Extramarital involvement occurs in happy marriages and is not necessarily a symptom of a distressed relationship.*[2]

When people marry, they bring almost mythic assumptions to the union, including these: *If we love each other, you will not cheat on me; if we have a good marriage, we will be safe from infidelity.* The truth is that not every person who is unfaithful is unhappily married. Marital distress can be seen as either the *cause* or the *consequence* of an infidelity. The marriage may not have caused the infidelity, but disclosure of infidelity will certainly damage the marriage.

Two partners in the same relationship may respond quite differently to the question "Does infidelity mean we have a bad marriage?" The involved partner, as happens frequently, may negatively rewrite the marital history in order to justify the affair. The betrayed partner may focus on the virtues of the marriage in order to eliminate self-blame and explain why he or she didn't see the catastrophe coming.

Regardless of what marital problems may or may not have preceded the affair, both partners need to use the aftermath, which can be from three months to two years, to strengthen the relationship. How long this takes depends on a lot of factors, including how distressed the marriage was before the affair. This time of rebuilding is designed to examine and strengthen. Needless to say, exploring problems in your marriage is not intended as a way to excuse the betrayal. A roof needs to be repaired regardless of whether it collapsed because of a slowly decaying frame or was in great shape before it was struck by lightning.

An essential part of the search for meaning is to discover what factors in the marriage could have set the stage for an affair. Even if your marriage has not been devastated by infidelity, the "Relationship Vulnerability Map" will point to cracks in the foundation that could cause a collapse under certain circumstances. If your marriage has been troubled—or just a little bit off track—going through this investigative process can help you build a stronger relationship.

Quiz: Relationship Vulnerability Map

There's no way to predict with certainty whether a specific couple is "affair-proof." Responding to the statements below will help identify relationship vulnerabilities that make marriages susceptible.

Directions: Circle the appropriate number to the left of each statement:
1 = **No,** disagree   2 = **Yes,** agree   3 = **Yes,** agree   NA = Not
   completely   somewhat   completely   applicable

1 2 3 NA   1. We had problems trusting each other before we got married.

1 2 3 NA   2. Our marriage revolves around our children.
              or (for childless couples)
              We disagree on whether or not to have children.

1 2 3 NA   3. My partner spends too much time away from home.

1 2 3 NA   4. My partner rarely takes my side in anything.

1 2 3 NA   5. We've grown apart.

1 2 3 NA   6. I have felt alone and unsupported at times of loss or crises.

1 2 3 NA   7. We don't have equal input for important decisions.

1 2 3 NA   8. We argue about the frequency of sex.

1 2 3 NA   9. Our interactions feel more like a parent-child relationship than one between equals.

1 2 3 NA 10. We are uncomfortable about exposing our inner selves to each other.

1 2 3 NA 11. We sweep things under the rug, so we hardly ever fight.

1 2 3 NA 12. There's a disparity in how invested we are in the relationship.

1 2 3 NA 13. I feel I can't influence my partner to do what I request.

1 2 3 NA 14. I don't know if I really love my partner.

1 2 3 NA 15. We don't know how to repair after a conflict.

1 2 3 NA 16. We don't have much in common.

Scoring Key:
Add up your total number of points to interpret your **relationship vulnerability score.**

Your marriage is in:
16–20 = A safe harbor
21–29 = Choppy waters
30–39 = Rough seas
40–48 = Watch out! You're headed for the rocks.

Take another look at those statements that you rated 2 or 3. You and your partner can work on these issues to build a better marriage. Sharing your responses will give you another way to discuss your marital lifeline and the relationship patterns discussed in this chapter.

It's important to realize that your relationship vulnerability score is *not a predictor of infidelity.* It is an assessment of your marital adjustment. Remember that affairs can and do happen in good relationships. Even a score that indicates high vulnerability does not mean that infidelity is inevitable. Just as there are happily married people who are unfaithful, there are also many dissatisfied individuals who remain faithful because of individual or cultural factors. The Relationship Vulnerability Map is one component that should be considered along with the vulnerability maps in the next two chapters.

The State of the Union

There's a lot to be learned by comparing the differences between monogamous marriages and those in which infidelity has occurred. The couples in my clinical practice fill out relationship questionnaires at the onset of marital therapy. The statistics presented in this section on "the state of the union" are the results of analyses from these clinical couples, unless otherwise indicated. I was interested in examining what relationship factors distinguish between faithful and unfaithful spouses of the same sex, and how unfaithful husbands differ from unfaithful wives. The case examples and my research findings may validate what you've observed in your own relationship, or they may not seem applicable. Nevertheless, knowledge is power. Understanding what (if anything) typifies the dissatisfactions of unfaithful partners can provide an informed perspective on your own marriage.

A common vulnerability leading to infidelity is the disillusionment that develops when expectations about marriage are not met. Individuals with high expectations can be easily dissatisfied because they expect more than any one relationship can reasonably provide. Unrealistically high expectations can lead to affairs, just as undeniably bad marriages can. For today's woman, a "good husband" has to be much more than a good provider; for today's man, a "good wife" has to be more than a good mother. *Both husbands and wives are looking to their spouses for love, companionship, intellectual stimulation, emotional support, and great sex in the high-stress environment of dual careers and Little League carpools.* An attractive person who appears to offer any of the components missing from this picture of perfection can be very tempting.

Because women appear to have higher relationship expectations than men, both faithful and unfaithful wives are much more dissatisfied with numerous aspects of marriage than are their husbands.[3] I see wives in marital therapy each week who begin with a proposed agenda for change and a list of specific complaints. They have thought long and hard about what is missing in their marriages. When I ask husbands what they would like to change, they frequently answer, "I just want her to be happy." Husbands report "We had a great week" because they had no conflict. Their wives will report about the same week "We had a terrible week" because they didn't have much verbal intimacy or emotional closeness.

Emotional affairs can be the consequence of emotional deprivation in the marriage, *or* they can be the source of diminishing emotional closeness. Unfaithful wives frequently are aware of being unhappy long before they get involved with another man. This is probably the underlying reason that wives and female therapists tend to blame infidelity on problems in the marriage more than do husbands and male therapists.

Unfaithful husbands, on the other hand, often regard their marriage as happy until they begin to make unfavorable comparisons between their wife and their affair partner. Randy became disappointed by the lack of intellectual interests he shared with Rianna *only after* he experienced Sophie as a kindred spirit. In the final analysis, he decided this was not a good enough reason to abandon his family and a devoted wife who had never been anything but loving toward him.

> My airport study indicated that 56 percent of the men and 34 percent of the women who had extramarital intercourse said that their marriage was happy.[4]

For men and women in empty marriages, affairs may provide what's missing; in stormy marriages, affairs may provide consolation and comfort. Unfaithful husbands and wives were more dissatisfied with marital companionship and being in love with their spouses than those who were faithful.[5] People in affairs with deep emotional attachment and sexual intercourse (combined-type affairs) are not only more likely to be unhappy with their marriages but are also more likely to end up divorced. Because more women engage in combined-type affairs than men, involved women are more dissatisfied with their marriages than are involved men.

Involved wives in marital therapy were also significantly more dissatisfied than the unhappy wives who had remained faithful. In contrast, involved husbands who engaged in primarily sexual affairs weren't any unhappier than noninvolved husbands. But husbands who described their affair as more emotional than sexual had much lower marital satisfaction than noninvolved husbands.

> In my clinical sample, among those who had engaged in extramarital sexual intercourse or other physical intimacies, 59 percent of men and 79 percent of women rated their marriage as unhappy.

John Cuber and Peggy Haroff conducted intensive interviews with almost 500 affluent Americans who were married for more than ten years and concluded that affairs may not only compensate for bad marriages, but also occur in marriages that were judged to be good. Reasons for infidelity were linked to the type of marriage: an outlet for hostility in "conflict-habituated" marriages, an outlet for boredom in a "passive-congenial" marriage, or the recapture of lost romance in a "devitalized" marriage. Infidelity was rare in "total" marriages, where partners were bound together by psychological, intellectual, and recreational compatibility.[6]

Sexual Compatibility

Exploring the sexual side of marriage is another crucial element for understanding infidelity. Talking openly, without blame or evasion, may expose sexual vulnerabilities that could have increased the allure of the affair, except when sexual involvement was an outgrowth of an emotional affair. Affairs that develop from friendships are usually influenced by emotional intimacy and sexual chemistry rather than by dissatisfaction with marital sex. Nevertheless, sexual frustrations or disappointments in the marriage are illuminated by comparisons with the exciting sex in the affair.

In general, husbands are disappointed with sexual frequency, whereas wives express greater concern about sex being linked to love and affection. When Ken and Kris discussed their sexual history, they realized that they had different perceptions of what constituted "good sex." He evaluated sex in terms of quantity, whereas she used a different barometer. Ken thought the sex was really good at the beginning of their marriage, and Kris said sex was really bad then. It was good for him because there was a lot of it; it was bad for her because she felt too pressured. Although she was exhausted by grad school, she felt she had to "let him" have sex, because he acted so disappointed if she turned him down. After awhile, she became angry with herself for always giving in just so that he wouldn't be upset.

By the time Ken had his affair, Kris was rejecting him almost every time he asked. Both of them were responsible for this sorry state of affairs. Ken could have been more sensitive to the signals that she was yielding reluctantly to sex on demand; Kris could have said *no* selectively, so that her *yes* indicated desire instead of duty. They developed greater empathy for each other after he discussed how it feels to experience sexual rejection, and she shared how it feels to experience sexual pressure.

Russ was understandably upset because Rita wasn't interested in having sex with him but then had sex with another man. Apparently, Rita enjoyed sex more with her affair partner than with her husband. Rita typifies many unfaithful wives.

Unfaithful wives are more dissatisfied with sexual enjoyment in their marriages than are faithful wives and unfaithful husbands. Surprisingly, unfaithful husbands enjoy marital sex as much as faithful husbands. Husbands and wives generally agree that husbands enjoy sex more than wives and want sex more often. However, both unfaithful husbands and unfaithful wives enjoy sex and desire sex on an equal basis with their affair partners.

One of the most frequent requests by husbands is for their wives to initiate sex. However, the partner who is perpetually pressed for sex before he or she senses any personal desire will never have the opportunity to feel

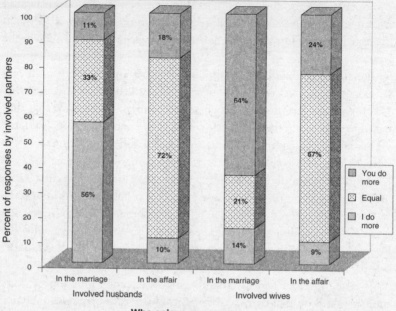

Who enjoys sex more

Equity in marriages and affairs of unfaithful spouses in clinical couples

enough desire to initiate lovemaking: "If you keep putting food in front of me whether I'm hungry or not, I will never have a chance to develop my own appetite."

Men often turn to sex to relax, whereas women usually have to *be* relaxed already to enjoy sex. One of the best ways a husband can help his wife relax enough to desire sex is to fold the laundry and help her put the kids to bed. A free mind will do more for her than twenty minutes of foreplay. One of the allures of an affair is that time for sex is scheduled, so the needs of both participants are considered.

It's unfair to compare the sexual warmth of a long-term marriage with the sizzling chemistry of a new, forbidden relationship. Although marriage does not have the same kind of "instant hot" as an affair, a good marriage combines sexual sensitivity and special meaning in lovemaking that can be like playing a familiar but subtly nuanced concerto on a cherished musical instrument.

Men are more interested than women in the pursuit of exciting sex with no strings attached. That's why some men who are "getting enough" and enjoying sex at home still engage in extramarital sex. For women, the physiological arousal of extramarital sexual intercourse creates a strong emotional bonding with her lover.[7]

> Unfaithful husbands and wives were more dissatisfied than faithful spouses with how exciting the sex was in their marriages.

Sexual enjoyment in the marriage can increase, decrease, or remain the same when one partner is sexually unfaithful, depending on the circumstances. There frequently is *no* impact on marital sex as long as a husband's sexual affairs remain secret. Wives, however, are more prone to withdraw from sex with their husbands after engaging in extramarital sex. After an affair is discovered, marital sex may either improve or deteriorate in the immediate aftermath. Some couples experience renewed passion and desire; other couples are haunted by the breach of sexual intimacy, avoid sexual contact, and recover very slowly—if at all.

> The impact of known affairs on *sexual satisfaction* in the marriage according to the unfaithful spouse: 19 percent observed *increased* sexual satisfaction, 36 percent observed *decreased* sexual satisfaction, and 45 percent observed *no effect* on sexual satisfaction.

The affair can be a catalyst for constructive discussions about sexuality. Sharing sexual preferences openly increases intimacy and can actually be sexually exciting: the turn-on for her is talking together in the den; the turn-on for him is an overt gesture such as touching his genitals. Good sex provides an incentive to overlook little annoyances or to rebound more quickly from arguments. A couple's sexual relationship creates a bond that can carry them through good and bad times.

Inequity

Inequitable relationships may result from one partner giving more than he or she receives or one partner being in a position of greater power than the other. Lack of balance in the marriage can lead either spouse to seek a more balanced relationship with another person.

Who Does More?

A common belief is that a person having an affair may not be "getting enough" at home. But the reality is that he or she may not be *giving* enough. Contrary to popular wisdom, people are not as satisfied in relationships where they are "overbenefited" as in relationships where there is more equity. In the most satisfying relationships, giving and receiving are balanced.

The involved spouse may be either an exhausted giver or an unappreciative recipient. Unfaithful spouses perceived more equity in their affairs than in their marriages.[8] Understanding was considered to be equal in 47 percent of marriages and in 70 percent of affairs.

Unfaithful husbands perceive more reciprocity with their affair partners than with their wives in *understanding problems and feelings.* However, there were as many unfaithful husbands who were overbenefited in their marriage as were "underbenefited": 25 percent rated their wives as more understanding, and 28 percent rated themselves as more understanding.

Unfaithful wives reported that they were more understanding than their husband, but they perceived understanding as a shared experience with their affair partners. The majority of these women were underbenefited in their marriage: 66 percent rated themselves as more understanding than their husbands, and 29 percent considered understanding to be equal in their marriage. In their affairs, only 9 percent said they were more understanding, and 87 percent said they were equal in understanding.

Here's how it works: It's easy for the person who is giving less to become involved with another person. Partners who give much less than they receive already have one foot out the door, so it's not difficult for them to break the loosely held connection to their marriages. The more you invest, the more committed you are and the more attached you feel.

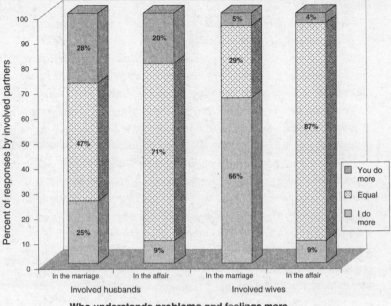

Who understands problems and feelings more

Equity in marriages and affairs of unfaithful spouses in clinical couples

The partner who has invested time and energy in the relationship is like someone who has just put new tires and new brakes on their car. When the transmission blows up, they think, "I've got too much invested to junk it now." There is a limit, however: if the investment is one-sided for too long, the underbenefited partner eventually gets burned up and burned out and seeks compensation somewhere else.

Luther depended on Lois for everything. While he was on call at the hospital for days on end, she managed the household, cared for the children, and was supportive and loving when he finally arrived home. He explained how his infidelity occurred: "My wife made it too easy for me. She was wonderful and giving. I didn't have to work at the marriage." This doesn't sound fair, but it's important to hear what he is saying.

When Lois discovered that Luther had been unfaithful for years, she probably felt that she was at home cleaning the barn while her less invested husband was out riding the pony.[9] When Lois decided she was through being a selfless, nondemanding wife, she wrote the following letter to Luther:

Dear Luther,

I looked upon our love as a nice comfortable burning ember after the blaze dies down, but you have stamped on it with both feet. If you want to keep my fire from being totally extinguished, you better start fanning the embers. You may be thinking I can't be serious, but I have never felt so strongly about anything in my life. I am tired of being the only one who is giving, so you better start giving too. Pretend I'm one of your girlfriends, not your wife who will always be there, because she won't be.

If you want to stay in the race with me you better start running, because I am tired of carrying the full load. This is a brand new marathon, and I want you to show me it's worth my time to stay in it. I refuse to run myself ragged anymore without active participation from you. I really want to go the whole 26K with you. I'll be at the finish line waiting for you. It's in your hands and you (not me) are going to have to go for the gold medal. If not, I'll have to start a new race without you on my team.

I love you,
Lois

Power Struggles

Infidelity can reflect an attempt by either spouse to correct an imbalance in power. Within the marriage, greater power is achieved through finances, competence, personality, or relative attractiveness. More powerful partners can feel entitled to indulge in the available alternatives without seriously considering the feelings of their partner. Conversely, less powerful partners can feel resentful and attempt to get even by having an affair. Individuals who feel one-down in their marriage may restore balance by satisfying their desires and preferences in an outside relationship.

Unfortunately, the power balance often shifts when couples go from a peer relationship to one with more traditional gender roles. Zachary and Zoë worked together as high-level executives in the same corporation. After they got married, each of them put a portion of their income into a common pool. They made all their financial decisions together. They decided to foster Zachary's career so Zoë could be a stay-at-home mom. After the birth of their third child, their heated arguments about spending money were really power conflicts. Zachary said, "You know that things are a little tight right now. What makes you think that you can build a new deck with *my money?*" Zoë hit the roof and yelled, "If we're so poor, then how did you go out and buy a new car without even consulting me?" Zoë felt frustrated and powerless because she had no earning power.

It was Zachary, however, who had an affair. His rationale was that he was tired of her constant (as he perceived it) complaining and lack of appreciation for what a good provider he was. It could just as easily have been Zoë who sought a partner who would treat her with respect.

Triangles: Two against One = Four
Extramarital triangles are not the only triangles that can cause marital distress. Other troublesome triangles also create an imbalance in the marriage when partners feel excluded by a bond between their spouse and some other person or activity. In the same way that workaholics are married to their careers instead of to their lonely spouses, partners can form alienating triangles with other family members, hobbies, serious avocations or artistic pursuits, athletic activities, volunteer work, and the obvious one: affair partners. Even a therapist working with an individual member of a couple can create a triangle harmful to the marriage by encouraging a stronger bond and greater intimacy within the therapy relationship than in the marriage.

Squaring the triangle: The danger of triangles is that the person who feels left out in the cold is at risk for seeking attention and support outside the marriage. An affair can sometimes be seen as a misguided attempt to square a troublesome triangle. That is when two against one often adds up to four.

Extended family: One of the first tasks in creating a marital bond is to create an attachment to each other that is stronger than attachments to siblings, parents, and grandparents. Obviously, the issue here is whether the young couple is able to pull away from family and be primarily committed to each other. The degree of dedication and unity the couple exhibits from the beginning obviously has implications for their loyalty to each other later.

A united front is epitomized in the words of the popular song "You and Me against the World." Husbands and wives should handle any difficulties caused by their own families in order to protect the fragile bond between their spouses and the in-laws. Furthermore, running "home" after a routine argument creates an unhealthy triangle in which one's spouse is portrayed as the villain, the returning adult child is the victim, and the parents are the rescuers.

Children: When parents triangle with the children, the children and the marriage are all losers. Clever children take advantage of any splits and play parents against each other by manipulating one parent for comfort after being disciplined by the other. An even worse scenario occurs when either parent feels humiliated and criticized in front of the children. In that degrading situation, the admiration and respect of an attractive colleague can look like an oasis in an arid desert.

Recreational activities: "Golf widow" is an apt description for wives whose husbands leave them to their own devices while they spend leisure time and weekends away from home. When the wives look for ways to fill up their empty time, their loneliness makes them susceptible to someone who values their companionship.

From Niagara to Viagra

Every marriage goes through ups and downs. There are natural peaks and valleys as we go from the high of the honeymoon through the challenges of child-rearing years to the empty nest. The particular stressors and joys that accompany each stage in the family life cycle cause shifts in satisfaction. *It's encouraging to learn that the majority of unhappy couples who weather marital storms eventually arrive at a safe harbor.*

> In a national sample analyzed by sociologist Linda Waite of people who stayed married, those in the worst marriages had the most dramatic turnarounds: 77 percent of those who first rated their marriage as "very unhappy" said that they were "very happy" or "quite happy" five years later.[10]

It's important to pay particular attention to new stressors or significant changes in the family environment during the two-year period before the affair began. Marital problems might first have surfaced right before the advent of the affair or could have been evident all along. It's also a possibility that there weren't any significant problems prior to the affair.

The Family Life Cycle

Of particular importance is *when* in the family life cycle the affair occurs. Couples in long-term marriages are usually more committed to staying together after an affair than those in younger marriages—particularly those without children. Affairs early in marriage are more likely to lead to divorce; they may indicate a fear of commitment or a belief that the marriage was a mistake. Every transition in the family life cycle necessitates a restructuring of the marital relationship and establishment of new priorities. Difficulties during each stage can create a vulnerability for infidelity, as follows:

- Young marriage: fear of commitment or lack of compatibility; faulty individuation from family of origin.
- Pregnancy: husband's fear of increased responsibility and feelings of entrapment.
- Transition to parenthood: husband's need for attention and his envy toward mother-infant bond.
- School-age: peak period of child-centered marriages and neglect of the couple.
- Teen years: escape from turbulence at home and nostalgia for own adolescence.
- Launching and empty nest: pondering bleak future together without children.
- Retirement: loss of work or professional identity and fear of aging.

Dating and Courtship

There may have been red flags or warning signs during courtship that were ignored. For example, a relationship may have started with trust issues and jealousy or by cheating on previous partners. When Kris met Ken in college, she thought he was "the perfect man." Ken was sophisticated, smart, and looked like Tom Cruise. They studied together and spent hours in the coffeehouse talking about what they were learning in class. Because Ken was living with another woman student at the time, he had to sneak out whenever they wanted to spend time together. Kris found their secret dating romantic and ignored the red flags of secrecy because their courtship was so passionate. She was shocked by Ken's infidelity after they married. Looking back, however, she realized that she should have been warned by the fact that their relationship began with sneaking around.

Trust issues are not the only warning signs. Inadequate bonding can be seen in misplaced loyalties. A bride-to-be struggled with constant conflicts while planning the wedding: "My parents want one thing and my fiancé wants something else. I think it's more important to please my parents. After all, they're my parents, and they are paying for everything." She was unaware that her wedding was a time to develop a united front with her husband-to-be. In the fifth year of their marriage, her husband had an affair. He had always felt like an outsider: when she said "my family," she still meant her parents and siblings—not her husband and children.

Newlyweds
Soon after Tom and Tamara got married, they agreed that Tamara would work full-time while Tom worked part-time to finish his MBA degree. He spent every hour working, studying, or (sometimes) sleeping and had no time to do the things they'd always enjoyed together. Tamara was lonely and unhappy. She was a geologist and filled up her empty hours in the company of an unmarried colleague. They shared an excitement about working outdoors in the field that she didn't share with Tom, because he was so busy and not very interested. Tom was relieved that Tamara had this friendship, because she was less upset with him for being unavailable.

You can guess the rest. Although Tamara and her friend never went any further than kissing, she began to ponder the implications of her attraction to another man. She had only been married a year; shouldn't she and Tom still be totally wrapped up in each other? She ended up leaving her marriage because even though her betrayal was only a kiss, it made her think of all the other ways she and Tom were not a good match. When she ended the marriage, Tom was devastated. He believed that the reason he'd worked so hard to advance his career was for *them*. He had difficulty imagining that he would ever risk marriage again.

Transition to Parenthood
The arrival of the first child causes many alterations in the marriage. When a wife becomes a mother, her husband can lose some of his erotic

feelings toward her. Mothers of newborns often experience a decrease in sexual desire because of hormonal changes and fatigue. The husband can feel neglected as the wife attends to the demanding physical and emotional needs of the infant. One wife told her husband how she felt after their baby was born: "I was tired but very happy," she said. Her husband confessed that he was tired but *not* happy: "You had no time for me anymore. I felt left out."

In addition to this new dynamic, both parents may feel trapped and ill prepared for the responsibilities they now have. An affair can represent an escape into a carefree zone. I have known couples where husbands had their first affair when their wives were pregnant. The men were anticipating the loss of freedom and fearing the additional responsibility. Mothers of preschool children seldom have affairs because they have insufficient time, energy, or opportunity.

Child-Centered Marriages
One of the most powerful vulnerabilities for infidelity is the child-centered marriage. Mothers and fathers make sacrifices for their children. Infants and school-age children test the bond you have with each other as you stretch to provide for their needs. Parents who worry about not giving enough time to the children plan their vacations and weekends around their children instead of making time for "the couple." Unfortunately, this is an oxygen-poor atmosphere for breathing life into romance.

Parenting has its pleasures and demands. In busy families, parents use whatever time they have to address the needs of their children. Even when they go out for a special occasion, such as a wedding anniversary, their romantic dinner turns into problem-solving sessions about their kids. They stare at each other across the candles and the flowers and don't have a lot to talk about except for vaccinations, school performance, or fussy bedtimes. Their "couplehood" is engulfed by their parenthood.

Ralph and Rachel clearly loved and respected each other. They had no terrible problems, but they also weren't paying attention to their vulnerabilities, their soft spots. The story of their marriage became the story of work and family routines almost exclusively. The demands of their alternating work schedules, household renovations, and learning-disabled son hardly gave them time for themselves as a couple.

After Ralph's affair, they did some soul searching about how they had drifted apart. Rachel gained some insight into her part in turning her marriage into a child-centered relationship: "Looking back on it, I can see how my being such a devoted mother made Ralph feel excluded. I was either helping our son with homework or driving our daughter to ice skating practice." Ralph realized that he hadn't let Rachel know how isolated he felt, nor had he given her the undivided attention he had given to Lara.

The Turbulent Teens

For many couples, the teenage years are the time when marital satisfaction is lowest. Opposing views about setting limits, premarital sex, and use of alcohol and drugs can escalate conflict between parents. Parents often feel alienated from their adolescent children, which can expand into alienation from each other. Either parent can be vulnerable to an affair that provides them with a temporary respite from the turbulence at home.

Besides the challenges inherent in shepherding teenagers toward adulthood, parents can become aware of yearnings they didn't know they had. One mother explained how she felt as she took a picture of her daughter and her date before they left for the prom: "It took me by surprise—how beautiful my daughter was, the handsome young man bringing her a gift, and the surprise limo I knew he had rented for later. I was overcome by feelings of nostalgia and longing." This mother identified her feelings as a "sweet yearning"; other parents can become jealous, envious, or downright competitive.

Launching

When children start to leave home, another critical point in the life of the marriage has been reached. Launching often comes at about the same time that husbands and wives are wrestling with their own middle age. This important transition in the family life cycle can be mistaken for a midlife crisis (which is a matter of age rather than a result of transitional life events).

The launching period is frequently a time when couples choose whether to "make it" or "break it." Marriages where the children are sources of conflict may experience a renaissance. Couples who depended on their children as the glue that kept them together will have to find new reasons to remain married. A college freshman told her mother, "Every week someone in my dorm finds out that their parents are divorcing." People who have their first affair at this critical time often use their extramarital relationship to exit from the marriage.

Another vulnerable time for couples is when adult children return home because of divorce, job loss, or emotional problems. Oscar and Opal had worked hard to recover from his prolonged affair, but she fell back into old habits of catering to her children after their daughter and son-in-law moved back home during graduate school. When Opal realized that her marriage was at risk, she announced to her daughter, "Mom doesn't live here anymore. You can do your own laundry and cooking from now on." As Oscar welcomed his wife back from her role as an ever-nurturing mother, they both realized how crucial it is to nurture *the couple.*

Empty Nests and Retirement Dreams
Empty nesters often find a resurgence of companionship and intimacy. Retirement poses new challenges associated with aging and the identity crisis caused by leaving the work setting. Couples experience conflicts and misunderstandings about how and where they want to spend their retirement. After George retired from his job, he spent all of his time planning a dream house of glass and cedar that would overlook the water.

When construction started, George was out there every day. Georgia begged him to take time off to take the trips she had always dreamed of, but George was totally absorbed in concrete and lumber and plumbing fixtures. Furthermore, he didn't want to spend any of their retirement funds on anything that might compromise plans for the house.

Georgia started taking short, inexpensive trips on her own with Elderhostel. She had to restrain herself from becoming emotionally involved with a widower who made time for travel and for her. When she told George about her close call, he felt wrecked. He thought he had been doing what Georgia wanted. Unlike Tom and Tamara's young marriage, which split up because Tamara felt abandoned, George and Georgia were committed to their marriage. They compromised to achieve a balance between traveling afar and watching the sunset from their waterfront veranda.

The Marital Lifeline: A Unique History

Exploring the context that set the stage for an affair must also include the unique events that illustrate each couple's marital history. It is stressful but enlightening to position the affair on the marital lifeline. The chaos and distress that follows disclosure can put a negative spin on memories of the past. Most people view the past through the bright or darkened lens of the present. Distressed couples tend to recount their history in terms of what went wrong and portray a distorted view unless they also revisit positive memories.

Until involved partners are fully committed to the marriage, they may claim that they were never in love with their spouse or paint a dismal picture of the entire marriage. However, they usually change their tune after the marital relationship is revitalized. Honest engagement in constructing the marital lifeline can transform black-and-white perspectives into a deeper, more comprehensive, and more sensitive understanding than any self-serving constructions created to account for the infidelity.

Your objective should be to figure out how the relationship got off track and how to get it back on course. This is hard to do if either partner's judgment is clouded by the censure and condemnation that obscure the delicate thread of shared truth. One of the challenges of discussing the events along the marital lifeline is to do it without casting blame. It's important to see what role each partner played in marital problems without holding the betrayed partner responsible for the affair. *Contributing to marital problems is not the same as causing infidelity.*

From Puppy Love to Mature Love

Marriage is not just a series of events but also a process of growth and development. Relationships progress through three stages, each of indeterminate length. The failure of some couples to mature together may be an indication that they have remained at one particular stage for too long.

- *Stage I:* The partners are typically quite enmeshed, like two peas in a pod. Flaws are almost invisible in a setting of romantic projections and idealistic thinking. It would be unthinkable to consider being with anyone else.

- *Stage II:* Their differences emerge and power struggles are frequent, along with disappointment and exaggeration of flaws. A disillusioned or angry spouse may try to recapture Stage I idealization through an affair.

- *Stage III:* Couples achieve a mature love with mutual respect and acceptance of defects. Couples who empathize with and accept each other after an affair often achieve this type of reality-based love.

Constructing the Marital Lifeline

Constructing a graph of the marital lifeline provides a self-guided discussion of the marital history. This graph can be as simple or as elaborate as you wish. Each partner should draw his or her own graph privately, although the objective is to share them. Use the illustration by Phil X, M.D., on page 238 to guide you.

1. At the bottom left-hand corner of the page, mark a zero point where the vertical and horizontal lines of the graph will meet.

2. Beginning at this zero point, draw a vertical line from the bottom to the top of the page. Put five ratings along this line from the bottom to the top: (1) *Very Unhappy,* (2) *Unhappy,* (3) *Average,* (4) *Happy,* (5) *Very Happy.* Refer to Figure 9-3 for clarification.

3. Beginning at the zero point, draw a horizontal line to the right that marks the bottom of the happiness scale. This horizontal line represents *the years of your relationship from the time when you seriously began dating.*

4. Place significant events during your marriage by using the timeline at the bottom of the page. You can use words, pictures, or a combination of words and pictures. Place your mark, symbol, or picture of the event up high if very happy, in the middle if average, or down low if very unhappy. Milestones you might want to include on your marital timeline are:

   • Moving to a different home

   • Career changes

   • Milestones with children, friends, or other family members

   • Special occasions: holidays, vacations, or gifts

   • Times of illness or the death of people close to you

   • Moments of triumph

   • Moments of disappointment

   • Beginning and ending of affair(s)

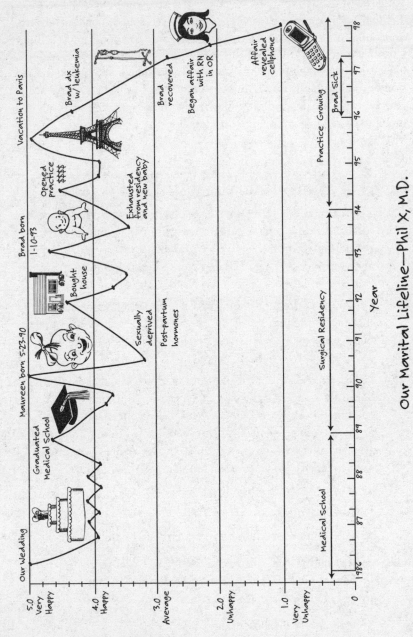

Our Marital Lifeline—Phil X, M.D.

Using the Marital Lifeline as the Basis of Discussion

Highlighting significant events that could have created the vulnerability for an affair is an effective way to strengthen your relationship. Recalling other challenges you faced and happier times you shared can inspire optimism about the future. One partner might say to the other, "I didn't realize we moved so often when we were first married" or "Look how much was going on when we had our third child" or "Remember how well we worked together when our house was flooded?"

Although partners may be able to agree on what happened, they often have different feelings about their shared experiences. Perhaps there was a time when one partner was happy and the other was miserable—when "her dream was his nightmare." Jessica recalled that the time she felt closest to John was when he was out of work. He was home every night for dinner, helped out with household tasks, and confided in her about his anxieties and frustrations. Despite their financial worries, she considered herself very happy with the marriage during his layoff. Although John agreed that Jessica had been very supportive, being out of work was catastrophic for him. He recalled that period in their marriage as very unhappy, without enough money to go out to dinner or have much fun.

Family Crises

Recall crises that could have brought you closer together or driven you further apart. A couple facing a family crisis can pull together with renewed dedication or withdraw into separate camps. Some partners need to connect and talk things over, whereas others avoid discussions of upsetting topics by pretending they didn't happen or dealing with them alone. A relationship can become very fractured when there is no healing communication about heart-rending events.

People handle grief and loss in different ways. Those who don't want to bring up painful memories can become estranged. You might remember Angela, whose husband Aaron had an affair right after her mother died. When Angela cried openly, Aaron backed away from her pain. He had adored her mother but didn't want to add to Angela's burden with his own grief. He shed his tears on the shoulder of the "friendly neighbor" who became his affair partner. Angela and Aaron eventually did their grieving together for the loss of her mother as they recovered from his betrayal.

Ignoring the wound is seldom a healing resolution. It is unfortunate when the outcome of a family tragedy is an affair or a divorce. In couples who stay married, unresolved grief and neglected issues can create a tremendous gulf between them.

Unresolved Issues
Often in long-term relationships, uncomfortable issues get swept under the carpet. You either don't discuss them at all or don't satisfactorily resolve them. You can build barriers to emotional and sexual intimacy. It is not uncommon for husbands or wives to stay silent about miscarriages, abortions, and stillbirths. A growing number of infertile couples can attest to the debilitating cycle of mechanical sex, high hopes, and crushing disappointments. Silent frustration and visible anguish can dominate their previously satisfying intimate relationship.

Stan and Stella never talked to each other about the meaning of their childlessness. Although they stopped using birth control after the first few years of marriage, she never got pregnant. He thought she didn't care that much about having children, and she thought he didn't care. When Stan had an affair ten years after they got married, his affair partner got pregnant because they didn't use any contraception. It was only then that he and Stella revealed how heartbroken each of them had been about not having any children of their own.

Physical Separations
Those who travel regularly on business, couples who work in different cities, or men and women in the military may be vulnerable to filling the void created by their partner's absence. A Naval officer told me that at his post, men and women receive a briefing from a military psychologist before they leave for a temporary duty assignment. They are warned that when they face difficult situations in close quarters with members of the opposite sex, they should not mistake adrenaline for attraction. Good advice, whether you are officially on duty or not.

Flashbacks can be triggered if the unfaithful partner used travel to sick family members, conferences, and educational activities as opportunities for infidelity. Any recovering couple who is going to be separated by travel in the future will need a plan for staying connected and establishing a sense of safety. You need to discuss any periods when you were deliberately living apart because your marriage had hit rock bottom, even though it can painful. Discussing what brought you back together and what you missed about each other during your marital separation can reinforce your commitment.

Joys and Triumphs
Be sure to point out those special times when you were joyful or triumphant together. Bask in the glow of recounting the events in your marriage that make you feel proud or that give you pleasure, such as the day you found out you were pregnant, the accomplishments of your children, your special anniversary trip, your starter home, or your dream house.

Mixed Feelings
Reviewing your marital lifeline has probably brought up some powerful emotions. Remembering the tender moments brings tears to your eyes, and the funny stuff brings tears of laughter. There are probably things you've forgotten, times you hadn't thought about for a while. Working on your history together not only co-constructs reality, it provides you with intriguing new information. You've probably shared things you haven't talked about before: you didn't know your partner was so proud of you when you were promoted, or you didn't realize that your partner was so resentful when you had to move to another city. Talking about the meaning of your joint experiences strengthens your bond.

Now that you have filled in your marital lifeline, you are ready to look carefully at the patterns of interaction that can create vulnerabilities for infidelity.

Relationship Dances

Every couple develops relationship dances. Through the years, interactions that were once fresh and even surprising can become well worn by repetition. Even the children can predict with some accuracy what Mom and Dad will do and say in their exchanges with each other. The advantage of having such unchanging scripts is familiarity. The disadvantage is that the dance can become inflexible and unyielding. What we see in these imperfect pairs is that each person is defined *in relation* to the other:

if one person steps forward, the other takes a corresponding step back. Although such movement can describe a beautiful dance, it can also describe the kind of lockstep that keeps both people imprisoned.

In a relationship that is enriching, opposite traits that may have been part of the initial attraction diminish as partners become more similar to each other. In a deteriorating relationship, differences between partners become more extreme and the negative cycles accelerate. Taking a closer look at relationship patterns reveals unrewarding interactions that may have made one partner susceptible to seeking solace outside the marriage. An affair can foster the opportunity for personal growth that fixed roles don't provide. Couples either handle the aftermath of an affair by replicating patterns that formed vulnerabilities in the first place, or they use the crisis to develop new patterns that are more rewarding.

Parent and Child

In some marriages, central issues take the form of a parent-child relationship. The parent-child dance between spouses can manifest itself in a variety of interactional patterns. The partner who is the "child" may not only admire but also resent the high esteem with which his or her partner is regarded by the outside world. The partner who takes the role of "parent" may envy the freedom and lack of responsibility that the "child" seems to enjoy. Either partner may become uncomfortable being in a sexual relationship with a spouse who appears parental or childlike because it feels too incestuous.

Dennis was older than his wife, Dora, by more than ten years. She looked up to him during the early years of their marriage because of his maturity and sophistication. After their children were in high school, Dora pursued a career in marketing. Her work outside the home increased her self-esteem, and she grew resentful that Dennis still didn't treat her as an equal. One day they had a huge argument. Dora took off her shoe and threw it across the room, where it landed against the opposite wall. Dennis turned to her and shouted, "Go to your room right now!" Dora shouted back, "You're not my father!"

You may remember that Dora is the woman who refused to stop playing tennis with her affair partner. His appeal was that she could be more spontaneous with him because he appreciated her free spirit. Although she was committed to saving her marriage, in her effort to avoid submitting to Dennis's reasonable request she was being as unreasonable as a defiant adolescent.

Saint and Sinner

In the saint-sinner dance, a "goody-goody" partner is intent on reforming a partner who is the "wild one." Blake grew up in a very strict family. He was grounded for the last two years of high school, after he got his nose pierced and his chest tattooed. When he got to college, he busted loose and vowed never to be controlled by anybody again. Although Brenda was attracted to his wild and winning ways during courtship, she tried to tame him after their first child was born. Their marriage soon replicated his childhood pattern. Brenda was stern and disapproving and lectured Blake when he drove fast or came home late at night. She thought he needed to be carefully monitored. What better way for him to rebel against her than to have an affair? After she discovered his affair, they sank even more deeply into their positions as "saint" and "sinner."

Bully and Sneak

In the bully-sneak situation, one partner is judgmental and intimidating, and the other resorts to subterfuge. As a child, Sandy learned that if she was going to do anything her parents might disapprove of, she'd better do it behind their backs. Whenever she bought something new for herself, her husband would question her purchase. Instead of asserting herself, she began to make secret purchases that she hid in the trunk of her car until the coast was clear. When she became friendly with a coworker, she hid the relationship because she didn't want to have to explain herself.

Sneaking around became such a pattern for Sandy that her ensuing affair was only one more secret she hid from her husband. When Sandy offered her house to Cheryl for her clandestine meetings, she was colluding in Cheryl's sneaking around. She justified lying to Cliff by seeing him as just another "bully."

Demand-Withdrawal Patterns

In patterns of demanding and withdrawing, one partner makes a request and the other delays or avoids carrying it out. As a reasonable request escalates into a coercive command, a subtle avoidance escalates into overt resistance. Nobody wins, and everybody loses—especially the relationship.

Pursuer and Distancer

One of the most common gender dances is that of wives pursuing emotional connection by talking about relationship problems, while their husbands distance to avoid conflict by withdrawing physically or emotionally. A vicious cycle occurs when pleas for intimacy that are ignored by the husband cause the wife to intensify her pursuit. His subsequent retreat triggers feelings of abandonment in the wife, who then attacks him with criticism and contempt . . . and the beat goes on.[11]

As long as wives are complaining about lack of closeness, they're still committed to their marriages. It's a serious sign that a marriage is in trouble when a wife finally withdraws. Wives stop pursuing when they've become discouraged about ever satisfying their emotional intimacy needs within the marriage. Ironically, husbands often react to the newfound peace and quiet with increased satisfaction. But it's a false sense of security.

I get frantic distress calls from husbands in this situation too late in the cycle to save their marriages. By the time the husband is concerned about his wife's detachment (often because she has also withdrawn sexually), she is either involved with another man or is making concrete plans to leave the marriage.

Clam and Stingray

In the clam-stingray dance, one partner attacks with barbed words while the other retreats into a shell. In some couples, both partners suppress expressions of anger, anxiety, fear, and disappointment toward each other. In other couples, conflict is the stuff of life. With the clam and the stingray, one partner loves conflict and the other is conflict-avoidant. Growing up in a home with a high sense of conflict can make some people comfortable with emotional explosiveness, whereas others are almost phobic about any sign of disagreement or tension.

Cecilia was one of three girls in a warm, passionate Italian family. The sisters exchanged clothes, had fun together, and also had terrible fights, after which they made up quickly. Cecilia's husband, Carl, grew up as an only child in a constricted Scandinavian family. When he did something that displeased Cecilia, she ranted and raved at him. As soon as her voice began to rise, Carl retreated as far away as he could. He felt like putting his hands over his ears. After decades of hiding his resentment over his wife's hot temper, Carl fell in love with a very gentle woman who was soft-spoken and sensitive. When Cecilia found out, she was shocked. She thought they had a great marriage because she acted as she pleased. As she said to him: "You never told me that I upset you. I was just being myself."

Fay also found it very difficult to stand up to differences of opinion or negative emotions in her marriage. She grew up in a conflict-habituated household where her parents shouted and argued a lot. As a little girl, she cowered alone in her bedroom, hoping she would be magically trans-ported to a safe place. After Fay got married, she darted back into her shell for protection whenever her husband, Fabian, was angry or even slightly peeved. She caved in almost immediately every time a dispute or disagree-ment arose. Holding back her feelings built a wall of unexpressed grudges and resentments.

Both Fay and Fabian would say that there wasn't very much intimacy in their marriage. He always felt like he was walking on egg shells around her. The pattern they developed kept them from honest sharing. Only after Fabian's affair did she begin to realize the damage that had been done to their marriage because she avoided telling or hearing about negative feelings. There was no way to deal with those unresolved problems in the marriage, so it had seemed easier for Fabian to start with a blank slate in a new relationship. Fay's rage over his betrayal unleashed a torrent of angry feelings that had been accumulating for years. Fabian's willingness to hang in and work it out with her was the beginning of genuine exchanges and more open communication.

Reminder and Procrastinator

In the reminder-procrastinator dance, one partner appears superresponsi-ble and the other appears to be a slacker. The partners might think of each other as "the nag" and "the mule." The reminder's scripts are: "When are you going to call the doctor?" "Have you sent in your taxes?" "Why do I have to do everything around here?" The procrastinator's sole script is: "Stop bugging me. I'll do it later." In this rough cycle, each brings out the worst in the other. The reminder may be overly compulsive or impatient, and the procrastinator may be disorganized or stubborn. The affair provides a release from this tension because responsibilities are more likely to be equally shared on a voluntary basis.

How to Begin a New Dance

If any of the preceding relationship patterns apply to your marriage, you can break the cycle. In the dysfunctional dances described above, the partners occupy the extreme ends of the spectrum of behavior. If one pursues, the other withdraws; if one controls, the other rebels; if one does too much, the other does too little. If you feel stuck in a groove that is confining you to a fixed role, there are other options besides seeking growth in a new relationship.

When you focus on trying some new and different steps in your existing relationship, you can achieve surprising changes.[12] If you're the one who pushes, you can back off a little. If you're the one who retreats, you can meet your partner halfway. If you don't like being reminded, you can volunteer before you're asked. Abandon the large pendulum swings of action and reaction in favor of the comfortable synchronization of give and take. When you moderate your reactions, you make it easier for your partner to moderate his or hers.

The Myth of the Low-Maintenance Marriage

You can't just show up at your job and expect to be successful; you put time and energy into it. By the same token, *you can't just show up for marriage.* Creating a marriage that is intimate and safe takes work, just like any other worthwhile human endeavor. You have to put time and energy into it too. Love is not enough to keep a marriage going. Enjoying your children and maintaining your home are not enough to keep the marriage going either. Only conscious and mutual efforts are enough—including wise decisions about keeping your commitments.

The story of your marriage is reflected in a variety of assets and deficits. You can see it in your satisfying sex life and in how good you feel in each other's company. Some couples are bonded because of a high level of understanding, affection, and companionship. Others are distanced by criticism, disrespect, and a failure to enhance each other's self-esteem.

Some couples love talking together about ideas and interests; others communicate mostly about schedules and the other mechanics of running a household.

Relationship factors do not account for involved people whose marriages are satisfying and loving. The story of your marriage is not the whole story. Other types of vulnerabilities also need to be explored. The story of individual vulnerabilities in attitudes, personality, and attachment style is presented in Chapter 10, and the influence of social factors such as friends, family, and community standards is presented in Chapter 11.

10

YOUR INDIVIDUAL STORIES

What kind of a person are you, anyway, to do what you did?

BETRAYED PARTNERS are disoriented by the revelation of infidelity. They confront the unfaithful partner: "Who are you? Everything I once believed about you is changed, now that I know what you are capable of." They're trying to assemble a new picture that incorporates the landscape of betrayal. Involved partners may also feel confused if they have fractured their self-image by acting against their own value system.

Some people in unhappy marriages don't have affairs and some people in happy marriages do have affairs. The explanation lies not in the marriage but in their individual stories. Russ rejected opportunities for extramarital affairs despite sexual deprivation and frustration in his marriage. Even after being shattered by Rita's infidelity, he was resolute in his own commitment to monogamy because of his personal and moral values. In contrast, Luther was unequivocally satisfied with his marriage but had no misgivings about engaging in extramarital sex.

Infidelity raises questions about personal factors that may not have surfaced until the affair came to light. Slowly, the couple pieces together the individual story that explains *why*. Trying to understand how it happened and why is much more than a diversionary tactic. Exploring the vulnerabilities in the personal background of unfaithful partners is a way for them to gain insight about themselves so they can avoid the slippery slope in the future.

Sometimes betrayed spouses are interested in the details of the affair but don't want to hear about individual motives or vulnerabilities because they're afraid to get sidetracked from their sense of having been wronged. They don't want to make the effort to understand what happened in case understanding becomes confused with condoning or excusing. *But understanding is not the same as excusing.* Gaining insight into what happened and why benefits both partners.

We have already discussed how the new crisis of infidelity is a product of increased opportunity in the workplace, but opportunity alone doesn't determine whether someone will be unfaithful. Some people accept the invitation, and others in comparable circumstances turn it down. Now it is time to look at those unique aspects of experience and personality that make each of us who we are as individuals. Personal factors such as attitudes, needs, personality, and character shape the actions and reactions of both partners before, during, and after the affair.

Quiz: Individual Vulnerability Map

There's no way to predict with certainty whether a specific individual is going to be unfaithful. Responding to the statements below will help identify attitudes and personality characteristics that increase an individual's vulnerability to opportunities for extramarital involvement.

Directions: Circle the appropriate letter to the left of each statement:
A = **Yes,** I agree.   D = **No,** I disagree.   NA = Not applicable.

Part I. I would feel *justified* having an extramarital relationship for the following reasons:

A   D   NA   1. If I fell in love with another person.

A   D   NA   2. For sexual excitement or sexual variety.

A   D   NA   3. To have someone understand my problems and feelings.

Part II. I would be *inhibited* from having an extramarital relationship for the following reasons:

A   D   NA   4. I would feel too guilty.

A   D   NA   5. It's against my moral, ethical, or religious principles.

A   D   NA   6. I wouldn't break my wedding vows or my commitment to my partner.

A   D   NA   7. I'm devoted to my partner.

Part III. I'd probably *get involved* with an attractive person who is interested in me because:

A D NA   8. I work hard, so I deserve to have some fun.

A D NA   9. I wouldn't be hurting anybody.

A D NA   10. It's okay to have sex as long as you don't get too emotionally involved.

A D NA   11. It's okay to fool around as long as you don't have intercourse.

A D NA   12. It's okay to be emotionally involved as long as there's no physical intimacy.

Part IV. The following statements reflect *my beliefs* about life:

A D NA   13. I thrive on risky, new adventures.

A D NA   14. Rules are made to be broken.

A D NA   15. Forbidden fruit is sweeter.

A D NA   16. Beginning a project is always more interesting than finishing it.

Part V. The following statements reflect *how I feel* about my relationship:

A D NA   17. I feel uptight if my partner tries to get too close.

A D NA   18. I feel anxious and rejected if my partner ignores me.

A D NA   19. I'm most comfortable being alone. I have little need to spend time with my partner.

Scoring Key:

*Add up your points to calculate your **individual vulnerability score:***
In Parts I, III, IV, and V: each Yes = 1, No = 0.
In Part II: each No = 1, Yes = 0.

Your score tells how close you are to the *slippery slope of infidelity.*
  0–4 = Safety zone
  5–9 = Proceed with caution
  10–14 = Slippery slope
  15–19 = Danger zone

Individual Attitudes about Infidelity

Our attitudes—what we believe about monogamy, commitment, honesty, loyalty, and extramarital sex—very definitely influence how we behave. Attitudes, not marital happiness, differentiate between people like Russ and Luther. It seems pretty obvious that people who have been unfaithful will have more approving attitudes toward infidelity than those who have never been involved. Our attitudes and values predict how likely it is that we would cheat in the first place and whether we would feel guilty afterward if we did. Permissive attitudes can move us to open the door of opportunity, whereas personal values and relationship considerations can inhibit us from crossing the threshold.

Justifications and Excuses

One man in my airport sample offered a unique justification on my research questionnaire; he wrote as his reason for having an extramarital relationship, "I never refuse a gift." His lighthearted approach was diametrically opposed to one women who felt she had violated her inner core. This unfaithful wife commented, "Nothing justified what I did, but I was feeling so lonely that I got involved. I regret it every day." Both of these individuals had extramarital intercourse, but one brushed it off and the other was seriously shaken. The first individual didn't value fidelity; the second one did.

Individuals who deliberately seek extramarital relationships justify their actions beforehand and feel little regret afterward. Unfaithful partners who are frustrated by inadequacies in their marriage can intentionally fulfill those unmet needs with someone else. For example, a spouse who feels emotionally deprived may justify an affair for its intellectual sharing and companionship—before falling in love or engaging in sex with someone who started out as "just friends."

On the other hand, others look for reasons to justify their betrayal after the fact. If they feel justified to have an affair because they fell in love with another person, then they claim that they never really loved their spouse. After their indulgence, when they are no longer simply talking to themselves (but actually justifying their behavior to others), they tend to cast blame. They create an explanation in which their own victimization absolves their transgressions: "My wife was frigid"; "My husband didn't talk to me"; "I was crazy from the all the stress at my job."

Some people offer *excuses*, such as "I was drunk" or "I was seduced." Offering excuses is not the same as offering justifications. Those who offer excuses are not blithely saying that they didn't do anything wrong; they are explaining why they did something wrong but are attempting to minimize their wrongdoing by giving a reason for their actions. "Justifiers" act self-righteous in efforts to validate the appropriateness of their behaviors; "excusers" are more willing to accept blame for their actions.

National surveys report that 85 percent of those polled disapprove of extramarital involvement, but these surveys define "extramarital involvement" with a single question about approval/disapproval of *extramarital sexual intercourse*. On my justification questionnaire, I offered people sixteen specific reasons that would justify an extramarital relationship for themselves. They were able to discriminate among specific justifications that were meaningful for them and rejected other reasons that were not acceptable to them.

The justifications that men and women offer for extramarital involvement often reflect different perspectives on sex and love. An unfaithful wife who was leaving her husband said, "I had an affair because I found someone who was understanding and affectionate. It would have been wrong to get involved for sexual reasons." A man who considered his sexual infidelities to be harmless diversions said, "Variety is the spice of life, but I'd never allow myself to get emotionally involved. That would be an unjustifiable offense."

Unfaithful husbands and wives in my clinical practice selected reasons for getting involved that represented emotional intimacy, love, sex, and ego enhancement. *Falling in love with another person* was a justification chosen by 64 percent of the husbands and 66 percent of the wives who admitted having extramarital sexual intercourse. These unfaithful wives felt justified by companionship and understanding more than unfaithful husbands did, whereas unfaithful husbands approved more of sexual justifications than did unfaithful wives.

Faithful spouses are vulnerable for an affair if they believe that getting involved would be acceptable under certain circumstances. For example, a still faithful partner who feels sexually deprived in the marriage could be receptive to a sexual invitation from an interested colleague at work. A partner who is not constrained by personal values will give off signals that he or she is ripe for the picking.

Percent of Unfaithful Spouses with Extramarital Intercourse Who Approved Specific Justifications for Extramarital Relationships

Justifications for Extramarital Relationships	Unfaithful Spouses	
	Husbands	Wives
Emotional intimacy justifications		
For intellectual sharing	45%	55%
For someone to understand problems and feelings	55%	76%
For companionship	47%	72%
Love justifications		
Falling in love with another person	64%	66%
To get love and affection	56%	66%
Sexual justifications		
To relieve sexual deprivation or frustration	67%	38%
To enjoy sexual relations	58%	41%
For sexual excitement	49%	48%
Ego enhancement justifications		
To be respected	30%	45%
To enhance self-confidence and self-esteem	33%	45%
Revenge		
To get even with spouse	11%	7%

Premarital Sexual Permissiveness

Thelma had sexual intercourse for the first time at age fifteen. She had many brief encounters and long-term sexual relationships before she met and married her husband, Trent. After she was married, she had extramarital sex with ten different men before Trent discovered her betrayal. Because of Thelma's extensive premarital experience, the extramarital sex act didn't seem momentous to her, but it did cause the destruction of her marriage.

More women are engaging in extramarital sex because more women have experienced premarital sex with men other than their husbands. Men and women with sexually permissive attitudes after marriage were often sexually permissive before marriage—particularly if they were sexually experienced with multiple partners and began at an early age. People who had a quick succession of lovers in the past more typically have extramarital affairs that are quickly consummated and just as quickly finished. On the other hand, *emotional affairs* begin slowly, have an extended duration, and are not predicted by premarital sexual permissiveness.

> Extramarital sex was reported by 48 percent of women whose first premarital sex occurred at age fifteen or younger, in contrast with 16 percent of women whose first premarital sex occurred after age twenty-one.[1]

Entitlement

Feelings of entitlement are plentiful among willful philanderers. Arnold was one of the few successful "dot com-ers" who continued to prosper during the economic downturn. He felt entitled to enjoy the fruits of his labor by availing himself of the enamored young women who worked for him. Part of the satisfaction for him was that desirable women had scorned him when he was just another "computer nerd" at the bottom of the corporate ladder. Now that he was the CEO of a thriving company, his sexual conquests gave him a special thrill. He felt no regret about betraying Alice, who had loved him unconditionally since their college days.

Men like Arnold can carry on their risky behaviors for decades without being detected, or they can suffer personal and professional catastrophe from their philandering. In either case, they regard themselves as committed to their wives and happily married all the while. The irony is that men who operate from a misguided sense of entitlement almost always restrict the women they love from engaging in the same behavior. When a wife asked her husband how he would feel if the shoe was on the other foot, he said, "I'd kill you. But I know you'd never do anything like that."

The stereotype of the powerful man and the trophy woman is consistent with research findings across cultures and across time that men are attracted to beauty and youth, and women are attracted to power and resources. Successful men who already view extramarital sex as a privilege of masculinity feel even greater entitlement by virtue of prominence and wealth. We have certainly had enough public scandals of politicians and religious leaders who felt entitled to take advantage of starry-eyed young women. *What the powerful man fails to comprehend is that he is the coveted trophy* who becomes attainable when he takes the giant step down from his lofty pedestal to unzip his fly. Stripped of his cloak of impenetrability, the seducer has become the seduced.

Power can be an aphrodisiac for high-status men and women. In couples where there is a high-status wife and a lower-status husband, the wife is likely to have more affairs than other women, and her husband is likely to have fewer affairs than other men.[2]

Personal Deterrents

The fact remains that lots of people who *don't* take a bite of the forbidden fruit are stressed out, have opportunities for affairs, and are unhappy in their primary relationships. Although they may feel tempted or needy, they don't act on their desires. Randy justified his affair with Sophie after he had fallen in love with her. If he had been truly dedicated to remaining faithful, he could have backed off as soon as he felt himself wanting to spend secret hours with her.

Individuals who believe that nothing justifies extramarital involvement make a special effort to avoid opportunities—even more so if they are feeling vulnerable. No matter what is going on, they uphold their commitment to be faithful. One man told me, "On a good day, when things are going well, I am committed *to my wife*. On a day when things are just okay, I am committed to *my marriage*. And on a day when things aren't so great, I satisfy myself by being committed to *my commitment*."

Our personal value system provides us with a green light that accelerates our movement toward an impending affair, or a cautionary yellow light that slows us down at the dangerous intersection of opportunity, or a flashing red light that tells us to brake at the sound of an approaching siren. Just as justifications and feelings of entitlement pave the road to infidelity, moral values and commitment to fidelity are the barriers on the highway to extramarital involvement.

There is a delicate balance between the factors that are vulnerabilities and those that act as deterrents. In general, vulnerabilities increase as a marriage ages. If we believe that falling in love with another person is justification for an affair, we avoid thinking about the deterrents that would inhibit us as we allow ourselves to fall in love. By the time we are accelerating our slide down the slippery slope, it may be too late to reverse direction. Those who honor their commitment in the face of a wavering focus draw on dedication to personal and relationship ideals.

Guilt and Shame

It's important not to confuse guilt with shame. Guilt is felt even if nobody else knows about the transgression. In the movie *City Slickers*, Billy Crystal's character turned down the idea of a fail-safe sexual affair. "It doesn't matter if nobody else would know. I'd know, and I wouldn't like myself." Shame is a reaction to external consequences that occurs when caught doing something "bad." When President Clinton apologized to the American public after many denials of infidelity, he discussed feeling *shame* but didn't mention feeling *guilt*. It appears that he regretted his actions after the fact because of their consequences.

Guilt

Guilt works as a deterrent for extramarital involvement only when you perceive it before you act. After noticing the first tugs of attraction, anticipatory guilt helps to frame the consequences of your impulses, pulls you back from the edge, and keeps you from acting on your desires. After a wrongful act, wallowing in self-recrimination can serve as a way to avoid changing your inappropriate behavior. *Allow yourself to feel guilty for five minutes only. Then it's time to take responsibility for reparation.*

We have learned something interesting about who is likely to feel guilty and who is not. People who purposefully set out to be unfaithful are usually guilt-free beforehand and afterward. Those who fall accidentally or unintentionally are more inclined to feel guilty.[3] Because the new crisis of infidelity is about people getting swept away by "friendship affairs," we can expect genuine remorse from these unintentional betrayers.

Shame

Shame doesn't deter infidelity in the first place, and a shamed response to being caught doesn't guarantee abstinence in the future. In fact, shame can generate a cycle that makes recurrence *even more likely.* For Donald, this shame cycle was powerful enough to become a compulsive pattern of Internet affairs. After his wife, Daphne, exposed his e-lovers, he felt ashamed. He told her, "I feel terrible. I know I've been bad. I'll try to do better." Although his feelings were genuine, they were all about *him* and how bad *he* felt. He wasn't able to empathize with his wife's pain because he was too self-absorbed. To escape from his misery, Donald turned once again to distract himself—in an Internet chatroom.

Donald and Daphne believed that his self-flagellation was a sign of rehabilitation. They didn't realize that shame frequently perpetuates the undesirable behavior. Shame is centered on the self. To heal the wound in his marriage, Donald had to stop the self-pity, take responsibility for what he had done, and enter more into Daphne's world. He showed true compassion for Daphne when he bolstered her safety by giving her the password for his e-mail. He took action by restricting his on-line activities to necessary business correspondence—and only when Daphne was at his side.

Inhibitors

I asked an unfaithful husband what had inhibited him from engaging in extramarital intercourse despite sixteen years of "fooling around" and enjoying oral sex with other women. He said that he restrained himself from going any further with these women because he was devoted to his wife and committed to his marriage. We wrestled with the concepts of *commitment* and *devotion* during the ensuing sessions, until he realized how his "inconsequential" behavior constituted an enormous betrayal. His value system was not unique: 100 percent of the husbands in my clinical practice who were sexually intimate without having intercourse said they were inhibited from further involvement by devotion to spouse and commitment to marriage. My data indicate that women view any type of sexual intimacy (even kissing) as crossing the line, but men are more apt to view sexual intercourse as the place to draw the line.

Relationship considerations and moral values were the strongest deterrents when all of the husbands and wives in my clinical practice were asked *what would inhibit their potential involvement* in extramarital relationships: 84 percent were inhibited by *devotion to spouse* and 91 percent by *commitment to marriage.* Only one-third of them were inhibited by *high marital satisfaction* because so many of them were unhappy in their marriages. Therefore, their commitment and devotion appear to be based on abstract principles and a sense of responsibility despite low marital sat-isfaction.

Moral values were a much greater deterrent than *religious beliefs.*[4] Moral values restrain women from having any type of sexual intimacy and restrain men from having sexual intercourse. People who attend religious services frequently were deterred from extramarital involvement by reli-gious beliefs. However, I must note that several of the errant spouses had met their affair partners at weekly services. Their original spiritual con-nection turned sexual by excluding their less observant spouse from their friendship.

It is no wonder that so many unfaithful spouses have unprotected sex because anticipation of negative consequences was not a very powerful inhibitor. *Fear of pregnancy* was a deterrent for only 12 percent of men and women. *Fear of disease* was a deterrent for 35 percent of husbands and 44 percent of wives. The plea of betrayed partners—"How could you have risked my health and my life?"—has no easy answers.

Conflict between Values and Behavior

As we know, many normally scrupulous people with "good values" are vi-olating their marriage vows. These are people who return a wallet full of money when they find one, volunteer their time to work in soup kitchens, and recycle. Yet they allow themselves to be drawn into illicit relation-ships, even though they don't think it's right. Their values aren't enough to keep them from lying and cheating, even though they may feel uncom-fortable about leading a double life.

It's easy to have values in the abstract. Many people find, though, that being face-to-face with someone who is captivating and available makes fidelity seem less critical (and perhaps less appealing) than it once did. In the absence of clearly stated, consistently reinforced boundaries, they suc-cumb to their romantic fantasies and the misery that ultimately comes from an affair.

I remember an unfaithful husband telling me with obvious distress about leaving his lover's house and inadvertently passing his wife on the street as he drove home. She was parked in front of the grocery store, wrestling their two young children into their car seats, and trying to load packages into the station wagon at the same time. She looked haggard and alone. He felt terrible about what he was doing to her but didn't terminate the affair because he was "hopelessly in love."

Some people resolve the inner conflict between values and behavior by ending the affair. Some eliminate the struggle by finding flaws in the marriage that justify their involvement. Others are driven to disregard their own principles because their psychological needs are too consuming for a single relationship to satisfy.

Running on Empty

Partners often turn to affairs to meet needs that are not being satisfied in their marriages. These needs may be reasonable, or they may be so unreasonable that *no* person or relationship could ever gratify them. Hunger for attention and affection may derive not from a love-starved marriage but from an insatiable appetite. Needs for admiration, romance, or sexual pleasure can be overwhelming in their extreme forms. Some people can't get enough sex, and others can't get enough love. Then there are those ego-starved individuals who can't get enough approval or positive stroking. The drive toward excitement can mask underlying depression, numbness, or emptiness. Multiple affairs can indicate a compulsive need for arousal that takes the form of an addiction to sex, love, or romance.

People who are running on empty may unconsciously seek an adrenaline high as a way to escape from an internal void or external stressors. An affair can provide an oasis in the midst of an arid desert or a refuge in a stormy sea. The quest for extramarital excitement can be an attempt to "fix" an internal problem, such as boredom, low self-esteem, or existential angst. This last is a little hard to define; one unfaithful husband summed it up by saying that his affair sharpened his sense that there was something worth living for.

The Need to Escape

Affairs provide an escape from a whole host of upsetting situations or memories. One dedicated husband and father discovered this when he had an affair two months after his son was in a near-fatal skiing accident. When he was home, he had to confront his injured child and deal with the worry and sadness that he and his wife were enduring. When he was with his affair partner, he could enter another world and escape from the concrete reminders of his unbearable emotional pain.

After putting forth incredible effort to end her affair and restore her marriage, Uma examined why she had let herself get involved after years of fending off unwanted male attention. In her therapy, she recalled how depressed she was about everything in her life in the months preceding her affair. She had hit a glass ceiling at work, and she was heartbroken that she had not been able to get pregnant. She was frustrated and disillusioned about her future. The affair offered intellectual stimulation and fun at a time when she was way down in the dumps. She began to recognize how she had used her lover as an antidepressant instead of getting professional help for her situational depression.

The Starving Ego

At least in the beginning, affairs are great ego boosters. Through them you can inhabit an enlarged version of yourself and enjoy the feedback that tells you that you are special and infinitely valuable. All you have to do is look into your lover's eyes to remind yourself that you have never been more worthy or more lovable. Idealization is a potent short-term remedy for low self-esteem.

As we have observed, the attraction of most affair partners is the positive mirroring they provide when you gaze into their eyes. Affair partners are generally no more attractive than the spouses they rival. What makes them irresistible is their gratification of an unquenchable thirst for approval. It's hard for an impoverished ego to resist a cornucopia of flattery and admiration.

The Need for Excitement

Type-T Personality
Thrill-seeking personalities prefer high-risk adventure, constant novelty, and high-intensity activities. Psychologist Frank Farley's Type-T theory explains the personality and behavior of individuals who seek stimulation and high arousal.[5] Type-T individuals can risk financial ruin by being constantly on the verge of bankruptcy or participate in dangerous sports,

such as bungee jumping and drag racing. On the positive side, these individuals may be enormously successful because they aren't afraid to shoot for the moon. On the negative side, their attraction to risky undertakings can endanger them. The appeal of infidelity for the Type-T personality is the thrill of flirting with danger and the challenge of avoiding detection by a suspicious spouse.

Alexythymia

A persistent desire for excitement and thrill seeking in all aspects of life may be an indication of *alexythymia*. Alexythymic individuals have difficulty naming emotions and describing what they feel. According to psychologist Ron Levant, alexythymia is common among American men because of early socialization experiences that teach them to keep a stiff upper lip.[6] Anger is one of the few emotions that can be identified or expressed by alexythymic males.

The alexythymic spouse's lack of sensitivity toward subtle emotions makes him somewhat impervious to feeling the gentle warmth and contentment of a stable relationship. Only the intense blaze of a new passion reaches his high threshold for detecting emotional states. He likes "hot" sex and being "in love" and strives for intensity instead of intimacy.

Bright Beginnings, Muddled Middles

Some people are sprinters, and others are long-distance runners. In the game of love, almost everybody can do the short course. Unfortunately, many eager beginners lose momentum or drop out of the race when they get to the demands of the middle phase. Each new experience and each new person offers the possibility of personal transformation. Each new start is the best that he or she has ever known, *until it isn't.*

A person who thrives on "beginnings" will have a life pattern of starting over and over and over: new careers, new hobbies, and new relationships. This person feels fully alive during the romantic wooing of a new partner and the uncertainty of conquest but has difficulty staying on course when no longer carried forward on the wings of arousal. Being in the middle of what was once new creates boredom. Many move from relationship to relationship in a pattern of "sequential monogamy." Others are able to sustain long-term marriage by fulfilling their need for new beginnings through a succession of extramarital affairs.

Getting High

Philandering can be a sign of addictive behavior, although the surface behaviors (and consequences) may look similar to those of the entitled philanderer. The addicted philanderer feels driven to seek opportunities rather than entitled to take advantage of opportunities that present themselves now and then. An addictive cycle begins with obsessions or feelings of anxiety that escalate until the need is satisfied. After the initial high, individuals often crash and burn. Their oaths to make this the last time are difficult to keep. However, those who are acting against their own value systems tend to benefit much more from individual and couple therapy than entitled philanderers.

> **In** a sexual addiction recovery program, 16 percent of all of the sex addicts were women.[8]

Addicted to sex: Sex addicts experience feelings of worthlessness. They are unable to resist their impulses despite possible embarrassment or risk to their family and career. They are driven toward orgasmic release, but the release is only temporary; the cycle of regret, anxiety, and risky behavior begins again. Compulsive masturbation, pornography, massage parlors, and one-night stands can become such a preoccupation that marital sex is no longer desired.

> **A** residential treatment center for addictions reported that 80 percent of the patients being treated for sexual addiction were corporate executives or high-level professionals.[7]

Discovery is shocking to spouses, who may have been attributing lack of marital sex to their partner's low libido. On the other hand, the fixation with sex may create demands for such frequent sex that the betrayed spouse is stunned by a revelation that extramarital sex was occurring in addition to twice daily sex in the marriage. Discovery is catastrophic if it occurs because of an arrest for soliciting prostitutes, a sexual harassment suit at work, or contraction of a sexually transmitted disease by the betrayed partner.

Addicted to love: Love addicts live for the heightened physical and emotional feelings that are part of falling in love with a new person: the passionate pursuit, the adoration, the thrill of infatuation. They experience physiological changes similar to those felt by a drug addict: an initial high or euphoria that doesn't last. The love addict enjoys falling, but soon after the object of pursuit reciprocates the attention, the clarity of daylight is a call to reality. This kind of love doesn't tolerate the earthiness of flesh-and-blood connections. However, the constant covering up required by infidelity can keep the illusion alive longer than an open relationship.

A betrayed wife was torn apart by the love letters she found, but by the time her husband was on his third affair she recognized the same passionate phrases and pronouncements of love that she had seen in the first two. She realized that he was in love with love, and that she could never compete with the intensity of his attachments to his fantasy loves.

Addicted to romance: People who are addicted to romantic love are really addicted to the romantic setting: candlelight and roses, violins playing love songs, and walks in the moonlight. More important than the specific person who is the object of desire are the circumstances of desire. I was touched and impressed by the romantic gestures that Oliver made toward his wife during their recovery from his infidelity. He planned a surprise weekend at a romantic place, covered the bed with roses, and bought her something special from Victoria's Secret. Unfortunately, one year later he was romancing yet another woman with his extravagant gestures, and his illicit courtship landed him in divorce court.

Addicted to the Internet: The Internet offers a perfect vehicle for pursuing addictions to sex, love, or romance. On-line activities often start out as entertainment or recreation but escalate into compulsions that are difficult to discontinue despite adverse consequences. It is clear that Donald went over the line when on-line sex and love threatened his career, his family life, and his marriage to Daphne.

Multiple addictions: People with an addictive personality are frequently addicted to getting high on more than one thing, for example, sexaholics can also be alcoholics or fanatic exercisers. Infidelity may be only one component of a compulsive pattern that includes the abuse of drugs or alcohol. The connection between substance abuse and infidelity is a familiar scenario. "I had too much to drink at the company party" is a common explanation for a one-night stand. Alcohol, marijuana, and cocaine loosen inhibitions and intensify sexual arousal. Occasional overindulgence may explain a brief fling, but getting high may be part of the camaraderie of a continuing affair. One man brought that home to me when he said, "When I got sober, I got faithful."

> Psychologist Kimberly Young found that 52 percent of Internet addicts were in recovery programs for alcoholism, chemical dependency, compulsive gambling, or chronic overeating.[9]

The drive to satisfy cravings for stimulation or approval can lead to invigorating adventures, extraordinary achievement, or self-destructive patterns. A quest for intensity is what characterizes all of these needs, desires, and addictions. Looking back at experiences from childhood and earlier relationships will help us understand where these excessive needs come from. Getting in touch with suppressed emotions will diminish the striving for intense stimulation.

Echoes from the Past

Our reactions to current situations resound with echoes from the past. When I am sitting on the sidelines at the tennis court because I haven't found someone to play with, I feel totally rejected and forlorn. These feelings are irrational because I usually have lots of people who want to play tennis with me. I recognize that I am reexperiencing rejections in junior high, where I was usually the last one to be picked for a team. My adult reactions at the tennis court are reverberating down the halls of memory to age thirteen. To get myself back to reality, I try to figure out whether what I am feeling is *live or Memorex.*

We bring to our current relationships all of our old tapes from the past. The way we react to present situations reflects the psychic wounds, adaptations, and survival skills we learned in earlier relationships. Our parents, teachers, lovers, and even our old classmates are sitting on our shoulders whispering messages into our ears. They influence how easily we trust others, how much closeness or distance we need, how much sex and affection we seek, and how threatened we are by criticism. Without conscious awareness, we've been evolving our emotional deficits and resources since infancy.

Old Family Tapes

The family is our first and foremost teacher about relationships. The child observes how family members relate to each other and is taught to take certain parts in the unfolding drama. The question here isn't as much about family history as about family roles. Some people become habituated to the roles they experienced in their family. Others rebel against their childhood roles and vow never to be in that position again. Our family constellation is the first drawing board for relationship triangles.

The Indulged Child

Not every entitled philanderer is a person of wealth and influence. Some adults were raised to feel privileged by virtue of their birth order, their special talents, their physical appeal, or their gender. The "golden child" in the family is indulged and pampered without any responsibilities, except to shine and make the parents proud. The "baby" or the "princess" may expect his or her spouse to cater to every whim without any expectation of reciprocity.

Sid was his family's shining star. He was an outstanding athlete and a brilliant scholar. He was treated differently from his siblings, who were expected to perform mundane chores. When Sally caught Sid with his affair partner after many false promises, she packed his suitcase and told him to leave. Sid said, "If you make me leave, then you have to take responsibility for breaking up this family." Sid felt entitled to do whatever he wanted and expected his wife to endure his deception because he had been indulged throughout his childhood, adolescence, and young adulthood.

The Chaste Mother

Men who perceive their mothers as pure and untouchable have a tendency to split women into two distinct groups: the virginal types that you marry and the wild women you have erotic sex with. This split between affection and sex is called the "Madonna-whore complex." You might remember how difficult it was for Gavin and Grace to arrive at a mutual understanding of his sexual fling with Tina. Gavin saw Grace as "a good woman" and Tina as "loose." This split allowed him to engage in casual sex with Tina while remaining committed to Grace.

Some men become constricted sexually with their wives after the first child is born because their exciting sex partner has now become a mother. An unfaithful husband sent sexually explicit greeting cards to his affair partner but never considered sending something like that to his wife. Even after his wife told him she would enjoy receiving a sexy card from him, he said, "I couldn't send something like that to you. You're my wife and the mother of my children."

The Laissez-faire Parents

Hilda's parents let her do pretty much as she pleased because they were preoccupied with their own lives. When her friends in high school had to rush home for curfews, Hilda could stay out as late as she wanted. Although she enjoyed this freedom, she felt neglected and uncared for. Her husband, Hale, was an easygoing guy who loved Hilda's free spirit. However, as the years went on, Hilda took his unflagging trust as lack of interest and caring.

One night, Hilda went out with a bunch of her girlfriends to a dance club, where she met an interesting man who invited her to his house. She called Hale at 2:00 A.M. and told him that she was going to be out all night. Hale's unexpected response stunned her. He said, "Either you get home in the next half hour, or you can pack your bags." Hilda drove home immediately, singing joyously at the top of her lungs. She took Hale's reaction as evidence that finally there was someone who loved her enough to set limits on her.

Our Parents as Partners

We learn not only from how our parents and family members treat us, but from how they treated each other. Sometimes people identify with the parent who, as they perceived it, was victimized in the marriage, and sometimes they identify with the one who they thought was stronger.

Sadie had a dominating father who was demeaning to her mother. After witnessing her mother's passivity and humiliation, Sadie vowed that she would never be like her mother. Her conscious decision to be different put into place an unconscious drive to model herself after her father, a notorious womanizer. In her own marriage, Sadie was "a control freak" and was unfaithful with several different men. She retained her "first-strike capability" as a defensive maneuver because what she feared most was being the type of woman who stayed at home, weeping over a philandering husband.

During his engagement, Ronald got involved briefly with an old girl-friend. A few months after he was married, he "fooled around" with a woman he met at a bar. In counseling he uncovered how leery he was of committing to one woman for life. He had watched his father become the unhappy caretaker of his difficult mother after she became chronically ill. He believed his father could have done so much better if he hadn't gotten stuck in a bad marriage.

Emotional Allergies

Excessive emotional reactions can be due to *emotional allergies* from the past that are unconsciously activated by minimal cues in the present.[10] Xandra and Edward developed extreme sensitivity (and therefore extreme reactions) to anything that looked or smelled like what they had experienced at the hands of their parents. Thus, their spouses unwittingly triggered emotional allergies by fairly innocuous behaviors.

Think of a woman who is allergic to peanuts. She may have eaten peanuts comfortably until the day that peanuts brought on an allergic reaction that was life-threatening. Since then, just the scent of peanuts is enough to start an automatic response, such as sensations that her throat is closing up. Even looking at pictures of peanuts, when no real peanuts are present, can trigger the same allergic reaction in some people.

Xandra felt like she was going to suffocate when her husband was even remotely solicitous. Her mother had been extremely overprotective and smothered Xandra with attention, advice, and her own anxieties. When Xandra got married, she imagined that she would be able to breathe free at last. When her husband simply mentioned that the weather report was predicting hazardous driving conditions, Xandra reacted as if he had just lit a fuse under her. She had an emotional allergy to his attention, advice, and anxieties (sound familiar?). She would plead, "I need space" without understanding the unconscious mechanisms. An affair gave Xandra the distorted perception that she was finally a freewheeling adult.

Edward grew up with a mother who was distracted and distant. The only attention he got from her was criticism. Edward's wife gave him a lot of physical and emotional support, but he was supersensitive to being neglected or criticized. Whenever she was preoccupied with work or tired at the end of the day, he would personalize her weariness as rejection and feel that she must not love him anymore. He heard her requests to help out more with the children as ego-shattering putdowns. The unconditional adoration of his secretary made him vulnerable for an affair. But he didn't get what he craved because his secretary soon began to complain that she wanted more time together—so he ended it.

Xandra's husband and Edward's wife were innocent victims of their partners' troubled childhoods. They were unfairly caught in reactions that their partners developed before they had ever met. Recognizing these patterns is an essential step in developing emotional antihistamines. Lori Gordon teaches in her PAIRS program that knowing what touches off our emotional allergies is the only way to determine whether we are in the presence of something harmless or harmful.[11]

Xandra and Edward can control their emotional allergies by reminding themselves, "You are not my toxic parent. You are my caring partner." And their spouses can be sensitive about triggering these allergies unnecessarily; for example, they can signal, "I'm having a rough day today, and it isn't anything you've done." A compassionate marriage is the safest place to heal; affairs can activate new emotional allergies in the unfaithful spouse *and* the betrayed spouse.

Survivors of Childhood Abuse

Men and women who were sexually abused during childhood or adolescence may engage in compulsive sexual behavior as a consequence of the earlier trauma. It is common for male and female sex addicts to be survivors of childhood sexual abuse.[12] Men who were molested during childhood or adolescence by adult men or women often turn to extramarital sex to validate their masculinity. Psychologist April Westfall has observed a significant number of incest survivors engaging in high-risk sexual behaviors.[13] Compulsive sexual acting-out replicates the earlier trauma through secrecy, shame, and high emotional intensity.

> Patrick Carnes reported that 81 percent of 600 sex addicts he surveyed had been sexually abused, 73 percent had been physically abused, and 97 percent had been emotionally abused.[14]

Adult survivors of sexual abuse may show a strong sexual desire at the beginning of a relationship. It is common for abuse survivors to have trouble integrating their sexual feelings with feelings of love. Therefore, they may withdraw sexually when a relationship becomes more emotionally intimate because the closeness recalls the discomfort of sexual molestation by caregivers. They may seek experiences with a new partner as their sexual feelings for a spouse taper off. This separation of feelings can make fidelity in marriage a real challenge for both spouses.

Spouses may not even be privy to this traumatic past. Sudden amorous gestures by an unknowing spouse can be experienced as aversive if they evoke memories of unwelcome intrusions into their partner's personal space. It's important for the sexually abused spouse to initiate and be in control of sexual encounters. Extramarital pursuits may be perceived as a way for him or her to be the more powerful partner, the one who can *do* rather than be *done unto*. The couple's recovery from infidelity will necessitate sharing not only the nature of the betrayal but also the history of sexual victimization in the unfaithful partner.

Attachment Styles

Attachment experiences with caregivers during infancy and early childhood have a profound effect on adult love relationships.[15] Researchers have demonstrated a link between the kind of bonding that people formed with their parents and the kind of bonding they will form later with sexual partners. A secure and trusting relationship with parents is likely to result in a secure and trusting relationship with a life partner. To extend that link even further, Elizabeth Allen's research demonstrated how adult romantic attachment styles predicted who was most likely to be unfaithful, what motivated extramarital involvement, and the likelihood of remorse over infidelity.[16]

Secure Attachment Style

Children who have been consistently well-loved from birth form secure attachments to their parents. They can count on their parents to be responsive to their needs. When these children are left with a baby sitter or day care provider, they are able to separate because they are secure in the belief that their parents will return. They are easily soothed. As adults, they are not concerned about abandonment or overdependency. They enjoy physical contact such as cuddling as well as sexual contact.

Adults with a secure attachment style are more likely to be faithful. Because they have the capacity to form deep emotional and sexual bonds, they are unlikely to have one-night stands and their infrequent affairs are more momentous when they do occur. Looking back at Ralph and Rachel, we can surmise that Ralph had a secure attachment style. His affair with Lara was a threat to his marriage because he became so attached to her. The closer he felt to Lara, the further he moved away from Rachel. He would never have been able to justify an affair just for the sex.

People with a secure attachment style usually form one bond at a time and are not comfortable leading a double life and loving two people at the same time. Loyalty to their lover inhibits them from having sex at home. They can't face the prospect that they are bad people who are abandoning good marriages, so they reframe their situation to make themselves into good people abandoning bad marriages. The internal pressure to resolve their divided commitments often leads them to divorce. They exemplify *monogamous infidels.*

Anxious Attachment Style

Children with anxious attachments have parents whose comforting and attention is unpredictable. Time together is arranged according to the needs of the parent, not the needs of the child. The children become anxious because they can't count on controlling the contact. Pleasurable connections with parents are erratic. The children cry profusely and are agitated when the mother or caretaker leaves, are angry upon her return, and are not easily soothed. They crave affection and need to be reassured of their self-worth. They cope by pulling away or clinging.

Anxious/fearful. Adults with an anxious/fearful attachment style are ambivalent and fearful of emotional closeness that they can't rely on. They need closeness but are afraid to open up too much and expose their vulnerabilities. Marriage can feel confining. They view an affair as a way to get "space" and autonomy. They can sometimes risk getting close in the affair because the constraints of an affair limit how much closeness is possible. An affair allows them to achieve some autonomy and increase their self-esteem.

Anxious/preoccupied: Adults with an anxious/preoccupied attachment style crave emotional closeness. They are insecure about the depth of their spouse's feelings and may view them as distant or neglectful. An affair offers them the intimacy and self-esteem they hunger for. They may develop a rapid and intense attraction to their affair partner, which fills them with both desire and anxiety. Although Elizabeth Allen found that women were more likely than men to cite intimacy as the reason for an affair, men with preoccupied attachment style were inclined toward intense, obsessive affairs.

Dismissive Attachment Style
Children with a detached or dismissive attachment style have very little interaction with their parents. They are rejected either physically or emotionally. As a consequence, they learn to suppress their own needs, don't rely on others, and appear independent. They feel safest by depending solely on themselves and may be seen as "lone wolves." They prefer flying solo and are uneasy collaborating with a copilot.

> Elizabeth Allen found that dismissive men had twice as many affairs as men with other attachment styles: 74 percent of married men with a dismissive attachment style had at least one affair.[17]

Adults with a dismissive attachment style don't open up easily (if at all) and don't ponder much about relationships. They are prone to have one-night stands and to engage in multiple infidelities. Engaging in extra-marital sex early in marriage is not uncommon and indicates a reluctance to make a lifetime commitment to one person. They experience their spouses as too intrusive and smothering, and they enjoy the increased distance, space, and freedom that infidelity provides.

Split Attachment Styles: The Double Life

I have observed that individuals who had an anxious attachment in childhood often try to repair it by marrying someone who will provide the secure base they longed for but didn't have. They look for a mate who will give them unconditional regard and will always be there for them. Although the marriage provides some healing, the longing for the parent who wasn't there never disappears completely.

When Ken married Kris, he felt really good being with a woman who could give him the steady loving attention he never got from his mother. Through the years, Ken could count on Kris's warmth and devotion. He gradually became more secure and confident as the deficit of his childhood was largely filled by Kris. Then Ken met Ilse, who was a lot like his mother: she had rapid mood swings, was seductive and elusive, and her interest in him was intermittent.

How could Ken cheat on his wonderful wife with a woman who wasn't nearly as loving or devoted? Because Ken's primary need for security and loving stability had been met by Kris, he then was driven to pursue his unconscious need to capture a woman who created an anxious attachment similar to that of his mother.

Childhood attachments can be either compensated or replicated in the marriage. An affair provides an alternative. There is usually a contrast in the type of attachment that is formed in these two relationships by an ambivalent spouse in a stable triangle. A clear picture of attachment style will bring insights into how and why someone becomes involved outside the marriage—whether he or she is seeking closeness, distance, or unpredictability.

Passages and Growing Pains

In Chapter 9 we explored the transition points in the family life cycle when an individual can be vulnerable to extramarital involvements. In this section, we will look at the *developmental* cycle, which charts the inner psychological evolution of the individual. These are passages from one stage to another when the individual asks "Do I want to keep on as I am, or am I ready for a change?" An affair can be a way to ask or answer that question.

To a great extent, how you cope with transitions in your life depends on how you perceive them. Transitions can be times of reflection or times of loss. Birthdays and anniversaries can be occasions to ask where you want to go or times of regret about where you've been. Instead of living fully in the present, some people dwell in the glories and regrets of the past; others live in dread or in eager anticipation of the future. Each new passage can be experienced as a challenge, a burden, or an accomplishment.

New Roles

An affair can represent a transition from the way we were to the way we would like to be. When Ilene married Ian, she was attracted to his strong sense of morality and religious principles. They belonged to a devout religious community. Ilene welcomed the structure and constraints because she had grown up in a chaotic family where rituals and routines were absent. However, as Ilene advanced in her career and became more involved in the secular world, she began to question the rigidity and constrictions that their religion placed on their lifestyle.

Instead of bringing her concerns to Ian, she had an affair with a man who professed to be an atheist. She enjoyed listening to his philosophy and liberated perspective. Although Ian began to notice that she was dressing in a less conservative manner, he didn't object. In fact, he sometimes complimented her on her makeup and attractive clothes. When Ilene's "adultery" was revealed, Ian was shattered. However, his dedication to his family kept them together until they were able to come to a mutual understanding about their beliefs. Ilene realized that she could be her own person within the marriage without violating the Ten Commandments.

Reluctant Grown-ups

Some individuals appear to have a prolonged adolescence. Although they age and advance in their careers, they are reluctant to grow up and assume the responsibilities of adulthood. When young adults become engaged, get married, or face the challenges of parenting, they may start to think: "Omigawd, now I have to be a real grown-up." Until this new event, they could pretend they were only "playing house." Now they have to come to terms with their adult commitments and responsibilities. One way to hold on to the illusion of an unencumbered life while married is to have an extramarital affair.

Midlife Reckonings

For many people, midlife is a time of turmoil, when they question their choices and experience the disappointment of unmet expectations. Family responsibilities are often heavy, and health problems may become apparent. It's not unusual for midlife couples to be raising teenagers and dealing with aging parents at the same time.

Death of a Parent
One common midlife reflection occurs when parents die. You are still a child as long as one of your parents is alive. When both parents are gone, the buffer between middle age and your own demise has disappeared. The bereaved children start to evaluate their own marriages if a parent dies after a life of misery in a bad marriage: "Do I want to spend what's left of my life in this empty marriage?" An affair can be used as a trial balloon to see whether a new partner offers a more promising future than the disappointing past.

No More Mountains to Climb
In another kind of midlife reckoning, people who appear to be highly esteemed and materially rewarded may be restless and unhappy. The unease for some is the failure to achieve incredible aspirations: economists who didn't win the Nobel prize; professional athletes who weren't inducted into the Hall of Fame; artists who weren't exhibited at the Metropolitan; and parents who failed to raise children who were designated as "gifted and talented."

Sid's story illustrates how midlife restlessness contributes to infidelity. From the time Sid was young, he had known he was going to be an attorney. His parents fostered his dreams and did everything they could to help him achieve his goals. He worked hard to get into an Ivy League college;

once there, he put his nose to the grindstone and achieved the excellence required for him to be admitted to a prestigious law school. After attaining a competitive edge through his appointment to the Law Review, he acquired a coveted position in a corporate law firm.

During law school, Sid and Sally got married. While he studied, she worked and handled the household responsibilities—just as his parents had done. He excelled in his profession. His Mercedes convertible and gorgeous home were outward signs of his success. Sally was able to stay home to raise their three outstanding children, but Sid worked so hard that his children were practically strangers to him.

At midlife, Sid found himself at the peak of his profession with no more mountains to climb. He asked himself "Is this all there is?" He felt empty because his life had always been about what he could achieve, rather than who he was or what kind of personal relationships he had. He was exalted by his colleagues and his clients, but Sally was less impressed because she had known him before he was such an important person. He started feeling bored with his life and his marriage.

And then he met an exciting female attorney who wasn't easily attainable. Pursuing her became his new undertaking. After a bitter divorce from Sally, Sid married his dream woman and bought an even more palatial house than before. Without Sally there to front for him, he had to establish an independent relationship with his children. They were devastated by the breakup of the family unit and began to have problems in school and at home.

Sid began to realize that he had always run away from the real issues in his life during the same time he was being lavishly rewarded. He started to wonder how he could be fulfilled without constantly reaching for the brass ring. It was too late to reclaim the fractured past, but he did become a better father and a more devoted husband in his second marriage—even after it was no longer exciting.

Never Too Old

I have encountered couples old enough for Medicare who were dealing with the trauma of infidelity. Just because you're grandparents and respected seniors in your community doesn't mean that the vulnerability for infidelity has vanished. Imagine the shock of finding out that your spouse is having an affair while you are sending out invitations for your fiftieth wedding anniversary or eagerly awaiting the birth of your first great-grandchild.

Getting older triggers fears about death, worries about physical health, and concerns about sexual potency or desirability. Occasional male erectile dysfunction is part of the normal aging process, and the increased arousal of extramarital sex can appear to provide a temporary cure. (Viagra is a more reliable route that helps to restore good marital sex.)

An affair can be an attempt to rekindle vitality and demonstrate that you're still alive and kicking. A new partner can feel like drinking from the fountain of youth. In the movie *Moonstruck,* the aging wife says to her philandering husband, "No matter where you go or what you do, you're going to die anyway." Nevertheless, men (with declining testosterone levels) have fewer affairs after their mid-sixties because they are afraid to risk family disapproval or lose the security of their marriages. Women having affairs in their sixties tend to be involved in long-term love affairs rather than brief casual affairs.[18] This suggests that they are seeking something much more than sexual excitement.

Retirement poses an identity crisis for people whose sense of self was dependent on their work. I have observed numerous individuals in the military who had their first affair as their service career was ending. They hardly knew who they were without their uniforms and stripes. The excitement of an affair was a way to experience a new beginning at a time when it felt like everything they had counted on for their sense of identity was coming to an end. Those who attributed their affairs to marital problems instead of to this major life transition often ended up divorced.

The Exception or the Rule?

Understanding the story of the individual helps to answer the burning question of whether deception and dishonesty are *the exception or the rule.* When Rachel first learned of Ralph's affair with Lara, she said, "I thought Ralph was an honest person. Now I have to ask myself whether I married a liar." Is the unfaithful partner a good person who did a bad thing, or is infidelity just another demonstration of poor character?

Faithlessness can be either an aberration or a life pattern. To determine whether infidelity is a matter of character or circumstance, you have to know the difference between behaviors that emanate from *states* versus those due to *traits*. For example, if your spouse comes home after work and is irritable and uncommunicative, you might conclude that he or she is tired and had a bad day at work (*situational—a temporary state*), or that he or she is simply an inveterate grouch who'll never change (*personality— a permanent trait*).

Although the focus of this book is not on pathological behavior, a brief review of traits that are indicative of narcissism and antisocial personality disorders might be helpful.[19]

Narcissism

Narcissists have an excessive preoccupation with their own distress and an inability to empathize with the pain caused by their betrayals. An attitude of entitlement is seen in the narcissist's lack of guilt over infidelity. Narcissists also have a grandiose sense of self-importance. They can be workaholics, noted philanthropists, or charming raconteurs. They see themselves as unique and demand special attention from doctors, restaurant hosts, and their romantic partners. They are often condescending to others and expect to be catered to; they get frustrated waiting in line with ordinary mortals. Although they appear arrogant, their own shaky self-esteem is dependent on high achievement and constant recognition.

Antisocial Behavior

Infidelity may just be one more manifestation of the deceit and manipulation for profit or pleasure that is characteristic of individuals with antisocial personality disorder. Antisocial personalities may have difficulty sustaining monogamy and may be exploitative in sexual relationships. They appear to have a faulty conscience and frequently deflect blame onto their spouses if their infidelity is disclosed.

Their disregard for others and failure to accept social standards and legal restrictions probably began before adulthood. They are frequently impulsive and irresponsible, but their superficial charm and winning ways with words can endear them to others. Their lack of empathy can be perceived in their cynicism and contempt over the suffering of others. They often have problems with authority that cause them to lose their jobs or fail to pay their taxes. Unscrupulous business deals, reckless driving, aggressiveness, or substance abuse may lead to getting in trouble with the law.

Chronic Lying

Lying can either represent a stable personality trait or be a situational arti- fact of the infidelity. Liars cheat on their taxes, make promises they don't keep, and blame other people for their mistakes. Pathological liars can tell such exaggerated versions of their exploits and accomplishments that they begin to believe their own stories. The chronic liar who cheats on a loving partner has no difficulty inventing ploys to escape detection and has no guilt about the betrayal.

Hope for Change

You can change attitudes, you can change behaviors, but you can't change character. The betrayed partner can determine whether the infidelity is a magnification of lying and cheating that is widespread. Exposing infi- delity can put other disturbing patterns into clearer focus.

To heal a marriage disrupted by infidelity, unfaithful partners have to empathize with the pain they've caused and take responsibility for their actions. If they have characterological flaws, such as the ones I've just mentioned, taking these two steps may seem beyond their capacity. Lack of empathy for others and unscrupulous behaviors are consistent traits in character disorders. Infidelity may reflect a pattern of deceit and selfish- ness that is persistent throughout their lives and is unlikely to change.

Individual values and attitudes are influenced by our friends and col- leagues, work environment, and ethnic background. In the next chapter we will explore how these outside influences create additional vulnerabil- ities for infidelity.

11

THE STORY OF OUTSIDE INFLUENCES

Practically everyone I know has cheated at least once.
I think that proves my point: Monogamy is unnatural.

MARRIAGES DON'T exist in isolation, and neither do affairs. The way we fall in love, commit our allegiance to another person, and break our commitments all happen within a larger social context. We are born male or female, thus automatically falling under certain expectations for our roles in life. Even when differences in sex are accounted for, personal and social filters still lead people to see the world in different ways. Our moral and religious values are derived from the neighborhood and family we grew up in. We are influenced by what we learned in school. We formed expectations based on the cultural messages we received as children and now receive as adults.[1] And, most important, we watch very closely what our friends and colleagues say and do.

These important but often overlooked outside influences can help explain why some spouses cross the line into infidelity and others do not. Along with individual and relationship vulnerabilities, social and cultural factors are the missing links. These factors account for why some people stay monogamous while others either seek opportunity or offer no resistance when opportunity knocks. Here is the irony: we live in a culture that professes to value monogamy *but at the same time* undercuts monogamy significantly by glamorizing illicit love affairs and commercializing sexual titillation. This is analogous to the way our society prizes thinness while it pushes junk food.

If you want to choose a mate who is likely to stay loyal, what would you look for? According to statistics, you should choose someone who

devotedly attends religious services, has friends who support a monogamous lifestyle, lives in a small community, and has parents and grandparents who are straight arrows. Your potentially faithful partner would work
alone, close to home, and wouldn't travel for business purposes.

If, on the other hand, you want to know whom to be wary of, statistics
would steer you clear of someone who works in a condoning or encouraging occupational environment with attractive coworkers, travels with
them to conferences, does not attend worship services or have strong religious beliefs, comes from a sexually liberal background, lives in a large
metropolitan area, and has a history of parental infidelity.

None of these factors is a *predictor* of marital infidelity in any particular individual. But they do point to who is more likely to be unfaithful
and who is more likely to be monogamous.

Many people who violate their vows begin marriage expecting to be
faithful. It's just that over the years, inner convictions begin to erode. Acceptance of infidelity increases in response to personal problems, relationship disillusionment, and a tolerant social environment.

Quiz: Social Vulnerability Map

There's no way to predict with certainty whether a specific individual is
going to be unfaithful. Responding to the statements below will help
identify the influence of your social environment. Rate these social-
cultural influences that increase individual vulnerability to extramarital
involvement.

Directions: Circle the appropriate letter to the left of each statement:
A = **Yes,** I agree.   D = **No,** I disagree.   NA = Not applicable.

A   D   NA   1. I have to travel a lot for my work.

A   D   NA   2. My work offers me the opportunity to interact
              with attractive colleagues whom my significant
              other might perceive as a threat.

A   D   NA   3. Nobody at my workplace would condemn me for
              an "office romance."

A   D   NA   4. I enjoy going to *Happy Hour* with my friends or
              colleagues.

A D NA   5. I have friends who confide in me that they are
            cheating on their partner.

A D NA   6. I have lots of fun with my single friends because
            they like to party.

A D NA   7. Most of my friends would be understanding if I
            cheated on my spouse.

A D NA   8. Hardly anybody I know is strictly monogamous.

A D NA   9. There is a history of infidelity in my childhood
            family or extended family.

A D NA   10. My father would support me and not condemn
            me if I cheated on my partner.

A D NA   11. My mother would support me and not condemn
            me if I cheated on my partner.

A D NA   12. My siblings would support me and not condemn
            me if I cheated on my partner.

Scoring Key:
Add up your points to calculate your **social vulnerability score.**
Each Agree = 1, Disagree = 0, NA = 0.

Your score shows the influence of your social-cultural environment:
0–2 = Clean air zone
3–5 = Smog warning
6–9 = Pollution alert
10–12 = Toxic air zone

Birds of a Feather Frolic Together

One of our most important filters is the social screen. Our vision is sharpened or blurred by what we see and hear from the people around us. You are more likely to be unfaithful if you are surrounded by friends and professional colleagues who are also unfaithful. Friends and acquaintances serve as socialization agents who may make cheating seem alluring or, at the very least, normal.

When you hear exciting confessions and philosophical rationalizations often enough, you can justify almost anything. Your best friend is glowing as she tells you how her lover fulfills her in ways her husband never would or could. When your friends glorify their affairs, you might start to think that marriage is not only dull but a serious impediment to personal growth.

> Opportunity and support of a male peer group were deciding factors in the extramarital sex of 41 percent of the prominent men studied by sociologist Robert Whitehurst.[2]

Occupational Vulnerability

Work settings and occupations can either foster opportunity for extramarital sex or place strict prohibitions against it. For people working in the entertainment industry or in professional sports, infidelity is a common practice. For people working in religious or conservative educational institutions, infidelity is an infraction of behavioral codes. Although workplace environments have become more sensitized to sexual harassment issues, a number of them still overlook or accept flirting and romantic involvements between coworkers. U.S. military policies have been a prime example of mixed messages. Although adultery has been severely punished by demotion or expulsion, male service personnel on foreign assignments have been supplied with prophylactics whether or not they were married.

Laurel Richardson found that married men who were involved with single women at work were not afraid that their affairs could become public knowledge. Their lack of concern was because of two factors: others seldom condemned them, and they were able to keep their wives away from their work setting.[3]

What we see depends on two things: what we are looking at, and who is doing the looking. This also holds true for how we view our opportunities for extramarital relationships. It depends partly on the setting and partly on how we assess the scene.

The story of the attorney, Karl, illustrates how widespread infidelity can be in some work settings. His wife, Karen, became suspicious when she went to Karl's office one day to take him out to lunch. While she was waiting for him, his paralegal, Britney, said to her, "You shouldn't have come here. Don't you know he's too busy to go out for lunch?" The inappropriateness of this remark led to Karen's uncovering of Karl's affair with Britney.

When Karen and Karl entered therapy to repair their marriage, it became clear that recovery could not occur as long as Britney continued to work closely with Karl. He told Karen that he could not fire her because of the risk of a sexual harassment suit. Karen suggested that he exchange paralegals with one of the other attorneys in his practice. Karl told her that was impossible because all the other attorneys in his office were having affairs with *their* paralegals and they would be opposed to making any changes in staffing.

> Bram Buunk and Arnold Bakker found that people are more influenced by their perception that persons of equal status are willing to engage in infidelity than by the perception that others will disapprove.[4]

Sometimes it's hard to tell which comes first, the act of betrayal or the rationale that justifies it. If your social setting isn't filled with people committing adultery, then you might fill in the gap with your own *projections,* ascribing to others the same motives and desires that are attracting you. Conscious or not, the projection of your desires onto other people serves to support your own course of action.

You may remember Luther, a popular physician in a prestigious hospital whose wife, Lois, did everything for him. He had many one-nighters with nurses in the on-call room, which were never detected by Lois. However, one of his flings turned into an intense affair that he had difficulty ending, even after Lois discovered it. During marital therapy, he was clear that his wife had nothing at all to do with his long-term promiscuity or his recent love affair. He loved and admired Lois. He was explicit about their great companionship and satisfying sex.

By way of explaining the apparent contradiction between his promiscuous behavior and his love for his wife, he talked about his early years as a resident. He explained how impressed he had been by the sexual exploits of his medical mentors. He thought it was "cool" to have all these different women at work and a wonderful wife at home.

After the pain and suffering he saw Lois endure, and after experiencing the tumultuous ending to his love affair, Luther had a major shift in attitude and perception. The physicians he came to respect were those with conservative ideals who valued monogamy and were unflinchingly devoted to their wives. Luther now saw the philanderers as immature and "uncool." He used to believe that practically everyone in his department "fooled around," but once he committed himself to fidelity, he noticed how many actually frowned on such antics.

> Anthony Thompson reported that people who are unfaithful may justify their behavior by overestimating how prevalent infidelity is.[5]

Faithless Friends

Lynne Atwater found that a woman's progression toward first extramarital sex is greatly influenced by the faithlessness of other women. The steps are knowing someone who has engaged in extramarital sex, talking to that person about it, and then thinking about it for an extended period of time after becoming aware of an opportunity. Nearly all of the women she interviewed said that they never intended to be unfaithful when they first got married.[6]

Before Cheryl betrayed her husband by having a two-year affair, her friend Sandy had started confiding in Cheryl that *she* was having an affair. Sandy went on and on about the special treatment she was enjoying. She told Cheryl that her lover bought her beautiful presents and treated her like a queen. Sensing that Sandy would be supportive about hearing a similar story from her, Cheryl told her about the exciting new man *she* was attracted to. The object of Cheryl's affection was the opposite of her husband; he reminded her of an old boyfriend who was quiet and outdoorsy. She told Sandy about her fantasies but also said she didn't want to do anything that would hurt her husband, Cliff.

Every time the two friends talked, Cheryl found herself thinking that a little romance on the side wouldn't be such a bad thing. It didn't have to mean anything. When Cheryl and her fantasy man finally got together, Sandy let them use her house as their private hideaway. When Cliff found out, his rage at Sandy was easy to understand. And he knew only the half of it. He knew that Sandy had loaned her house; he never realized what role Sandy's encouragement had played in his wife's predisposition for getting involved in the first place.

It is not unreasonable for worried partners to insist that their spouses terminate or limit friendships that encourage infidelity. To make the marriage safe, it may be necessary to sacrifice friends of the same sex who are not friends of the marriage.

When Vince was first married, he never looked at other women. He only had eyes for his wife, Viola. Every day he went to his desk job in a large utility, processed his paperwork, and was eager to come home to his beautiful wife. Five years down the road, he was tired of sitting around all day indoors and going home to sit some more, so he signed up to play in his company's softball league. He enjoyed the outdoor exercise and had fun with the guys (and the occasional athletic woman).

After a game Vince and his teammates would go to a favorite hangout, have a couple of beers, and shoot some pool. Over the course of several months, he got to know these guys well. The three who were still married were openly contemptuous of men who buckled under to their wives; the five others were either single or divorced. Vince's buddies began to tease him for being "pussy whipped" and having to go home after the second beer. They pointed out to him a couple of attractive young women who seemed interested in him.

Soon Vince started to wonder whether sexual freedom was the norm and monogamy the exception. He started to think that his marriage could be in jeopardy because his commitment to being faithful was starting to waver. Viola was angry and anxious about his nights out, and they started to fight. After months of dissension at home, Vince began to realize that his "friends" were egging him on to destroy his marriage. He decided that he would continue to play softball but go home immediately after the games, without stopping for a beer with his buddies.

The Family Tree

"The apple doesn't fall far from the tree." Like most popular sayings, this one has a large measure of truth in it. In the context of our discussion, it predicts a link between the characteristics of parents and their offspring. In fact, that is what therapists and researchers have observed as they've studied patterns of infidelity across generations within the same family.[7] Nonmonogamous families seem to produce sons who betray their wives, as well as daughters who either accept their husbands' betrayals as normal or are unfaithful themselves.

Carol Ellison's research with over 2,000 women found a definite link between parental affairs and extramarital sexual permissiveness. Of the affair-prone women she studied, 13 percent had five or more affairs. Many of them had grown up in a childhood environment where a parent or a parental figure had engaged in affairs.[8]

Multigenerational family trees often show consistent patterns of infidelity or monogamy. One study based on an analysis of twelve couples found that each family had a unique pattern, ranging from virtually no affairs in the entire family to multiple affairs in all three generations.[9] In the nonmonogamous families, the affair partners were remarkably similar. For example, in the case of one couple, two generations of men had affairs with baby sitters; in that of another couple, a number of affairs in the family had involved coworkers.

The Kennedy family presents us with a well-known example of multigenerational infidelity. The patriarch, Joseph Kennedy, provided the model for his sons, who followed in his footsteps, not only by getting involved in politics but by having affairs with many women, including famous actresses. President Bill Clinton's grandfather was a very well-liked, friendly man; however, his grandmother was frequently angry at his grandfather because he was "too friendly" with other women.[10] In trying to explain Clinton's philandering, the model of his beloved grandfather could be more significant than all of the public speculation about possible problems in his marriage.

Some people are able to make the "family connection" as a result of bitter personal experience. Hannah was engaged to a man she felt she could trust: "I feel safe with Herman. I really do believe he'll be totally faithful to me because his family's like that. They believe in monogamy, just like my family." Hannah had divorced her first husband because he showed no inclination to be faithful, even after she caught him many times with different women. She described him as someone who "has an amazing ability to lead a double life." He came from a family where his mother and father both cheated on each other. She said, "To them, fidelity meant nothing."

Unfortunately, it's hard to make predictions about how parental infidelity will play out in a child's adulthood. A parent's infidelity creates vivid impressions that usually lead to one extreme reaction or the other. Eric's father took him along to Gentlemen's Clubs when Eric reached adolescence. He admired his father and was easily indoctrinated into a world of macho men and easy women. Although he married "the girl of his dreams," he did not expect to be sexually faithful.

In a contrasting example of the effect of paternal behavior, Patrick was disgusted when his father started taking him along to meet his "mistresses." He was appalled by the disregard for his mother's feelings. He vowed then and there that he would never do that to his wife. Although Patrick's marriage was conflicted, he remained faithful and was never tempted by another woman.

The World We Live In

The family patterns described above are often part of a larger cultural context that accepts infidelity by men and abhors infidelity by women. Society plays a large role in setting the standard for what is acceptable and what is not. The fact that there is a standard at all is evidence of how powerful social norms and expectations can be in regulating private behavior. You may think you are making completely independent decisions about your romantic life, but all of us are influenced by our culture's ideas about what is appropriate, what is desirable, and *especially* what is unacceptable.

The Double Standard Is Alive and Well

The *double standard*—one standard for women and another, less strict standard for men—is the primary example of a social norm that influences sexual behavior. In fact, a double standard of infidelity is more prevalent among those from cultures with traditional gender roles.[11] As a general rule, societies that give higher status to men promote a double standard.

Despite the many ways we are moving toward an egalitarian society, the double standard still exists. Society easily accepts and excuses men who engage in premarital and extramarital sex. Women who engage in similar behaviors are condemned and suffer severe consequences. The double standard has never been applied in a reverse pattern; men have never been subjected to a double standard in the past or the present, according to a study of sixty-two cultures by anthropologist Suzanne Frayser.

> Husbands, but not wives, were allowed to have extramarital sex in 26 percent of the societies studied by Frayser.[12]

A *single standard* of sexual behavior for both men and women is most likely when a society is either extremely permissive or extremely conservative, according to sociologist Harold Christensen.[13] His study showed that in the extremely permissive Danish culture, women were as sexually liberated as men; in the extremely restrictive American intermountain society, men were as constrained as women.

Condoning Men

In some quarters, a man gains prestige and respect from other men as a result of his sexual conquests. Boasting about extramarital adventures can be almost as important as, if not more important than, the experience itself.[14] Peggy Vaughan spoke to men who missed the camaraderie of talking with other men about their exploits after they had stopped having affairs.[15] These men impressed their friends with their "successful" affairs but were seen as failures if they got caught and brought pain to their wives.

Surprisingly, some wives tolerate the double standard. There are wives who put up with their husband's philandering as part of the spoken or unspoken "deal" they've made in their marriage. These are often the wives of high-status men who provide substantial material and social benefits. These eminent corporate and political figures are enculturated to have affairs with women who are mostly their subordinates. Jan Halper studied 4,126 male business leaders, executives, and professionals and found that the more successful a man was and the greater his income, the more likely he was to have an affair.[16]

> The proportion of British men who began marriage assuming that they need not be faithful was almost three times higher than the rate for women.[17]

Alice and Arnold initiated couple therapy to deal with her distress about his philandering. You may recall that he was the CEO of a highly successful computer company; she was a devoted mother, active on behalf of the homeless, and a dedicated volunteer at the art museum. I soon realized that they had come into therapy with separate agendas. Alice was hoping that I would persuade Arnold to stop having affairs; Arnold hoped I would persuade his wife to accept his sexual flings as harmless diversions.

When it became apparent that Arnold had no intention of stopping, Alice seemed to accept his behavior as part of their evolving marital contract. She took stock of the pluses and minuses and figured she was better off staying married and enjoying the privileges of being his wife than filing for divorce. It is not unusual in this situation for the wives of prominent men to accept their husband's philandering and do the best they can to develop separate lives.

Condemning Women
Women in nearly all cultures and eras have been punished much more severely than men for extramarital relationships. In 54 percent of the societies for which Suzanne Frayser had data, husbands had the option to kill unfaithful wives. There was *no* culture that was less punitive toward women than toward men.[18]

Fear of public exposure is a real deterrent, especially for women. Public opinion is not so kind toward a woman who admits enjoying the physical fulfillment of illicit affairs. If you listen carefully when people talk about the affairs of others, you will notice a bias that runs in favor of men and against women. What you will hear most often is that the affair is the woman's fault. A woman who is caught in an affair is blamed for having loose morals. A woman *whose husband* is caught in an affair is blamed for not meeting his needs.[19] In reality, this is the opposite of the truth: men tend to have extramarital sex regardless of their satisfaction with the marriage, but women are unlikely to engage in extramarital sex unless they are unhappy.

Matthew was beside himself with rage when he discovered that his wife had been having an affair for four months. In fact, he was ready to end the marriage on the spot. In therapy he was able to gain a more balanced perspective. He finally admitted that he himself had had several "mini-affairs" that he didn't think amounted to much. Like many men, Matthew didn't hold himself to the same standard of monogamy as he held his wife. In the ethnic neighborhood he had grown up in, men bragged about their sexual mastery *and* their ability to keep their wives in line. The women knew what was going on but looked the other way. The entire community ostracized an unfaithful married woman, but an involved man was accepted without any moral outrage.

Trends

In general, the more premarital sexual activity you engage in, the more likely it is that you will be involved in an extramarital affair. Because girls are more sexually active at younger ages than they used to be, married women are not nearly as inhibited about crossing the line as earlier generations of women were. Sexually active girls frequently have mothers and grandmothers who had limited experience with men other than their husbands.

Let's compare Virginia with her old college roommate, Thelma. They both dated men in the same fraternity, and they both got married one year apart after graduation. But after that the similarity ended. When Thelma had her first affair during the second year of marriage, Virginia was shocked. She continued to be dismayed as Thelma had one affair after another.

What accounts for the contrast between them? The answer lies in the difference between the communities they grew up in. The two women were shaped by environments with different standards and expectations. Thelma lost her virginity at fifteen, her sophomore year in high school, as did most of her girlfriends. Virginia and her friends signed abstinence oaths in high school, so it was a momentous event when she had intercourse with her steady boyfriend in her junior year of college. By the time Virginia had her first sexual experience with the man she later married, her precocious roommate had already had multiple partners. We could have predicted from this small bit of information alone that these two women would have different odds of remaining monogamous after marriage.

It is still true that many more women than men disapprove of and reject casual sex, and it is still true that men tend to hold more permissive sexual attitudes about their own involvement than women do. But women are beginning to catch up. Using premarital sexual data alone, we could guess that more women are betraying their husbands than ever before. And that is, in fact, the case.

> Analysis of a national survey concluded that the incidence of extramarital sex did not differ for men and women under forty.[20]

Modern husbands are aware that their wives were not virgins when they first met. A man who knows about his wife's sexual experiences before marriage may be more able to work through disclosure of infidelity than men who perceive their wives as pure and chaste. The influx of sexually experienced women into the workplace is undoubtedly a factor in the prevalence of affairs with professional colleagues.

Sin Cities

The community where people live or travel to can affect the likelihood that they will be unfaithful. Male extramarital sexual opportunities are often promoted and solicited in cities such as Las Vegas and New York, where it is easy to find places to obtain willing partners.[21]

According to several studies, husbands and wives who lived in or near large metropolitan centers were more approving of premarital and extramarital sex than those in small communities or rural areas.[22]

We have seen that every person has a story, or more accurately, several stories. Infidelity is a complex phenomenon involving multiple factors: family traditions and the social-cultural setting influence individual attitudes and values and therefore have an effect on behavior, and individual and relationship vulnerabilities also play a major role.

Before completing the picture, we need to understand more fully the third person in the drama: the lover. Affair partners provide the context for attraction and opportunity, but they come with their own set of vulnerabilities and personal histories. The next chapter discusses the stories of unmarried affair partners with their unique issues.

12

THE STORY OF THE AFFAIR PARTNER

*I knew we were meant for each other. I was waiting
for him to leave his wife . . . and then he ended it.
My pain is so unbearable, but all I hear from
my friends and family is, "What did you expect?"*

IN DECEMBER 2001, a man wrote a letter to a popular newspaper advice columnist confessing that after twenty-five years of happy, faithful marriage, he found himself sexually attracted to an unmarried younger woman who worked in his office. In her reply, the columnist referred to the young woman as a "home-wrecking wench." [1] This is without knowing any more about her than that she was young, attractive, and, according to the letter writer, showing some interest in him.

Such epithets are dehumanizing. Once we label and vilify the affair partner, we don't have to understand or empathize with him or her.

Because the unmarried female is the most common affair partner, this chapter focuses on understanding her story. I am aware, however, that the single affair partner may be a man, for whom many of the characterizations in this chapter may be helpful. Understanding the reasons that single people get involved in illicit relationships with other people's spouses will enlighten both the affair partners and the recovering couples.

Quiz: Single Woman's Vulnerability Map

There's no way to predict with certainty whether a specific unmarried woman is going to get involved with a married man. Responding to the statements below will help you identify your vulnerability to being the "other woman" in an extramarital triangle.

Directions: Circle the appropriate letter to the left of each statement:
A = **Yes,** I agree.　　D = **No,** I disagree.　　NA = Not applicable.

A D NA　1. Married men are not "off limits" to me.

A D NA　2. Married men love to confide in me about their bad marriages.

A D NA　3. Nobody at my workplace would condemn me for an "office romance."

A D NA　4. Most wives don't appreciate their husbands enough.

A D NA　5. My friends wouldn't condemn me for getting involved with a married man.

A D NA　6. My father made me feel special, but he neglected my mother.

A D NA　7. I prefer relationships with no strings attached.

A D NA　8. I would rather turn to men than women for companionship and support.

A D NA　9. My mother was a doormat who put up with my father's infidelity.

A D NA　10. I find myself attracted to older men who can look out for me.

A D NA　11. I can get almost any man to fall for me by turning on my sexual charms.

A D NA　12. I'd rather be a man's part-time lover than his full-time wife.

Scoring Key:

Add up your points to calculate your **single lover vulnerability score.** Each Agree = 1, Disagree = 0, NA = 0.

Your score indicates how likely you are to be *the other woman* in an
  extramarital triangle:
0–2 = Not the type
3–5 = Slippery slope
6–9 = Danger zone
10–12 = Fatal attraction

The majority of single women hope and believe that their married
lovers will leave their wives. In contrast, the majority of single men involved
with other men's wives tend to be commitment-phobic; they may be especially attracted to married women who have no intention of leaving their
husbands. Single men having affairs with married women have a perspective similar to that of unfaithful husbands and wives for whom the affair is
a *sideshow*, whereas for single women it is often the *main event*. The married
affair partner is best understood in the role of the unfaithful spouse.

Married women who have sexual affairs look for different traits in
lovers than in husbands, according to Dalma Heyn's findings.[2] They often
choose younger men because of their endearing personal traits and disregard their inadequate financial, social, or professional status. This is analogous to married men who have affairs with women they do not consider
to be "wife material."

Experts on infidelity agree that affair partners are not superior *or* infe-
rior to the spouses they compete with. They are just different (except
when they are a younger version of an aging partner). Betrayed spouses
generally believe otherwise and often have a distorted view that either
they or their rival must be inadequate and out-classed.

If you believe your partner was hypnotized by the depraved magic of a
sorcerer or a sex goddess, then you may also believe there's not much to
say except "Bad luck!" Stereotyping may be easier for you than the hard
work of internal examination. When you see your unfaithful husband as
the innocent target of an evil seducer, you'll need to maintain vigilance to
keep him from falling prey to the next siren singing on the rocks as his
ship sails by.

The wronged wife isn't the only one prone to witch hunting. The affair
partner may also have typecast the wife as a submissive *homebody* in the
same way that she herself has been labeled a licentious *home wrecker*. To
protect herself from the reality of what she's been doing, the affair partner
may also dismiss the wife as demanding, stupid, or "frigid."

Both women—the wife and the affair partner—need to gain a fuller understanding of each other as people in order to recover.

The Story through the Lens of the Other Woman

As we have seen in the earlier chapters of this book, most affairs start from the innocent spark of friendship. Two people find themselves spending time together, enjoying each other's conversation, and the attraction starts to burn. They don't intend to get involved past the boundaries of being friends, colleagues, or associates. When they do fall for each other, they fall deeply because the relationship has developed over time and is based on an intense intimacy. They have a hard landing if the affair ends because they are plunging from the height of romantic love.

Some affair partners, like Sophie, are eventually able to bounce back and get on with their lives after being rejected by a married partner. Others, like Peggy, are shattered by the crash landing of a prolonged affair. The following stories of Sophie and Peggy describe an affair through the eyes of the other woman.

Sophie's Lost Friendship

Sophie and Randy were professional colleagues who never expected to have an affair. He was devoted to his wife, Rianna, and he had strong religious principles. He and Sophie did not recognize the signs that they were on the slippery slope; their love affair developed slowly over a three-year period and lasted one year before his guilt drove him to confess to his wife. This is their aborted love story.

Falling: Sophie and Randy loved working together at the bank and brainstorming about new projects. She savored his willingness to open up to her. She listened as he disclosed his worries about work-related problems. When she responded to him with humor or insight, he made her feel brilliant and extraordinarily wise. She often thought about how lucky she was that this wonderful man had chosen her as his confidant.

As their intimacy deepened, he told her more about his wife and children. He never said anything negative, so she convinced herself that her relationship with Randy was just a friendship—not a betrayal. Gradually, however, he admitted to Sophie that they shared similar interests that he did not have in common with his wife. Sophie began to think that his home life was barren and that he would be much better off with a wife who shared his intellectual and cultural interests.

Enjoying: This was the golden era of their relationship. They were clearly crazy about each other. They mostly hung out at lunch and after hours at work. They couldn't take a chance on being seen together publicly. He brought her books to read, videotapes of movies to watch, and CDs to listen to, which they spent hours discussing in their offices and on their cell phones. Months later, at her apartment, they tentatively began touching each other. Once they had crossed that physical barrier, it was inevitable that they would go on to lovemaking during their next tryst. She felt that no one had ever loved her body as much as he did. They regarded each other as true soul mates.

Waiting and wondering: They lived from interlude to interlude. Sophie planned her life around the times they could be together. If he suddenly became available, she cancelled plans with her friends. Seeing each other at work provided continuity and a connection that she treasured, but the strain of secrecy and a part-time romance was taking its toll on her. She wanted to shout from the rooftops that she had found the love of her life. Occasionally, the unpleasant thought surfaced that because he was lying to his wife about her, maybe he was lying to her about his wife.

Daydreaming: In spite of herself, Sophie started daydreaming about being married to Randy. She instinctively felt that this was what he wanted too. She visualized living with him in a house just as nice as the one he was living in now. She pictured them sitting in front of the fireplace listening to symphonic music, going to the theater together, and having friends over for gourmet dinners and political discussions. She longed for the time when they could be together openly.

Worrying: The full force of her situation was hitting her. Although she liked to think that their relationship was unique, she recognized that she had joined the large group of women who get "stolen hours" while the wife gets weekends, holidays, and birthdays. When her best friend got married, Sophie was jealous and wondered if it would ever be her turn to have a full-time partner.

Regretting: After Randy confessed everything to his wife, he called Sophie. He told her that he didn't know how things were going to fall out in his marriage, but he still loved her. His words sounded hollow. Secretly, she had wished that Rianna *would* find out. She had been sure that once he was pushed to make a choice, he would choose her. Now she wasn't so sure.

> Of the 4,100 prominent men surveyed by Jan Halper, 85 percent who cheated on their wives stayed in their marriages. Only 3 percent of the men who got divorced during an affair ended up marrying their illicit lovers.[3]

While Randy was resolving his ambivalence, he went back and forth between the two women. One day, during his period of indecision, it came to Sophie in a rush that he would choose his wife. She was the one who would be abandoned with nothing to show for it. She was right. When Randy got back in touch with his religious principles, he realized he couldn't leave his wife and family and start a new relationship based on immorality and deception.

Not only did Sophie lose the love of her life, she also lost her best friend. Every time she bumped into him at the bank, she tried to tell him how much she missed him. She needed to hear that he loved her as much as she loved him. At first he showed concern and caring, but then he became increasingly distant. She realized she couldn't stand to see him at the bank every day and act as if they meant nothing to each other. She applied for a transfer to another branch.

Obsessing: Even though Sophie tried to get Randy out of her mind, she found herself calling his answering machine just to hear his voice. She rode past his house and looked longingly through the picture window and imagined him listening to one of their favorite symphonies. She found excuses to call him for advice on business decisions at her branch. She was mortified and humiliated when he called her one night and told her that he was changing his telephone service to an unlisted number. That was not why he called, however; he wanted her to know that he and his wife would issue a restraining order if she continued to *harass* him.

Sophie couldn't believe how low she had sunk. If it hadn't been for her parents and her adoring dog, she would have taken her life that night.

Rebounding and realizing: Sophie was badly shaken. She knew she had to do something to get a grip on herself. She began therapy and started taking antidepressants to get her through the agony of letting go. Gradually, she was able to replace her romantic fantasies of marrying Randy with a more realistic view. She resumed contact with her old girlfriends, who had been neglected while she was sneaking around with Randy.

As difficult as it was to be dumped, it might have been worse for Sophie if Randy had actually left his wife, kids, and job to be with her. He had financial responsibility for his family, still cared about the well-being of his wife, and would have been torn apart by the pain of his children over a divorce. Sophie realized that Randy might have begun to blame her for the breakup of his marriage and his fall from grace. His teenage children would never have accepted the woman who broke up their family. She would still have been competing for his time and money. Instead of *happily ever after,* her story would have turned into *jealously ever after.*

She eventually realized that he had done her a favor by not continuing with her in an eternal triangle. It frightened her that she might have allowed herself to give him the best years of her life. She was still young and could fulfill her dreams of a home and family with someone who held similar visions for the future.

The next story, about Peggy's clandestine love affair, is Sophie's nightmare come true.

Peggy's Lost Years

Peggy had waited fifteen years for Elliott to leave Elsa, but there was always one more family milestone for him to get through. After each milestone passed, Elliott found another reason to stay married. Every time her hopes were dashed, Peggy was heartbroken and threatened to leave the relationship in an attempt to start her life over. Elliott always came back with heartfelt apologies and seductive promises. She viewed her new SUV and beautiful condo as expressions of his commitment to her, not as expensive bribes to pacify her.

Then, when Elliott's last child got married, he did finally leave his wife. After his divorce was final, Peggy waited excitedly for a diamond ring. Two weeks later, he told her he was getting married—to another woman whom Peggy didn't even know existed. She was crushed to find out that she wasn't the only "other woman" in his life.

She walked into my office in a state of hysteria. How could this have happened to her? When she recalled the years she'd spent bolstering this man, postponing her own personal goals, and settling for the left-overs, she was furious. She felt stupid for believing him when he said they'd be together. He had cheated on her just as he had cheated on his wife.

Peggy was twenty-four years old when she met Elliott. Now she was thirty-nine, and her biological clock had been ticking away during all those years. Her rage that she had given him her prime years was directed more at herself than at him. She realized she had been a willing accomplice in her own victimization. His help in her climb up the corporate ladder was no compensation for the sacrifice of her personal life. She needed to understand what it was in her own family background that made her vulnerable to being the other woman. She also needed to understand how she had subjugated herself to a powerful, older man like Elliott.

Power Balance: Who's on Top?

There is an imbalance of power in the affair when one individual is viewed as a subordinate or is more dependent on the relationship than the other. Peggy's reliance on Elliott for sex, love, and career advancement gave him greater power in their relationship. Although Sophie and Randy were on an equal footing in their careers, Sophie had less power because she had nobody but him, and he had his wife. As we shall see, however, there is a new breed of women who retain power by being emotionally *independent* from their married lovers.[4]

Dependent Women

The dependent affair partner settles for stolen moments and relinquishes weekends, holidays, and special occasions. She is on call, like a genie in a bottle sitting on the shelf until she's asked to appear. When her lover summons her, she drops whatever she is doing to be available. She, on the other hand, is seldom able to get an immediate response from her lover when she is feeling lonely for companionship and attention.

Not all single women who become involved with married men have made a rational choice to do so. Naïve young women can find themselves in tricky situations at work. When I was writing an on-line advice column, I received e-mails from single women who were on the slippery slope at work with married men, often their bosses. They were flattered by the attention, confused about the intentions of these powerful men, and worried about doing anything that would jeopardize their jobs.

> According to marital therapists Anthony Schuham and Waldo Bird, 60 percent of the affair partners of prominent men were secretaries or office assistants, and the remaining 40 percent were from lower socioeconomic backgrounds.[6]

Here is an abridged correspondence with a confused employee:[5]

Dear Dr. Glass,

I am falling in love with my boss. I know he has feelings for me, too. He always takes breaks with me and covers up for me if I'm late. He puts his arm around me as we are walking and talking. There is one small problem. He's married!!! Whenever the subject of his wife comes up, he walks away from me. I know that it would not be right for me to go after a married man. What should I do? I do wonder what's on his mind.

Just call me "Confused"

Dear Confused,

Catch yourself before you go any further. Married men who pursue younger women at work are usually just looking for a little fun on the side and rarely leave their wives. His refusal to discuss his wife with you maintains his loyalty to her and keeps his family and office lives completely separate.

You show him that his attention is pleasing to you by not pulling away when he puts his arm around you. Avoid being alone with him, and discourage his friendliness. Be very professional in your demeanor and only talk to him about business. If he continues to pursue you, tell him that you are not interested in a personal relationship. If he bothers you with unwanted sexual remarks or inappropriate affec-

tionate gestures, then you are being sexually harassed. Confide in a friend or family member to get support while you try to disengage. If you can't control your feelings for him, then you should consider looking for another job.

> *Reflectfully yours,*
> *Shirley Glass*

In Peggy's situation, financial incentives became a gilded cage that helped to sustain an unhealthy relationship. An older man can also act as a mentor who takes a promising young woman under his wing and fosters her career. His marital status seems irrelevant as he shares his expertise and prestigious connections with his eager young disciple. A woman whose father was physically or emotionally unavailable can be more vulnerable to moving into an affair with her mentor because she craves the attention and encouragement she missed during childhood.

> Laurel Richardson interviewed fifty-five single women who had affairs with married men. In almost 30 percent of the affairs, the men had supervised or mentored the women.[7]

Independent Women

The *new other woman* is a term used by Laurel Richardson to describe independent single women who deliberately choose married men with whom they can relate on an equal or superior level. These career-minded women relish their freedom, so they prefer a relationship with no strings attached. They get to love their men *and* send them home. Let their wives worry about the bills, the laundry, and the kids. They will end the relationship if the man becomes too emotionally attached or demanding of their time.

Helen's first marriage had ended in divorce after two years because her job was a greater priority than her husband. When she considered her parents' marriage and her own, the whole marriage setup looked like a trap. She liked being accountable only to herself. She made time for her married lover when it fit into *her* schedule. She could enjoy the best parts of him and be free of any need to change him. If he was irresponsible with money or too indulgent with his kids, she was glad to look the other way. She liked to tease that she was a "low-maintenance mistress" because she made no demands of time or money—just good sex and sparkling conversation. If one of her lovers began to feel deeply about her or hinted that he might leave his wife for her, she dumped him.

The Guilt-Free Affair

Many single women who have affairs with married men appear to experience very little guilt. A magazine survey of 4,700 single women involved with married men revealed that 84 percent knew that their lovers were married. Although very few of them had reservations about sharing a man with his wife, 61 percent said that they would break off the relationship if he had another lover besides them.[8]

> In the survey of "the other woman" in *Woman* magazine, 30 percent said they felt *no* guilt, and 32 percent had *very little* guilt.

The married lover frequently feeds into the other woman's perception that she is doing no harm. To keep his affair partner on the string, he feeds into her belief that he is stuck in an empty-shell marriage because of family responsibilities. But no matter how her married lover may have demeaned his wife, the affair partner who turns his wife into a nonperson is devaluing women, in general.

The other woman may use rationalization, denial, or unconscious mechanisms to avoid feeling guilty. In some cases, she simply has no conscience about what she is doing and no empathy for the wife and children she is sabotaging. There are as many variations of guilt-free affair partners as there are guilt-free philanderers.

- *Antagonist:* This woman betrays other women by stealing their husbands. She views other women as rivals and feels no need for loyalty to or identification with her own gender. She does not regard herself as a "sister" to other women. She seldom has other women as friends and leans on men to enhance her fragile ego and gratify her emotional needs.

- *Antitraditionalist:* Another guilt-free affair partner is the unconventional woman who opposes the institution of marriage as being outdated. She asserts that all marriages are flawed, so why should she restrict herself to an ancient contract whose main purpose is to suppress women? There's no reason to constrain the richness of life just because the man you love happens to be married. While she shares some characteristics with the New Other Woman, the antitraditionalist has a philosophical abhorrence for marriage as an institution.

- *Escapist:* To deny the existence of his wife and family, the escapist affair partner puts the marriage out of mind and out of sight. She never asks questions about his other life. She doesn't consider any repercussions from their illicit affair because the time she spends with her lover is an escape into an alternate reality.

- *Family counselor:* Assuming the role of family therapist is another way to assuage guilt. The other woman offers insights to improve her lover's communication with his children and to help him understand his wife's point of view. Acting partly out of real concern and partly out of self-preservation, she tries to make things better. Laurel Richardson says that the single woman affair partner does "feminist social work among the married." As a result, the affair partner perceives herself as a good person who makes positive contributions to her lover's family life.

- *Unwitting participant:* Finally, the affair partner may not feel guilty because she doesn't know that she is the "other woman." Some men pretend to be single as part of their "dating" strategy, especially on the Internet. The unwitting participant in his infidelity doesn't know that she isn't his one and only.

When Kayla began her on-line romance with Melvin, it never occurred to her that he might be married. Two days before Melvin was due to fly out to meet Kayla in person, she received a phone call ending their relationship. He told her that he was married and that he loved his wife, Mollie. Kayla was so shocked she couldn't get over it. She e-mailed him to get some closure, but he didn't respond. She called him, but he was cold and distant. Kayla learned the hard way to always verify independently that a man pursuing her is free of other commitments.

Getting to the Root of It

Although many women have no guilt about being involved with married men, only a few survive with no regrets. Connecting with a married man may be a one-time aberration or a lifelong pattern that is a connection between the unmarried affair partner and her past. The other woman is often replicating dysfunctional triangles in her family of origin or other significant roles from her childhood relationships.

Family Triangles

The childhood stories of many single women who get involved with married men reveal patterns of triangulating with mothers, siblings, grandparents, or the illicit lovers of parents. In what amounts to emotional incest, some fathers shower their daughter (instead of their wives) with compliments and attention.[9] In other cases, girls jealously watch as their fathers' attention is directed toward other women, at the expense of their wives and children. In both scenarios, the daughter sees that the wife gets the short end of the stick: all of the pain and none of the pleasure. The mother is perceived by her daughter as a negative role model who is either weak or unappealing. The daughter does not want to end up like her mother.

Many of these girls grow up with an unconscious drive to be the other woman in an extramarital triangle. Rather than being a deterrent, the fact that the men whom these women get involved with are married is part of the attraction. They are very much aware of the wife and are competing with her in an attempt to replace her, outdo her, or rescue their married lover from her grasp.

Daddy's Girl

After Karl ended their affair, Britney was heartbroken. In therapy, she recounted a series of affairs with married men. I made the observation that Britney's relationships had been not only with the men, but with their wives. Her affairs had been contests for love, and the prize had been the victory over the wife as much as the man himself. She was competing to be the favorite. That's why she was so nasty when Karen, Karl's wife, showed up at the law office.

Britney's role as the wife's rival reflected her early relationship with her parents. Her father inappropriately confided in his daughter the details of his disappointing marriage. On Valentine's Day, Britney got a box of candy from her father, but her mother got nothing. Britney had mixed feelings: although she liked her father's attention, she saw how hurt her mother was. To alleviate her guilt, she convinced herself that her mother didn't deserve anything because she was distant and unaffectionate. Britney didn't realize that her mother's coldness was a depressed response to her husband's neglect.

Daddy's Other Women

Zelda remembered how her father had humiliated her mother by flirting with other women every time they went out together as a family. As a little girl, she had learned about his secret life when she caught him kissing the lady next door and saw her holding a jewelry box. Zelda felt so sorry for her mother that she vowed she would never allow herself to be in the position of the rejected wife. The position of the other woman looked much more appealing. Zelda's seduction of Al was just another manifestation of her drive to repeat this early triangle by becoming the other woman over and over again.

Saving Daddy from a Bad Marriage

Unless the affair partner knows the wife personally, the unfaithful husband can give the false impression that he and his wife don't love each other anymore and that they never have sex. Samantha saw her mother treat her father badly, so she had no trouble believing that Jerry's wife was doing the same to him. She didn't see him as a saint, but she had no trouble seeing him as saintly for putting up with years of celibacy. Samantha was shocked when June confronted her at the airport and shouted, "Remember when you called the other night? We were making love! We do that a lot." No wonder Samantha felt betrayed. She had been led to believe that Jerry reserved his sexual pleasure for her alone.

A Sexy Veneer

The other woman who is seductive in behavior and appearance uses sexuality as a way to attract men. She longs for someone who will value her for herself, but her sexual favors are the only personal merchandise she has confidence in. As soon as she seeks a deeper relationship she is rejected by the married lover, who was interested in her only as the playmate she pitched herself to be. To the outsider it might look like a "bait and switch" routine: she offers the promise of no-hassle fun and games but then begins to realize that she wants and needs more. It's sad that so many beautiful and intelligent young women have been shaped by unfortunate early circumstances, so that they take on behavior that is ultimately destructive to themselves and the marriages they disrupt.

Tina was sexually molested during her childhood by her uncle and also by a teenage baby sitter. She was extremely confused by these experiences; although they made her feel like she was "special," they left her with a "yukky" sensation in the pit of her stomach. She never resisted because she was a lonely girl who was hungry for affection and attention. During her teen years, she attracted lots of boys by being "easy," but she never had a real boyfriend.

After high school graduation, she rejected the advances of coworkers who were interested in her. She didn't ever want any man to take advantage of her again. Then she discovered she could gain more control by becoming the one who made sexual overtures rather than the one who was always being "hit on." She felt a greater sense of power by deliberately seducing Gavin, who was committed to his wife, than by falling prey to a man who was obviously on the prowl.

Although Tina's lifestyle gave her the illusion of power, she could easily have become a victim of her own self-destructive behaviors because she did not protect herself against infection, pregnancy, or rejection. Her search for intensity masked the hollow life she was leading. After Grace made Gavin stop seeing her, she yearned for a companion of her own to grow old with. She was thirty-two years old, and the longest relationship she had ever had lasted ten months. The question was: Could she be happy with a man who was committed to her, or would she feel smothered and controlled by allowing herself to be dependent on a man?

A Heart of Gold

Isabel had a soft heart. So much so that she sometimes felt like a cliché. She took in stray cats and contributed her hard-earned money to every sad-eyed supplicant on the sidewalks of New York City. The trouble was that her heart of gold didn't stop at cats and street people.

When Isabel was first introduced to Wayne at a party, they clicked immediately. She listened empathically as he recounted his recent run of bad luck. He told her that his wife was an extravagant spender who was furious with him for losing his job.

At first Isabel met him regularly at restaurants and coffee shops just to give him moral support. As time went on, though, she found herself getting more and more involved. She helped him get over his marijuana habit and used her connections to get him a new job. Then he started coming over to her studio apartment for breakfast and dinner. In less than a month, they became lovers and he moved in with her.

Isabel paid for almost everything because Wayne's money went to helping out his wife and children. He told Isabel that he no longer loved his wife, but he felt a little guilty about leaving her in the lurch. Nevertheless, he didn't feel any guilt about leaving Isabel in the lurch when one day he just up and left. Isabel was shattered.

As usual, Isabel had given so much and had asked for so little in return. She was always taking on the problems of men who leaned on her because of her competence and understanding. Three of these relationships had been with married men. It's true that they made her feel good about herself, but it's also true that she took on the emotional burdens of a wife without any of the benefits.

In Isabel's family, she had assumed the role of the caretaker. Her father had been a weak, inadequate man, and her mother had suffered from a chronic medical condition. Isabel's older sister ran away from home at age sixteen, and her younger sister was self-centered and demanding. It fell to

Isabel to see that everyone was happy. Her selflessness extended into her
adult relationships, where she gave and gave with little expectation of receiving anything in return.

Lessons for the Affair Partner

If you are trying to heal from a broken affair, there are ways to help yourself. You might have lost an important person in your life, but you don't
have to lose those important parts of yourself that grew during that experience. Focus on what you can learn from this life-altering event:

* *Think about how easy it is to idealize a relationship when it's not
  based in real life.* Because you didn't live with your lover, you never
  lived with the day-to-day grind of real-life issues. The very qualities in him that you found so attractive could very well have driven
  you nuts after a while. The way he made time for you by deceiving
  his wife could come back to haunt you. A man with a history of
  infidelity is not the best candidate for a life partner.

  Nobody can know what it's like to live with another person
  without taking *Shirley's Toothpaste Test.* Sharing the same tube of
  toothpaste is one of those tests of a relationship that you can't possibly capture in a hit-and-run romance. Does he squeeze from the
  bottom or the top? Does he leave the cap off? These are the minu-
  tiae upon which a marriage often revolves. So, unless you and your
  affair partner survive the toothpaste test—or some variation of
  it—together, you'll never know whether it would have worked out.

* *Give yourself time to mourn and feel the depth of your grief.* Before
  you can move on, you must express your feelings and share your
  memories with someone. You have suffered a significant loss. Cry
  when you feel like it and give yourself as much time as you need to
  return to normal. Talk to someone who can listen and support
  you. Stay away from people who say "I told you so." You need to
  feel the enormity of your loss before you will be ready to do a post-
  mortem on the wouldas, shouldas, and couldas.

* *Cultivate friendships with other women.* Instead of seeing other
  women as rivals, look at them as friends and positive role models.

If you like men better than you like women, it is possible that you are having trouble accepting your own feminine role. The sisterhood of other women provides an emotional connection that is irreplaceable. Even women who have wonderful marriages rely on their women friends to understand and share their experiences in a way that is out of reach for men.

- *Seeing the wife in a more sympathetic light is a sign of moving on.* The wife is rarely as bad as you may have painted her. To get on with your life, you need to develop some understanding and empathy for the woman you were trying to displace. When you can see the wife as a human being whose actions and feelings have validity, then you can remove your own blinders and carry your sharpened vision and newfound empathy into future relationships.

Lessons for the Couple

The basic guidelines for healing are the same for the betrayed spouse and the affair partner: once the affair is over, mourn your losses, understand yourself better in the context of the affair, humanize your rival, and get on with your life. You don't have to see the affair as a story that is confined to perpetrators and victims.

Part of the work of healing for the couple involves resolving the contrasting perceptions of the affair partner. If the betrayed partner continues to demonize and the involved partner continues to idealize the affair partner, they are drawing emotional resources away from their own relationship. The betrayed spouse may think the affair partner deserves to suffer because of the suffering she caused. Focusing all of your outrage on her is a way to deny the complicity and duplicity of the unfaithful spouse. It always feels safer to blame the outlander than to assess the weakness in your own camp. The betrayed partner will have to accept some of the affair partner's positive human qualities, and the involved partner will have to accept some of her imperfections. *There are no winners in the resolution of extramarital triangles—only survivors.*

In the final section of the book, we conclude the healing journey by tackling unfinished business and impediments to forgiveness. Then we move on to rituals for a renewed commitment and signs of a strengthened relationship.

The last chapter is for those of you who are going to do your healing alone. You will be inspired by stories on how to live fully and happily as a single person after recovering from your loss during this next phase of your life story.

PART IV

The Healing Journey

In the last part of this book, I'll help you to craft an approach to healing that allows you to move forward. Whether your healing is accomplished with your partner or alone, you can once again find love, joy, and purpose in life. In difficult times, we all need to be reminded that insight and strength are born from pain and struggle. Moving forward means letting go of the anger and suffering that keep you tied to the past.

Healing takes time. No matter how many times you hear it, it's still true. For recovering couples, patience is more than a virtue—it's a prerequisite. In my experience, it takes several months to get over the initial shock, and full recovery and healing can take several years. Traumatic reactions such as flashbacks and hypervigilance become a rare occurrence but can still be triggered years later.

In the final steps of recovery, couples must work together to complete unfinished business and develop a united front. You can reconstruct a stronger marriage by addressing the relationship vulnerabilities exposed by the affair. Your healing will be delayed if questions remain unanswered or if you're not convinced of your partner's honesty and fidelity. Regardless of whether you continue your journey as part of a couple or as a single person, forgiveness means you let go of anger and pain but remember the lessons.

In the Afterword, I summarize the major points of the book to help you remember how to maintain safe friendships and preserve committed relationships. I include essential facts about infidelity and love, and pointers on how to prevent infidelity and recover from betrayal. A vulnerability chart helps you compare the individual, relational, and social-cultural factors that could make your relationship vulnerable to infidelity.

13

HEALING TOGETHER

Most days, I can't believe how close we are.
That's why it's such a surprise to us when something
unexpectedly triggers another "day from hell."

Y OU'VE MADE an effort to rebuild your marriage. Your communication is now more honest and more caring. You've talked about your personal backgrounds, your marriage, and the meaning of the affair. You cherish the special moments when you feel secure and happy together. No wonder it's so confusing and upsetting when you run up against things that you expected to be over and done with long before now.

During their recovery, Ralph and Rachel handled some troubling incidents with exceptional togetherness. Rachel burst into tears in the middle of making love because she was struck by the bittersweet joy of their renewed sexual intimacy, and Ralph held her tenderly in his arms without any defensiveness or resentment while she cried. When Rachel had a flashback while they were watching a movie, Ralph turned off the VCR to handle the disturbing memories together. When Rachel became anxious that Ralph had to go away to a weekend conference, she arranged for a baby sitter so they could have a mini-vacation together without the children.

An affair is like a radioactive substance: dangerous and potentially lethal, but also a powerful agent of change. Energy that's released by the affair gradually launches new insights and improved interactions that revamp the marriage. Relationships are often remarkably revitalized.

The road to recovery and healing is marked by hard work and heartbreaking events. If you are like other couples, you've had to alter your perceptions of what you want and what it is possible for you to get from your relationship. You will probably still mourn the loss of the assumptions and dreams you held about the marriage or the affair as you work on the painstaking task of rebuilding, moment by moment.

Recovering means that the infidelity is no longer the focus of daily life: each partner has regained equilibrium and is able to perform normal activities, and you can work together when you need to. *Healing* means that most of the time it hardly hurts at all: Both partners have regained hopefulness, confidence, and the resilience to recover from whatever losses may occur in the future. The healing couple proceeds in an atmosphere of safety, shared meaning, caring, commitment, and honest communication.

You will know that the recovery process is on track if the affair is over, the unfaithful partner is visibly moving back into the marriage, and you're addressing the betrayed partner's unhealed wounds. Betrayed spouses who are recovering respond positively to the efforts of unfaithful partners to provide reassurance and reestablish trust. The goal is to reestablish identity as a couple and put the past into perspective—in spite of the pain that persists.

This chapter describes how to complete unfinished business, repair the remaining wounds, and reconstruct a stronger relationship as you move ahead together into the future.

How Long Is It Supposed to Take?

Reconstructing the marriage is usually a long-term process lasting *at least* one or two years. Unfortunately, the challenges inherent in the process of recovering from the trauma can put many couples at risk for repeating harmful patterns that preceded the infidelity. It is unreasonable to expect that the trauma can be brought to closure until the first year anniversary dates of the discovery and aftershocks have passed and been reflected on.

Four Steps Forward and One Step Back

During the final stage of recovering and healing, couples improve by taking *four steps forward and one step back*. Because negative experiences tend to carry more emotional weight than positive ones, "one step back" can appear to cancel out "four steps forward" in the eyes of either partner. Setbacks will become a familiar part of the journey, but these impediments to healing can be temporary roadblocks rather than a major breakdown.

Recovery is not a linear progression, but a series of positive and negative cycles. During these cycles, however, you will make progress. You will need to try to use each as a learning experience. Each time you encounter a setback, avoid getting stuck in it. Use the struggle to generate new insights about how to make the changes that will pull you through to the daylight.

Patience Is Essential

Men and women who were involved in passionate love affairs need time to make the transition back into the marriage. After ending the affair and recommitting to the marriage, unfaithful partners can take weeks or months to reconnect wholeheartedly with their spouses. They will probably continue to have lingering attachments to their affair partners in their thoughts and affections, at least for a while, as well as some grief at the loss of a deep relationship.

Betrayed partners will be making their own transitions back into the marriage. On some days they feel totally committed to working it out; on other days they feel foolish for staying with a partner who deceived them. They will continue to be insecure and preoccupied if the involved spouse has not yet returned emotionally to the marriage.

Both partners have to be patient during this recovery process. During the transition, it is especially important to talk and interact with each other in a way that sends a clear signal of dedication. It may take time before they can say "I love you" in words, but actions can send an undeniable message of devotion and caring.

When Warren discovered that Wendy was losing weight and buying sexy underwear for another man, one of his first remarks was, "Why didn't you do that for me?" After Wendy ended the affair, Warren was acutely aware that she came to bed every night in her old flannel nightgown. He watched and waited silently week after week for some sign of sexual interest on her part. Several months later she put on black lace before bedtime, and Warren breathed a sigh of relief that his wife was finally back.

Completing Unfinished Business

To recover fully, betrayed partners need to know that vestiges of the affair have been fully dealt with. The road to healing is often cluttered with the unfaithful partner's cherished mementos of the affair, ambiguous or unconvincing good-byes to the affair partner, or unexplored details of the infidelity. Swift, sure action that burns the remaining bridges with the affair partner is a vital step in clearing away the leftover debris. Unfinished business that is not addressed doesn't go away; it just goes underground until it surfaces at a later time to contaminate your relationship.

Getting Rid of Reminders

It's especially offensive for the betrayed partner to see the unfaithful partner holding on to cherished mementos of the lost love. Francesca in *The Bridges of Madison County* kept a scrapbook of her stolen days with her lover. Other involved partners hold on to letters, books, cards, recordings, jewelry, dried flowers, photographs, and articles of clothing. These "souvenirs" are links to a chapter in their lives that is now closed.

Both as a symbol and as a commonsense tactic for moving past the affair, unfaithful partners should dispose of these physical reminders of the affair. Getting rid of the offending bed, disinfecting or trading in the family automobile that was violated, or destroying souvenirs of the affair can be cleansing. Destroying the love letters together can symbolize the ending of a traumatic era. Betrayed partners need to decide if they will be helped more by reading the letters before turning them into ashes or by protecting themselves from the pain of romantic phrases burned into memory.

Warren had trouble trusting that Wendy was really committed to him. When he was asked what stood in the way of his healing, he said, "I want my wife to get rid of the orchid in her office that *he* gave her." Whenever Warren went to her office, the plant was like a knife in his heart. This seemed like a reasonable request. When Wendy hesitated, it looked as if she was still attached to her affair partner, but the reality was that Wendy was attached to *the plant*. She just couldn't destroy it. They finally resolved their dilemma when Wendy gave the orchid to a female coworker who had admired it.

Even though she believed that Oren's affair was over, Olivia was still troubled by visions of him having sex with his lover in the upstairs office. The next time they went to his office together she told him she would like him to get rid of the futon upstairs because it was a constant reminder to her that he used it for sex. Oren said, "Of course. I didn't know it bothered you. I'll do it tomorrow." Oren demonstrated empathy for Olivia in his willingness to dispose immediately of this blatant reminder of his affair.

The Final Farewell

If the ending of the affair was ambiguous or uncertain, it's hard for the betrayed partner to be convinced that it's really over. Betrayed spouses often cannot let go until their partner has agreed to end the affair with conviction and finality. Unfaithful spouses may have to send unmistakable messages to their former lover in letters or phone calls saying that they have chosen to stay in the marriage "for love" and *not* "out of duty" or "for the sake of the children."

The nature of these final farewells should be a collaborative effort that attends to the sensitivities of both spouses. It is usually necessary to have some proof that the call was made or the letter was sent, so I strongly support the desire of the betrayed partner to witness the phone call or the e-mail correspondence. A decisive good-bye helps all three individuals in the extramarital triangle get closure.

Randy realized that he had unintentionally fed into Sophie's obsession with him. From his point of view, he was just being nice when he tried to end their relationship gently and lovingly, but the effect on Sophie was to allow her to think that there was still a chance. Unfortunately, Sophie finally got the message to stay away when Randy and Rianna threatened to get a restraining order. Not until then did Sophie pull herself together and get some help to get over him.

The Unanswered Questions

As I said earlier, it is essential for the unfaithful partner to satisfy the betrayed partner's need to understand the meaning of the affair. If the betrayed partner still wants answers that are not forthcoming, recovery will be delayed or even halted. Unfaithful partners frequently get exasperated because it seems to them that they are being tortured with the same questions over and over again. However, each discussion and permutation may shed new light or provide more extensive elaboration. Painful topics that were put on hold earlier in the process can be shared more easily now that you've established an empathetic, caring atmosphere. Betrayed partners may deliberately put aside sensitive issues that appeared to be pressing at the beginning because the answers are no longer important, or because they want to avoid further wounding.

Harold realized that the more information he provided on his own, the less pressure and tension he felt from Hope. He began volunteering information about his sexual affair with his workout partner to his wife without being prodded. Hope said, "It used to be that I would say, 'Was it like this?' and he would say 'Yes' or 'No.' I felt like I was suggesting possible scenarios for a movie and all he did was approve or disapprove of my version. Now he paints the scene for me because he knows that it's important for me to be able to visualize what happened."

Some questions are difficult to answer. *Why did you do it?* is a complex question that may require more introspection and soul searching than some individuals can manage. Although one couple had discussed all of the minute details of the husband's sexual infidelities, they had gone round and round with this frustrating question and couldn't seem to get anywhere. The only answer the unfaithful husband offered was that he was curious.

I asked the unfaithful husband if he could say what explanations for infidelity *did not apply* to him. He readily came up with a long list of reasons why he did *not* do it: "I didn't do it because she was more attractive or something was missing at home. I didn't do it for love or companionship. I didn't do it out of any resentment toward my wife." Although he was unable to provide a direct answer to the burning question "Why?" his wife was able to slowly move forward because she was finally beginning to understand his infidelity.

Repairing the Damage

Recovery cannot occur if you don't work together to repair the damage that resulted from the betrayal and its aftermath. Some repairs can be done with a one-time effort; others require constant maintenance. Traumatic wounds will fade as you restore trust, loyalty, and honesty. Reversing walls and windows, reclaiming lost territories, and cleaning up the fallout from the infidelity will help you to restore a healthy marriage.

Mending the Trauma Wounds

Flashbacks, intrusive thoughts, and hypervigilance will usually persist well into the recovery period. The smallest event or sensory perception may trigger painful memories or flashbacks of earlier, insecure times. When these symptoms erupt, you can work as a couple to mend the wounds.

The unfaithful partner must keep evolving from being the one who has been hurtful to the one who soothes the hurt. That requires a level of patience and caring that he or she may seldom have shown before. Betrayed partners must be able to respond positively to efforts to console and reassure them. Both must get past their anger, blame, and loss to heal their wounds and move beyond the trauma.

Jim's desire to avoid and minimize Janet's deep anguish made her recovery extremely erratic. Whenever she told Jim about a flashback, he would have to steel himself to stay with her instead of following his inclination to run away and hide. Reaching out to hold her physically or accept her emotions was more than he could do. He was proud of himself for enduring her traumatic symptoms, but he was not able to engage in a positive way.

One day when Jim got home from work, Janet was curled up on their bed crying. When he asked what was wrong, she said, "Everything flooded in on me. I feel so hopeless. I can't believe what you did to me." His response was to freeze and not say anything. What went through his mind was: "Not *again*. I can't keep going through this." He knew enough not to voice *those* thoughts, but he couldn't stay with her in her pain. So he said, "Well, let me leave you alone so you can pull yourself together. Why don't I take the boys out for pizza?" Not the worst response, but not as helpful as if Jim had been able to say, "I'm so sorry you are feeling this way. I know you can't help it. I'm here for you."

Harold was able to provide more comfort than Jim because he understood that Hope wasn't being emotional or bringing up upsetting thoughts on purpose. Hope and Harold approached their healing and their lives as a team. Hope had learned that when she was upset about an intrusive thought, she should bring it up in a gentle way without accusing Harold. She knew it was painful and embarrassing for him to recall his shameful behavior. The way they handled the following incident is indicative of how they learned to confront the trauma wounds directly instead of shying away from reminders.

One day as their relationship was growing stronger, Hope wanted to hear more about the fitness center where Harold had met his affair partner. Every time Hope had driven past it, she had experienced a strong visceral reaction of nausea and panic. Hope and Harold decided to go there together. They toured the facility, and Harold gently and thoroughly answered her questions. As she visualized him there with his affair partner, she began to tremble and shake. They went outside and he held her until she was no longer agitated. Harold was comforting and reassuring. After that experience, the gym no longer held the power to upset her when she was driving by.

Reversing Walls and Windows

Reversing walls and windows that were inappropriately positioned during the affair helps to redirect positive energy back into the marriage. Opening windows and erecting a protective wall keeps secrets inside and intruders outside. Just as the recovering couple deals with traumatic symptoms together, they also deal with outside threats together. They handle encounters with the affair partner side by side and guard against other relationships that could compromise their intimacy. Potential attractions are kept at bay and friends are kept safely as "just friends" (in the truest sense). The couple is also sensitive to potential splitting caused by family members, leisure activities, good causes, and even their children.

Putting the Betrayed Partner on the Inside

Recovery can continue in the face of encounters with the affair partner if the couple deals with them together. After his affair ended, Ralph still saw Lara at work for three months until she moved to another city. The only thing that made it bearable for Rachel was that Ralph volunteered information about when he saw Lara and what they said to each other. If Ralph had claimed he never saw Lara or had given accounts that were superficial or unrealistic, Rachel would not have trusted him. In the absence of credible information, she would have filled in the blanks herself with her worst fears.

Rita opened a window with Russ despite her failed attempt to put up an airtight wall against her affair partner. When she caught sight of her ex-lover walking toward her at an airport, she felt as if everything were happening in slow motion. Out of nervousness more than a real desire to know, she asked him how he was doing. He managed to convey a lot of information to her in a short period of time, including the fact that he and his wife had divorced. All Rita could think about on the flight home was how much she wanted to tell Russ about her encounter. Russ was reassured when she told him, "I was mad at myself. I shouldn't have stopped to ask him how he was. If it ever happens again, I won't ask. I'll just keep walking."

Hope feared what would happen if she and Harold ever ran into his affair partner. She told him that she was worried about whom he would show the most concern for. One day while driving to a shopping center, Harold was able to demonstrate his loyalty to Hope. While stopped for a red light, they saw the affair partner in the right-hand lane adjacent to them. Harold slipped his arm around Hope's shoulders and drew her close. Hope felt an enormous sense of relief and closure. Both she and the affair partner could see who was on the inside track with Harold.

Cementing the Wall with the Affair Partner

Angela had a very difficult time recovering from Aaron's affair with their neighbor. She became upset when a friend reported that she had seen Aaron's supposedly former affair partner seated next to him wearing his coaching jacket at a Little League game. When Angela asked him, "Why were you sitting next to her in the first place?" he said, "She came over to ask me something about her son's playing. Then she sat down next to me and told me she was cold, so I loaned her my jacket. It was all public—out in the open."

Although her husband's behavior at the game did not mean he had resumed his affair, it did mean that he had not constructed a big enough wall between himself and his ex-lover. When Angela explained how uncomfortable this made her feel, Aaron suggested that she come to the next game and sit beside him. Angela agreed to come if Aaron would let her wear his jacket, because she knew that would send a clear message. Whenever Angela stayed home from subsequent games, Aaron was less passive and more aloof if his affair partner attempted to enter his space. He always told Angela about these incidents, so she didn't have to hear about them through the grapevine.

Letting Each Other In

Keeping any secrets, even if they are not about the affair or the affair partner, can evoke feelings of being shut out. Ken didn't tell Kris that a friend of theirs was cheating on his wife. When Kris found out about it from someone else, she felt as if Ken was condoning infidelity by keeping the secret from her. To Ken it was a matter of not betraying his male friendship. He complained, "Even if it's about somebody else, Kris turns it into something about us. She holds me guilty for stuff I'm not doing myself."

Kris regarded his reluctance to share this information as evidence that he wasn't totally open with her. She said, "The room was dark even before the affair. When he shares things with me, he lifts the shades." She conceded that his lack of openness made it hard for her to relax: "Since his affair, I've become high-maintenance. I'm not nearly as easygoing as I was before." They finally came to an understanding about what it meant for them to be "best friends." She agreed that she would hold his confidences if he would share openly with her, and he agreed to trust her enough to let her in.

Restoring Broken Trust

Innocence is one of the casualties of betrayal. Never again will the betrayed partner have the same kind of unquestioning faith that marked the beginning of their relationship. Unfaithful partners fear that they will never be free of "trust tests." Reestablishing trust requires sustained effort by both partners over a long period of time. You'll restore your belief in your partner's love and devotion gradually through mutual affection, communication, and understanding. All of the trust-building approaches that I suggested you try during the aftermath of disclosure will continue to be necessary because the injured partner will remain hypervigilant for any signs of deception or further betrayal.

Proof Positive

Trust cannot be earned by oaths of allegiance. The secrecy, deception, and alibis that accompany a secret affair are usually more destructive than the actual acts of infidelity. The antidote is openness, accountability, and honesty. When a partner has been dishonest and deceptive, the only reality that can be trusted is concrete evidence that the affair is over.

A year after Melissa had discovered Morty's one-night stand by calling his hotel room, she became upset when Morty left their romantic Valentine's Day dinner to see an emergency client. Melissa didn't like the feeling of being suspicious, but she couldn't stop herself. She drove over to his office to see if he was really there. She sat in the waiting room until he came out with a client. Morty was sympathetic to her need to check up on him, and he considered her presence an opportunity to reassure her about his fidelity.

Accountability

Actions speak louder than words. By definition, an infidelity is a breach of trust, and only being trustworthy can heal the rupture. Willingness to be accountable is essential. In everyday terms that means that unfaithful partners need to answer questions about where they are going, what they are doing, and with whom. Without accountability, there's no reason to believe their word that the affair is over.

Once Drew told Debbie who his Internet affair partner was, they were able to start the engine of their recovery. Drew had several ideas to help restore Debbie's confidence in him. First, whenever he used the computer, he invited her to sit beside him and read a book. Second, because he had fabricated a web of lies to cover his face-to-face meetings with his on-line lover, he made himself totally accessible to Debbie when he traveled; he brought back items such as restaurant receipts and hotel bills as proof of where he had been.

Respecting Boundaries

After an infidelity, trustworthiness can be reestablished only through specific changes in behavior. One way to increase safety and security is to make significant changes in the kinds of behavior that led to infidelity. In situations where the unfaithful partner had inappropriate boundaries that led to an affair, evidence of stricter boundaries will help to rebuild fractured trust.

Although Ken was careful to be businesslike with attractive women, sometimes he still slipped up. Kris became incensed and accused him of flirting after he went up to the well-endowed produce clerk at the grocery

store and asked, "Got any nice ripe melons?" Ken was initially defensive
and protested his innocence, but he agreed to make a stronger effort to
avoid making these kinds of suggestive remarks.

Loosening the Cord

It can become exasperating for the unfaithful partner to be tethered to
such a short string. One unfaithful partner said, "You'll just have to trust
me or get rid of me." However, it's not that simple. Being accountable and
maintaining appropriate boundaries goes a long way in helping the betrayed partner to gradually lengthen the string. The autonomy of the involved partner should be respected as long as there continues to be honest
communication and no evidence of further deception.

Reclaiming Lost Territories

Healing couples overwrite anniversary dates of traumatic memories by creating their own new memories. In this way, you can reclaim territory, activities, and settings that were connected to the affair. Although you cannot
erase the painful past, you can create promising new chapters. For example,
if last year's wedding anniversary was contaminated by the affair, you can
honor this year's anniversary date with a memorable celebration. Next year's
anniversary date will recall that special vacation, party, romantic dinner, or
house gift from this year instead of the upset from the year before.

When you as a couple are able to reclaim territories where the affair occurred, you are healing. To do this, however, you may have to wait until
the betrayed partner is strong enough to venture into settings that could
trigger flashbacks. Ken first slept with his affair partner at the annual convention hosted by his company. He complied with Kris's request that he
not attend the convention during the year after the end of the affair.

One year later, Kris felt that she was ready to go along with him to the
convention. He promised to tell her if his affair partner was in atten-
dance, and they planned together how they would act if they ran into her.
On the third day they stepped onto an elevator and Ken signaled to Kris
that his ex-lover was standing next to them. Kris felt as if she were going
to faint, but Ken held her hand. Kris was surprised that this woman wasn't
nearly as attractive as she had imagined. Ken and Kris managed to have a
wonderful time afterward. They talked a long while and he answered a
bunch of new questions. Kris and Ken now consider the convention *their*

territory and wonder whether the affair partner will be gutsy enough to venture there again.

Cleaning Up the Fallout

The consequences of infidelity have ripples far beyond the intimate relationship of the recovering couple. Friends, family members, and children are often put into difficult positions by the infidelities of the people they are close to. If others knew about the affair but didn't say anything, betrayed partners may feel that their silence was a form of approval. Those who took sides during the crisis by badmouthing the unfaithful partner may remain alienated from the couple and critical of their reconciliation.

The cleanup may also involve any pregnancies, sexually transmitted diseases, job losses, debts that might have been incurred, or legal problems resulting from drug use or illegal sex. Betrayed partners must decide what they are willing to do by way of active support and plan how to handle the repercussions together. Fallout resulting from the affair may need to be addressed head-on with professional help.

Weaving Broken Threads with Family and Friends

Friends and family members can sometimes be an impediment to recovery. They may have heard the shocking details of the betrayal, but they may not witness how you are drawing together again as a couple. They may have been outraged by the news of the affair, but if they continue to demonize the unfaithful partner, they make it harder for both of you to recast the marriage in a more satisfying mold.

Wounded partners should be cautious about whom they talk to and what they share about their problems. Friends and family remember whatever you tell them—forever. An unhappy spouse who laments bitterly to anyone willing to listen will find it harder to get support for reconciling with an errant partner at a later time. It's also difficult for maligned partners to recover from knowing that others have been privy to the unfortunate details of their private lives.

Friends and family members are often reluctant at first to welcome back the person who hurt their loved one because they are afraid that further pain will be inflicted. They usually come around after they see evidence that their loved one is being treated well and is truly happy in the relationship.

Family

When Rachel confided in her parents about Ralph's affair, they offered her their total support. Her father had a few choice words for the jerk who had hurt his beloved daughter. He vowed that he would never forgive Ralph and advised Rachel to divorce him.

After Rachel decided to stay in the marriage, she tried to convey the extraordinary effort Ralph was making. Although she told her parents and her sister that Ralph was a better partner than he had ever been before, they only reiterated that Ralph wasn't good enough for her. When she looked at him through their eyes, his faults were magnified, but she persevered in spite of her family's opposition and their obvious animosity toward him at family gatherings.

Ralph and Rachel had alternated visits between their families at Christmas. However, the year after his affair they went to his family's home out of sequence because Ralph was too embarrassed to face Rachel's family. They had always treated him lovingly and he felt terrible about disappointing them. Rachel continued throughout the following year to give a detailed picture of how happy she now was and how devoted Ralph had been.

As it became clear that their marriage was strong and loving, her parents softened. Although Ralph remained apprehensive about visiting her family, they agreed on a simple overnight visit the following Christmas. Rachel's mother opened the door and put her arms around Ralph in a big hug. Her father remained aloof until they were ready to leave, and then he shook Ralph's hand.

Friends

Ralph felt so bad about the rift his affair had caused between Rachel and her family that he worked extra hard to repair the damage with their friends. He wanted them to know that he and Rachel were now solidly *together*. Rachel was pleased to overhear one of her friends remarking to another, "I don't understand it, after all she's been through, but she seems happy." She and Ralph were relieved to know that other people were responding to the positive signals they were sending out that they were happy and united.

Friends who are not supportive of the marriage need to be excluded.

Cheryl understood that in order to heal her marriage, she had to part with her friend Sandy, who was not a friend of the marriage. In addition, Cheryl and Cliff decided to socialize only with other couples who had loving relationships. Husbands and wives who constantly fight and don't respect each other can negatively affect your relationship. Spending time with people who honor marriage, in word and deed, made it easier for Cheryl and Cliff to honor their own.

What to Tell the Children

Children should be told as little as possible about a parent's affair. The major reasons to share information with children are (1) if they have already observed evidence or heard the parents discussing the infidelity or (2) if they are going to read about it in the newspaper or hear about it from outside sources.

In some instances, telling the children is the only way they will be able to make sense of what has been happening in the family. However, a child should never be told about an affair and admonished to keep it secret. There is a fine line between maintaining your privacy and answering their questions honestly. If the marriage is rebuilding and there is no pressing reason to tell them, it is better to be discreet.

Cameron's twelve-year-old daughter asked him about a fight she had overheard when he was accusing his wife of having an affair with his business partner. He blurted out that her mother was having sex with another man, which was inappropriate to tell her to begin with, but then he compounded the damage when he told her not to share this information with anyone else. He regretted his outburst later, when he and his wife were rebuilding and when he understood what a psychological and emotional burden he'd placed on his young daughter.

Parents may find it necessary to say something if the children have been upset by conflict or are asking why their parents go to counseling every Monday night. It's best for parents (even separating couples) to sit down with the children together, so the children can have the security of seeing their parents functioning as a unit.

> *Preschoolers* can be told: "Mommy and Daddy have some disagreements that have nothing to do with you. We both still love you, so you don't have to worry."

Grade-school children are sensitive about secrecy and tension in their household because they know other kids whose parents are divorced. Ask what they've noticed and what they are afraid of. Stress that although you are having problems getting along, you still want to stay together.

Preteens and teenagers are dealing with their own sexuality and are more likely to suspect infidelity. If your child asks you directly, be honest without going into detail. You can say, "Yes, Dad got too friendly with another woman, but he realizes that he really loves me and wants us to stay together."

What children most want to know is whether their family life will be disrupted. Disclosing an affair without making it clear that parents are committed to making the marriage work creates tremendous uncertainty. Just like betrayed spouses, poorly informed children will imagine the worst in the absence of evidence to the contrary.

Life-altering Consequences

For the majority of recovered couples, the traces of infidelity are in the painful memories. For an unfortunate minority, the negative consequences are life-altering. Unprotected extramarital sex carries the risk of pregnancy and sexually transmitted diseases that are often mentioned in the aftermath as dangerous possibilities, but in some cases are the tragic realities. I have been impressed with how many couples are able to deal with this kind of near disaster together and come out stronger than those couples who can't get beyond the initial revelation of infidelity.

Pregnancy
You may remember that Stan got his affair partner pregnant. He and his wife, Stella, became involved in the child's life far beyond the legal requirements. For them, open involvement with Stan's daughter was the best way to handle this difficult situation.

If a child is the outcome of an infidelity, the married couple needs to decide from the outset what role they want to play in the child's life. They can fulfill the ethical, legal, and financial obligations as though the child were the product of a one-night stand. The other option is to do what

Stan and Stella did and make the child a part of their own family. Including the child in the family is analogous to raising a child from a previous marriage that ended in divorce. Of course, the outrage and shame of other members of the immediate or extended family must be contended with.

If the child is not integrated into the marriage, the unfaithful partner should *not* be involved in coparenting the child with the affair partner, nor should he or she ever go to the affair partner's residence alone to see the child. This situation creates too great a risk to the marriage. Whatever the married couple decides to do should be a joint decision that they can both accept.

Loss of Job

Donald and Daphne worked hard to rebuild their marriage despite many challenges that would have torn most couples apart. Donald lost his job when his employer found out that he was using company time and the company computer to carry on his Internet romances. Daphne stood by him because of Donald's serious efforts to end his Internet addiction and deal with related issues in therapy. She was also aided in her commitment to him by his obvious devotion and caring for her.

Daphne had to go back to work full time as a waitress at night while Donald looked for a job during the day. By the time he found work in his profession, they were heavily in debt. They managed to give their children a stable environment and acted lovingly toward each other with a minimum of blaming. When Daphne was finally able to return to her normal routine, they had a unique relationship that their friends admired.

Reconstructing a Stronger Marriage

The work of recovery is designed to help you uncover whatever relationship vulnerabilities there may have been in the structure of your relationship, repair them, and emerge with a stronger bond. Caring and consideration ensure that you'll have sufficient emotional reserves and energy to draw on whenever you're hit with negative backlash from the affair. When you have reconstructed a stronger marriage after the trauma of infidelity, you will exhibit the following characteristics:

- Compassionate communication is the essence of your healing.
- Your sexuality is a mutually desired expression of love, affection, and eroticism.
- You have replaced any rigid patterns with flexible interactions: shared intimacy, power, and respect.
- Conflicts are resolved and don't escalate; you don't avoid them.
- Neither of you feels overbenefited or underbenefited because you are equally invested in the relationship.
- You have a united front in dealing with others, a co-constructed story about the meaning of the infidelity, and a shared vision of monogamy.

Addressing Relationship Vulnerabilities

For many couples, infidelity presents an opportunity to examine the individual, relational, and social factors that created the vulnerabilities for the hurtful behavior. By addressing these problem areas, you can build a much stronger marriage than you had before the betrayal.

Child-centered Marriages

Ralph and Rachel realized that their child-centered marriage had created the vulnerability for an affair. To transform their relationship into a couple-centered marriage and keep their connection alive as a two-career couple with school-age kids, they made a concerted effort to share their excitement and their worries about work with each other. Instead of their son's reading comprehension problems, they talked about the volatile stock market. They went out with other couples socially, planned an overnight at a bed and breakfast every few months, and developed an identity as a couple separate from their identity as "Mom and Dad."

Incompatible Sexual Interests

Different perspectives about sexuality evolved into a problem for Ken and Kris once the excitement of their passionate beginning had faded. Ken wanted lots of sex, and Kris wanted sex that was an outgrowth of physical affection and emotional intimacy. In the years prior to Ken's affair, their sexual relationship had become practically nonexistent because Kris began rejecting his sexual advances.

Ken didn't have a good role model. His mother had appeared seductive in her dress and mannerisms, but his parents never touched each other and didn't even sleep together. What he had been looking for in his affair was exciting sex with no strings. In contrast to Ken's parents, Kris's parents hugged and kissed each other a lot. When Kris was young, she would hear her parents giggling in the bedroom next to hers. She remembered thinking, "That's what I want to have when I get married."

The challenge for Ken was to engage with Kris in a more loving way that did not always lead to sexual intercourse. After several months, he was able to say, "I get so much pleasure from cuddling. This is almost better than sex." The challenge for Kris was to be more receptive to Ken's overtures, even if she was tense or tired. Kris shyly admitted that sometimes a "quickie" was just fine.

Lack of Common Interests

After Randy fell in love with Sophie, he justified his affair by telling himself that she offered him greater intellectual interests than he had with Rianna. His affair was a wake-up call to revitalize common interests. After a tortured period of ambivalence, Randy recommitted to the marriage. He and Rianna had a frank discussion and recognized that although their relationship had been warm and loving, it had become complacent and boring.

They decided to take an adult education course together at the local community college on spirituality and religion. They had many lively conversations about what they were learning in their class. They then attended a series of lectures and Bible study courses at their church that reinforced their shared religious convictions. They volunteered to teach Sunday School and met other parents and children who were a good match with their own family interests and values. Randy and Rianna grew to appreciate how much they really did have in common.

Learning New Dances

The recovering couple is able to identify and dance away from old patterns of relating to each other in imbalanced ways, such as pursuer-distancer or parent-child interactions. They equalize power and responsibility through compassionate communication and mutual respect. Their approach to problems is solution-oriented instead of blame-oriented.

Blake and Brenda cast aside their unrewarding roles as "saint" and "sinner" after his affair. Brenda was even more fed up than Blake that she had turned into being the judge, jury, and prison guard. Blake had to decide whether he wanted to assume responsibilities at home or continue to pursue the wild life as a single person. He recognized that he had been attracted to Brenda because he could depend on her, but now he chose to be a "grown-up" that she could depend on. When they saw themselves slipping back into old dances, they teased each other in an affectionate manner with reminders such as "Yes sir, Sergeant," and "Hey, Kiddo."

Cecelia didn't take Carl's complaints seriously about how her ranting and raving was such a turn-off to him until she discovered his affair with a very gentle woman. Cecelia had not liked it when Carl escaped into his clamshell, but she had never expected him to betray her. For them to retire their roles as "stingray" and "clam," Cecelia inhibited her family's pattern of unbridled emotions. She would always be more emotionally expressive than Carl, but she didn't blow him away anymore with her barbed tongue. Carl let her know when he was unhappy with her, so he didn't build up resentment. It was more comfortable for her when he came out of his shell than when he clammed up.

Shifting the Balance of Power

Fred and Frieda's story is an example of how an affair can change the balance of power in a marriage. When they first met, Frieda had interpreted Fred's domineering ways as a strength that she could depend on. She was not tuned in to how overpowering he was. After they got married, she chose to go along with him to avoid his temper outbursts, but she hated herself for being such a wimp and became depressed about her own passivity.

After years of being pressured by Fred, Frieda reluctantly agreed to engage in swinging with other couples. During their sexual adventures with one particular couple, Frieda experienced a greater degree of affection, warmth, and sensitivity with the other man than she had ever had with her husband. The consequence was that she had a secret love affair with him. After two years of sneaking around, she confessed to Fred about the affair and told him that she was *this* close to leaving him. In couple therapy, she confronted Fred with how much he had hurt and scarred her, and she admitted that she didn't know whether she wanted to remain with him. Although the decision was anguished, both of them made the commitment to remain married and work on their problems.

The shock of the affair combined with Frieda's newfound determination to speak up for herself shifted the balance of power in the marriage. The most significant changes were that Frieda began to talk and Fred began to listen. She was assertive about what she wanted and needed, and he developed the capacity to empathize and be influenced by her. A year later, neither of them could believe how much had changed. They had largely liberated themselves from their old roles of Fred as all-powerful and Frieda as powerless. They discovered that new behaviors could emerge out of the chaos that results from the revelation of an affair.

Fostering New Roles

One way to diminish the void caused by the loss of the affair is for the betrayed spouse to foster the positive new roles that the unfaithful spouse experienced with the affair partner. The challenge is to find a way to bring those elements back into the marriage. Rita felt sexually liberated in her affair, and she was afraid she would never experience that kind of freedom to express herself with Russ. Russ was a good person, but he had grown up in a sexually constricted environment. With him, Rita was afraid to be sexually aggressive or to suggest new approaches.

After her affair, Russ wanted to know how to increase Rita's interest and pleasure. He was open but somewhat shy at first about following her suggestions to shower together and to make love at nontraditional times and in unexpected places. Rita was overjoyed that she could stay married without losing a vital part of herself that had been unleashed in the affair. Admittedly, Russ occasionally felt nauseous when he visualized Rita experiencing these sexual adventures with another man. However, he appreciated the fact that they had never been as sexually active as they were now, and both of them delighted in their newfound sexual pleasure.

Equalizing Give and Take

We have seen that often there is greater reciprocity (and thus greater satisfaction) in the affair than in the marriage. When you and your partner are unequally invested in the marriage, you need to develop a better balance between giving and receiving. Regardless of which partner has been unfaithful, the overbenefited partner needs to *give* more and the underbenefited partner has to give less and expect more. Less committed partners will be moved as much or more through their own caring behaviors as by those of their spouse's.

Remember Luther, the physician who had multiple infidelities, and his wife, Lois? During their recovery, one of the most significant issues they worked through was the inequity that had existed in their marriage. Without realizing the full implications, Lois and Luther had relegated Luther to a peripheral role in their family life. He was passionate about his job and was free to concentrate on it, to the exclusion of everything else. He benefited from his marriage with a minimal investment of time and attention on his part. The marital crisis after his affair inspired him to shift his priorities.

As part of the rebuilding process, Luther took a more active role in home life. He modified his work schedule to be at Little League games. Whenever possible, he drove the kids to activities, attended school plays, and went to parent-teacher meetings. His participation in the family allowed Lois to go back to graduate school for an MBA degree. Luther realized how shallow his life had been before. He was amazed at how fulfilling it was to be an involved father and husband. His children began to count on his presence, and he became a favorite with their friends because of his playful, engaging personality.

Forming a United Front

When you achieve your goals and solve problems together, convey respect and affection for each other, and put your relationship ahead of other distractions and obligations, you have effectively formed a united front. This is essential but difficult after an affair because of all the splintered pieces you have to pick up and reassemble into a new, durable mosaic. You have achieved true solidarity when you speak with a single voice to friends, family, and children but also maintain your individuality.

Potential distractions come wrapped up in all kinds of tempting packages, but the couple still has to be aware of people and activities that draw precious resources away from their relationship. Whatever the outside interest is, it has to be reformulated so that it strengthens the couple's relationship instead of weakening it.

Shared Responsibility

Both of you are responsible for healing your relationship, but the affair has to be indisputably over for the recovery process to stay on track. You can tell that couples are recovering when they are more resilient and handle traumatic symptoms together. They are responsive to each other's efforts to provide reassurance and reestablish trust. A healing process reflects equal effort and participation. Both partners have to breathe life into the embers so the fire doesn't go out.

Shared Intimacy

Couples with a united front turn to each other with their deepest thoughts and feelings more readily than they turn to anyone else. Ralph and Rachel came into therapy one day and mentioned that they had stayed up late one night talking about a particularly sensitive issue. I was thrilled when they said that they preferred to keep their discussion private because it was too personal to reveal in therapy. It is crystal clear that a couple has achieved genuine intimacy and comfort when they feel safer talking confidentially to each other than to their therapist.

Shared Meaning

Having a shared meaning about the infidelity is a vital element for recovering couples. Gavin's affair with Tina was a grave breach of faith to Grace, whereas Gavin considered it meaningless fun. For several months, their inability to arrive at a common understanding impeded their recovery. Although they were ultimately able to bridge the gap with mutual understanding, they had to acknowledge that they would never be able to erase the gap entirely between their dissimilar perspectives.

It's important to iron out differences and do everything possible to see things through the other person's eyes, but sometimes the couple must let go of the need to regard the affair in the same way in order to move on. Randy could not gratify Rianna's wish and say that he had never loved Sophie. Although this was hurtful to Rianna and not what she wanted to hear, she came to accept that this was consistent with Randy's character—that he would never have had a casual affair. As long as Rianna was convinced that Randy loved her, she was able to let go of her obsession with the reality that he had been in love with Sophie.

Rianna also got some comfort from knowing that Randy regretted going against his personal values. They were able to establish a greater sense of unity around his regrets; he said that if he could go backward in time, he'd never cross the line in the first place. He felt terrible that others were hurting because he wasn't mindful of his vows.

Shared Vision of Monogamy

Recovering couples have a shared vision of fidelity. The partner with more permissive attitudes commits to exclusivity because of the pain his or her behavior has caused and because another incident could end the marriage. You recognize and avoid opportunities for infidelity, such as office parties without spouses, singles bars, and gatherings with friends who do not support monogamy. You do not quarrel about this any longer because you are on the same side of the fidelity fence. It is not a question of autonomy—it is a question of common sense. *People who are committed to marriage don't act like they're single.*

In the next chapter, we discuss how partners can embark on a process of forgiving, in stages, over time. We also address how to overcome obstacles to forgiveness, while acknowledging that some situations may be unforgivable.

14

FORGIVING AND MOVING FORWARD

It was so hard to forgive you, but when I was finally
able to do it, I felt a great burden lift from my heart.

FORGIVING IS not a single event, but a gradual process of increasing
compassion and reducing resentment. You couldn't have gotten this
far in healing and recovery if you hadn't already done some forgiving.
Suggesting forgiveness too early, while you were still stinging from the af-
tershock of betrayal, would have been out of touch with the reality of
your deep wounds and suffering.

As you established safety, goodwill, and compassionate communication, *you were letting go of anger.* As you were searching for the meaning of
the events of your life together, *you were gaining empathy for each other.* Although forgiveness is not a precondition for recovery, it is essential for
healing. Now is the right time for you to make a conscious choice to seek
and grant forgiveness.

The reason we discuss forgiveness in the next to last chapter is because
forgiveness is at the end of a long journey of healed wounds. It is time to
forgive when shattered assumptions have been reconstructed in a meaningful way. There should be no additional surprises or shoes dropping after forgiveness: the full extent of the betrayal and all of the significant
details are known. Forgiveness is appropriate when there is evidence of intent to change; for example, troubled partners are working in therapy or a
support group on their individual problems, such as addiction, codependency, or echoes from the past.

The steps that lead to granting forgiveness closely parallel the steps for
trauma recovery. As you have followed the trauma model of recovery and
healing in this book, you have been building a bridge to forgiveness. Your

hearts have been opened to each other slowly by your positive interactions. With each caring gesture, each episode of attentive listening, each effort to understand the other's experience, you have strengthened the empathy and understanding that are the essential conditions for forgiveness. When I see people stuck in revenge or retaliation, I know they are not healing.

Olivia wasn't sure if she could forgive Oren, even after he had ended his affair and disposed of the offending futon. Olivia said, "My mother and my girlfriend think I should forgive Oren and get over it because he's been great in so many ways. What bothers me is that forgiving him would be saying that his feelings are more important than mine."

Olivia was confused about the meaning of forgiveness. Like many people, she thought that forgiving Oren would send him the message that she was condoning what he had done. She was afraid that if she let him off too lightly, she would make it easy for him to betray her again. Sometimes, her strongest feeling was one of revenge—she wanted him to suffer in the same way she was suffering. She even thought of having an affair herself to even the score.

It's possible to reach a functional level of *recovery* without forgiveness, but it's not possible to achieve final *healing* of yourself or your relationship without forgiveness. In this chapter we talk about the complexities of forgiving and not forgiving. Some people get stuck in the mire of blame, recrimination, and punishment and are not able to seek or grant forgiveness. Others get beyond these barriers by *developing compassion* for their partner and *letting go of anger and resentment.*

What Is Forgiveness?

Forgiveness is not just an ideal that only saints can achieve. Although Alexander Pope's assertion, "To err is human, to forgive, divine," expresses the high value placed on forgiving, it overlooks how frequently ordinary people demonstrate in extraordinary situations that forgiving is not only a common human experience, but a humane one.[1]

> In one survey of partners of sex addicts, 63 percent said they had mostly or totally forgiven their spouses.[2]

Because so many people are confused about what it means to forgive, I begin with a discussion about what forgiveness *is not* and follow with a discussion about what forgiveness *is*.

Clarifying What Forgiveness Is *Not*

Saying "I forgive you" is not the same as saying "It's all right. No big deal. Let's forget it." *The process of forgiving is about as far away from "no big deal" as you can get.* Each of the following statements addresses misconceptions about forgiveness and describes what forgiveness *is not:*

- *Forgiveness is **not** forgetting or pretending it didn't happen.* Forgiveness allows you to move forward into the future without being stuck in the past, but the lessons and meaning of the event are an essential part of the remainder of your life's journey.

- *Forgiveness is **not** excusing or condoning the behavior.* In fact, a behavior that can be easily excused does not have to be forgiven. The necessity of forgiving an act means that a grievous injury occurred.

- *Forgiveness is **not** reconciliation.* You can forgive someone and let go of your need for revenge without wishing to reconcile with that person.

- *Forgiveness is **not** giving permission to continue the behavior.* Forgiveness cannot occur unless you are safe from further hurt.

Defining What Forgiveness Is

- *Forgiveness is a gift you give to yourself.* If you are able to free yourself from the anguish and burden of the past through forgiveness, you will move forward in your life journey with a lighter step. You will begin the next chapter of your life with more self-awareness and more options than you had before.

- *Forgiveness is a choice.* You choose not to be held hostage in the present to the injustices that occurred in the past. Authentic forgiveness acknowledges the wound and is the result of conscious effort.

- *Forgiveness is a process.* In couples who heal together, forgiveness is built on the sincere remorse of the unfaithful partner. It involves both of you. Over time, you have made good on your intention to reconcile and have demonstrated (through specific acts of relationship building) a commitment to each other.

- *Forgiveness is letting go of obsessiveness, bitterness, and resentment.* Forgiveness is built on a sincere desire to let go of anger and resentment and a conscious decision to take positive steps to move on with your life.

- *Forgiveness is letting go of the pain.* When you forgive, you free yourself from continual suffering without minimizing the injury. Forgiving is a personal act that directly affects the quality of your inner life.

- *Forgiveness is letting go of revenge and the need to punish.* You make the decision to live in the self-created atmosphere of solutions rather than blame. Rachel looked for ways to let Ralph know that she had forgiven him and relished their relationship. Privately, she told herself that her greatest gift to him was to hold her tongue and not bring up Lara's name or past incidents that she knew would embarrass him.

The Personal Benefits of Forgiveness

Forgiving someone fosters your own well-being. As you begin to let go of the resentment and punishing scenarios, you gain energy that was frozen by vindictiveness and pain. The release of rancor allows the sweetness of serenity to seep into your life.

Forgiveness activates the transformation from victim to survivor. Forgiveness frees you from the tyranny of people and events from the past and decreases the likelihood that you will misdirect your anger in other relationships. How good it feels to cast yourself as the master of your own life rather than as the victim of circumstances!

Forgiving is good for your psychological and physical health. The Stanford Forgiveness Project demonstrated the benefits of teaching people how to dispel the aggravation and anger of holding grudges. The process of forgiving reduced significant risk factors (stress, anger, and depression) for heart disease, stroke, and other serious diseases. People who learned to forgive had lower blood pressure, improved immune function, and a reduction in a host of health complaints, such as headaches, stomach distress, muscle aches, dizziness, and heart palpitations.[3]

Emotionally, people who learned to forgive were able to improve their psychological and spiritual functioning. Forgiving increased hope, optimism, and the likelihood of developing an enhanced spiritual point of view. Replacing negative emotions with positive ones enlarged the capacity for feelings of connection, trust, and affection.

Are Some Things Unforgivable?

There are some situations in which trying to forgive is inappropriate, as well as impossible. As we've said, first you must ensure your own safety. Forgiving wrongful behavior that has not stopped is like absolving a debt that was paid off with a bad check. It's also difficult, if not impossible, to forgive someone who shows no regret. Apologies must be sincere and backed up with action. Addicts such as alcoholics, gamblers, and philanderers often feel real remorse and promise to change, but then go on doing the same things. It makes little sense to forgive a repeat offender who exhibits extremely self-centered or uncaring behavior unless you are protected from further hurt by removing yourself from the relationship.

Betrayed and unfaithful partners must make their own decisions about whether to forgive partners who betrayed or hurt them. Forgiveness by the betrayed partner may not be possible if the deception went on too long and the unfaithful partner shows no compassion. Forgiveness by the unfaithful partner may not be possible if any disillusionment and deprivation that preceded the affair went on too long and if the betrayed partner is unwilling to take responsibility for repairing the problems in the marriage.

Is There a Right Time to Forgive?

For everything there is a season and a time for every matter under the heaven . . . A time to weep and a time to laugh . . . A time to mourn and a time to rejoice . . . A time to forgive and a time to be forgiven. A time to hurt and a time to heal. Ecclesiastes 3:1, 4.

Waiting too long to forgive can reinforce your hopelessness and despair. On the other hand, premature or inappropriate forgiveness can give a false sense of healing that is out of sync with your underlying emotions. Forgiving too soon can lower your feelings of self-worth, whereas appropriate forgiving is often empowering. Pseudo-forgiving is done begrudgingly on demand or because it is "the right thing to do." Forgiving that is not heartfelt or genuine only erects more barriers to intimacy and honest communication.

Forgiving Too Soon

A common mistake is wanting to move away from the pain and anger too soon. After a couple of weeks, the unfaithful partner has seen the error of his or her ways, confessed some transgressions, and is ready to stop processing the infidelity. The betrayed partner, anxious to get past the stress of the crisis, colludes with this "flight into health." Perhaps they agree that the infidelity was just a little bump in the road, or maybe a boulder, but the guilty party has apologized and that's the end of it. Easy forgiveness can be perceived as license to continue the hurtful behavior. This kind of denial and superficiality may be a reflection of how a couple has conducted their whole relationship.

> Psychologists Kristina Gordon and Donald Baucom found that forgiveness develops in sequential stages after infidelity. Spouses who were "true" forgivers felt much closer to each other than spouses who were "false" forgivers.[4]

Beware of Pseudo-forgiveness

Either or both partners may eagerly embrace a kind of pseudo-forgiveness in an effort to spare themselves the unpleasantness of confrontation. You can't pretend that the infidelity never happened. Rushing to quick solutions does more to perpetuate denial than to offer real resolution.

Forgiveness that feels like a fast food drive-thru can result in lingering yet deeply harbored resentment.

Pseudo-forgiveness does not benefit either partner. It may even create a perpetual cycle of betrayal followed by apologetic confessions. Unfortunately, some unfaithful partners calculate the cost-benefit ratio of infidelity, go through a little bit of hell, and repeat the pattern. They're willing to pay the cost of their partner's brief unhappiness in order to experience the thrill of forbidden love. *Some people choose to get forgiveness after the fact when they can't get permission before the act.*

Why Can't You Forgive Me?

Let's focus now on the difficulties a betrayed partner may have in moving away from bitterness toward a position of understanding and forgiveness. If the betrayed partner is stuck in the mind-set of a victim who keeps reiterating "You have ruined my life," forgiveness will be impossible to attain. In fact, for true forgiveness to occur, both partners must be willing to stop competing for the part of the suffering or outraged spouse.

Even after going through six months of recovery work, Rianna still felt she couldn't forgive Randy because he was not the moral person she had thought he was. In her mind, she hadn't done anything wrong that could "justify" his betrayal. As long as she perceived herself as the saintly victim of a brazen sinner, she was stuck in a rut of indignation and self-righteousness. She even blamed Randy for turning her into a vindictive, cynical person.

One day in church, Rianna had an epiphany: she realized that her inability to forgive Randy meant that she wasn't the spiritual person she had aspired to be. She was then able to start a process of relinquishing her illusion of the perfect marriage and herself as a perfect human being. Once she saw herself as imperfect, she was able to accept and begin to forgive Randy's human weaknesses.

Lingering Suspicion

If a couple has worked for many months through all of the stages of recovery and nothing relieves the suffering of the betrayed partner, it's time to ask what else is going on. A betrayed partner who does not respond to the goodwill, good faith efforts of a contrite and well-intentioned partner may be afraid that the unfaithful partner is still ambivalent or that the infidelity is continuing in secret. Betrayed spouses often have a sensitive "radar" for their partner's ongoing involvement, even when it appears to outside observers that the affair is over.

You cannot move on and you cannot forgive if you are not safe. If the threat of reinjury is real and imminent, the imperiled partner has no choice but to stay on the defensive and remain alert to any hint of attack. Obviously, a betrayed partner who continues to respond as though the affair were still alive and well and is *right* (i.e., it has *not* ended) has reason to be obsessed and hypervigilant. If the current affair is over but there's no reasonable assurance against future infidelity, staying stuck in unmitigated suffering protects the betrayed partner from the devastation of being unprepared for the next act of treachery.

Reverberating Pain from the Past

If betrayed partners continue to experience lingering pain and suspiciousness after the affair is *indisputably* over and after the unfaithful partner has made sincere efforts to make amends, they may be reacting to more than the affair. There may be unresolved injuries in the betrayed partner's life that were reawakened by the affair.

For some betrayed partners, the affair is further evidence that the world is a harsh and unjust place where they were born to be victimized. They may have been treated unfairly and hurt by their families or previous relationships. Exploring the relationship history of an unremittingly wounded partner may reveal infidelities by parental figures, exploitation or sexual molestation by trusted adults, bullying by the peer group, or persistent doubts about personal attractiveness and self-worth.

Georgia's rage over George's daily coffee breaks with a young woman coworker was so intense and prolonged that it appeared to be an extreme overreaction. Georgia understood the rejuvenation George felt from the sexual innuendos and lively conversations. She accepted his claim that there had been no sexual intercourse or strong emotional attachment. She knew that George had terminated all contact with his "friend." She even admitted that their marital bonds were based on love and companionship.

In spite of this understanding, though, Georgia became physically aggressive on several occasions and threatened to end the marriage. She rejected George's efforts to comfort and reassure her. When she was sarcastic and brutal to him, he drove away in his car for hours on end. Georgia's family history revealed that she still harbored tremendous bitterness over her father's desertion of her mother for a younger woman thirty years earlier. When she found out that George had spent so much time with another woman, it unleashed her basic distrust of men and love-hate feelings toward her father.

George and Georgia were both so miserable that they finally negotiated a truce. She agreed not to attack him verbally or physically. He agreed that if she expressed her hurt without yelling and screaming, he would stay and listen to her. As Georgia shared her fears with him, they grew closer. She asked him to forgive her for her unrelenting cruelty, and he asked her to forgive him for violating her trust and opening up old wounds.

Like George and Georgia, most couples do recover over time. However, if the tone of the marriage continues to be punishment and retribution, the marriage will be unable to get the traction it needs to move forward into healing.

Accusatory Suffering

It must be acknowledged that some betrayed partners never get past their initial despair. They become a living memorial to the betrayal. They keep blowing on the live coals of their misery to keep it alive. It may be hard to understand why betrayed spouses would want to perpetuate suffering by intentionally probing an open wound. Whenever the wound starts to close, they poke it again, ensuring that it doesn't heal. These betrayed partners are similar to victims of incest and domestic violence who do not permit their psychic wounds to heal. *Accusatory suffering* is the term used by Elizabeth and Arthur Seagull to describe this never-ending pain.[5]

Some people pass through this accusatory stage on their way to a more accepting and understanding stance. Others get stuck in this punishing place forever. One of the keys to accusatory suffering is that it is unconscious. The victims unconsciously believe that if they make a full recovery, the person who hurt them will be exonerated from blame and get off too easily. If they are no longer visibly in pain, the injury might look like a small scratch instead of a deadly back-stabbing. They're afraid that unless they continue to suffer, they might forget the depth and breadth of their own injury. To prevent this, the betrayed partner becomes a living, breathing memorial to the betrayal, a living accusation of the suffering the unfaithful partner has inflicted.

The irony is that an unfaithful partner may respond to a persistent lack of forgiveness by getting emotional support from a sympathetic colleague or friend and end up crossing the line again. What difference does it make if your spouse will never trust you anyway? It's not hard to understand that kind of hopelessness, but the choice and the responsibility for fidelity lies with the involved partner rather than with the injured partner.

Self-absorbed Unforgiving

Betrayed partners who are able to forgive are willing to relinquish their role as victim and see things through their partner's eyes. Tyler exemplifies someone who was too self-absorbed in his own injury to make room for compassion and forgiveness. For nineteen years he lived and breathed the story of how his wife, Tanya, had wounded him with an unforgivable transgression before they got married. He was blind to how he had wounded her.

After they had been engaged for only three weeks, Tyler decided he wasn't ready for marriage and broke off their engagement. Tanya was distraught about his abandonment and had a one-night stand with someone she met at a bar. She felt numb and didn't care what happened to her. After several months, Tyler realized how much he missed her and they went ahead with their wedding plans.

Because she didn't want there to be any secrets between them, Tanya confessed to Tyler that she had had casual sex with someone else during their separation. Tyler's reaction was explosive and frightening. His cherished vision of her as "pure" was destroyed forever. He stayed angry throughout their many years of marriage. His parents had held lifetime grudges and had been bound together by mutual spite and rancor. Tanya's "sin" gave Tyler the perfect opportunity to practice the unforgiving behaviors he had observed at home.

His refusal to get past Tanya's "disloyalty" weakened their bond and adversely affected their lives on many levels. For one thing, Tyler never fully invested in their marriage, just in case it didn't work out. In the back of his mind was the nagging thought that by next month they might be separated. After they had a child, he told himself he was staying only un-til their daughter graduated from high school. When he occasionally soft-ened toward Tanya, he then immediately reverted to picturing her acting like a "slut" and goading himself into another fit of righteous indignation. Tanya never knew when he would bring up her "sin." She accepted her perpetual punishment because she had never been able to forgive herself for going against her own values.

A breakthrough occurred when Tyler actually listened to Tanya for the first time and allowed himself to hear that her act of desperation was caused by his abandonment. He realized how much he had hurt her and how much she had suffered. He was not the sole casualty of their broken engagement! Allowing himself to experience her pain pulled him out of the pit he had been digging for almost twenty years. He couldn't believe how much better he felt without the weight of his vindictiveness.

Rituals of Forgiveness

Compassion for the other person is what makes forgiveness possible. The most important element of being able to achieve a state of forgiveness is mutual empathy. Insight into the mistakes made by the person to be for-given helps in replacing anger with understanding. Both partners must seek and grant forgiveness for the part they played in marital problems that preceded the infidelity or for hurtful behaviors that followed the rev-elation of the betrayal.

One partner's capacity to forgive depends on the other partner's sin-cere efforts to make amends. Unfaithful partners must seek forgiveness for the acts of betrayal; betrayed partners must be willing to acknowledge what they regret about their own behavior before or after the affair. Nev-ertheless, it may be unrealistic to expect the betrayed partner to show re-morse for having made malicious statements about the affair partner. Needless to say, neither partner is ever justified in inflicting cruelty as a re-action to his or her own injury.

The majority of couples forgive each other in a gradual process that is subtle but unmistakable. They show they have let go of the past when they risk being vulnerable to each other again. They deal with repercus-sions of the affair together in an atmosphere of affection and sensitivity. Carolyn overheard a group of women at church discussing how aggressively her husband, Chas, had pursued his affair partner, Roxie, despite Roxie's reluctance to get involved. Carolyn knew this was an unfounded rumor because she had witnessed how Roxie had flirted and made obvious moves on Chas. When Carolyn shared these offensive remarks with him, he put his arms around her and said, "I'm so sorry you had to listen to this upsetting gossip because of what I did." Carolyn felt how genuine his remorse was and was comforted because his primary concern was protecting her instead of defending his own actions.

Other couples benefit from a more structured ritual where forgiveness for specific injuries is formally sought and granted. They have a need to hear precise apologies and see concrete signs of forgiveness. Even if one partner is clearly cast as the perpetrator and the other as the innocent victim, the following approach is suitable for couples who are ready to forgive and be forgiven through a formal ritual of letting go.

Seeking Forgiveness

These forgiveness rituals have the most profound impact on healing when both partners are willing to seek forgiveness. I knew a betrayed spouse who was testifying in divorce court about how terrible her marriage had been. Her husband's attorney asked her, "Didn't *you* do anything wrong?" She responded, "Yes, I was wrong to put up with it for so long." Perhaps that really was her only mistake, but since perfect partners and perfect marriages are rare, betrayed partners can usually express true regret about their own actions, inactions, or reactions during the marriage and after the affair.

1. *Forgive yourself.* Stop chastising yourself and learn from your mistakes. You may be unable to forgive your partner if you have not yet forgiven yourself. Betrayed partners may have to forgive themselves for having been too gullible and trusting.

2. *Identify your transgressions.* Enumerate what you wish to be forgiven for. Articulate all of the ways you failed to protect the relationship. This is not a confession, but an assumption of personal responsibility. Regardless of how upset you might have been, it is important to acknowledge your own hurtful behaviors, such as verbal or emotional abuse, signs of contempt, or nasty put-downs.

Rachel told Ralph, "I got so wrapped up in the children that I didn't notice how lonely you were." Ralph told Rachel, "I lied to you and made you think you were crazy. I didn't tell you I felt lonely and didn't give us a chance to work it out together. Worst of all is how I deceived you and gave to somebody else what I promised to share only with you."

3. *Make a heartfelt apology.* The unfaithful partner needs to apologize for fracturing the trust. If you are the unfaithful partner, you must show genuine compassion and make a sincere apology for the pain and mistrust your actions created. If you cannot apologize for having the affair because you view it as a special event in your life, you can apologize for the anguish that your adventure caused your spouse.

Jim told Janet, "I hope you can forgive me for all of the pain I caused you. I never internalized my marriage vows. I was sexually and emotionally unfaithful. I'm so sorry I did this to you. I realize that I protected you from everybody but me. I can't stop thinking about how you deserved better."

If you are the betrayed partner, it might be appropriate to apologize for being too controlling or too distant or for not meeting your partner's emotional or sexual needs. If the affair was not a reflection of relationship vulnerabilities, you can probably recall some action or reaction during the recovery period when you put the kids or family members in the middle or when you could have been less attacking or more understanding.

4. *Make a formal request to be forgiven:* "Please forgive me."

5. *Offer some tangible action to back up your words.* Ralph offered to give Rachel a weekend at a spa while he took care of the children, so she could relax and be pampered. Victor had postponed getting married and had cheated on his fiancée, Valerie, on several business trips. Valerie got upset when his work team was scheduled to go to Paris and only married partners were allowed to come along. She said, "If I can't come, promise me you won't go either." After a long period of recovering from his infidelities, they decided to engage in the forgiveness ritual. Victor backed up his remorse by saying, "I know you're anxious about

my traveling abroad. If they restrict it to spouses, I'll make sure we're married first."

Granting Forgiveness

It's easier to forgive if your partner feels your pain, doesn't want to hurt you again, and follows words of apology with actions. Before you are prepared to forgive, you need to have done some work on your own. The steps in granting forgiveness are as follows:

1. *Acknowledge your own pain and express your emotions clearly without yelling or attacking.* You can say, "The worst thing you did to me was to look me straight in the eyes and lie to me. I doubted my own sanity."

2. *Understand the personal weaknesses and emotional vulnerabilities of your partner.* You still hold your partner accountable for his or her behaviors, but you are no longer angry because you have some compassion for his or her frailties.

3. *Be specific about what you expect and what you cannot tolerate.* There are some things that are not negotiable. You might decide to tell your partner that you can forgive him or her for past hurts, but you cannot stay in the relationship if he or she ever hurts you in the same way again.

4. *Be specific about what you are forgiving your partner for.* Respond to your partner's request for forgiveness by enumerating the transgressions you are forgiving him or her for.

5. *Perform an overt act of forgiveness verbally, physically, or in writing.* After Rachel told Ralph that she forgave him for his affair with Lara, she reached out and gave him a big hug. Tears welled up in both their eyes as they clung to each other and dedicated themselves to their future together.

6. *Stop blaming and start living.* After you have granted forgiveness to each other, searching for who's to blame is over and done with. It's time to get on with your life and enjoy the liberation of letting go.

Once Rachel had truly forgiven Ralph, her loving acts were

spontaneous—out of devotion and not out of duty or fear of loss. She welcomed him back with open arms. She purposely looked for ways to please and surprise him: she bought his favorite preserves when she was in the up-scale supermarket; sometimes she surprised him by playing his favorite Billy Joel CD upon his arrival home from work; she occasionally wrote him limericks that she thought would amuse him; and she reorganized and cleaned out their gardening shed, something she knew would thrill him almost more than sex.

Ralph wanted to show Rachel that she was on his mind during the day. He started bringing home precious little tokens: sometimes he bought her a small present, like a book he thought she would enjoy; at other times, he handed her a funny story he had seen on the Internet or brought her a special dessert he saved from a business luncheon. These small tokens made Rachel feel special.

An unmistakable measure of forgiving is when the betrayed partner can refer to events related to the affair with humor. Les and Lisa experienced together the healing symbolism of a good laugh. Lisa knew that Les was attracted to Fiona's long blond hair, which was very different from Lisa's dark curls. One night, when Les got home from work, Lisa called to him from the bedroom. He opened the door and there was Lisa, sitting in bed wearing a skimpy nightgown and a long blond wig. They collapsed in laughter, and then they made love.

Rituals of Recommitment

Many couples have found it quite meaningful to engage in symbolic rituals to mark the end of infidelity and a new beginning in their marriage. One ritual suggested by Rona Subotnik and Gloria Harris is to mark the end of the affair by making a list of wrongful acts, tearing it up, and throwing it into a river.[6] Burning the mementos and burying the ashes is a variation that symbolizes a funeral for the affair. Couples who feel their wedding vows have been shattered may need to go through a period of courtship and formal ceremony to renew their vows.

Courtship

It is very hurtful when courtship activities such as thoughtful notes and romantic dinners were absent in the marriage but were enjoyed in the affair. Unfaithful partners should initiate courtship behaviors to compensate betrayed partners by giving them the same kind of attention and thoughtfulness that was given to the affair partner. Ralph brought Rachel simple bouquets of her favorite flowers and read love poems to her. Rachel planned dates to go out dancing and to concerts that revived the fun and excitement they had enjoyed during their courtship.

Renewing Vows

Many couples have found profound meaning and comfort by renewing their vows in an informal or formal ceremony, exchanging new wedding rings, or going on a second honeymoon. After their reconciliation, Randy and Rianna invited their children and some close friends to a private church service in which they renewed their vows. They picked the verses together, and Randy spent hours choosing the musical selections as a surprise for Rianna. The ceremony had special significance for them because they delayed having sex until they had pledged themselves to each other.

Randy and Rianna went to Hawaii to celebrate, and they regarded their idyllic vacation as their second honeymoon. They thought of their renewal ceremony as the beginning of a new era of compatibility. From that time on, they celebrated two anniversaries every year: one on the date they had first married, and the other on the date they had recommitted themselves to each other and to their marriage. Twice a year they paused in their busy lives to reaffirm how important their relationship was to them.

Forgive the Pain but Remember the Lesson

One of the greatest fears couples have is that "things will never be the same again." The reality is that things will never be the same again—no matter how spectacular the recovery and how sincere the apologies. The knots of infidelity are now woven within the threads of your marital quilt. Yet, like many other couples who have healed, you are likely to find that your relationship is unique and special. Because the two of you have been to hell and back together, you can discuss your most hidden thoughts and feelings about almost any subject on earth.

After forgiving each other, you'll be able to remember the past without reliving the pain. Nevertheless, you don't want to forget the lessons you've learned. You have learned to be more sensitive to each other. You understand each other better and are cautious about triggering each other's wounds.

How Do *We* Know You Won't Betray Again?

Regardless of the quality of your renewed relationship, the betrayed partner is still plagued by the nagging concern "How do I know you won't betray me again?" This question should also be of concern to the unfaithful partner who doesn't want to relapse. Unfortunately, there are no guarantees that infidelity won't occur again—only probabilities. Part of the lesson you have learned is how to identify and address vulnerabilities. The following checklist will allow you to validate your positive resources and how hard you have worked to get to this point.

- You both have increased clarity about appropriate thresholds in friendships.
- You make sure that all of your friends are friends of the marriage.
- You agree on what commitment and exclusivity mean.
- You can talk together about individual vulnerabilities and danger signs without defensiveness.
- You recognize problems in the marriage that could threaten your commitment.
- You show understanding for each other in everyday interactions.
- Your relationship is a priority that comes before everything and everyone else.

If you feel comfortable right now that your partner is not violating your trust, don't sacrifice the pleasure of today because of what might happen tomorrow. If you had a serious illness that was successfully treated, you'd be told the probability of a recurrence. If you were fully recovered, you wouldn't want to waste your healthy days preoccupied with the possibility of a relapse in one year, five years, fifteen years, or maybe never. As long as you're doing everything in your power to have a thriving relationship, you have to transform your suffering into appreciation for how far you've come. *Worrying won't change tomorrow. It just takes the enjoyment out of today.*

Ralph and Rachel were amazed at how happy they were after their recovery from Ralph's affair. Their older son was responding to Rachel's efforts to help him with his learning disability and was taking less of her time and attention. The boys teased their father when they observed how he continued to enjoy courting their mother. Best of all, both sons often talked to their friends about how much fun and laughter they had at home. They told each other that they hoped to have a good marriage when they grew up—just like their parents!

What Choices Does the Betrayed Partner Have?

You may have been dealt a hand you didn't choose. Almost everyone has been scarred to some degree by people and events that have treated them roughly, or even unjustly. The question is: What are you going to do now? Is the memory of your wound going to poison you, or are you going to find a way to use your painful memories to grow beyond the boundaries of your injuries?

Hopefully, the betrayed partner has been able to forgive and reconcile with the unfaithful partner. That is the preferred option. However, if your partner refuses to do what's necessary to rebuild trust, you may choose to do your healing alone. The next chapter discusses under what conditions you might be in the position of healing alone. Remember: you can forgive without reconciliation. In fact, it might be possible for you to forgive only after you have separated yourself from a destructive relationship.

15

HEALING ALONE

When I look back, I can't believe how hard it's been,
and how glad I am to be where I am now.

As we've seen, couples who can weather the storm of infidelity together emerge stronger than before. But not every marriage will make it through the challenging steps that define the road to recovery. Regardless of whether or not they choose it, some people find themselves facing the future alone. It's a hard truth that *it takes two people to make a marriage and only one person to make a divorce.* There are many routes through infidelity that lead to divorce.

Sometimes the affair is an exit out of a dead marriage. In some relationships, the infidelity is a graphic symbol of irreconcilable differences and serves as an announcement that the marriage is over. No amount of recovery coaching can restore shattered trust or refresh vanished desire. The affair is perceived to be "the last straw" for both partners, and so it becomes.

Sometimes unfaithful partners choose to leave for their lovers. They use the revelation of the affair as a springboard to leave the marriage. Once the story breaks, they're gone. They often cover up their real intention, which is to pursue the affair, by giving lame excuses such as "I need some space right now" or "This isn't about you, it's about me."

Betrayed partners who are left behind are often ready to forgive and work through the problems but have no say in the matter. They were powerless to stop the affair, and they end up being powerless to preserve the marriage. Many are abandoned against their wishes and against their values. They may consider divorce unacceptable and be horrified at the thought of their children being raised without two parents at home. They have to live with the reality that they failed to keep their family together, despite how desperately they tried.

Being left peremptorily and prematurely can leave the betrayed partner with a number of unresolved issues. Psychologically, one of the greatest difficulties is the lack of closure. If the unfaithful partner left early in the aftermath of the affair, the betrayed partner may never know the whole story of what happened. The crucial steps of recovery—getting the facts, searching for meaning—are never completed. The one who is left must formulate the story alone, without the input of the central character in the drama. It's like trying to build a building without ever having seen a blueprint.

You may remember that Rachel blurted out to Ralph that it would have been easier if he had died. She meant that enduring his loss would have been easier than enduring his betrayal. She felt this way even in the face of Ralph's remorse and his commitment to stay and rebuild their relationship. Think about what it's like for those who are both betrayed and abandoned. They lose both their relationship *and* any conviction that their partner once loved them and cared about them.

Sometimes betrayed partners leave because they can't trust the involved partner to be honest or faithful. They know that as long as they are uncertain about these core issues, they cannot remain in the marriage. You may remember Thelma, who had ten affairs while she was married to Trent. After her last affair was exposed, she begged Trent for another chance. She said she would go to counseling and do anything he wanted to prove that she had stopped sleeping around. But Trent thought about all her infidelities and couldn't imagine ever being able to trust her. With unrelenting rage and profound sorrow, he filed for divorce.

Although Trent never wavered from his decision to divorce Thelma, it's not uncommon to hear from both betrayed and unfaithful partners that they live with a lingering regret that they might have done more to save their marriage. If only they had been more understanding, worked at it harder, stayed together longer . . . They have discovered that being on their own is harder than they thought, and from this perspective, the insurmountable problems in the marriage seem more surmountable than they appeared at the time.

Sometimes one partner or the other gives up during the struggles of the recovery period. One partner may have begun the recovery process in good faith, intending for it to work, without the other partner's being fully on board. The less committed partner doesn't have the heart for the challenges of reconstruction. The marriage ends because one partner is too exhausted or too disillusioned to put it back together. In the end, he or she is not able to follow the trail of caring and honesty to the final reward.

Sometimes a separation is only temporary. It's worth remembering that even if a couple does separate, the final outcome is not necessarily a foregone conclusion. The separation may be a prelude to the final dissolution or, in defiance of the odds, may end up being only temporary. I have seen people surprise everyone, including themselves, by reuniting after a time apart—even after the divorce decree. Either they underestimated the depth of their attachment to each other, or the ones who left to be with their affair partners discovered that their "soul mates" had annoying habits, made stressful demands, and brought unanticipated baggage. They find their new love to be an illusion, and the romantic bubble is burst. After that, the spouses may reconcile, falling in love again from an older and wiser perspective. I don't want to give you false hope, but it's never over till it's over.

I Never Intended to Be Just Another Statistic

Very few people begin marriage thinking that they will end up being just another statistic in infidelity surveys or the rising divorce rates. Although the majority of marriages affected by infidelity do not end in divorce, the probability of divorce is significantly greater among unfaithful spouses. In my clinical practice, only 10 percent of couples separated when neither partner was unfaithful, but 35 percent of couples separated when there was an infidelity by one or both partners. Infidelity was the single most frequently cited cause of divorce out of forty-three causes in a study of 160 cultures by researcher Laura Betzig.[1] Infidelity is more likely to lead to divorce when the unfaithful spouse is the wife. Annette Lawson found that women were likely to separate if they had only one liaison, but unfaithful men were unlikely to divorce unless they had a serious affair.[2]

In my clinical practice, couples were more likely to be separated at the end of therapy if:

1. *The unfaithful partner did not end the extramarital involvement.*
   In these situations, the betrayed partner may have asked the involved partner to leave, or the involved partner may have decided to ride off into the sunset with the affair partner.

2. *The affair was a combined-type involvement with deep emotional
   attachment and extramarital sexual intercourse.* Wives' affairs
   were more often combined-type involvement.

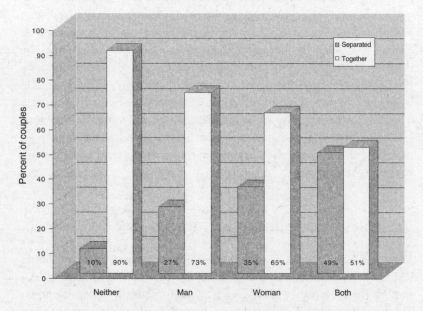

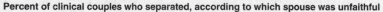

Percent of clinical couples who separated, according to which spouse was unfaithful

3. *Both spouses had experienced extramarital involvement.* Forty-
   nine percent of the marriages ended when both the husband
   and wife engaged in an extramarital relationship.

4. *Unfaithful wives were younger than thirty-one years old.* Young
   wives in childless marriages appeared to use affairs as an exit out
   of a marriage that appeared to be a mistake.

5. *Unfaithful husbands in long-term marriages described their affairs
   as more emotional than sexual.* Men whose affairs were primarily
   sexual seldom chose to leave.

6. *Commitment to working on the marriage was low at the beginning of therapy.* Involved spouses who were not committed to do everything possible to save their marriage were more likely to drop out of therapy quickly and leave the marriage.

Therefore, no matter how hard you may have worked to save the marriage, if your partner was unwilling to end an affair in which there was a deep emotional involvement, you were fighting an uphill battle.

The Hard Adjustment

Individuals adjust in many different ways to the ending of a marriage, just as they vary greatly in their reactions to discovering a partner's infidelity. How difficult it is for you depends on a whole host of personal, social, and financial factors. But no matter who you are, going from being married to being single is a tremendous adjustment. Even people who had a miserable marriage and wanted to leave do not slide seamlessly into an unmarried state. At the very least, being alone is unsettling and unfamiliar. Most likely, there is an emotional legacy of anger and sadness that lies heavy on the heart.

The Unfairness of It All

One of the most difficult things betrayed spouses have to deal with is the apparent injustice of it all. They've been hurt, and there doesn't seem to be any restitution or compensation for their suffering. Although they perceive themselves as having been loyal, supportive, and giving throughout the marriage, they may have to endure unfair disparities between their circumstances and their ex-partner's. Number one on the list is that they are alone while their unfaithful spouse blissfully revels in the company of a new love—at least for a while.

I agree with Rabbi Harold Kushner that it's distressing and incomprehensible *"when bad things happen to good people."*[3] I have observed that it's even more distressing *when good things happen to bad people.* We can't control what happens to others; we can control only how we choose to respond.

It's not unusual for betrayed partners to watch ex-partners openly engage in activities and interests they avoided or disdained during the marriage. One wife had stubbornly refused to allow her husband to have any pets in the house because she hated animals. When her boyfriend moved in, he bred black Labradors at the house that had been off-limits to goldfish and box turtles. An ex-wife couldn't believe it when she saw her former husband at the symphony, after she had begged him for years to accompany her to concerts. "Why couldn't he have done that for me?" she asked.

For many ex-wives, the injustice involves more than animals and music. There ends up being a real disparity in lifestyle. The wife and kids live in cramped housing while the husband builds a fabulous dream house. Or the kids from the first marriage go to college on scholarships and loans while a college trust accumulates for the new baby in the second marriage.

> In a sample of divorces in Los Angeles County, the standard of living declined by 27 percent for women and increased by 10 percent for men.[4]

The divorce process can deepen traumatic reactions, especially in the betrayed spouse. Betrayed partners who expect a judge to compensate them for their suffering are usually very disappointed. A law school research paper by Janis Haywood reported that in a majority of jurisdictions, the financial settlement is not affected by proof of an adulterous relationship. Furthermore, an extramarital relationship carries little weight in child custody battles, unless the infidelity interferes with the capacity to parent.[5]

The Financial Nightmare

Divorce is notoriously difficult financially. Both partners often feel that the divorce settlement is unfair. Preexisting power struggles and new hostilities are acted out over the division of assets and liabilities. Unfortunately, couples can deplete their funds by spending tens of thousands of dollars in legal fees to triumph over material goods that are often worth considerably less than the cost of "winning."

Coming to an agreement about division of assets is often so contentious that some couples turn to a judge to make the final decision. This is an unfortunate choice. Do you want a judge who doesn't know you and doesn't know your children to be the one to make decisions that you will have to live with the rest of your life? Couples who leave it up to the court system are more adversarial and tend to be more dissatisfied with the terms of settlement than those who are able to negotiate their own agreement through mediation.

After divorce, a woman who formerly enjoyed a high standard of living in an affluent community can suddenly find herself living in a small apartment, working at a low-paying job, and trying to be both mother and father to her troubled children. A man, too, may be relegated to low-rent living and working overtime to meet court-ordered payments to his former wife and children and still have enough to live on. Even very affluent men can feel constant pressure to maintain their current lifestyles and still make alimony payments to first and second wives.

The Loneliness

Most people go through a period of mourning after the divorce. Even those betrayed partners who could hardly wait to get rid of their cheating spouse will discover moments when they miss their former partner. They begin longing for the good old days, before the relationship soured. It takes a while to become accustomed to the silence. (If you are afraid or sad about being home alone at night, consider installing a home security system or getting a dog.)

Being alone, after so many years of being coupled, colors almost every moment of daily life because you are dealing with so many losses. You miss the companionship: Whom will you tell your good news to or complain to, and whom will you worry with? You miss having someone around to help out: there's no one to go to the drugstore when you're sick, move the piano, or look for the lost dog. You miss the physical presence of someone warming up the bed. If you don't mourn the loss of your mate as a person, you mourn the loss of your dreams of growing old together. You grapple with the loss of identity and self-concept that being married represents.

New Scenarios with Old Friends

The whole social scene is an intimidating new game. Individuals with a strong commitment to marriage and family can feel embarrassed to present themselves publicly as divorced. A newly divorced woman often feels like a third wheel in social situations. If she has retained the friends she had when she was married, most of them are probably couples. Being the only single person in a couple-centered universe can feel awkward.

One woman told me that when she joined her friends for dinner, they always insisted on paying for her meal. Their well-intentioned generosity put her in a quandary about whether to continue to accept this one-sided arrangement and feel like a freeloader or refuse their invitation and stay home alone. She hated having to deal with a problem that was evidence of her awkward status. She finally resolved her dilemma by initiating the invitation and arranging with the restaurant beforehand for payment by credit card. She also held small dinner parties as a way to reciprocate to the couples who so kindly included her in their plans.

Starting Over

Starting over is a challenge you may have preferred to avoid. But starting over does not mean starting from scratch. You enter this new phase of your life with greater self-knowledge and life experience than you had when you were first married. I know that it's hard to contemplate that the affair partner might benefit from the insights and skills that you helped your spouse develop (while you were working so hard to save the marriage), but you too can take what you've learned about relationships into the future. You've been exposed to deception and mistrust, but you've also been exposed to empowering information about compassionate communication and the dynamics of relationships.

Wallowing Never Gets You Anywhere

In a real sense, betrayed partners have been victimized. No matter what the circumstances, the fact remains that a trusted partner violated the basic assumptions of the relationship. Life may appear to favor the deceitful partner, but in my experience, the abandoned partner often ends up with a better life than before.

In the beginning it's important to feel whatever anger, bitterness, despondency, or hopelessness there is. But after a while, it's equally important to ask: *Do I want to remain stuck in these events?* If I stay stuck in the rage, I become angry and embittered. If I stay stuck in the punishment, I punish myself. If I stay stuck in the hurt, I let my partner continue to control my feelings. By letting that happen, I allow someone else's offense to become a permanent part of who I am. I limit my own options if I allow myself to wallow in self-pity.

An antidote to feeling victimized is the conscious cultivation of your own inner resources and goals. You know you can survive in the face of tremendous obstacles, so, step by step, you will become more independent. It will take some time to reach wholeness, but you do not need to do your healing alone. Call on your friends and family for help. Tell others what you want and need from them. Teach the people who care about you how to help you through the dark times. One of the most important things you can do is cultivate single friends who can do things with you such as going to movies or out to dinner—especially when your children are not at home with you. Join a group for separated and divorced people offered by religious groups, community colleges, and independent organizations. Many of these groups provide structured guidance for moving from being married to being single.

If you need more help than you can get from your support groups, you should consider going to a mental health professional. Find an experienced therapist who can help you and your children with the adjustment to separation and divorce through individual or group therapy. Get a referral for a psychiatrist who is an expert in psychopharmacology to evaluate whether you would benefit from medication for depression, anxiety, disordered sleeping, or loss of appetite. You can refer to the Appendix in the back of the book for suggested readings, 12-step programs, and helpful Web sites.

The New Learning Curve

You will stretch and grow as you assume the roles that you depended on your partner for. You may have relied on your mate to do a thousand things that you now have to do by yourself. If one partner had primary responsibility for household financial decisions and record keeping, the other may initially find these duties unfamiliar and confusing. Separated partners who step immediately into another relationship may be deprived of the opportunity to be self-sufficient and learn brand new skills.

Wounded partners are transformed once they've made the decision to move forward. To the extent that traditional roles operated in the marriage, men and women must learn how to navigate the foreign waters of child care, finances, or mechanical repairs without their spouse around. Men go on preschool field trips, arrange play dates for their kids, and launder their own clothes. Women learn how to cope with flat tires and broken lawn mowers.

In the transition from a traditional marriage to single parenting, fathers often become more nurturing and mothers become more career-oriented. I can't count how many divorced women I've worked with who went back to school, completed an undergraduate or graduate degree, and derived enormous personal satisfaction from their late arrival as working professionals. Men enjoy parenting in a way they never imagined when they can no longer rely on their wife to stand in for them at PTA meetings. They learn to cook nourishing meals for their children, drive carpools to ballet class, and monitor homework assignments.

In the earlier parts of this book, you learned valuable information about how to have a healthier relationship, which you can implement with a new partner. So many people starting over have said to me, "I can't believe how much easier this new relationship is. I don't have to work nearly as hard, and I feel so much better about myself." If you've spent most of your life putting others first, it's time to discover and express your own needs and preferences. On the other hand, if you realize you may have been self-absorbed or controlling, you can focus on being more tuned in to what others want.

The Dating Game

You can look at dating as an opportunity to continue your learning curve rather than as frightening foreign territory. Many divorced people haven't dated for decades (or they may think of themselves as *never* having been part of the singles scene), and they have no idea what the current rules and expectations are. Some people make the mistake of jumping into the game too quickly without giving themselves enough time to grieve their recent losses. They amaze themselves and everyone else by becoming obsessed with capturing a new partner. Their sense of well-being and self-esteem is overly dependent on whether they've "met somebody" or whether they've received a call for another date.

Other people wish fervently for a partner but do nothing to find one except cross their fingers. Admittedly, it isn't always easy to meet the kind of person you'd want to spend your life with, but we know for sure that Santa Claus isn't going to come down the chimney with the perfect man or woman for Christmas just because you put it on your wish list. So where can you look? The best place is friends and acquaintances: let them know that you are ready for dating so they can introduce you to someone they think you would be compatible with.

Over the years, I've seen divorced people find wonderful partners using these ideas:

- Attend events that provide a structure, such as museum tours, hiking clubs, and concerts.
- Enroll in stimulating courses.
- Become a member of a single-parent group, such as Parents Without Partners (PWP).
- Join an organization that offers social opportunities for single people of the same religion.
- Go to singles events such as organized dances with other single friends.

I have even known people who were successfully matched through Internet special interest groups or religion-specific Web sites for singles. Obviously, that option requires that you be careful and keep your wits about you. Before you make arrangements to meet Internet acquaintances in person, check out the authenticity of the phone number and home address. Come in your own car, meet in a public place, and let your friends know what you're doing. I know a woman who had her friends sit at the next table when she went to meet a man for a first date.

People have told me they are turned off by dates who appear too needy or too bitter about their failed marriage. Don't look too hungry for approval or take an obvious initiative in furthering the relationship. Be receptive and interested without appearing overly eager. Don't do more for the other person than the other person does for you. Don't drive 60 miles to make it convenient for your date if he or she isn't willing to do the same. Remember: in the most satisfying relationships, the giving and receiving are equitable.

Don't appear too embittered about the loss of your marriage. If you badmouth your ex-partner, you can appear to be a male basher or a woman hater. If you convey the message that you are still suffering from your victimization, you may appear pitiful and undesirable. If you are brimming over with details about how badly your marriage ended, you may appear to be too tied up in the past to share your future with a new partner. Think about how much more appealing someone would be to you if he or she demonstrated understanding toward an ex-partner or told you what was learned as a result of that relationship ending.

Parents with children at home need to temper their dating behavior with an awareness of their children's needs and developmental stages. Wait until you're in a committed relationship before involving your children. It's hard on kids when they become attached to their parents' girlfriends or boyfriends, only to watch them leave and be replaced by newer models.

It's potentially harmful for parents to have dates sleep over. Ask yourself what message you want to send to your children about premarital sex. They won't be impressed if you tell them that it's okay because you're a grown-up. Exposing youngsters to their mother's or father's sexuality can be damaging at any time, but especially when the child's world has already been rocked by the turmoil of divorce.

The Matter of Children

Having children makes starting over both easier and harder. Childless couples can sever their ties completely and don't have to deal with each other once the divorce is final. Couples with children will never be totally disengaged. They will need to talk to each other on behalf of their children and attend events and special celebrations throughout their lives.

Parents who are going through the breakup of their marriage not only contend with their own pain and loss but also feel responsible for the pain and loss their children are experiencing. Some parents tell me that not having children would have made the infidelity and its aftermath easier to deal with. Already emotionally and physically exhausted, they found coping with their children's new needs almost more than they could manage. Other parents say the opposite: they couldn't have gotten through the tough times if they hadn't had their children to care for and focus on.

Older divorcing couples may be surprised that their grown-up offspring react so strongly to the infidelity and the resulting divorce. Just because children are no longer dependent doesn't mean they're not affected. Older children may develop bitter feelings toward the parent who defected. If that parent introduces the affair partner as a new member of the family at family gatherings, the negative reactions can be either very cold or very hot, depending on whether disapproval is expressed by snubbing or provoking. If divorcing parents model considerate and dignified behavior when dealing with each other, the chances are that their children will also.

A childless spouse who divorces may feel especially rootless. Your marriage coming apart can make you feel like a castaway being thrown up on an alien shore. Other childless partners thank their lucky stars that they haven't dragged children into the mess they've created. If marital problems caused a delay in childbearing, childlessness could be another devastating consequence for women whose biological clock has run down.

Breaking the Bad News

In Chapter 13, we discussed how to talk with children about a parent's affair and the turmoil it may have created in the household. The suggestions below are intended to help you prepare your children for the impending separation.

- *Tell your children together of your decision to divorce* if at all possible. Keep it simple, but answer their questions directly. If your partner is leaving the marriage to be with another person, you cannot hide that reality. However, this information should be discussed calmly, with both parents present, without blaming or maliciousness. No matter how hard this might be, you owe it to your children not to involve them in any bitterness. You might say, "Mommy doesn't love me anymore the way married people are supposed to love each other. I don't want her to leave, but she loves somebody else now."

- *Reassure your children that there was nothing they did to cause the divorce and that there is nothing they can do to keep you together.* If the affair is over and no longer a factor in the divorce, use explanations that fit in with their observations, such as, "We just can't get along together any more. We don't agree on things, and we're too different from each other to live together." As incomplete as that may sound to you, it will at least not suggest to a child that the strain is his or her fault.

- *Reassure your children that you still love them and will continue to love them.* Children might be afraid that if Mommy and Daddy can stop loving each other, they might also stop loving them. Let them know that you will work *together* on their behalf. One couple I knew bought their son a bicycle for his birthday during their separation and presented it to him together as a surprise.

- *Validate how sad this is for everyone.* Let them know that it's normal to feel sad and scared about the breakup of the family. Everybody will be grieving. Let them know that you will be there for them when they feel sad or lost or fearful. Let them know about any changes that will occur in their lives as a result of the separation or divorce. Take them to see their bedroom at the new apartment, and involve them in choosing the decor.

Protecting Your Children from the Fallout

Your job as a parent is to protect your children; your children aren't there to protect you or to compensate you for a lost relationship or for a poor marriage. Here are some guidelines adapted from pediatrician Herman Frankel on how to protect your child by maintaining appropriate boundaries:[6]

- *You are the caretaker—not your child.* Although it's important to acknowledge your own feelings of loss, it's up to you to nurture and look out for your children, not the other way around. For example, nine-year-old girls shouldn't have the responsibility of cooking for their inexperienced fathers or taking care of the younger children for their depressed mothers.

- *Your child is not your confidante.* Even if your child is an adult, confiding about matters pertaining to you and the other parent is a violation of emotional boundaries. Don't burden your child with details of the legal proceedings or how you've been wronged. This often backfires when the child pulls away from the parent who shared too much.

- *Your child is not your companion.* Don't expect to fill up your empty social life with your child. Your child needs to be with his or her peers. Your need for companionship cannot be met by making your child your best friend; your child needs you to be a parent, not a pal. For example, you can certainly take your son to the movies because you would have done that before the separation, but don't ask him to watch a rented video with you on a lonely Saturday night instead of going to a sleepover with his school friends.

- *Your child is not your ally.* No matter how much you are tempted to find out what's going on in the life of your ex-partner, don't ask your child to spy or give you information. Don't expect your child to take your side against the other parent. And let the child form his or her own opinion about the affair partner: their relationship is not contingent on how badly you might have been betrayed.

The most important advice I can give is what you've heard before: Your goal is to provide your children with the best possible parenting under these trying new circumstances. Whether your children are grown or not, do not badmouth the other parent and do not involve them in your private business or your conflict with your ex-spouse. If your ex-spouse forms a committed relationship with the affair partner, you will need the support of your friends to attend special events where the affair partner will be present. You should not create turmoil that would hurt your children, or they will end up resenting you.

Survivors of Infidelity

Survivors of infidelity appear in many different guises. Some people heal without impairment, walking with more joy and confidence than they've ever felt before. Others are visibly crippled by their injury and continue to limp throughout their lives. Fortunately, most betrayed partners who are completely demoralized at the point of revelation of the affair often gain a different perspective as the years go by. They are able to create a new life for themselves that is fuller and richer than what they had before.

I want to end with the stories of four survivors of infidelity you have not met yet. Each of them was severely rocked by his or her partner's infidelities, but all four of them went on to live fulfilling lives. Although their healing journeys vary in length and outcome, each illustrates my belief that recovery is possible for anyone who is starting over alone.

Nancy: Always on Guard

Nancy's story is the most sobering. Although she recovered from her divorce and resumed a fulfilling life, the magnitude of her husband's betrayal left her uninterested in ever having another romantic relationship.

Nancy and Nathan had been married for twenty years when he told her that he had been falsely accused of sexual harassment by an administrative assistant in his firm. Nancy completely believed in his integrity and agreed with him that the woman who had accused him of sexual harassment was nuts. They relocated to a neighboring state, where he found an even better career opportunity. Although this meant that Nancy would have to give up the dynamic, high-paying job she loved, she never questioned the move.

After Nathan left for his new job, Nancy stayed behind a few months with their three children to train her successor at work, complete the school year, and sell their house. When she finally arrived at their new home, she discovered evidence that Nathan was having an affair. When she cornered him, he confessed that he had been involved with other women throughout their marriage. He cruelly added that he had never loved her and wanted a divorce—now that his children had been moved by her to the new location. She realized how naïve she had been to believe she had a devoted partner when what she really had was a philandering, narcissistic husband.

Nancy was severely traumatized. Everything she had believed about her husband was false. In a strange city without a job, she felt she had no choice except to take her children and move back home into her parents' house. For almost two years the only task she could handle was caring for her children. The only time she left the house was for child-related events and errands. She stayed home to avoid seeing men who might resemble her manipulative, lying husband. Her post-traumatic reaction was so extreme that she had a panic attack if a man approached her in a public place to ask her for directions.

Nancy did recover from her traumatic symptoms, but she was never again interested in intimate relationships with men. Her relationships with the opposite sex are cordial but always somewhat distant. No amount of time or therapy can erase the traumatic injury by a man she innocently trusted. The worst aspect for her was that she didn't trust her own judgment because she had been so bamboozled by her husband's glib talk and charming ways.

After three years, however, she was able to go back to work and build what eventually became a wonderful career. She came to treasure her independence and reveled in the freedom to develop her own interests. She resumed her profession, but in an environment that was all female. She took flute lessons and became an expert in rock gardening. If you met her, you would admire her zest for life.

Kimberly: Bridge to a New Life

Kimberly became suicidal and was hospitalized after her husband, Konrad, told her he'd been unhappy for years and wanted a legal separation. When she was released from the hospital, they started couple therapy, but all he did was unleash an avalanche of stored-up resentments from twenty-six years of marriage. It was clear that Konrad wanted only to enumerate his complaints without giving Kimberly a chance to rectify any of the things he was unhappy with. After he left for good, she learned that he was having an affair with an employee who doted on him.

Kimberly began to rebuild her life slowly, bit by bit. Fortunately, her children needed little from her because they had families of their own, and she had sufficient financial resources. She immersed herself in the people and activities she found healing. She spent as much time as she could with her children and grandchildren. She had a number of close women friends who looked out for her and had fun with her.

She knew she was making real progress when she felt like playing bridge again. She had always enjoyed bridge, but had given it up because Konrad didn't like to play. She became a Life Master and started teaching other people. She began dating a man she met through her interest in bridge, and they played in tournaments together.

Kimberly launched an exciting venture when she was recruited to teach bridge to passengers on cruise ships. She didn't receive a salary, but all of her expenses were paid; she traveled to ports all over the world whenever she chose to accept the many offers from different cruise lines. She became engaged to her bridge partner, and they started cruising together to exotic ports, where they taught the classes as a team.

Kimberly says that even though it's been five years since the divorce, there are some things that are still hard. She never thought that she and Konrad would end up divorced. Konrad's marriage to his affair partner has caused a great deal of tension. His adult children are still angry about his infidelity because he was always a rather sanctimonious, moralistic man before his defection. Every time there is a family gathering, Konrad brings his new wife and everyone ends up being upset. Most of the time, though, Kimberly is very happy. She has a wonderful man in her life who shares her interests and appreciates her for who she is.

Evan: Better the Second Time Around

Evan felt he was the luckiest man on earth the day he married Emily. She was so sure of herself and sophisticated in a way that he had never encountered before. Evan was much more of a homebody, and Emily liked to be on the go. He fell in love with all the ways she was different from him.

Evan's happiness was short-lived. Soon after the honeymoon, Emily's time and attention shifted away from the marriage. Evan had known that she was ambitious and career-centered, but he didn't realize how much of her time and energy would be invested in her job. When he asked her to spend more time with him, she told him, she needed "more space." Eight months after the wedding, he learned that Emily was sexually involved with her boss. After a nasty confrontation, she told Evan that she should never have gotten married in the first place and didn't want to be married anymore.

Evan couldn't believe what was happening. He was personally shattered and publicly humiliated. His parents were still paying for their share of the wedding. After the divorce, his friends tried to fix him up, but he definitely wasn't interested in dating yet. He didn't trust himself to make a good choice. He put his efforts into crafting a beautiful home. He was very handy and spent most of his free time building himself a comfortable nest.

A couple of years later, he met Elizabeth at his congregation's discussion group for singles. He felt safe with Elizabeth because she was a few years older than he and had a two-year-old son, Kyle. Evan liked to spend time with her, but he knew he'd never allow himself to get involved with a woman who already had a child. Elizabeth was in awe of the way Evan had created such a beautiful home. She loved to come over with Kyle and just hang out on the deck talking. Evan enjoyed going places like the zoo with the two of them.

Evan was surprised when his feelings for Elizabeth began to change. They had so much in common. He admired her devotion to Kyle, and he felt himself flowering under her kind and supportive attention. They shared similar visions of married life: they both wanted several children and believed it is best if mothers stay home and devote themselves to their children during the formative years. After they got engaged, Evan told her, "This will be my second wedding, but it will be my first real marriage. If Emily hadn't left me, I'd never have the kind of home life I always dreamed about." The last time I saw Evan, he was wheeling a stroller with an adorable little girl, and Kyle and Elizabeth were walking along at his side.

Heather: Becoming Whole Again

Six months ago, Heather got married again at the age of seventy-five. She told me, "I feel like I have lived a miracle. You have no idea where the power to heal is going to come from. You have to have faith that when one door closes, a new door will open."

Heather was divorced twenty-eight years ago from the high school sweetheart who had turned into an unfaithful alcoholic. Heather and Horace had fallen in love at first sight. She said, "Our love was so overpowering, it was awesome. I had met the person I wanted to spend the rest of my life with. I never dated anyone else after I met him." He was handsome, brilliant, talented, and had a great sense of humor. Their early years of marriage were full of love, laughter, and music.

During their life together, Horace became an eminent trial attorney, but he was abusive and neglectful of Heather and their three children. As she says, "I never knew what was going to come through that door at night." Her life was falling apart. She suspected for a number of years that Horace was having an affair with his secretary. He told her that if she left, he would use his legal connections to get custody of the children, and she would end up penniless. She felt trapped and unable to find a way out, so she held on.

She waited until her two older children were on their own before she allowed herself to think about leaving. She was at the end of her rope. One night, she collapsed to the floor in the laundry room and cried out to her God for help. She was rescued by her spiritual connection. She felt lifted up by her faith from the "miry clay" and placed upon a solid rock: "I knew then that I had the courage and strength to carry on and go through a divorce." She realized that the man she used to love no longer existed: "I didn't love the man he had become. I mourned the man he had been. He was not the same person. I looked in his face and saw betrayal and lying."

Although she wanted to take back her life, contemplating divorce was hard for Heather. Nobody in her family had ever been divorced. She felt like a failure and was ashamed to face people, as if it had been her fault. She thought that when she married, her vows were for life. She was relieved when her minister advised her that her marriage vows didn't require her to stay in an abusive relationship with an adulterous husband. Her friends from church also rallied around her and supported her during the tortuous divorce proceedings.

Heather's divorce and the time afterward were difficult emotionally and financially. She and her ten-year-old daughter could barely subsist on her meager child support and her part-time job as a nursery school teacher. She was forced to get a full-time job as a librarian at a private boy's school, but, Heather says, "It was one of the best things that ever happened to me." She not only improved her financial situation, but she found the work intellectually stimulating and the collegial environment warm and friendly.

In spite of her new life, Heather was still plagued by bitterness toward her ex-husband and his new wife (the loyal secretary). She said, "By that time I was sick and tired of being sick and tired. My anger and resentment were hurting me more than him." She realized that she had to let go of the negative emotions that were robbing her of being the loving person she had always been. Until she released the anger that was holding her captive, she was destroying herself and was unable to experience the full power of a loving God.

When her younger daughter got married, Heather was able to greet Horace and his secretary/lover/wife with equanimity. During the wedding reception, she kissed Horace on the cheek. As she says, "At that moment, I knew I was healed." She had gotten to the point where she could even look at him with some compassion for his ruined life. Their two older children would have nothing to do with him.

Heather was not interested in getting married again. Horace had been the love of her life, and she doubted that she could ever love anyone that way again. To her great surprise, she fell in love again twenty-seven years after her divorce. She had known Harrison and his wife for many years. After his wife died, they started going out to dinner and spending time together. She suddenly felt like a teenager again: "The relationship just flowed naturally. I fell in love in a way I never expected to happen again."

Heather attributes her healing to her faith and the important role of God in her life. She was able to forgive her husband because she believed he was a lost soul whom she was finally able to pray for. She believes that releasing her hurt and anger was what allowed her to become whole again.

Living Well Is the Best Revenge

For Heather, healing came from the power of the love that springs from her religion. For others, it comes from the power of love in other forms—through friends, or children, or good causes. Still others find what they need through therapy or through the lasting power of a happy childhood. No matter where the energy comes from, the process is the same. Let go of the hurt and the anger, and get on with your own life.

There is no revenge as sweet as living a joyful life. Through the years, I've suggested to certain betrayed partners that some day they might feel like writing a Thank You note to the lover who took a cheating spouse off their hands. At the time, these wounded partners didn't know how they were going to be able to survive the affair, the divorce, and the aftermath. Several ex-wives have smiled at me years later and said, "You were right. She did me a favor. I hear she's as unhappy now as I once was. I really should write that Thank You note." One betrayed wife admitted that she even felt a little sorry for the affair partner, who had been deliberately taunting during the affair. The affair partner was now taunted herself by the self-centered ways of her stolen "prize."

It may be hard to let go of the knot of anger that keeps you connected to your ex-spouse. Marla's best friend accepted an invitation to an open house hosted by Marla's ex-husband and his affair partner. Marla was indignant: "Why would you go, knowing how he abandoned me?" After Marla regrouped, she asked her friend if she would act as a spy and tell her what his new house was like and how he treated his new wife.

At that point, I interrupted her: "Why do you want to know what kind of furniture they have or what his wife was wearing? If you care about those things, you have not broken your attachment to him. You are as involved with him in your resentment as you were when you were in love with him. Your goal is to get to the point where his life isn't of interest to you anymore." When Marla can tell her friend that she doesn't care to hear anything about it, she'll know that she is healed.

Until you are no longer preoccupied with your ex-partner, you are letting him or her take up space in your heart and brain. You may be legally divorced, but you are as emotionally tied to your former partner as if you were still married. If you enlist friends and children to bring back information about your ex-spouse, you remain shackled to the past.

Elsa moved from rage and pain to detachment. When she saw Elliott a couple of years after their divorce, she commented, "It was like seeing somebody I used to know a long time ago. He couldn't trigger feelings in me anymore. I didn't feel the connection in the way I would have with an old friend. There was no warmth, but there was also no animosity." Displays of ill will demonstrate as much emotional connection as displays of affection. One of the great lessons of healing is *The opposite of love is not hate; it's indifference.*

The catalyst for this process of replacing a poisonous relationship with an indifferent one is forgiveness. As we said in Chapter 14, forgiveness is a gift you give yourself. When you're able to unknot the cord that has kept you bound to your ex-partner, you set yourself free. You realize that you are the creator of your own life.

AFTERWORD:
MINI-GUIDE TO SAFE FRIENDSHIPS
AND A SECURE MARRIAGE

So we end where we began, with real people wishing they had had the foresight to prevent infidelity before it wreaked havoc. When they say "I wish I could go back in time before the affair," I ask what information would have helped and what they would say to others. They tell me that they didn't know how easily good friendships could imperceptibly cross the line. They never comprehended that you could love two different people at the same time. It never occurred to them that good people in good marriages could be vulnerable to betraying their partners. Some say they would have worked to fix their marriages instead of running away from problems. Many never considered how much pain their actions would cause, or how long it would take to heal.

After reading this book, you are now more conscious of the threat of platonic friendships that evolve into romantic love affairs. You know how to recognize individual, relational, and social vulnerabilities. You have seen how the revelation of infidelity leads to shattered assumptions and traumatic reactions. You have also observed dedicated couples rebuilding their relationships with greater intimacy and honesty than ever before.

Facts about infidelity and love that have been explored in depth throughout the preceding pages are summarized here. Pointers on how to maintain safe friendships and preserve committed relationships are intended for those who are still on safe ground and those who need to step back from the edge of the slippery slope. These pointers are also directed toward couples who are recovering from infidelity—so they will never again have to face the trauma of betrayal in the form of a relapse or a new affair.

Seven Facts You Need to Know about Infidelity

1. A happy marriage is not a vaccine against infidelity.

2. The person having the affair may not be giving enough at home rather than not getting enough.

3. It is normal to be attracted to another person, but fantasizing about what it would be like to be with that other person is a danger sign.

4. Flirting is crossing the line because it is an invitation that indicates receptivity.

5. Infidelity is not only about love or sex—it's about maintaining appropriate boundaries with others and being open and honest in your committed relationship.

6. You do not have to have sexual intercourse to be unfaithful. Passionate kissing or oral sex is a violation of your commitment to your partner.

7. Emotional affairs are characterized by secrecy, emotional intimacy, and sexual chemistry. Emotional affairs can be more threatening than brief sexual flings.

What You Need to Know about Love

- People compare and confuse the intensity of being "in love" during an affair with the secure, comfortable feeling of reality-based "loving" that occurs in long-term relationships.
- The feeling of being "in love" is linked to Stage I idealization, passion and infatuation.
- True love, which you grow into, is characterized by acceptance, understanding, and compassion. That is why so few people end up marrying their affair partner, and those who do have an extremely high probability of divorce.

• Once the affair is no longer the forbidden relationship that takes place in a golden bubble, the cold light of day soon bursts the romantic fantasies.

Seven Tips for Preventing Infidelity

1. *Maintain appropriate walls and windows.* Keep the windows open at home. Put up privacy walls with others who could threaten your marriage.

2. *Recognize that work can be a danger zone.* Don't lunch or take private coffee breaks with the same person all the time. When you travel with a coworker, meet in public rooms, not in a room with a bed.

3. *Avoid emotional intimacy with attractive alternatives* to your committed relationship. Resist the desire to rescue an unhappy soul who pours his or her heart out to you.

4. *Protect your marriage by discussing relationship issues at home.* If you do need to talk to someone else about your marriage, be sure that person is a friend of the marriage. If the friend disparages marriage, respond with something positive about your own relationship.

5. *Keep old flames from reigniting.* If a former lover is coming to the class reunion, invite your partner to come along. If you value your marriage, think twice about having lunch with an old flame.

6. *Don't go over the line when you're on-line with Internet friends.* Discuss your on-line friendships with your partner and show him or her your e-mail if he or she is interested. Invite your partner to join in your correspondence so your Internet friend won't get any wrong ideas. Don't exchange sexual fantasies on-line.

7. *Make sure your social network is supportive of your marriage.* Surround yourself with friends who are happily married and who don't believe in fooling around.

Critical Elements for Healing the Trauma of Infidelity

- Recovery requires reversing the walls and windows in the extra-marital triangle to place the betrayed partner inside and the affair partner outside.
- Healing cannot begin without safety. The first step in establishing safety is to stop all contact with the affair partner.
- Rebuilding trust after deception and lying is achieved by complete honesty about the infidelity. Voluntarily sharing all unavoidable encounters with the affair partner is an essential trust builder.
- Discussing the story of the affair is crucial for understanding the meaning of the infidelity.

Vulnerability Maps

Look back at the scores you achieved on each vulnerability map in Chapters 9, 10, and 11. Circle your ratings on the chart below.

	VULNERABILITY MAPS		
RATINGS	Marital Relationship	Individual Factors	Social Environment
Safety Zone	16–20 Safe Harbor	0–4 Safety Zone	0–2 Clean Air Zone
Caution	21–29 Choppy Waters	5–9 Proceed with Caution	3–5 Smog Warning
Slippery Slope	30–39 Rough Seas	10–14 Slippery Slope	6–9 Pollution Alert
Danger Zone	40–48 Headed for the Rocks	15–19 Danger Zone	10–12 Toxic Air Zone

We have explored three types of vulnerability for infidelity: relationship issues, individual factors, and social-cultural influences. Comparing your ratings on this chart will alert you to the areas where you and your partner are most vulnerable, so you can take corrective steps.

APPENDIX: RESOURCES

I have collated a list of books, Web sites, and support groups that have been useful to people recovering from the trauma of infidelity. Some are specifically targeted at affairs; others are of general interest and very helpful for improving relationships. I have also included some information for those whose marriages are ending.

Suggested Readings

Infidelity, Addiction, and the Internet

Carnes, Patrick. 1983. *Out of the shadows: Understanding sexual addiction.* Minneapolis: CompCare.

Forward, Susan. 1999. *When your lover is a liar.* New York: HarperCollins.

Lusterman, Don-David. 1998. *Infidelity: A survival guide.* Oakland, CA: New Harbinger Publications.

Maheu, Marlene M., & Subotnik, Rona B. 2001. *Infidelity on the internet: Virtual relationships and real betrayal.* Naperville, IL: Sourcebooks, Inc.

Pittman, Frank. 1989. *Private lies: Infidelity and betrayal of intimacy.* New York: Norton.

Schneider, Jennifer P. 1988. *Back from betrayal: A ground-breaking guide to recovery for women involved with sex-addicted men.* New York: Ballantine Books.

Schneider, Jennifer P., & Schneider, Burt. 1999. *Sex, lies, and forgiveness: Couples speaking on healing from sex addiction.* Tucson, AZ: Recovery Resources Press.

Schneider, Jennifer, & Weiss, Robert. 2001. *Cybersex exposed: Simple fantasy or obsession?* Center City, MN: Hazelden.

Spring, Janis Abrahms, & Spring, Michael. 1997. *After the affair: Healing the pain and rebuilding trust when a partner has been unfaithful.* New York: HarperCollins.

Subotnik, Rona, & Harris, Gloria. 1999. *Surviving infidelity: Making decisions, recovering from the pain.* Holbrook, MA: Bob Adams Press.

Vaughan, Peggy. 1998. *The monogamy myth: A personal handbook for recovering from affairs.* New York: Newmarket Press.

Marriage

Doherty, William. 2001. *Take back your marriage.* New York: Guilford Press.

Gordon, Lori. 2000. *Passage to intimacy.* New York: Fireside.

Gottman, John M., with Silver, Nan. 1994. *Why marriages succeed or fail . . . and how you can make yours last.* New York: Simon & Schuster.

Gottman, John M., & Silver, Nan. 2000. *The seven principles for making marriage work.* New York: Crown.

Markman, Howard J., Blumberg, Susan L., & Stanley, Scott M. 2001. *Fighting for your marriage: Positive steps for preventing divorce and preserving a lasting love.* New York: Wiley.

Notarius, Clifford, & Markman, Howard. 1994. *We can work it out: How to solve conflicts, save your marriage, and strengthen your love for each other.* New York: Penguin/Putnam.

Weiner-Davis Michelle. 2001. *The divorce remedy: The proven 7-step program for saving your marriage.* New York: Simon & Schuster.

Love and Intimacy

Hendrix, Harville. 1990. *Getting the love you want.* New York: Harper & Row.

Levine, Janice, & Markman, Howard, Eds. 2000. *Why do fools fall in love? Experiencing the magic, mystery, and meaning of successful relationships.* New York: Wiley.

Love, Pat. 2001. *The truth about love: The highs, the lows, and how you can make it last forever.* New York: Simon & Schuster.

Pines, Ayala Malach. 1999. *Falling in love: Why we choose the lovers we choose.* New York: Routledge.

Sex

Barbach, Lonnie. 2000. *For yourself: The fulfillment of female sexuality.* New York: NAL Penguin/Putnam.

Gray, John. 1995. *Mars and Venus in the bedroom.* New York: HarperCollins.

Love, Pat, & Robinson, Jo. 1995. *Hot monogamy: Essential steps to more passionate, intimate lovemaking.* New York: Plume/Penguin.

Zilbergeld, Bernie. 1999. *The new male sexuality.* New York: Random House.

Divorce

Ahrons, Constance R. 1995. *The good divorce: Keeping your family together when your marriage comes apart.* New York: HarperTrade.

Hetherington, E. Mavis, & Kelly, John. 2002. *For better or for worse: Divorce reconsidered.* New York: Norton.

Mercer, Diana, & Pruett, Marsha Kline. 2001. *Your divorce advisor: A lawyer and a psychologist guide you through the legal and emotional landscape of divorce.* New York: Fireside.

Neuman, M. Gary. 1999. *Helping your kids cope with divorce the sandcastles way.* New York: Random House.

Ricci, Isolina. 1997. *Mom's house, Dad's house: A complete guide for parents who are separated, divorced, or remarried.* New York: Simon & Schuster.

Wallerstein, Judith S., Blakeslee, Sandra, & Lewis, Julia M. 2001. *Unexpected legacy of divorce: The 25 year landmark study.* New York: Hyperion.

Understanding Yourself

Beattie, Melody. 2001. *Codependent no more and beyond codependency.* New York: Fine Communications.

Carnes, Patrick. 1997. *The betrayal bond: Breaking free of exploitive relationships.* Deerfield Beach, FL: Health Communications.

Hayes, Christopher L., Blau, Melinda, & Anderson, Deborah. 1994. *Our turn: Women who triumph in the face of divorce.* New York: Pocket Books.

Lew, Mike. 1990. *Abused boys: The neglected victims of sexual abuse.* Lexington, MA: Lexington.

Love, Pat, with Robinson, Jo. 1991. *Emotional incest: What to do when a parent's love rules your life.* New York: Bantam.

Maltz, Wendy. 1991. *The sexual healing journey: A guide for survivors of sexual abuse.* San Francisco: HarperCollins.

McGraw, Phillip C. 2001. *Self matters: Creating your life from the inside out.* New York: Simon & Schuster.

Web Sites

BAN—Beyond Affairs Network, by Peggy Vaughan. *www.dearpeggy.com.* An international support group for people recovering from a partner's affair.

Divorce Busting Center, by Michelle Weiner-Davis. *www.divorcebusting.com.* On-line support forum.

Divorce Information. *www.divorceinfo.com.* A clearinghouse for divorce information, including articles and research.

Marriage Builders, Inc., founded by Willard Harley Jr., Ph.D. *www.marriagebuilders.com.* Links to articles to build mutually enjoyable marriage and section on recovery from infidelity.

Smart Marriages, founded by Diane Sollee, Director of Coalition for Marriage, Family and Couples Education, LLC. *www.smartmarriages.com.* Articles, books, audiotapes and videotapes, directory of marriage education programs, annual conference.

Support Groups

Co-Dependents Anonymous. *www.codependents.org.* 12-step program to develop healthy relationships.

S-Anon. *www.sanon.org.* 12-step program for partners and families of sex addicts.

SA—Sexaholics Anonymous. *www.sa.org.* 12-step program.

SAA—Sex Addicts Anonymous. *www.sexaa.org.* 12-step program.

SLAA—Sex and Love Addicts Anonymous. *www.slaahouston.org.* 12-step program.

SRA—Sexual Recovery Anonymous. *www.ourworld.compuserve.om/homepages/sra.*
    12-step program based on rational recovery instead of "higher power."

CHAPTER NOTES

Introduction

1. The incidence of extramarital coitus was 26 percent of wives and 50 percent of husbands in Alfred C. Kinsey, Wardell B. Pomeroy, Clyde E. Martin, and Paul H. Gebhard (1953), *Sexual behavior in the human female,* Philadelphia: W.B. Saunders; 36 percent of wives and 40 percent of husbands in Robert Athanasiou, Philip Shaver, and Carol Tavris (1970), Sex, *Psychology Today* (July), 37–52; 26 percent of women and 35 percent of men in S.S. Janus and D.L. Janus (1993), *The Janus report on sexual behavior,* New York: Wiley. It is noteworthy that a *Playboy* magazine survey that elicited 100,000 responses from 5 million readers (1.3 percent) obtained a comparable incidence finding: 34 percent of women and 45 percent of men were unfaithful. James R. Petersen (1983), The *Playboy* readers' sex survey. *Playboy, 30*(3), 90ff.

2. Surveys measuring the incidence of extramarital relationships are difficult to compare because sample characteristics create wide variations in self-reports. Magazine surveys and volunteer populations preserve anonymity at the cost of nonrepresentative samples, which may overestimate incidence. Extramarital behavior is typically defined as extramarital sexual intercourse. Methodological issues also impact how honest people are in their self-reports. Anonymity is compromised in national studies because individuals are contacted at home and given an envelope to mail back with confidential information. Studies optimize reporting when individuals are primed by first asking them about specific reasons or situations that would justify extramarital involvement. Comparable findings in a number of studies suggest that a reasonable estimate for lifetime incidence of extramarital intercourse is 25 percent of women and 50 percent of men. However, the incidence of actual extramarital involvement is increased by 15 to 20 percent if sexual intimacies and emotional involvements are included.

3. The *Psychology Today* study was reported in Shirley P. Glass and Thomas L. Wright (1977), The relationship of extramarital sex, length of marriage, and sex differences on marital satisfaction and romanticism: Athanasiou's data reanalyzed, *Journal of Marriage and the Family, 39*(4), 691–703.

4. The findings of the airport/downtown Baltimore study of a nonclinical sample were reported in Shirley P. Glass (1981), Sex differences in the relationship between satisfaction with various aspects of marriage and types of extramarital

involvements (Doctoral dissertation, Catholic University, 1980), *Dissertation Abstracts International, 41*(10), 3889B; Shirley P. Glass and Thomas L. Wright (1985), Sex differences in type of extramarital involvement and marital dissatisfaction, *Sex Roles, 12*(9/10), 1101–1119; Shirley P. Glass and Thomas L. Wright (1992), Justifications for extramarital involvement: The association between attitudes, behavior, and gender, *Journal of Sex Research, 29*(3), 1–27.

5. A survey of 122 members of the American Association of Marriage and Family Therapy and members of the Division of Family Psychology of the American Psychological Association reported that therapists rated affairs as the third most difficult problem to treat and as the second most damaging problem that couples face. This survey was by Mark A. Whisman, Amy E. Dixon, and Benjamin Johnson (1997), Therapists' perspectives of couple problems and treatment issues in couple therapy, *Journal of Family Psychology, 11*(3), 361–366.

1: I'm Telling You, We're Just Friends

1. "Get Over It," *This American Life,* Public Radio International. First aired on November 22, 1996.

2. Research findings about an increase in infidelity by married women are described in the studies below; current trends are for increased extramarital sex by younger women, and earlier gender differences are disappearing. In a 1994 population survey by the National Opinion Research Center, the lifetime incidence of extramarital sex in women and men younger than forty did not differ. Michael W. Wiederman (1997), Extramarital sex: Prevalence and correlates in a national survey, *Journal of Sex Research, 34*(2), 167–174. A 1988 British study by Annette Lawson and Colin Samson found that the pattern of multiple extramarital liaisons among women under thirty-five was more like the pattern of their male contemporaries than that of older groups of women. In Age, gender, and adultery, *British Journal of Sociology, 39*(3), 409–440. Gender differences in a 1977 Dutch study of extradyadic sex could not be replicated by the same researchers in a 1992 study. In Bram Buunk and Arnold Bakker (1995), Extradyadic sex: The role of descriptive and injunctive norms, *Journal of Sex Research, 32*(4), 313–318.

3. Frank Pittman (1993), Beyond betrayal: Life after infidelity, *Psychology Today,* 35.

4. Researchers have found an association between dedication to the marriage and avoidance of opportunities for extramarital relationships. Husbands and wives who were less dedicated spent more time thinking about alternatives. Dedication was manifested by not thinking about alternatives, even during tough times. Scott Stanley and Howard Markman (1992), Assessing commitment in personal relationships, *Journal of Marriage and the Family, 54,* 595–608. Dedicated spouses perceived attractive alternatives as a threat to their relationship and internally devalued the attractiveness of the alternatives to protect their commitment. Dennis J. John-

son and Caryl E. Rusbult (1989), Resisting temptation: Devaluation of alternative partners as a means of maintaining commitment in close relationships, *Journal of Personality and Social Psychology, 57,* 967–980.

5. Research studies on jealousy consistently support opposite patterns, in that husbands are more jealous of their wives' sexual involvement, whereas wives are more jealous of their husbands' emotional intimacy with other women. David Buss (1994), *The evolution of desire: Strategies of human mating,* New York: Basic Books; Janice L. Francis (1977), Toward the management of heterosexual jealousy, *Journal of Marriage and Family Counseling, 3,* 61–69; Anthony P. Thompson (1984), Emotional and sexual components of extramarital relations, *Journal of Marriage and Family, 46*(1), 35–42.

6. An analysis of a national population study by the National Opinion Research Center was reported by Michael Wiederman (1997), Extramarital sex: Prevalence and correlates in a national survey, *Journal of Sex Research, 34*(2), 167–174.

7. The concept of "walls and windows" was first introduced by Shirley Glass and Tom Wright at the 1990 annual conference of the American Association of Marriage and Family Therapists. The use of this metaphor in therapy is described in Shirley P. Glass and Thomas L. Wright (1997), Reconstructing marriages after the trauma of infidelity, in W.K. Halford and H.J. Markman (Eds.), *Clinical handbook of marriage and couples interventions,* New York: Wiley; Shirley P. Glass (2002), Couple therapy after the trauma of infidelity, in A.S. Gurman and N. Jacobson (Eds.), *The clinical handbook of couple therapy,* New York: Guilford Press.

8. The following studies have found that men seek opportunity more than women and cite lack of opportunity more frequently as a reason for not having engaged in extramarital relationships. In my airport sample, three times as many non-sexually involved men as women were deterred by lack of opportunity; 33 percent of noninvolved men versus 11 percent of noninvolved women cited lack of opportunity as a reason inhibiting potential extramarital relationship. Ralph Johnson also found that more noninvolved men than women attributed their lack of extramarital involvement to lack of opportunity: 48 percent of husbands and 5 percent of wives without opportunity said they would like such an experience. Ralph E. Johnson (1970), Some correlates of extramarital coitus, *Journal of Marriage and the Family, 32*(3), 449–456. A *Playboy* magazine survey with 100,000 respondents found that women who are sexually satisfied in their marriage are less likely to engage in extramarital sex, but men "cheat" despite the quality of marital sex; 75 percent of the women versus 50 percent of the men believed that an affair indicates a problem in the marriage. James R. Petersen (1983), The *Playboy* readers' sex survey, *Playboy, 30*(3), 90ff.

9. Annette Lawson and Colin Samson (1988) reported on a British survey of 340 women and 234 men, primarily white middle-class adults. Nearly 40 percent of the unfaithful men had a single partner for the first and most recent liaison. Men

typically were found to have more adulterous liaisons than women because more married men choose single women as affair partners and married women more often choose married men as affair partners. Age, gender, and adultery, *British Journal of Sociology, 39*(3), 409–440.

10. Happily married women often have a "filter" that screens out potential affair partners. They seem to tune out possible opportunities if they are satisfied with their marital relationship. For women only, high marital satisfaction was associated with less frequent opportunity for extramarital relationships. Shirley P. Glass and Thomas L. Wright (1988), Clinical implications of research on extramarital involvement, In R. Brown and J. Field (Eds.), *Treatment of sexual problems in individual and couples therapy,* New York: PMA.

11. Additional findings of the prevalence of workplace affairs were also found by other researchers. In a survey of marital therapists, work relationships accounted for the affairs of 39 percent of husbands and 36 percent of wives who were in therapy. Frederick G. Humphrey (1985, October), *Extramarital affairs and their treatment by AAMFT therapists,* paper presented at American Association of Marriage and Family Therapy, New York. In her on-line dissertation research, Debbie Layton-Tholl (1998) found that 41 percent of an Internet sample of 583 married persons met their affair partner through work. Extramarital affairs: The link between thought suppression and level of arousal, unpublished doctoral dissertation: Miami Institute of Psychology of the Caribbean Center for Advanced Studies. A national sample of 2,600 individuals found that the likelihood of infidelity during the prior twelve months was associated with jobs that required touching, talking, or being alone with others. Judith Treas and Deirdre Giesen (2000), Sexual infidelity among married and cohabiting Americans, *Journal of Marriage and the Family, 62* (February), 48–60.

12. Researchers have associated the increase in women's infidelity with the increase of women in the workplace. Anthony Pietropinto (1986) studied sex in the workplace and concluded that an influx of well-educated women into the workforce undoubtedly contributed to the rise in female infidelity. Sex in the workplace, *Medical Aspects of Human Sexuality,* July, 17–22. The highest incidence of infidelity in a *Redbook* survey of 100,000 women was for wage-earning women who were thirty-five to thirty-nine years old. Robert J. Levin and Amy Levin (1975), The *Redbook* report on premarital and extramarital sex, *Redbook,* October, 38ff. Annette Lawson (1988) found that 33 percent of all British wives who had had affairs met their lovers at work, but 44 percent of younger women met their affair partners through work. *Adultery: An analysis of love and betrayal,* New York: Basic Books.

13. My research and the research of others point to opportunity as a primary factor in the occurrence of extramarital involvements. An "opportunity theory" was supported by findings that the rates of extramarital sex for part-time workers and for housewives who do volunteer work fell exactly between the rates for full-time

workers and full-time housewives. Carol Tavris and S. Sadd (1977), *The Redbook report on female sexuality,* New York: Dell. Opportunity and social context were deciding factors in male sexual involvement for 41 percent of the men in a study of prominent upper-middle-class men. Robert Whitehurst (1969), Extramarital sex: Alienation or extension of normal behavior, in G. Neubeck (Ed.), *Extramarital relations,* Englewood Cliffs, NJ: Prentice-Hall.

14. Cup-of-coffee syndrome is a reason given for extramarital sex by Fred Humphrey (1983). Affairs resulting from attractions that are initially quite innocent and asexual may begin with a cup of coffee at work or somewhere else. The individuals soon develop the "habit" of meeting regularly and sharing more and more details of their lives and feelings, and they develop a dependence on these coffee talks. When "magical sex" enters as the next level of involvement, "It just happened." *Marital therapy,* Englewood Cliffs, NJ: Prentice-Hall, 47–66.

15. Janice Saunders and John Edwards (1984) found that extramarital sexual behavior is facilitated by separation of workplace from home. Extramarital sex was associated with the degree of autonomy (defined as "freedom from constraint") men and women experienced. The low autonomy group consisted of housewives not employed outside the home, the moderate group consisted of dentists and dental assistants, and the high autonomy group consisted of male and female real estate agents. Overnight traveling was associated with greater opportunity because of increased autonomy. Women reported less autonomy than men: 1 percent of the men compared with 13 percent of the women said that they had seldom or never had an opportunity. Extramarital sexuality: A predictive model of permissive attitudes, *Journal of Marriage and the Family, 46*(4), 825–835.

16. Married persons who were sexually involved with coworkers were compared to individuals who intentionally sought extramarital involvement for excitement and enhanced self-esteem. Those who were involved with coworkers were happily married and highly compatible with their spouses but proximity and common interests drew them into relationships with coworkers. The researchers concluded that some infidelity is associated with circumstantial, environmental events rather than low marital satisfaction or poor fit of personalities. James D. Wiggins and Doris A. Lederer (1984), Differentiated antecedents of infidelity in marriage, *American Mental Health Counselors Association Journal, 6,* 152–161.

17. Men learn to be situationally more expressive and relate to their wives with greater emotional expressiveness than to women in general. Jack O. Balswick and Charles W. Peek (1971), The inexpressive male: A tragedy of American society, *Family Coordinator, 20,* 363–368.

18. Nancy Kalish (1997) listened for two years to over one thousand "lost and found lovers" in print, by phone, in person, and by computer. She heard numerous stories in which lost lovers who were happily married and had been entirely faithful

met for a simple lunch together and rekindled the fire. More than 30 percent of renewed romances were secret, extramarital affairs. *Lost and found lovers: Facts and fantasies of rekindled romances,* New York: Morrow.

19. This true story, "I Met Him in the Yogurt Store, but Now He's Not the Leader of My Pack," was related on public radio on Valentine's Day 1998, on *This American Life.* The couple were Linda Howard and Richard Bloom of Boca Raton, Florida. The name of the old flame has been changed.

20. Debbie Layton-Tholl (1998), Extramarital affairs: The link between thought suppression and level of arousal, unpublished doctoral dissertation: Miami Institute of Psychology of the Caribbean Center for Advanced Studies.

21. Jim O'Connor developed this quiz for the web site ComPsych.com using material from an article I had written for *Electra@aol.com* entitled "On-line Attractions."

2: Crossing into a Double Life

1. In a British survey, 90 percent of women and 80 percent of men intended to remain sexually faithful at the time they got married, but their attitudes changed and they became more permissive during their marriage. Annette Lawson (1988), *Adultery: An analysis of love and betrayal,* New York: Basic Books.

2. James B. Stiff, Hyun J. Kim, and Closepet N. Ramesh (1992), Truth biases and aroused suspicion in relational deception, *Communication Research, 19*(3), 326–345.

3. "The idealization of romantic love is like a vanity mirror with tiny bulbs all around the perimeter reflecting a rosy glow. Reality-based love is more like the makeup mirror which magnifies our wrinkles." Shirley P. Glass (2000), The harder you fall, the farther you fall, in J.R. Levine and H.J. Markman (Eds.), *Why do fools fall in love?* New York: Jossey-Bass.

4. Frank Pittman (1989), *Private lies: Infidelity and the betrayal of intimacy,* New York: Norton.

5. Annette Lawson (1988), *Adultery: An analysis of love and betrayal,* New York: Basic Books.

6. David Buss (1994), *The evolution of desire: Strategies of human mating,* New York: Basic Books.

7. When my clinical sample was asked what would inhibit potential involvement in an extramarital relationship, moral values were a deterrent that discriminated between women with no sexual involvement at all and women who had engaged in any type of sexual intimacy. Men, on the other hand, were deterred by moral values only if they had not engaged in extramarital sexual intercourse. Men who were sexually intimate were more similar to noninvolved men than to men who had sexual intercourse.

8. The "monogamous infidel" is a fundamentally monogamous individual who tries to justify an extramarital relationship by the belief that he or she fell in love, retrospectively rewrites the marital history, and may even deny ever having loved his or her spouse. Because these individuals are unable to be in two relationships at the same time, they withdraw from the marriage sexually and emotionally and feel unfaithful to the lover when they are intimate with the spouse. Shirley P. Glass and Thomas L. Wright (1997), Reconstructing marriages after the trauma of infidelity, in W.K. Halford and H.J. Markman (Eds.), *Clinical handbook of marriage and couples interventions,* New York: Wiley.

3: Reaching the Moment of Revelation

1. The *New York Times* (April 7, 2000) published a poll by Blum and Weprin in which a random sample of 1,003 adults in all fifty states asked whether individuals were "absolutely certain" that their partner had been faithful; 86 percent responded "yes." A survey of female readers in *New Woman* magazine (cited in Schneider, 1988) reported that 41 percent of women had one or more affairs, but only 19 percent knew for certain that their husband or lover had cheated on them. Lewis Yablonsky (1979) reported that 80 percent of husbands involved in "extra-sex" relationships never told their wives, nor were they found out. *The extra-sex factor: Why over half of America's married men play around,* New York: Times Books.

2. A 1997 study by Todd Shackelford and David Buss asked 204 men and women to list cues that would evoke suspicions of either sexual or emotional infidelity. Sexual signals were detecting sexual odors or other unfamiliar scents and abrupt or unexpected changes in sexual interest. Other signals were changes in clothing style or taste in books or music. Most devastating was accidentally calling one's spouse by another person's name. Cues to infidelity, *Personality & Social Psychology Bulletin, 23* (10), 1034–1045.

3. Sweethearts and cheating hearts: For private eyes on adultery cases, Valentine's Day is a bonanza, *Baltimore Sun* (February 14, 1993).

4. Many partners suspected correctly that extramarital sex was occurring long before disclosure took place; 53 percent were suspicious enough to confront, but 84 percent who were confronted initially denied any wrongdoing. Jennifer P. Schneider and Burt Schneider (1999), *Sex, lies, and forgiveness: Couples speaking on healing from sex addiction,* Tucson, AZ: Recovery Resources Press.

5. The case of Betty Broderick and her diagnosis of post-traumatic stress disorder subsequent to the discovery of protracted marital infidelity was presented by Don-David Lusterman in 1992 in a workshop, The Broderick Affair, which was presented at the annual meeting of the American Association of Marriage and Family Therapy in Miami, Florida.

6. Annette Lawson (1988), *Adultery: An analysis of love and betrayal,* New York: Basic Books. Confessing an extramarital affair appears less risky for men than for

women. However, negative consequences were three times more frequent for men when their wives discovered their affairs (58 percent) than for those who voluntarily confessed (18 percent). Forty percent of women and 30 percent of men said telling had adverse consequences for marriage. Women who confessed were more likely than men to be divorced. How husbands found out about wives' infidelity made no significant difference. The most common reason for telling was desire to stop deceit and be open. Only 6 percent of women and 3 percent of men admitted to hostile goals, such as wishing to hurt spouse, to exact revenge, or to inflict loss of face.

4: In the Wake of Discovery

1. Anxiety was assessed on the Burns Anxiety Inventory; among the revealed infidelities, 30 percent of betrayed husbands and 45 percent of betrayed wives had scores ranging from severely anxious to extremely anxious.

2. Depression was assessed on the Beck Depression Inventory; among the revealed infidelities, 30 percent of betrayed husbands and 29 percent of betrayed wives had scores ranging from moderately depressed to extremely depressed.

3. The world of European starlings is described in David P. Barash and Judith Eve Lipton, *The myth of monogamy: Fidelity and infidelity in animals and people*, W.H. Freeman, 2001.

4. Annette Lawson (1988), *Adultery: An Analysis of love and betrayal*, New York: Basic Books.

5. Judith L. Herman (1992), *Trauma and recovery*, New York: Basic Books.

6. Several men who had seen their mother engage in sexual infidelity when they were young adolescents had a form of pathological jealousy and an inability to let go of a wife's betrayal. John P. Docherty and Jean Ellis (1976), A new concept and finding in morbid jealousy, *American Journal of Psychiatry*, 133(6), 679–683.

7. In a study of eighty-two sex addicts, their partners were angry about stepwise disclosure in which significant information was initially hidden. Disclosure was a process, not a one-time event. Healing was achieved most easily when initial disclosure included all major elements of the acting-out behaviors but avoided the "gory details." Jennifer P. Schneider, Deborah M. Corley, and Richard R. Irons (1998), Surviving disclosure of infidelity: Results of an international survey of 164 recovering sex addicts and partners. *Sexual Addiction and Compulsivity*, 5, 189–217.

8. Mark Pazniokas, 2001, 1 man, 2 women, countless lies (Hartford) *Courant* (October 3).

5: Should You Pick Up the Pieces or Throw in the Towel?

1. Psychologists Notarius and Markman suggest that for some couples filing or seeking a divorce may be the first stage of transformation. Clifford Notarius and Howard Markman (1993), *We can work it out*, New York: Putnam, 137.

2. In the Spanier Dyadic Adjustment Scale, the strength of commitment to continue a particular marital relationship is measured on a 6-point scale, ranging from (1) "I want desperately for my marriage to succeed, and I would go to almost any length to see that it does" to (6) "My marriage can never succeed, and there is no more that I can do to keep the marriage going." In my clinical sample, 52 percent of men and 41 percent of women whose commitment ranged from 4 to 6 were separated, versus 18 percent of men and 21 percent of women whose commitment ranged from 1 to 2. The Dyadic Adjustment Scale is described in a journal article by Graham Spanier (1976), Measuring dyadic adjustment: New scales for assessing the quality of marriage and similar dyads, *Journal of Marriage and the Family, 38,* 15–28.

3. Jennifer Schneider and her associates found that once sex addicts made their initial disclosure, threats to leave by their partners were very common: 60 percent of partners reported making such threats. However, these threats usually were not carried out, as three-fourths of those who threatened to leave never did, even temporarily. Jennifer P. Schneider, Deborah M. Corley, and Richard R. Irons (1998), Surviving disclosure of infidelity: Results of an international survey of 164 recovering sex addicts and partners, *Sexual Addiction and Compulsivity, 5,* 189–217.

4. Wallerstein did a longitudinal study on the effects of divorce on children and found that the breakup and its aftermath were life-shaping events. The effects of parental divorce appeared to be cumulative and were evident throughout adolescence and adulthood. Her findings are discussed in Judith S. Wallerstein, Sandra Blakeslee, and Julie Lewis (2001), *The unexpected legacy of divorce: A 25 year landmark study,* New York: Hyperion.

5. Cited in E. Mavis Heatherington and John Kelly (2002), *For better or worse: Divorce reconsidered,* New York: Norton, 272.

6. Rekindled romances that ended up in marriage had the extremely high rate of 72 percent who stayed together. For couples who were each other's first love, the rekindled stay-together rate was even higher: 78 percent. These couples said that they shared emotional and sexual satisfaction unequaled by any other relationship. Nancy Kalish (1997), *Lost and found lovers: Facts and fantasies of rekindled romances,* New York: William Morrow.

7. Vaughan's on-line survey of 1,083 betrayed spouses assessed their experiences with marital counseling. Among those who sought counseling, 27 percent had one counselor, 26 percent had two, and 48 percent sought counseling from three or more therapists. Based on their first or only counselor, 20 percent found it very helpful; 23 percent found it helpful, but not as much as they would have liked; and 57 percent found it mostly frustrating. Only 14 percent of counselors were perceived to have dealt very directly with the issue of affairs; 28 percent dealt with affair issues but not as strongly or as clearly as the betrayed spouses would have liked; and 59 percent focused mainly on general marital problems. Peggy Vaughan (1999), Partial results of survey on extramarital affairs, http://www.dearpeggy.com/results.html.

6: How to Cope with Obsessing and Flashbacks

1. Herman presents her approach to traumatic recovery with victims of sexual and physical abuse, natural disasters, and violence in Judith L. Herman (1992), *Trauma and recovery*, New York: Basic Books.

2. The diagnostic criteria for post-traumatic stress disorder (309.81) is presented in American Psychiatric Association (1994), *DSM-IV: Diagnostic and statistical manual of mental disorders, fourth edition,* Washington, D.C.: Author.

3. The advantages of journaling are discussed in an on-line article by Ray Bruce, Ph.D. (1998, May 29), "Strange but true: Improve your health through journaling," *Selfhelp Magazine*, www.shpm.com.

4. Rona Subotnik and Gloria Harris (1999) made many helpful suggestions about dealing with obsessive thoughts in their book *Surviving infidelity: Making decisions, recovering from the pain*, Holbrook, MA: Bob Adams Press.

5. In their book *The trauma response: Treatment for emotional injury,* New York: Norton, Diana S. Everstine and Louis Everstine (1993) present the stages of trauma recovery for clinicians.

6. Norman Cousins (1989) describes research on the positive effects of laughter on the immune systems of medically ill patients in his book *Head first: The biology of hope and the healing power of the human spirit*, New York: Penguin Books.

7: Repairing the Couple and Building Goodwill

1. Michelle Weiner-Davis (1992) suggests that unhappily married individuals can get on track through envisioning the end product by asking future-oriented questions, *Divorce busting*, New York: Simon and Schuster.

2. Research on couples married more than fifty years conducted by Fran C. Dickson (1995) appeared in The best is yet to be: Research on long-lasting relationships, in J.T. Wood and S. Duck, (Eds.), *Understanding relationship processes: Off the beaten track,* Beverly Hills, CA: Sage.

3. Rabbi Harold S. Kushner (1996) says that "we have the power to choose happiness over righteousness." Righteousness is remembering hurts and disappointments, and happiness means giving others the right to be human, weak, and selfish. *How good do we have to be? A new understanding of guilt and forgiveness*, New York: Little, Brown.

4. John M. Gottman, with Nan Silver (1994), *Why marriages succeed or fail,* New York: Simon and Schuster.

5. The concept of bull's-eye caring was introduced by Dr. Tom Wright in our cotherapy sessions with distressed couples.

6. The two exercises, "What Pleases Me About You" and "The Newlywed Game" were adapted from a Caring Behaviors questionnaire by Richard B. Stuart (1993), *Couples pre-counseling inventory,* Champaign, IL: Research Press.

7. Judith S. Wallerstein and Sandra Blakeslee (1995) studied fifty couples in which both husband and wife regarded the marriage as very happy. They were married at least nine years, and their ages ranged from 32 to 74. *The good marriage: How and why love lasts,* New York: Warner Books.

8. Researchers Clifford Notarius and Howard Markman (1993) asserted: It takes one put-down to undo hours of kindness you give to your partner. *We can work it out: How to solve conflicts, save your marriage, and strengthen your love for each other,* New York: Penguin Putnam.

9. Ibid.

10. John M. Gottman and Nan Silver (1999), *The seven principles for making marriage work,* New York: Three Rivers Press.

11. Adapted from the technique of "intentional dialogue" as described in the writings of Harville Hendrix. Dr. Hendrix (1997) writes extensively about intentional dialogue in *Giving the love that heals,* New York: Pocket Books. There are three steps in his process: mirroring, validating, and empathizing. Validating centers on the idea of affirming the other person's right to think and feel the way he or she does, regardless of whether you agree with the content of what he or she is saying.

8: The Story of the Affair

1. Telling the story of the traumatic event is an essential part of the recovery process, according to trauma experts. Diana Everstine and Louis Everstine (1993) state that repeating what happened is an attempt to gain mastery over the experience by reinterpreting it again and again until it makes sense. *The trauma response: Treatment for emotional injury,* New York: Norton. Judith Herman (1992) states that in the second stage of recovery, the survivor tells the story of the trauma by reviewing life before the trauma and the circumstances that led up to the event. This provides a context to understand the meaning of the trauma. *Trauma and recovery,* New York: Basic Books.

2. Peggy Vaughan's survey through her Web site (*http://www.dearpeggy.com/results.html*) reported on responses by 1,083 betrayed spouses regarding the impact of discussing questions about the affair: (a) still married and living together were 55 percent who talked very little, 78 percent who talked a good bit, and 86 percent who talked a lot; (b) trust was rebuilt in 31 percent where unfaithful spouse refused to answer questions, 43 percent where some questions were answered, and 72 percent where all questions were answered; (c) somewhat healed were 41 percent

where unfaithful spouse refused to answer questions, 51 percent where some questions were answered, and 55 percent where all questions were answered; (d) the relationship was better than before the affair in 21 percent where the situation was discussed very little, 43 percent where they discussed it a good bit, and 59 percent where they discussed it a lot.

3. Findings of a survey of eighty-two sex addicts with 3.4 yrs of recovery and their spouses were: (a) disclosure is not a one-time event; even in the absence of relapse, withholding of information is common; (b) half of the sex addicts reported one or more major slips or relapses that necessitated additional decisions about disclosure. Jennifer P. Schneider, Deborah M. Corley, and Richard R. Irons (1998), Surviving disclosure of infidelity: Results of an international survey of 164 recovering sex addicts and partners, *Sexual Addiction and Compulsivity, 5,* 189–217.

4. Jennifer Schneider (1988) wrote about her study of betrayed women and their codependency issues in *Back from betrayal: A ground-breaking guide to recovery for women involved with sex addicted men,* New York: Ballantine Books.

5. In 1997 *The bridges of Madison County,* by Robert James Waller, was published as a paperback and released as a video by Warner Home Video.

6. Researchers consistently found that the powerful emotional component involved in secret relationships was associated with obsessive preoccupation and an increase in the attractiveness of the secret partner. Daniel M. Wegner, Julie D. Lane, and Sara Dimitri (1994), The allure of secret relationships, *Journal of Personality and Social Psychology, 66,* 287–300.

7. Debbie Layton-Tholl (1998) found that married persons whose affair has ended will experience greater arousal with thought of the lover if they have not disclosed the affair to the spouse. She suggested that disclosure may be the only form of relief from the constant demand of behavioral and physiological work that is required to keep the secret. Extramarital affairs: The link between thought suppression and level of arousal, unpublished doctoral dissertation: Miami Institute of Psychology of the Caribbean Center for Advanced Studies.

8. Ibid.

9. Kristina Coop Gordon and Donald H. Baucom (1999), A multitheoretical intervention for promoting recovery from extramarital affairs, *Clinical Psychology: Science and Practice, 6*(4), 382–399.

10. In a 1983 *Playboy* magazine survey with 100,000 respondents, James Peterson reported that women who are sexually satisfied in their marriages are less likely to engage in extramarital sex, but men cheat despite the quality of marital sex. The *Playboy* readers' sex survey, *Playboy, 30*(3), 90ff. The Kinsey Report found that sexual variety appears a reasonable desire to men, but most women could not understand how a "happily married man" would want sexual intercourse with another

woman. Alfred C. Kinsey, Wendell B. Pomeroy, Clyde E. Martin, and Paul H. Gebhard (1953), *Sexual behavior in the human female,* Philadelphia: W.B. Saunders.

11. Debbie Layton-Tholl (1998), Extramarital affairs: the link between thought suppression and level of arousal, unpublished doctoral dissertation: Miami Institute of Psychology of the Caribbean Center for Advanced Studies.

12. A 1997 study by Bram Buunk and Arnold Bakker in The Netherlands found that approximately 75 percent of individuals who engaged in extradyadic sex had unprotected vaginal intercourse while simultaneously having unprotected intercourse with their steady partner. Commitment to the relationship, extradyadic sex, and AIDS preventive behavior, *Journal of Applied Social Psychology, 27*(14), 1241–1257.

13. The data from the National AIDS Behavioral Survey was described in an article by Kyung-Hee Choi, Joseph A. Catania, and Margaret M. Dolcini (1994), Extramarital sex and HIV risk behavior among U.S. adults: Results from the National AIDS Behavioral Survey, *American Journal of Public Health, 84*(12), 2003–2007.

9: The Story of Your Marriage

1. In a *Redbook* magazine survey of 100,000 women, half of the sexually involved women reported that they were happily married and sexually satisfied with their husband. Robert J. Levin and Amy Levin (1975, October), The *Redbook* report on premarital and extramarital sex, *Redbook,* 38ff. Ninety-one interviews and 360 questionnaires were the basis for Morton Hunt's finding that one-half the men and one-third the women who engaged in extramarital sex reported happy marriages. Morton Hunt (1969), *The affair,* New York: World Publishing.

2. A statistical analysis found a significant difference between male and female therapists in the association between infidelity and marital dissatisfaction: men were more likely than women to believe that an affair is not necessarily a symptom of an unhappy marriage.

3. Involved and non-involved wives were less satisfied than their husbands with emotional intimacy (understanding, companionship), ego bolstering (respect and enhancement of self-confidence), fun, romance, love and affection, and help with household tasks.

4. In my clinical sample, unfaithful husbands were also more dissatisfied than monogamous husbands with sharing intellectual interests. Unfaithful wives were more dissatisfied than monogamous wives with fun and romance.

5. Significant sex differences in the marital satisfaction of men and women who engaged in extramarital sexual intercourse were reported in Shirley P. Glass and Thomas L. Wright (1985), Sex differences in type of extramarital involvement and marital dissatisfaction, *Sex Roles, 12*(9/10), 1101–1119.

6. John F. Cuber and Peggy B. Haroff (1965), *The significant Americans: A study of sexual behavior among the affluent,* New York: Appleton Century Crofts.

7. Oxytocin (a peptide secreted by the pituitary gland) plays a central role in the urge to bond. Just before orgasm, this hormone spikes to levels three to five times higher than usual. It is more intense in females than in males, so women have a stronger sense of bonding with a sex partner than do men. Theresa L. Crenshaw (1997), *The alchemy of love and lust: How our sex hormones influence our relationships,* New York: Pocket Books.

8. In the airport sample and in the clinical sample, husbands and wives both perceived greater equity in their affairs than in their marriages.

9. The metaphor "riding the pony" versus "cleaning the barn" was first introduced by Daniel Casriel and is included in the PAIRS marriage education program developed by Lori Gordon (personal communication with Lori Gordon, 2/19/2002).

10. Linda Waite analyzed the marital satisfaction of married respondents in the National Survey of Families and Households in 1987–1988 who were still married to the same people in 1992–1994. On a scale of marital happiness from 1 = Very unhappy to 7 = Very happy, 77 percent of those who had rated their marriage at 1 subsequently rated it at 6 or 7 five years later. Linda J. Waite and Maggie Gallagher (2000), *The case for marriage: Why married people are happier, healthier, and better off financially,* New York: Doubleday.

11. Research consistently finds that male withdrawal signals likelihood of future distress unless the pattern is altered. When females withdraw later in the relationship, this is a sign of serious current problems and is a predictor of divorce unless help is sought. Cliff Notarius and Howard Markman (1993), *We can work it out: Making sense of marital conflict,* New York: Putnam.

12. Michelle Weiner-Davis (1993) states that one person can make changes that radically shift destructive relationship patterns. Making a 180-degree turn in your own actions is a marriage-saving approach in her solution-oriented brief therapy. *Divorce busting: A revolutionary and rapid program for staying together,* New York: Simon and Schuster.

10: Your Individual Stories

1. The results of a survey of 100,000 women appeared in Robert J. Levin and Amy Levin (1975, October), The *Redbook* report on premarital and extramarital sex, *Redbook,* 38ff.

2. Annette Lawson (1988), *Adultery: An analysis of love and betrayal,* New York: Basic Books.

3. Intent was found to be inversely related to the amount of guilt respondents reported following the infidelity. Paul A. Mongeau, Jerold L. Hale, and Marmy

Alles (1994), An experimental investigation of accounts and attributions following sexual infidelity, *Communication Monographs, 61,* 326–343.

4. In my clinical practice, moral values were an inhibitor for 90 percent of men who were sexually intimate, compared with 61 percent who engaged in extramarital intercourse. Moral values was a deterrent for 95 percent of the women who had no sexual involvement at all, compared with 79 percent of women who were sexually intimate and 78 percent who had extramarital intercourse. Religious beliefs were a deterrent for 41 percent of men and 54 percent of women with no sexual involvement, and for approximately 25 percent of men and women who had any type of sexual intimacy.

5. Frank Farley (1990) theorizes that Type-T personality and behavior ranges from *Big T* (high-risk, thrill and stimulation seeking) at one end to *small t* (low-risk, avoidance of thrill or stimulation seeking) at the other end. *T+* is risk taking and thrill seeking that is positive, healthy, and constructive. *T-* is negative and destructive risk taking and thrill seeking. Type-T behavior and families: Introduction and background to a new theory, *Family Psychologist, 6*(4), 24–25.

6. Alexythymia is defined as the inability to identify and describe one's feelings in words. Psychologist Ronald Levant (1992) suggests that alexythymia is common for men in our culture because of the way they are socialized. Toward the reconstruction of masculinity, *Journal of Family Psychology, 5*(3–4), 379–402.

7. One-third of the patients at residential treatment center, Sierra Tucson, were sex addicts. Betsy Morris (1999, May 10), Addicted to sex, *Fortune,* 66ff.

8. Jennifer P. Schneider and Burt Schneider (1999) *Sex, lies, and forgiveness: Couples speaking on healing from sex addiction,* Tucson, AZ: Recovery Resources Press.

9. Kimberly S. Young (1998), *Caught in the Net: How to recognize the signs of Internet addiction—and a winning strategy for recovery,* New York: Wiley.

10. Lori Gordon writes, "Anything in our lives that has caused us pain or disappointment or distrust can develop into an 'emotional allergy,'" regardless of whether the memory is conscious or unconscious. Lori H. Gordon with Jon Frandsen (1993), *Passage to intimacy,* New York: Fireside/Simon and Schuster.

11. PAIRS (Practical Application of Intimate Relationship Skills) is an intensive relationship-enrichment program in which specific exercises, such as "A Museum Tour of Past Hurts," are used to reconnect with the sources of emotional allergies.

12. Many affair-prone women in Carol Ellison's survey (2000) had personally suffered childhood sexual abuse. *Women's sexualities.* Oakland CA.: New Harbinger.

13. April Westfall (1995), Working through the extramarital trauma: An exploration of common themes, Gerald R. Weeks and Larry Hof (Eds.), *Integrative solutions: Treating the most common couple problems,* New York: Brunner/Mazel.

14. Patrick Carnes (1991), *Don't call it love,* New York: Bantam Books.

15. Attachment styles influence not only the way people act in romantic relationships and caregiving patterns, but also in their sexuality. Ayala Pines (1999), *Falling in love: Why we choose the lovers we choose,* New York: Routledge.

16. Elizabeth Allen's dissertation research analyzed attachment styles and infidelity patterns of 251 married adults: 46 percent had at least one affair; 90 percent of them involved sexual intimacy such as oral sex or intercourse. Preliminary results were reported in Elizabeth Sandin Allen and Donald H. Baucom (2001), Attachment styles and their relation to patterns of infidelity, paper presented at Conceptualization and Treatment of Infidelity symposium, annual conference of Association for Advancement of Behavior Therapy, Philadelphia.

17. Ibid.

18. Dalma Heyn (1993), *The erotic silence of the American wife,* New York: Signet Books.

19. The diagnostic criteria for 301.81 Narcissistic Personality Disorder (pp. 658–661) and 301.7 Antisocial Personality Disorder (pp. 645–650) are presented in (1994), *DSM-IV: Diagnostic and statistical manual of mental disorders, fourth edition,* American Psychiatric Association, Washington, D.C.: Author.

11: The Story of Outside Influences

1. The United States was one of the most sexually conservative among twenty-four countries that were studied. Eric D. Widmer, Judith Treas, and Robert Newcomb (1998), Attitudes towards nonmarital sex in 24 countries, *Journal of Sex Research, 35,* 349–359.

2. In the absence of group support from male peers, a man was less likely to find opportunity unless he was a singular deviant who operated in terms of hiding behavior from practically all others. Robert N. Whitehurst (1969), Extramarital sex: Alienation or extension of normal behavior, in G. Neubeck (ed.), *Extramarital relations,* Englewood Cliffs, NJ: Prentice-Hall.

3. Laurel Richardson (1985), *The new other woman: Contemporary single women in affairs with married men,* New York: Free Press.

4. In two studies of extradyadic relationships in The Netherlands, with 125 men and 125 women in each study, sanctions from the group when deviating from prevailing group standards predicted willingness to engage in extradyadic sex (e.g., "If most of my friends do not play around, there must be good reasons not to do so"). Bram P. Buunk and Arnold B. Bakker (1995), Extradyadic sex: The role of descriptive and injunctive norms, *Journal of Sex Research, 32*(4), 313–318.

5. Anthony Thompson's (1984) study of Australian married and cohabiting couples found that involved persons may justify their own behavior by perceiving

extradyadic activity as more prevalent; involved individuals gave higher estimates than noninvolved regarding what percentage of men and women participated. Thompson concluded that friends and acquaintances serve as adult socialization agents, whereby extramarital behaviors become likely and desirable. Emotional and sexual components of extramarital relations, *Journal of Marriage and Family, 46,* 35–42.

6. Lynn Atwater (1982) conducted in-depth interviews with forty women recruited through an ad in *Ms* magazine asking for women with current or past extramarital relationships. *The extramarital connection,* New York: Irvington.

7. Affairs are more likely to occur among those whose parents had affairs. Emily Brown (1991), *Patterns of infidelity and their treatment,* New York: Brunner/Mazel. Over the course of marital therapy for infidelity, 90 percent of Bonnie Eaker Weil's patients found that at least one partner was the adult child of an adulterer—sometimes involving four generations. Bonnie E. Weil and R. Winter (1993), *Adultery: The forgivable sin,* New York: Birch Lane Press.

8. In-depth interviews were conducted with seventy women age 23 to 90, and a sixteen-page questionnaire that was developed with Bernie Zilbergeld surveyed 2,362 women throughout the United States about sexuality. Carol R. Ellison (2000), *Women's sexualities.* Oakland, CA: New Harbinger.

9. Sally D. Stabb, Brandi Ragsdale, Alison J. Bess, and Heather Weiner (2000), *Multigenerational patterns of infidelity and their relationship to attachment,* paper presented at annual convention of American Psychological Association, Washington, DC.

10. David Maraniss (1995), *First in his class: The biography of Bill Clinton.* New York: Simon and Schuster.

11. Studies of traditional cultures with a double standard of infidelity included Hispanic Americans, African Americans, and Asian Americans. Societies that provide higher status to men may give wives few options except to tolerate their husband's infidelity. Christie D. Penn, Stacy L. Hernandez, and J. Maria Bermudez (1997), Using a cross-cultural perspective to understand infidelity in couples therapy, *American Journal of Family Therapy, 25*(2), 169–185.

12. Suzanne Frayser (1985), *Varieties of sexual experience: An anthropological perspective,* New Haven: HRAF Press.

13. Harold T. Christensen (1962), A cross-cultural comparison of attitudes toward marital infidelity, *International Journal of Comparative Sociology, 3,* 124–137.

14. Male extra-sex behavior is more likely to be a result of sexual drives in the context of societal norms than a result of marital distress. Lewis Yablonsky (1979), *The extra-sex factor: Why over half of America's married men play around,* New York: Times Books.

15. Vaughn (1999), *http://www.dearpeggy.com/results.html.*

16. Jan Halper (1988), *Quiet desperation: The truth about successful men,* New York: Warner Books.

17. Annette Lawson and Colin Samson (1988), Age, gender, and adultery. *British Journal of Sociology, 39*(3), 409–440.

18. Under Muslim law, a man may freely murder his wife if she is discovered having extramarital sex; in modern Saudi Arabia she could be stoned to death. Suzanne Frayzer (1985), *Varieties of sexual experience: An anthropological perspective,* New York: HRAF Press. Most cultures have punished women more severely than men for extramarital transgressions. Husbands could protect their honor and kill wandering wives in traditional Greek culture. Until quite recently in France, the *crime passionel* was acceptable for men, and in Belgium only the wife's infidelity constituted legal grounds for divorce. Robert G. Bringle and Bram Buunk (1991), Extradyadic relationships and sexual jealousy, in K. McKinney and S. Sprecher (eds.), *Sexuality in close relationships,* Hillsdale, NJ: Erlbaum.

19. College students judged women more harshly than men who were portrayed in exactly the same vignette of sexual infidelity. Paul A. Mongeau, Jerold L. Hale, and Marmy Alles (1994), An experimental investigation of accounts and attributions following sexual infidelity, *Communication Monographs, 61,* 326–343. A severe double standard among Asian Americans illustrates how women are blamed for the infidelity of either spouse. Infidelity is deemed more acceptable for men and is not tolerated for women. The high status of males puts them into a "no-fault position" in which male affairs are either blamed on the wife's not being there for him, or on the other woman who took him away from his family. C.D. Penn, S.L. Hernandez and J.M. Bermudez (1997), Using a cross-cultural perspective to understand infidelity in couples therapy, *American Journal of Family Therapy, 25*(2), 169–185.

20. In an analysis of the National Health and Social Life Survey, it was concluded that similar incidence findings among men and women under forty years of age signified that either the previous double standard regarding extramarital sex did not exist among the younger generation, or that older women displayed a response bias as far as admitting extramarital sex. Edward O. Laumann, John H. Gagnon, Robert T. Michael, Stuart Michaels (1994), *The social organization of sexuality: Sexual practices in the United States,* Chicago: University of Chicago Press.

21. Lewis Yablonsky (1979), *The extra-sex factor: Why over half of America's married men play around,* New York: Times Books.

22. Husbands and wives who were more likely to approve of premarital and extramarital sex resided in or near large metropolitan centers rather than in rural areas and were unhappily married. David L. Weis and Joan Jurich (1985), Size of community of residence as a predictor of attitudes toward extramarital sexual relations,

Journal of Marriage and the Family, *47*(1), 173–178. Greater opportunity and Central City residence were associated with a higher incidence of sexual infidelity during the preceding twelve months in a national sample. Judith Treas and Deirde Giesen (2000), Sexual infidelity among married and cohabiting Americans. *Journal of Marriage and the Family, 62,* 48–60.

12: The Story of the Affair Partner

1. Ann Landers (2001, December 27), column, *The Oregonian,* Portland.

2. In a dramatic departure from their usual way of choosing men, married women chose extramarital partners without considering age or employment, social, financial, or marital status. They based their selection on his body and his smile; his credentials as friend, lover, and nurturer; and whether he treated her respectfully, kindly, and as an equal. Dalma Heyn (1993), *The erotic silence of the American wife,* New York: Signet Books.

3. Jan Halper (1988), *Quiet desperation: The truth about successful men,* New York: Warner Books.

4. This study of "the new other woman" used a structured interview of two to five hours with fifty-five women volunteers who were age 24 to 65 at the time of the interview but 18 to 56 years old when the affair began. The median age was 28, and for the most part the men were older and better established. Laurel Richardson (1985), *The new other woman: Contemporary single women in affairs with married men,* New York: Free Press.

5. This e-mail from "Confused" was posted on my advice column "Reflections by Glass." It is published with permission by Oxygen Media, LLC.

6. Anthony Schuham and Waldo H. Bird (1990), Marriage and the affairs of the anxious man of prominence, *American Journal of Family Therapy, 18*(2), 141–152.

7. Laurel Richardson (1985), *The new other woman: Contemporary single women in affairs with married men,* New York: Free Press.

8. Most of the affairs began as innocent flirtations at work. Craig Wilson reported in *USA Today* (April 4, 1988) about an upcoming survey by Gail North on "the other woman" in the May 1988 issue of *Woman* magazine.

9. Emotional incest syndrome occurs when parents are overly dependent on a child to meet their own emotional needs. Patricia Love with Jo Robinson (1990), *The emotional incest syndrome: What to do when a parent's love rules your life,* New York: Bantam.

14: Forgiving and Moving Forward

1. Alexander Pope (1953). Essay on criticism, in George K. Anderson and Karl J. Holzknecht (Eds.), *The literature of England,* Chicago: Scott, Foresman.

2. Jennifer P. Schneider and Burt Schneider (1999), *Sex, lies, and forgiveness: Couples speaking on healing from sex addiction*, Tucson, AZ: Recovery Resources Press.

3. Fred Luskin (2002), *Forgive for good: A proven prescription for health and happiness*, New York: Harper Collins, 86–92.

4. Kristina Gordon and Donald Baucom (1998), "True" forgiveness vs. "false" forgiveness: Further validation of a cognitive-behavioral stage model of forgiveness, poster session presented at the annual meeting of Association for Advancement of Behavior Therapy, Washington, D.C.

5. Elizabeth Seagull and Arthur A. Seagull (1991), Healing the wound that must not heal: Psychotherapy with survivors of domestic violence, *Psychotherapy: Theory/Research/Practice/Training, 28*(1), 16–20.

6. Rona Subotnik and Gloria Harris (1999), *Surviving infidelity: Making decisions, recovering from the pain*, Holbrook, MA: Bob Adams Press.

Chapter 15: Healing Alone

1. Laura Betzig (1989), Causes of conjugal dissolution: A cross-cultural study, *Current Anthropology, 30*, 654–676.

2. Annette Lawson (1988), *Adultery: An analysis of love and betrayal*, New York: Basic Books.

3. Harold S. Kushner (1982), *When bad things happen to good people*, New York: William Morrow.

4. Richard R. Peterson (1996), An evaluation of the economic consequences of divorce in L.A. County, *American Sociological Review, 61*, 528–536.

5. Janis A. Haywood (2001) read legal cases across the country and interviewed people who work in court services. She found that affairs seldom influence financial settlements or child custody awards. Child custody awards: Are parental extramarital affairs significant in the 1990's?, *www.affairs-help.com*.

6. Herman M. Frankel, M.D. (2000), *Dealing with loss: A guidebook for helping your children before and after divorce* (available from author; see appendix).

REFERENCES

Allen, E.S., & Baucom, D.H. (2001). *Attachment styles and their relation to patterns of infidelity.* Paper presented at Conceptualization and treatment of infidelity symposium, annual conference of Association for Advancement of Behavior Therapy, Philadelphia.

American Psychiatric Association. (1994). *DSM-IV: Diagnostic and statistical manual of mental disorders, fourth edition.* Washington, D.C.: Author.

Athanasiou, R., Shaver, P., & Tavris, C. (1970). Sex. *Psychology Today* (July), 37–52.

Atwater, Lynne. (1982). *The extramarital connection: Sex, intimacy and identity.* New York: Irvington.

Balswick, J.O., & Peek, C.W. (1971). The inexpressive male: A tragedy of American society. *Family Coordinator, 20,* 363–368.

Barash, D.P., & Lipton, J.E. (2001). *The myth of monogamy: Fidelity and infidelity in animals and people.* New York: W.H. Freeman.

Betzig, L. (1989). Causes of conjugal dissolution: A cross-cultural study. *Current Anthropology, 30,* 654–676.

Bringle, R.G., & Buunk, B.P. (1991). Extradyadic relationships and sexual jealousy. In K. McKinney & S. Sprecher (Eds.), *Sexuality in close relationships.* Hillsdale, NJ: Erlbaum.

Brown, E.M. (1991). *Patterns of infidelity and their treatment.* New York: Brunner/Mazel.

Bruce, R. (1998). Strange but true: Improve your health through journaling. *Self-help Magazine* (*www.shpm.com*), May 29.

Buss, D. (1994). *The evolution of desire: Strategies of human mating.* New York: Basic Books.

Buss, D. (2000). *The dangerous passion: Why jealousy is as necessary as love and sex.* New York: Free Press.

Buunk, B.P., & Bakker, A.B. (1995). Extradyadic sex: The role of descriptive and injunctive norms. *Journal of Sex Research, 32*(4), 313–318.

Buunk, B.P., & Bakker, A.B. (1997). Commitment to the relationship, extradyadic sex, and AIDS preventive behavior. *Journal of Applied Social Psychology, 27*(14), 1241–1257.

Carnes, P. (1991). *Don't call it love: Sex addiction in America.* New York: Bantam.

Choi, K., Catania, J.A. & Dolcini, M.M. (1994). Extramarital sex and HIV risk behavior among U.S. adults: Results from the National AIDS Behavioral Survey. *American Journal of Public Health, 84*(12), 2003–2007.

Christensen, H.T. (1962). A cross-cultural comparison of attitudes toward marital infidelity. *International Journal of Comparative Sociology, 3,* 124–137.

Cousins, N. (1989). *Head first: The biology of hope and the healing power of the human spirit.* New York: Penguin Books.

Crenshaw, T.L. (1997). *The alchemy of love and lust: How our sex hormones influence our relationships.* New York: Pocket Books.

Cuber, J.F., & Haroff, P.B. (1965). *The significant Americans: A study of sexual behavior among the affluent.* New York: Appleton Century Crofts.

Dickson, F.C. (1995). The best is yet to be: Research on long-lasting relationships. In J.T. Wood & S. Duck (Eds.), *Under-studied relationships: Off the beaten track.* Beverly Hills, CA: Sage, 22–50.

Docherty, J.P., & Ellis, J. (1976). A new concept and finding in morbid jealousy. *American Journal of Psychiatry, 133*(6), 679–683.

Ellison, C.R. (2000). *Women's sexualities.* Oakland, CA: New Harbinger.

Everstine, D.S., & Everstine, L. (1993). *The trauma response: Treatment for emotional injury.* New York: Norton.

Farley, F. (1990). Type-T behavior and families: Introduction and background to a new theory. *Family Psychologist, 6*(4), 24–25.

Francis, J.L. (1977). Toward the management of heterosexual jealousy. *Journal of Marriage and Family Counseling, 3,* 61–69.

Frayser, S. (1985). *Varieties of sexual experience: An anthropological perspective.* New Haven: HRAF Press.

Glass, S.P. (1981). Sex differences in the relationship between satisfaction with various aspects of marriage and types of extramarital involvements. (Doctoral dissertation, Catholic University, 1980). *Dissertation Abstracts International, 41*(10), 3889B.

Glass, S.P. (2000). The harder you fall, the farther you fall. In J.R. Levine & H.J. Markman (Eds.), *Why do fools fall in love?* New York: Jossey-Bass.

Glass, S.P. (2002). Couple therapy after the trauma of infidelity. In Alan S. Gurman & Neil S. Jacobson (Eds.), *Clinical handbook of couple therapy.* 3d ed. New York: Guilford.

Glass, S.P., & Wright, T.L. (1977). The relationship of extramarital sex, length of marriage, and sex differences on marital satisfaction and romanticism: Athanasiou's data reanalyzed. *Journal of Marriage and the Family, 39*(4), 691–703.

Glass, S.P., & Wright, T.L. (1985). Sex differences in type of extramarital involvement and marital dissatisfaction. *Sex Roles, 12*(9/10), 1101–1119.

Glass, S.P., & Wright, T.L. (1988). Clinical implications of research on extramarital involvement. In R. Brown & J. Field (Eds.), *Treatment of sexual problems in individual and couples therapy.* New York: PMA.

Glass, S.P., & Wright, T.L. (1992). Justifications for extramarital involvement: The association between attitudes, behavior, and gender. *Journal of Sex Research, 29*(3), 1–27.

Glass, S.P., & Wright, T.L. (1997). Reconstructing marriages after the trauma of infidelity. In W.K. Halford & H.J. Markman (Eds.), *Clinical handbook of marriage and couples interventions.* New York: Wiley.

Gordon, K.C., & Baucom, D.H. (1998). "True" forgiveness vs. "false" forgiveness: Further validation of a cognitive-behavioral stage model of forgiveness. Poster session presented at the annual meeting of Association for Advancement of Behavior Therapy, Washington, DC.

Gordon, K.C. & Baucom, D.H. (1999). A multitheoretical intervention for promoting recovery from extramarital affairs. *Clinical Psychology: Science and Practice, 6*(4), 382–399.

Gordon, L., with Frandsen, J. (1993). *Passage to intimacy.* New York: Fireside/Simon & Schuster.

Gottman, J., with Silver, N. (1994). *Why marriages succeed or fail.* New York: Simon & Schuster.

Gottman, J.M., & Silver, N. (1999). *The seven principles for making marriage work.* New York: Three Rivers Press.

Halper, J. (1988). *Quiet desperation: The truth about successful men.* New York: Warner Books.

Haywood, J.A. (2001). Child custody awards: Are parental extramarital affairs significant in the 1990s? *www.affairs-help.com*

Heatherington, E.M., & Kelly, J. (2002). *For better or worse: Divorce reconsidered.* New York: Norton.

Hendrix, H. (1997). *Giving the love that heals.* New York: Pocket Books.

Herman, J.L. (1992). *Trauma and recovery.* New York: Basic Books.

Heyn, D. (1993). *The erotic silence of the American wife.* New York: Signet Books.

Humphrey, F.G. (1983). *Marital therapy.* Englewood Cliffs, NJ: Prentice-Hall.

Humphrey, F.G. (1985, October). *Extramarital affairs and their treatment by AAMFT therapists.* Paper presented at American Association of Marriage and Family Therapy, New York.

Hunt, M. (1969). *The affair.* New York: World Publishing.

Janus, S.S., & Janus, D.L. (1993). *The Janus report on sexual behavior.* New York: Wiley.

Johnson, D.J., & Rusbult, C.E. (1989). Resisting temptation: Devaluation of alternative partners as a means of maintaining commitment in close relationships. *Journal of Personality and Social Psychology, 57,* 967–980.

Johnson, R.E. (1970). Some correlates of extramarital coitus. *Journal of Marriage and the Family, 32*(3), 449–456.

Kalish, N. (1997). *Lost and found lovers: Facts and fantasies of rekindled romances.* New York: William Morrow.

Kinsey, A.C., Pomeroy, W.B., Martin, C.E., & Gebhard, P.H. (1953). *Sexual behavior in the human female.* Philadelphia: W.B. Saunders.

Kushner, H.S. (1982). *When bad things happen to good people.* New York: William Morrow.

Kushner, H.S. (1996). *How good do we have to be? A new understanding of guilt and forgiveness.* New York: Little, Brown.

Laumann, E.O., Gagnon, J.H., Michael, R.T., & Michaels, S. (1994). *The social organization of sexuality: Sexual practices in the United States.* Chicago: University of Chicago Press.

Lawson, A. (1988). *Adultery: An analysis of love and betrayal.* New York: Basic Books.

Lawson, A., & Samson, C. (1988). Age, gender, and adultery. *British Journal of Sociology, 39*(3), 409–440.

Layton-Tholl, D. (1998). Extramarital affairs: The link between thought suppression and level of arousal. Unpublished doctoral dissertation: Miami Institute of Psychology of the Caribbean Center for Advanced Studies.

Levant, R.F. (1992). Toward the reconstruction of masculinity. *Journal of Family Psychology, 5*(3/4), 379–402.

Levin, R.J. & Levin, A. (1975). The *Redbook* report on premarital and extramarital sex, *Redbook,* October, 38ff.

Love, P., with Robinson, J. (1990). *The emotional incest syndrome: What to do when a parent's love rules your life.* New York: Bantam.

Luskin, F. (2002). *Forgive for good: A proven prescription for health and happiness.* New York: HarperCollins.

Maraniss, D. (1995). *First in his class: The biography of Bill Clinton.* New York: Simon & Schuster.

Mongeau, P.A., Hale, Jerold, L., & Alles, M. (1994). An experimental investigation of accounts and attributions following sexual infidelity. *Communication Monographs, 61,* 326–343.

Morris, B. (1999). Addicted to sex. *Fortune.* May 10, 65–80.

Notarius, C., & Markman, M. (1993). *We can work it out: Making sense of marital conflict.* New York: Putnam.

Oliver, M. (1992). The summer day. *New and selected poems.* Boston: Beacon Hill Press.

Pazniokas, M. (2001). 1 man, 2 women, countless lies. (Hartford) *Courant,* October 3.

Penn, C.D., Hernandez, S.L., & Bermudez, J.M. (1997). Using a cross-cultural perspective to understand infidelity in couples therapy. *American Journal of Family Therapy, 25*(2), 169–185.

Petersen, J.R. (1983). The *Playboy* readers' sex survey. *Playboy, 30*(3), 90ff.

Peterson, R.R. (1996). An evaluation of the economic consequences of divorce in L.A. County. *American Sociological Review, 61,* 528–536.

Pietropinto, A. (1986). Sex in the workplace. *Medical Aspects of Human Sexuality,* July, 17–22.

Pines, A. (1999). *Falling in love: Why we choose the lovers we choose.* New York: Routledge.

Pittman, F. (1989). *Private lies: Infidelity and the betrayal of intimacy.* New York: Norton.

Pittman, F. (1993). Beyond betrayal: Life after infidelity. *Psychology Today,* May/June, 33–38, 78–82.

Pope, A. (1953). Essay on criticism. In G.K. Anderson & K.J. Holzknecht (Eds.), *The literature of England.* Chicago: Scott, Foresman.

Richardson, L. (1985). *The new other woman: Contemporary single women in affairs with married men.* New York: Free Press.

Saunders, J.M., & Edwards, J.N. (1984). Extramarital sexuality: A predictive model of permissive attitudes. *Journal of Marriage and the Family, 46*(4), 825–835.

Schneider, J.P. (1988). *Back from betrayal: A ground-breaking guide to recovery for women involved with sex-addicted men.* New York: Ballantine Books.

Schneider, J.P., Corley, M.D., Irons, R.R. (1998). Surviving disclosure of infidelity: Results of an international survey of 164 recovering sex addicts and partners. *Sexual Addiction and Compulsivity, 5,* 189–217.

Schneider, J.P., & Schneider, B. (1999) *Sex, lies, and forgiveness: Couples speaking on healing from sex addiction.* Tucson, AZ: Recovery Resources Press.

Schuham, A., & Bird, W.H. (1990). Marriage and the affairs of the anxious man of prominence. *American Journal of Family Therapy, 18*(2), 141–152.

Seagull, E.G., & Seagull, A.A. (1991). Healing the wound that must not heal: Psychotherapy with survivors of domestic violence. *Psychotherapy: Theory/Research/Practice/Training, 28*(1), 16–20.

Shackelford, T.K., & Buss, D.M. (1997). Cues to infidelity. *Personality & Social Psychology Bulletin, 23*(10), 1034–1045.

Spanier, G.B. (1976) Measuring dyadic adjustment: New scales for assessing the quality of marriage and similar dyads. *Journal of Marriage and the Family, 38,* 15–28.

Stabb, S.D., Ragsdale, B., Bess, J.A., & Weiner, H. (2000). *Multigenerational patterns of infidelity and their relationship to attachment.* Paper presented at annual convention of American Psychological Association, Washington, DC.

Stanley, S., & Markman, H. (1992). Assessing commitment in personal relationships. *Journal of Marriage and the Family, 54,* 595–608.

Stiff, J.B., Kim, H.J., & Ramesh, C.N. (1992). Truth biases and aroused suspicion in relational deception. *Communication Research, 19*(3), 326–345.

Stuart, R.B. (1983). *Couples pre-counseling inventory.* Champaign, IL: Research Press.

Subotnik, R., & Harris, G. (1999). *Surviving infidelity: Making decisions, recovering from the pain.* Holbrook, MA: Bob Adams Press.

Tavris, C., & Sadd, S. (1977). *The Redbook report on female sexuality.* New York: Dell.

Thompson, A.P. (1984). Emotional and sexual components of extramarital relations. *Journal of Marriage and Family, 46*(1), 35–42.

Treas, J., & Giesen, D. (2000). Sexual infidelity among married and cohabiting Americans. *Journal of Marriage and the Family, 62,* 48–60.

Vaughan, P. (1999). Partial results of survey on extramarital affairs. Available on-line: *http://www.dearpeggy.com/results.html.*

Waite, L.J., & Gallagher, M. (2000). *The case for marriage: Why married people are happier, healthier, and better off financially.* New York: Doubleday.

Wallerstein, J.S., & Blakeslee, S. (1995). *The good marriage: How and why love lasts.* New York: Warner Books.

Wallerstein, J.S., Blakeslee, S., & Lewis, J. (2001). *The unexpected legacy of divorce: A 25 year landmark study.* New York: Hyperion.

Wegner, D.M., Lane, J.D., & Dimitri, S. (1994). The allure of secret relationships. *Journal of Personality and Social Psychology, 66*(2), 287–300.

Weil, B.E., & Winter, R. (1993). *Adultery: The forgivable sin.* New York: Birch Lane Press.

Weiner-Davis, M. (1992). *Divorce busting: A revolutionary and rapid program for staying together.* New York: Simon & Schuster.

Weis, D.L., & Jurich, J. (1985). Size of community of residence as a predictor of attitudes toward extramarital sexual relations. *Journal of Marriage and the Family, 47*(1), 173–178.

Westfall, A. (1995). Working through the extramarital trauma: An exploration of common themes. In G.R. Weeks & L. Hof (Eds.), *Integrative solutions: Treating the most common couple problems.* New York: Brunner/Mazel.

Whisman, M.A., Dixon, A.E., & Johnson, B. (1997). Therapists' perspectives of couple problems and treatment issues in couple therapy. *Journal of Family Psychology, 11*(3), 361–366.

Whitehurst, R.N. (1969). Extramarital sex: Alienation or extension of normal behavior. In G. Neubeck (Ed.), *Extramarital relations.* Englewood Cliffs, NJ: Prentice-Hall.

Widmer, E.D., Treas, J., & Newcomb, R. (1998). Attitudes towards nonmarital sex in 24 countries. *Journal of Sex Research, 35,* 349–359.

Wiederman, M.W. (1997). Extramarital sex: Prevalence and correlates in a national survey. *Journal of Sex Research, 34*(2), 167–174.

Wiggins, J.D., & Lederer, D.A. (1984). Differentiated antecedents of infidelity in marriage. *American Mental Health Counselors Association Journal, 6*(4), 152–161.

Wilson, C. (1988). "Other woman" says she feels little guilt. *USA Today,* April 4.

Yablonsky, L. (1979). *The extra-sex factor: Why over half of America's married men play around.* New York: Times Books.

Young, K.S. (1998). *Caught in the Net: How to recognize the signs of Internet addiction—and a winning strategy for recovery.* New York: Wiley.

INDEX

Fictional names appear in "quotation marks" and follow topics they illustrate.

ABOUT THE AUTHORS

Shirley P. Glass, Ph.D., is a licensed psychologist with a diplomate in family psychology. She is also a licensed marriage and family therapist and a Fellow of the American Psychological Association. *The New York Times* has referred to Dr. Glass as "the godmother of infidelity research." She has been conducting research on extramarital relationships since 1975. Her relationship expertise has made her a media favorite who is frequently cited in *USA Today,* the *Los Angeles Times, Psychology Today, Redbook, Glamour, Ladies Home Journal, Men's Health,* and *Newsweek.* She has appeared on *Good Morning America, Oprah, The Today Show,* and *Fresh Air* on NPR. She has been married for more than forty years and has three adult children, one of whom, Ira, hosts the popular radio show, *This American Life.* Visit the author at her web site, www.shirleyglass.com.

Jean Staeheli lives in Portland, Oregon. She is an experienced coauthor with several nationally acclaimed books to her credit.